INFORMATION GOVERNANCE

Founded in 1807, John Wiley & Sons is the oldest independent publishing company in the United States. With offices in North America, Europe, Asia, and Australia, Wiley is globally committed to developing and marketing print and electronic products and services for our customers' professional and personal knowledge and understanding.

The Wiley CIO series provides information, tools, and insights to IT executives and managers. The products in this series cover a wide range of topics that supply strategic and implementation guidance on the latest technology trends, leadership, and emerging best practices.

Titles in the Wiley CIO series include:

The Agile Architecture Revolution: How Cloud Computing, REST-Based SOA, and Mobile Computing Are Changing Enterprise IT by Jason Bloomberg

Big Data, Big Analytics: Emerging Business Intelligence and Analytic Trends for Today's Businesses by Michael Minelli, Michele Chambers, and Ambiga Dhiraj

The Chief Information Officer's Body of Knowledge: People, Process, and Technology by Dean Lane

CIO Best Practices: Enabling Strategic Value with Information Technology (Second Edition) by Joe Stenzel, Randy Betancourt, Gary Cokins, Alyssa Farrell, Bill Flemming, Michael H. Hugos, Jonathan Hujsak, and Karl Schubert

The CIO Playbook: Strategies and Best Practices for IT Leaders to Deliver Value by Nicholas R. Colisto

Enterprise Performance Management Done Right: An Operating System for Your Organization by Ron Dimon

Executive's Guide to Virtual Worlds: How Avatars Are Transforming Your Business and Your Brand by Lonnie Benson

IT Leadership Manual: Roadmap to Becoming a Trusted Business Partner by Alan R. Guibord

Managing Electronic Records: Methods, Best Practices, and Technologies by Robert F. Smallwood

On Top of the Cloud: How CIOs Leverage New Technologies to Drive Change and Build Value Across the Enterprise by Hunter Muller

Straight to the Top: CIO Leadership in a Mobile, Social, and Cloud-based World (Second Edition) by Gregory S. Smith

Strategic IT: Best Practices for Managers and Executives by Arthur M. Langer and Lyle Yorks

Transforming IT Culture: How to Use Social Intelligence, Human Factors, and Collaboration to Create an IT Department That Outperforms by Frank Wander

Unleashing the Power of IT: Bringing People, Business, and Technology Together by Dan Roberts

The U.S. Technology Skills Gap: What Every Technology Executive Must Know to Save America's Future by Gary J. Beach

Information Governance: Concepts, Strategies and Best Practices by Robert F. Smallwood

INFORMATION GOVERNANCE

CONCEPTS, STRATEGIES AND
BEST PRACTICES

Robert F. Smallwood

WILEY

Library of Congress Cataloging-in-Publication Data:

Smallwood, Robert F., 1959-
    Information governance : concepts, strategies, and best practices / Robert F. Smallwood.
        pages cm. — (Wiley CIO series)
    ISBN 978-1-118-21830-3 (cloth); ISBN 978-1-118-41949-6 (ebk); ISBN 978-1-118-42101-7 (ebk)
    1. Information technology—Management.   2. Management information systems.   3. Electronic
records—Management.   I. Title.
    HD30.2.S617 2014
    658.4'038—dc23

                                                                                    2013045072

Printed in the United States of America

10 9 8 7 6 5 4 3 2 1

For my sons

and the next generation of tech-savvy managers

CONTENTS

PART FOUR—Information Governance for Delivery Platforms   239

CHAPTER 12 Information Governance for E-Mail and Instant Messaging   241

CHAPTER 13 Information Governance for Social Media   253

By Patricia Franks, Ph.D, CRM, and Robert Smallwood

PREFACE

nformation governance (IG) has emerged as a key concern for business executives and managers in today's environment of Big Data, increasing information risks, colossal leaks, and greater compliance and legal demands. But few seem to have a clear understanding of what IG is; that is, how you define what it is and is not, and how to implement it. This book clarifies and codifies these definitions and provides key insights as to how to implement and gain value from IG programs. Based on exhaustive research, and with the contributions of a number of industry pioneers and experts, this book lays out IG as a complete discipline in and of itself for the first time.

IG is a super-discipline that includes components of several key fields: law, records management, information technology (IT), risk management, privacy and security, and business operations. This unique blend calls for a new breed of information professional who is competent across these established and quite complex fields. Training and education are key to IG success, and this book provides the essential underpinning for organizations to train a new generation of IG professionals.

Those who are practicing professionals in the component fields of IG will find the book useful in expanding their knowledge from traditional fields to the emerging tenets of IG. Attorneys, records and compliance managers, risk managers, IT managers, and security and privacy professionals will find this book a particularly valuable resource.

The book strives to offer clear IG concepts, actionable strategies, and proven best practices in an understandable and digestible way; a concerted effort was made to simplify language and to offer examples. There are summaries of key points throughout and at the end of each chapter to help the reader retain major points. The text is organized into five parts: (1) Information Governance Concepts, Definitions, and Principles; (2) IG Risk Assessment and Strategic Planning; (3) IG Key Impact Areas; (4) IG for Delivery Platforms; and (5) Long-Term Program Issues. Also included are appendices with detailed information on taxonomy and metadata design and on records management and privacy legislation.

One thing that is sure is that the complex field of IG is evolving. It will continue to change and solidify. But help is here: No other book offers the kind of comprehensive coverage of IG contained within these pages. Leveraging the critical advice provided here will smooth your path to understanding and implementing successful IG programs.

Robert F. Smallwood

ACKNOWLEDGMENTS

I would like to sincerely thank my colleagues for their support and generous contribution of their expertise and time, which made this pioneering text possible.

Many thanks to Lori Ashley, Barb Blackburn, Barclay Blair, Charmaine Brooks, Ken Chasse, Monica Crocker, Charles M. Dollar, Seth Earley, Dr. Patricia Franks, Randy Kahn, Paula Lederman, and Barry Murphy.

I am truly honored to include their work and owe them a great debt of gratitude.

PART ONE

Information Governance Concepts, Definitions, and Principles

CHAPTER 1

The Onslaught of Big Data and the Information Governance Imperative

The value of information in business is rising, and business leaders are more and more viewing the ability to govern, manage, and harvest information as critical to success. Raw data is now being increasingly viewed as an asset that can be leveraged, just like financial or human capital.[1] Some have called this new age of "Big Data" the "industrial revolution of data."

According to the research group Gartner, Inc., Big Data is defined as "high-volume, high-velocity and high-variety information assets that demand cost-effective, innovative forms of information processing for enhanced insight and decision making."[2] A practical definition should also include the idea that the amount of data—both structured (in databases) and unstructured (e.g., e-mail, scanned documents) is so massive that it cannot be processed using today's database tools and analytic software techniques.[3]

In today's information overload era of Big Data—characterized by massive growth in business data volumes and velocity—the ability to distill key insights from enormous amounts of data is a major business differentiator and source of sustainable competitive advantage. In fact, a recent report by the World Economic Forum stated that data is a new asset class and personal data is "the new oil."[4] And we are generating more than we can manage effectively with current methods and tools.

The Big Data numbers are overwhelming: Estimates and projections vary, but it has been stated that 90 percent of the data existing worldwide today was created in the last two years[5] and that every two days more information is generated than was from the dawn of civilization until 2003.[6] This trend will continue: The global market for Big Data technology and services is projected to grow at a compound annual rate of 27 percent through 2017, about six times faster than the general information and communications technology (ICT) market.[7]

Many more comparisons and statistics are available, and all demonstrate the incredible and continued growth of data.

Certainly, there are new and emerging opportunities arising from the accumulation and analysis of all that data we are busy generating and collecting. New enterprises are springing up to capitalize on data mining and business intelligence opportunities. The U.S. federal government joined in, announcing $200 million in Big Data research programs in 2012.[8]

> The onslaught of Big Data necessitates that information governance (IG) be implemented to discard unneeded data in a legally defensible way.

But established organizations, especially larger ones, are being crushed by this onslaught of Big Data: It is just too expensive to keep all the information that is being generated, and unneeded information is a sort of irrelevant sludge for decision makers to wade through. They have difficulty knowing which information is an accurate and meaningful "wheat" and which is simply irrelevant "chaff." This means they do not have the precise information they need to base good business decisions upon.

And all that Big Data piling up has real costs: The burden of massive stores of information has increased storage management costs dramatically, caused overloaded systems to fail, and increased legal discovery costs.[9] Further, the longer that data is kept, the more likely that it will need to be migrated to newer computing platforms, driving up conversion costs; and legally, there is the risk that somewhere in that mountain of data an organization stores is a piece of information that represents a significant legal liability.[10]

This is where the worlds of Big Data and business collide. For Big Data proponents, more data is always better, and there is no perceived downside to accumulation of massive amounts of data. In the business world, though, the realities of legal **e-discovery** mean the opposite is true.[11] To reduce risk, liability, and costs, it is critical for unneeded information to be disposed of in a systematic, methodical, and "legally defensible" (justifiable in legal proceedings) way, when it no longer has legal, regulatory, or business value. And there also is the high-value benefit of basing decisions on better, cleaner data, which can come about only through rigid, enforced **information governance** (IG) policies that reduce information glut.

Organizations are struggling to reduce and right-size their information footprint by discarding superfluous and redundant data, e-documents, and information. *But the critical issue is devising policies, methods, and processes and then deploying information technology (IT) to sort through which information is valuable and which no longer has business value and can be discarded.*

IT, IG, risk, compliance, and legal representatives in organizations have a clear sense that most of the information stored is unneeded, raises costs, and poses risks. According to a survey taken at a recent Compliance, Governance and Oversight Counsel summit, respondents estimated that approximately 25 percent of information stored in organizations has real business value, while 5 percent must be kept as business records and about 1 percent is retained due to a litigation hold. *"This means that*

> Big Data values massive accumulation of data, whereas in business, e-discovery realities and potential legal liabilities dictate that data be culled to only that which has clear business value.

> Only about one quarter of information organizations are managing has real business value.

> With a smaller information footprint, it is easier for organizations to find the information they need and derive business value from it.

[about] 69 percent of information in most companies has no business, legal, or regulatory value. Companies that are able to dispose of this data debris return more profit to shareholders, can leverage more of their IT budgets for strategic investments, and can avoid excess expense in legal and regulatory response" (emphasis added).[12]

*With a smaller **information footprint**, organizations can more easily find what they need and derive business value from it.*[13] They must eliminate the data debris regularly and consistently, and to do this, processes and systems must be in place to cull valuable information and discard the data debris daily. An IG program sets the framework to accomplish this.

The business environment has also underscored the need for IG. According to Ted Friedman at Gartner, "The recent global financial crisis has put information governance in the spotlight. . . . [It] is a priority of IT and business leaders as a result of various pressures, including regulatory compliance mandates and the urgent need for improved decision-making."[14]

And IG mastery is critical for executives: Gartner predicts that by 2016, *one in five chief information officers in regulated industries will be fired from their jobs for failed IG initiatives.*[15]

Defining Information Governance

IG is a sort of super discipline that has emerged as a result of new and tightened legislation governing businesses, external threats such as hacking and data breaches, and the recognition that multiple overlapping disciplines were needed to address today's information management challenges in an increasingly regulated and litigated business environment.[16]

IG is a subset of corporate governance, and includes key concepts from records management, content management, IT and data governance, information security, data privacy, risk management, litigation readiness, regulatory compliance, **long-term digital preservation**, and even business intelligence. This also means that it includes related technology and discipline subcategories, such as document management, enterprise search, knowledge management, and business continuity/ disaster recovery.

> IG is a subset of corporate governance.

> IG is a sort of superdiscipline that encompasses a variety of key concepts from a variety of related disciplines.

Practicing good IG is the essential foundation for building legally defensible disposition practices to discard unneeded information and to secure confidential information, which may include trade secrets, strategic plans, price lists, blueprints, or personally identifiable information (PII) subject to privacy laws; it provides the basis for consistent, reliable methods for managing data, e-documents, and records.

Having trusted and reliable records, reports, data, and databases enables managers to make key decisions with confidence.[17] And accessing that information and business intelligence in a timely fashion can yield a long-term sustainable competitive advantage, creating more agile enterprises.

To do this, organizations must standardize and systematize their handling of information. They must analyze and optimize how information is accessed, controlled, managed, shared, stored, preserved, and audited. They must have complete, current, and relevant policies, processes, and technologies to manage and control information, including *who* is able to access what information, and *when*, to meet external legal and regulatory demands and internal governance policy requirements. In short, IG is about information control and compliance.

IG is a subset of corporate governance, which has been around as long as corporations have existed. IG is a rather new multidisciplinary field that is still being defined, but has gained traction increasingly over the past decade. The focus on IG comes not only from compliance, legal, and records management functionaries but also from executives who understand they are accountable for the governance of information and that theft or erosion of information assets has real costs and consequences.

"Information governance" is an all-encompassing term for *how an organization manages the totality of its information.*

According to the **Association of Records Managers and Administrators** (ARMA), IG is "a strategic framework composed of standards, processes, roles, and metrics that hold organizations and individuals accountable to create, organize, secure, maintain, use, and dispose of information in ways that align with and contribute to the organization's goals."[18]

IG includes the set of policies, processes, and controls to manage information in compliance with external regulatory requirements and internal governance frameworks. Specific policies apply to specific data and document types, records series, and other business information, such as e-mail and reports.

Stated differently, IG is "a quality-control discipline for managing, using, improving, and protecting information."[19]

> Practicing good IG is the essential foundation for building legally defensible disposition practices to discard unneeded information.

IG is "a strategic framework composed of standards, processes, roles, and metrics, that hold organizations and individuals accountable to create, organize, secure, maintain, use, and dispose of information in ways that align with and contribute to the organization's goals."[20]

IG is how an organization maintains security, complies with regulations, and meets ethical standards when managing information.

Fleshing out the definition further: "Information governance is policy-based management of information designed to lower costs, reduce risk, and ensure compliance with legal, regulatory standards, and/or corporate governance."[21] IG necessarily incorporates not just policies but information technologies to audit and enforce those policies. The IG team must be cognizant of information lifecycle issues and be able to apply the proper retention and disposition policies, including digital preservation where records need to be maintained for long periods.

IG Is Not a Project, But an Ongoing Program

IG is an ongoing program, not a one-time project. IG provides an umbrella to manage and control information output and communications. Since technologies change so quickly, it is necessary to have overarching policies that can manage the various IT platforms that an organization may use.

Compare it to a workplace safety program; every time a new location, team member, piece of equipment, or toxic substance is acquired by the organization, the workplace safety program should dictate how that is handled. If it does not, the workplace safety policies/procedures/training that are part of the workplace safety program need to be updated. Regular reviews are conducted to ensure the program is being followed and adjustments are made based on the findings. *The effort never ends.*[22] The same is true for IG.

IG is not only a tactical program to meet regulatory, compliance, and litigation demands. It can be *strategic*, in that it is the necessary underpinning for developing a management strategy that maximizes knowledge worker productivity while minimizing risk and costs.

Why IG Is Good Business

IG is a tough sell. It can be difficult to make the business case for IG, unless there has been some major compliance sanction, fine, legal loss, or colossal data breach. In fact, *the largest*

IG is a multidisciplinary program that requires an ongoing effort.

impediment to IG adoption is simply identifying its benefits and costs, according to the Economist Intelligence Unit. Sure, the enterprise needs better control over its information, but how much better? At what cost? What is the payback period and the return on investment?[23]

It is challenging to make the business case for IG, yet making that case is fundamental to getting IG efforts off the ground.

Here are eight reasons why IG makes good business sense, from IG thought leader Barclay Blair:

1. *We can't keep everything forever.* IG makes sense because it enables organizations to get rid of unnecessary information in a defensible manner. Organizations need a sensible way to dispose of information in order to reduce the cost and complexity of the IT environment. Having unnecessary information around only makes it more difficult and expensive to harness information that has value.

2. *We can't throw everything away.* IG makes sense because organizations can't keep everything forever, nor can they throw everything away. We need information—the right information, in the right place, at the right time. Only IG provides the framework to make good decisions about what information to keep.

3. *E-discovery.* IG makes sense because it reduces the cost and pain of discovery. Proactively managing information reduces the volume of information exposed to e-discovery and simplifies the task of finding and producing responsive information.

4. *Your employees are screaming for it—just listen.* IG makes sense because it helps knowledge workers separate "signal" from "noise" in their information flows. By helping organizations focus on the most valuable information, IG improves information delivery and improves productivity.

5. *It ain't gonna get any easier.* IG makes sense because it is a proven way for organizations to respond to new laws and technologies that create new requirements and challenges. The problem of IG will not get easier over time, so organizations should get started now.

6. *The courts will come looking for IG.* IG makes sense because courts and regulators will closely examine your IG program. Falling short can lead to fines, sanctions, loss of cases, and other outcomes that have negative business and financial consequences.

7. *Manage risk: IG is a big one.* Organizations need to do a better job of identifying and managing risk. The risk of information management failures is a critical risk that IG helps to mitigate.

8. *E-mail: Reason enough.* IG makes sense because it helps organizations take control of e-mail. Solving e-mail should be a top priority for every organization.[24]

Failures in Information Governance

The failure to implement and enforce IG can lead to vulnerabilities that can have dire consequences. The theft of confidential U.S. National Security Agency documents by Edward Snowden in 2013 could have been prevented by properly enforced IG. Also, Ford Motor Company is reported to have suffered a loss estimated at $50 to $100 million as a result of the theft of confidential documents by one of its own employees. A former product engineer who had access to thousands of trade secret documents and designs sold them to a competing Chinese car manufacturer. A strong IG program would have controlled and tracked access and prevented the theft while protecting valuable intellectual property.[25]

Law enforcement agencies have also suffered from poor IG. In a rather frivolous case in 2013 that highlighted the lack of policy enforcement for the mobile environment, it was reported that U.S. agents from the Federal Bureau of Investigation used government-issued mobile phones to send explicit text messages and nude photographs to coworkers. The incidents did not have a serious impact but did compromise the agency and its integrity, and "adversely affected the daily activities of several squads."[26] Proper mobile communications policies were obviously not developed and enforced.

IG is also about information security and privacy, and serious thought must be given when creating policies to safeguard personal, classified or confidential information. Schemes to compromise or steal information can be quite deceptive and devious, masked by standard operating procedures—if proper IG controls and monitoring are not in place. To wit: Granting remote access to confidential information assets for key personnel is common. Granting medical leave is also common. But a deceptive and dishonest employee could feign a medical leave while downloading volumes of confidential information assets for a competitor—and that is exactly what happened at Accenture, a global consulting firm. During a fraudulent medical leave, an employee was allowed access to Accenture's Knowledge Exchange (KX), a detailed knowledge base containing previous proposals, expert reports, cost-estimating guidelines, and case studies. This activity could have been prevented by monitoring and analytics that would have shown an inordinate amount of downloads—especially for an "ailing" employee. The employee then went to work for a direct competitor and continued to download the confidential information from Accenture, estimated to be as many as 1,000 critical documents. While the online access to KX was secure, the use of the electronic documents could have been restricted even *after* the documents were downloaded, if IG measures were in place and newer technologies (such as information rights management [IRM] software) were deployed to secure them directly and maintain that security remotely. With IRM, software security protections can be employed to seal the e-documents and control their use—even after they leave the organization. More details on IRM technology and its capabilities is presented later in this book.

Other recent high-profile data and document leakage cases revealing information security weaknesses that could have been prevented by a robust IG program include:

- Huawei Technologies, the largest networking and mobile communications company in China, was sued by U.S.-based Motorola for allegedly conspiring to steal trade secrets through former Motorola employees.

Ford's loss from stolen documents in a single case of intellectual property (IP) theft was estimated at $50 to $100 million.

■ MI6, the U.K. equivalent of the U.S. Central Intelligence Agency, learned that one of its agents in military intelligence attempted to sell confidential documents to the intelligence services of the Netherlands for £2 million GBP ($3 million USD).

And breaches of personal information revealing failures in privacy protection abound; here are just a few:

■ Health information of 1,600 cardiology patients at Texas Children's Hospital was compromised when a doctor's laptop was stolen. The information included personal and demographic information about the patients, including their names, dates of birth, diagnoses, and treatment histories.[27]
■ U.K. medics lost the personal records of nearly 12,000 National Health Service patients in just eight months. Also, a hospital worker was suspended after it was discovered he had sent a file containing pay-slip details for every member of staff to his home e-mail account.[28]
■ Personal information about more than 600 patients of the Fraser Health Authority in British Columbia, Canada, was stored on a laptop stolen from Burnaby General Hospital.
■ In December 2013, Target stores in the U.S. reported that as many as 110 million customer records had been breached in a massive attack that lasted weeks.

The list of breaches and IG failures could go on and on, more than filling the pages of this book. It is clear that it is occurring and that it will continue. *IG controls to safeguard confidential information assets and protect privacy cannot rely solely on the trustworthiness of employees and basic security measures.* Up-to-date IG policies and enforcement efforts and newer technology sets are needed, with active, consistent monitoring and program adjustments to continue to improve.

Executives and senior managers can no longer avoid the issue, as it is abundantly clear that the threat is real and the costs of taking such avoidable risks can be high. A single security breach is an IG failure and can cost the entire business. According to Debra Logan of Gartner, "When organizations suffer high-profile data losses, especially involving violations of the privacy of citizens or consumers, they suffer serious reputational damage and often incur fines or other sanctions. IT leaders will have to take at least part of the blame for these incidents."[29]

Form IG Policies, Then Apply Technology for Enforcement

Typically, some policies governing the use and control of information and records may have been established for financial and compliance reports, and perhaps e-mail, but they are often incomplete and out-of-date and have not been adjusted for changes in the business environment, such as new technology platforms (e.g., Web 2.0, social

IG controls to safeguard confidential information assets and protect privacy cannot rely solely on the trustworthiness of employees and basic security measures.

media), changing laws (e.g., U.S. Federal Rules of Civil Procedure 2006 changes), and additional regulations.

Further adding to the challenge is the rapid proliferation of mobile devices like tablets, phablets, and smartphones used in business—information can be more easily lost or stolen—so IG efforts must be made to preserve and protect the enterprise's information assets.

Proper IG requires that policies are flexible enough not to hinder the proper flow of information in the heat of the business battle yet strict enough to control and audit for misuse, policy violations, or security breaches. This is a continuous iterative policy-making process that must be monitored and fine-tuned. Even with the absolute best efforts, some policies will miss the mark and need to be reviewed and adjusted.

Getting started with IG awareness is the crucial first step. It may have popped up on an executive's radar at one point or another and an effort might have been made, but many organizations leave these policies on the shelf and do not revise them on a regular basis.

IG is the necessary underpinning for a legally defensible disposition program that discards data debris and helps narrow the search for meaningful information on which to base business decisions. IG is also necessary to protect and preserve critical information assets. An IG strategy should aim to minimize exposure to risk, at a reasonable cost level, while maximizing productivity and improving the quality of information delivered to knowledge users.

But a reactive, tactical *project* approach is not the way to go about it—haphazardly swatting at technological, legal, and regulatory flies. A proactive, strategic *program*, with a clear, accountable sponsor, an ongoing plan, and regular review process, is the only way to continuously adjust IG policies to keep them current so that they best serve the organization's needs.

Some organizations have created formal governance bodies to establish strategies, policies, and procedures surrounding the distribution of information inside and outside the enterprise. These governance bodies, steering committees, or teams should include members from many different functional areas, since proper IG necessitates input from a variety of stakeholders. Representatives from IT, records management, corporate or agency archiving, risk management, compliance, operations, human resources, security, legal, finance, and perhaps knowledge management are typically a part of IG teams. Often these efforts are jump-started and organized by an executive sponsor who utilizes third-party consulting resources that specialize in IG efforts, especially considering the newness of IG and its emerging best practices.

So in this era of ever-growing Big Data, leveraging IG policies to focus on retaining the information that has real business value, while discarding the majority of information that has no value and carries associated increased costs and risks, is critical to success for modern enterprises. This must be accomplished in a systematic, consistent, and legally defensible manner by implementing a formal IG program. Other crucial elements of an IG program are the steps taken to secure confidential information by enforcing and monitoring policies using the appropriate information technologies.

Getting started with IG awareness is the crucial first step.

CHAPTER SUMMARY: **KEY POINTS**

- The onslaught of Big Data necessitates that IG be implemented to discard unneeded data in a legally defensible way.

- Big Data values massive accumulation of data, whereas in business, e-discovery realities and potential legal liabilities dictate that data be culled to only that which has clear business value.

- Only about one quarter of the information organizations are managing has real business value.

- With a smaller information footprint, it is easier for organizations to find the information they need and derive business value from it.

- IG is a subset of corporate governance and encompasses the policies and leveraged technologies meant to manage what corporate information is retained, where, and for how long, and also how it is retained.

- IG is a sort of super discipline that encompasses a variety of key concepts from a variety of related and overlapping disciplines.

- Practicing good IG is the essential foundation for building legally defensible disposition practices to discard unneeded information.

- According to ARMA, IG is "a strategic framework composed of standards, processes, roles, and metrics that hold organizations and individuals accountable to create, organize, secure, maintain, use, and dispose of information in ways that align with and contribute to the organization's goals."[30]

- IG is how an organization maintains security, complies with regulations and laws, and meets ethical standards when managing information.

- IG is a multidisciplinary program that requires an ongoing effort and active participation of a broad cross-section of functional groups and stakeholders.

- IG controls to safeguard confidential information assets and protect privacy cannot rely solely on the trustworthiness of employees and basic security measures.

- Getting started with IG awareness is the crucial first step.

Notes

1. The Economist, "Data, Data Everywhere," February 25, 2010, www.economist.com/node/15557443
2. Gartner, Inc., "IT Glossary: Big Data," www.gartner.com/it-glossary/big-data/ (accessed April 15, 2013).
3. Webopedia, "Big Data," www.webopedia.com/TERM/B/big_data.html (accessed April 15, 2013).

4. World Economic Forum, "Personal Data:The Emergence of a New Asset Class"(January 2011), http://www3.weforum.org/docs/WEF_ITTC_PersonalDataNewAsset_Report_2011.pdf
5. Deidra Paknad, "Defensible Disposal: You Can't Keep All Your Data Forever," July 17, 2012, www.forbes.com/sites/ciocentral/2012/07/17/defensible-disposal-you-cant-keep-all-your-data-forever/
6. Susan Karlin, "Earth's Nervous System: Looking at Humanity Through Big Data," www.fastcocreate.com/1681986/earth-s-nervous-system-looking-at-humanity-through-big-data#1(accessed March 5, 2013).
7. IDC Press Release, December 18, ,2013, http://www.idc.com/getdoc.jsp?containerId=prUS24542113 New IDC Worldwide Big Data Technology and Services Forecast Shows Market Expected to Grow to $32.4 Billion in 2017
8. Steve Lohr, "How Big Data Became So Big," *New York Times*, August 11, 2012, www.nytimes.com/2012/08/12/business/how-big-data-became-so-big-unboxed.html?_r=2&smid=tw-share&
9. Kahn Consulting, "Information Governance Brief," sponsored by IBM, www.delve.us/downloads/Brief-Defensible-Disposal.pdf (accessed March 4, 2013).
10. Barclay T. Blair, "Girding for Battle," *Law Technology News*, October 1, 2012, www.law.com/jsp/lawtechnologynews/PubArticleLTN.jsp?id=1202572459732&thepage=1
11. Ibid.
12. Paknad, "Defensible Disposal."
13. Randolph A. Kahn, https://twitter.com/InfoParkingLot/status/273791612172259329, November 28, 2012.
14. Gartner Press Release, "Gartner Says Master Data Management Is Critical to Achieving Effective Information Governance," www.gartner.com/newsroom/id/1898914, January 19, 2012
15. Ibid.
16. Monica Crocker, e-mail to author, June 21, 2012.
17. Economist Intelligence Unit, "The Future of Information Governance," www.emc.com/leadership/business-view/future-information-governance.htm (accessed November 14, 2013).
18. ARMA International, *Glossary of Records and Information Management Terms*, 4th ed., 2012, TR 22–2012.
19. Arvind Krishna, "Three Steps to Trusting Your Data in 2011," *IT Business Edge*, posted March 9, 2011, www.itbusinessedge.com/guest-opinions/three-steps-trusting-your-data-2011. (accessed November 14, 2013).
20. ARMA International, *Glossary of Records and Information Management Terms*, 4th ed., 2012, TR 22–2012.
21. Laura DuBoisand Vivian Tero, "Practical Information Governance: Balancing Cost, Risk, and Productivity," IDC White Paper (August 2010), www.emc.com/collateral/analyst-reports/idc-practical-information-governance-ar.pdf
22. Monica Crocker, e-mail to author, June 21, 2012.
23. Barclay T. Blair, *Making the Case for Information Governance: Ten Reasons IG Makes Sense*, ViaLumina Ltd, 2010. Online at http://barclaytblair.com/making-the-case-for-ig-ebook/ (accessed November 14, 2013).
24. Barclay T. Blair, "8 Reasons Why Information Governance (IG) Makes Sense," June 29, 2009, www.digitallandfill.org/2009/06/8-reasons-why-information-governance-ig-makes-sense.html
25. Peter Abatan, "Corporate and Industrial Espionage to Rise in 2011," Enterprise Digital Rights Management, http://enterprisedrm.tumblr.com/post/2742811887/corporate-espionage-to-rise-in-2011. (accessed November 14, 2013).
26. BBC News, "FBI Staff Disciplined for Sex Texts and Nude Pictures," February 22, 2013, www.bbc.co.uk/news/world-us-canada-21546135
27. Todd Ackerman, "Laptop Theft Puts Texas Children's Patient Info at Risk," *Houston Chronicle*, July 30, 2009, www.chron.com/news/houston-texas/article/Laptop-theft-puts-Texas-Children-s-patient-info-1589473.php. (accessed March 2, 2012).
28. Jonny Greatrex, "Bungling West Midlands Medics Lose 12,000 Private Patient Records," *Sunday Mercury*, September 5, 2010, www.sundaymercury.net/news/sundaymercuryexclusives/2010/09/05/bungling-west-midlands-medics-lose-12-000-private-patient-records-66331-27203177/ (accessed March 2, 2012).
29. Gartner Press Release, "Gartner Says Master Data Management Is Critical to Achieving Effective Information Governance."
30. ARMA International, *Glossary of Records and Information Management Terms*.

CHAPTER 2

Information Governance, IT Governance, Data Governance: What's the Difference?

There has been a great deal of confusion around the term **information governance (IG)** and how it is distinct from other similar industry terms, such as **information technology (IT) governance** and **data governance**. They are all a subset of corporate governance, and in the above sequence, become increasingly more granular in their approach. Data governance is a part of broader IT governance, which is also a part of even broader information governance. The few texts that exist have compounded the confusion by offering a limited definition of IG, or sometimes offering a definition of IG that is just plain *incorrect*, often confusing it with simple data governance.

So in this chapter we spell out the differences and include examples in hopes of clarifying what the meaning of each term is and how they are related.

Data Governance

Data governance involves processes and controls to ensure that information at the *data* level—raw alphanumeric characters that the organization is gathering and inputting—is true and accurate, and unique (not redundant). It involves **data cleansing (or data scrubbing)** to strip out corrupted, inaccurate, or extraneous data and **de-duplication,** to eliminate redundant occurrences of data.

Data governance focuses on information quality from the ground up at the lowest or root level, so that subsequent reports, analyses, and conclusions are based on clean, reliable, trusted data (or records) in database tables. Data governance is the most rudimentary level at which to implement information governance. Data governance efforts seek to ensure that formal management controls—systems, processes, and accountable employees who are stewards and custodians of the data—are implemented to govern critical data assets to improve data quality and to avoid negative downstream effects of poor data. The biggest negative consequence of poor or inaccurate data is poorly and inaccurately based decisions.

Data governance uses techniques like data cleansing and de-duplication to improve data quality and reduce redundancies.

Data governance is a newer, hybrid quality control discipline that includes elements of data quality, data management, IG policy development, business process improvement, and compliance and risk management.

Data Governance Strategy Tips

Everyone in an organization wants good-quality data to work with. But it is not so easy to implement a data governance program. First of all, data is at such a low level that executives and board members are typically unaware of the details of the "smoky back room" of data collection: cleansing, normalization, and input. So it is difficult to gain an executive sponsor and funding to initiate the effort.[1] And if a data governance program does move forward, there are challenges in getting business users to adhere to new policies. This is a crucial point, since much of the data is being generated by business units. But there are some general guidelines that can help improve a data governance program's chances for success:

- *Identify a measureable impact.* A data governance program must be able to demonstrate business value, or it will not get the executive sponsorship and funding it needs to move forward. A readiness assessment should capture the current state of data quality and whether an enterprise or business unit level effort is warranted. Other key issues include: Can the organization save hard costs by implementing data governance? Can it reach more customers or increase revenue generated from existing customers?[2]
- *Assign accountability for data quality to business units, not IT.* Typically, IT has had responsibility for data quality, yet it is mostly not under that department's control, since most of the data is being generated in the business units. A pointed effort must be made to push responsibility and ownership for data to the business units that create and use the data.
- *Recognize the uniqueness of data as an asset.* Unlike other assets, such as people, factories, equipment, and even cash, data is largely unseen, out of sight, and intangible. It changes daily. It spreads throughout business units. It is copied and deleted. Data growth can spiral out of control, obscuring the data that has true business value. So data has to be treated differently, and its unique qualities must be considered.
- *Forget the past; implement a going-forward strategy.* It is a significantly greater task to try to improve data governance across the enterprise for existing data. Remember, you may be trying to fix decades of bad behavior, mismanagement, and lack of governance. Taking an incremental approach with an eye to the future provides for a clean starting point and can substantially reduce the pain required to implement. A proven best practice is to implement a from-this-point-on strategy where new data governance policies for handling data are implemented beginning on a certain date.

Good data governance ensures that downstream negative effects of poor data are avoided and that subsequent reports, analyses, and conclusions are based on reliable, trusted data.

- *Manage the change.* Educate, educate, educate. People must be trained to understand why the data governance program is being implemented and how it will benefit the business. The new policies represent a cultural change, and people need supportive program messages and training in order to make the shift.[3]

IT Governance

IT governance is the primary way that stakeholders can ensure that investments in IT create business value and contribute toward meeting business objectives.[4] This strategic alignment of IT with the business is challenging yet essential. IT governance programs go further and aim to "improve IT performance, deliver optimum business value and ensure regulatory compliance."[5]

Although the CIO typically has line responsibility for implementing IT governance, the CEO and board of directors must receive reports and updates to discharge their responsibilities for IT governance and to see that the program is functioning well and providing business benefits.

Typically, in past decades, board members did not get involved in overseeing IT governance. But today it is a critical and unavoidable responsibility. According to the IT Governance Institute's *Board Briefing on IT Governance*, "IT governance is the responsibility of the board of directors and executive management. It is an integral part of enterprise governance and consists of the leadership and organizational structures and processes that ensure that the organization's IT sustains and extends the organization's strategies and objectives."[6]

The focus is on the actual software development and maintenance activities of the IT department or function, and IT governance efforts focus on making IT efficient and effective. That means minimizing costs by following proven software development methodologies and best practices, principles of data governance and information quality, and project management best practices while aligning IT efforts with the business objectives of the organization.

IT Governance Frameworks

Several IT governance frameworks can be used as a guide to implementing an IT governance program. (They are introduced in this chapter in a cursory way; detailed discussions of them are best suited to books focused solely on IT governance.)

IT governance seeks to align business objectives with IT strategy to deliver business value.

Although frameworks and guidance like **CobiT®** and **ITIL** have been widely adopted, there is no absolute standard IT governance framework; the combination that works best for an organization depends on business factors, corporate culture, IT maturity, and staffing capability. The level of implementation of these frameworks will also vary by organization.

CobiT®

CobiT (Control Objectives for Information and related Technology) is a process-based IT governance framework that represents a consensus of experts worldwide. Codeveloped by the IT Governance Institute and ISACA (previously known as the **Information Systems Audit and Control Association),** CobiT addresses business risks, control requirements, compliance, and technical issues.[7]

CobiT offers IT controls that:

- Cut IT risks while gaining business value from IT under an umbrella of a globally accepted framework.
- Assist in meeting regulatory compliance requirements.
- Utilize a structured approach for improved reporting and management decision making.
- Provide solutions to control assessments and project implementations to improve IT and information asset control.[8]

CobiT consists of detailed descriptions of processes required in IT and also tools to measure progress toward maturity of the IT governance program. It is industry agnostic and can be applied across all vertical industry sectors, and it continues to be revised and refined.[9]

CobiT is broken out into three basic organizational levels and their responsibilities: (1) board of directors and executive management; (2) IT and business management; and (3) line-level governance, and security and control knowledge workers.[10]

The CobiT model draws on the traditional "plan, build, run, monitor" paradigm of traditional IT management, only with variations in semantics. The CobiT framework is divided into four IT domains—(1) plan and organize, (2) acquire and implement, (3) deliver and support, and (4) monitor and evaluate—which contain 34 IT processes and 210 control objectives. Specific goals and metrics are assigned, and responsibilities and accountabilities are delineated.

The CobiT framework maps to the international information security standard, ISO 17799, and is also compatible with **IT Infrastructure Library** (ITIL) and other "accepted practices" in IT development and operations.[11]

ValIT®

ValIT is a newer value-oriented framework that is compatible with and complementary to CobiT. Its principles and best practices focus is on leveraging IT investments to gain maximum value. Forty key ValIT essential management practices (analogous to CobiT's control objectives) support three main processes: value governance, portfolio management, and investment management. ValIT and CobiT "provide a full framework and supporting tool set" to help managers develop policies to manage business risks and deliver business value while addressing technical issues and meeting control objectives in a structured, methodic way.[12]

CobiT is process-oriented and has been widely adopted as an IT governance framework. ValIT is value-oriented and compatible and complementary with CobiT, yet focuses on value delivery.

ITIL

ITIL (Information Technology Infrastructure Library) is a set of process-oriented best practices and guidance originally developed in the United Kingdom to standardize delivery of IT service management. ITIL is applicable to both the private and public sectors and is the "most widely accepted approach to IT service management in the world."[13] As with other IT governance frameworks, ITIL provides essential guidance for delivering business value through IT, and it "provides guidance to organizations on how to use IT as a tool to facilitate business change, transformation and growth."[14]

ITIL best practices form the foundation for ISO/IEC 20000 (previously BS15000), the International Service Management Standard for organizational certification and compliance.[15] ITIL 2011 is the latest revision (as of this printing), and it consists of five core published volumes that map the IT service cycle in a systematic way:

1. ITIL Service Strategy
2. ITIL Service Design
3. ITIL Service Transition
4. ITIL Service Operation
5. ITIL Continual Service Improvement[16]

ISO 38500

ISO/IEC 38500:2008 is an international standard that provides high-level principles and guidance for senior executives and directors, and those advising them, for the effective and efficient use of IT.[17] Based primarily on AS 8015, the Australian IT governance standard, it "applies to the governance of management processes" that are performed at the IT service level, but the guidance assists executives in monitoring IT and ethically discharging their duties with respect to legal and regulatory compliance of IT activities.

The ISO 38500 standard comprises three main sections:

1. Scope, Application and Objectives
2. Framework for Good Corporate Governance of IT
3. Guidance for Corporate Governance of IT

ITIL is the "most widely accepted approach to IT service management in the world."

ISO 38500 is an international standard that provides high-level principles and guidance for senior executives and directors responsible for IT governance.

It is largely derived from AS 8015, the guiding principles of which were:

- Establish responsibilities
- Plan to best support the organization
- Acquire validly
- Ensure performance when required
- Ensure conformance with rules
- Ensure respect for human factors

The standard also has relationships with other major ISO standards, and embraces the same methods and approaches.[18]

Information Governance

Corporate governance is the highest level of governance in an organization, and a key aspect of it is IG. IG processes are higher level than the details of IT governance and much higher than data governance, but both data and IT governance can be (and should be) a part of an overall IG program. The IG approach to governance focuses not on detailed IT or data capture and quality processes but rather on *controlling the information that is generated* by IT and office systems.

IG efforts seek to manage and control information assets to lower risk, ensure compliance with regulations, and improve information quality and accessibility while implementing information security measures to protect and preserve information that has business value.[19] (See Chapter 1 for more detailed definitions.)

Impact of a Successful IG Program

When making the business case for IG and articulating its benefits, it is useful to focus on its central impact. Putting cost-benefit numbers to this may be difficult, unless you

IG is how an organization maintains security, complies with regulations and laws, and meets ethical standards when managing information.

also consider the worst-case scenario of loss or misuse of corporate or agency records. What is losing the next big lawsuit worth? How much are confidential merger and acquisition documents worth? How much are customer records worth? Frequently, executives and managers do not understand the value of IG until it is a crisis, an expensive legal battle is lost, heavy fines are imposed for noncompliance, or executives go to jail.

There are some key outputs from implementing an IG program. A successful IG program should enable organizations to:

- *Use common terms across the enterprise.* This means that departments must agree on how they are going to classify document types, which requires a cross-functional effort. With common enterprise terms, searches for information are more productive and complete. This normalization process begins with developing a standardized corporate taxonomy, which defines the terms (and substitute terms in a custom corporate thesaurus), document types, and their relationships in a hierarchy.
- *Map information creation and usage.* This effort can be buttressed with the use of technology tools such as **data loss prevention**, which can be used to discover the flow of information within and outside of the enterprise. You must first determine *who* is accessing *which* information *when* and *where* it is going. Then you can monitor and analyze these information flows. The goal is to stop the erosion or misuse of information assets and to stem data breaches with monitoring and security technology.
- *Obtain "information confidence"*—that is, the assurance that information has integrity, validity, accuracy, and quality; this means being able to *prove* that the information is reliable and that its access, use, and storage meet compliance and legal demands.
- *Harvest and leverage information.* Using techniques and tools like data mining and business intelligence, new insights may be gained that provide an enterprise with a sustainable competitive advantage over the long term, since managers will have more and better information as a basis for business decisions.[21]

Summing Up the Differences

IG consists of the overarching polices and processes to optimize and leverage information while keeping it secure and meeting legal and privacy obligations in alignment with stated organizational business objectives.

IT governance consists of following established frameworks and best practices to gain the most leverage and benefit out of IT investments and support accomplishment of business objectives.

Data governance consists of the processes, methods, and techniques to ensure that data is of high quality, reliable, and unique (not duplicated), so that downstream uses in reports and databases are more trusted and accurate.

CHAPTER SUMMARY: **KEY POINTS**

- Data governance uses techniques like data cleansing and de-duplication to improve data quality and reduce redundancies.

- Good data governance ensures that downstream negative effects of poor data are avoided and that subsequent reports, analyses, and conclusions are based on reliable, trusted data.

- IT governance seeks to align business objectives with IT strategy to deliver business value.

- CobiT is processoriented and has been widely adopted as an IT governance framework. ValIT is valueoriented and compatible and complementary with CobiT yet focuses on value delivery.

- The CobiT framework maps to the international information security standard ISO 17799 and is also compatible with ITIL (IT Infrastructure Library).

- ITIL is the "most widely accepted approach to IT service management in the world."

- ISO 38500 is an international standard that provides high-level principles and guidance for senior executives and directors responsible for IT governance.

- Information governance is how an organization maintains security, complies with regulations and laws, and meets ethical standards when managing information.

Notes

1. "New Trends and Best Practices for Data Governance Success," SeachDataManagement.com eBook, http://viewer.media.bitpipe.com/1216309501_94/1288990195_946/Talend_sDM_SO_32247_EBook_1104.pdf, accessed March 11, 2013.
2. Ibid.
3. Ibid.
4. M.N. Kooper, R. Maes, and E.E.O. RoosLindgreen, "On the Governance of Information: Introducing a New Concept of Governance to Support the Management of Information," *International Journal of Information Management* 31 (2011): 195–120, http://dl.acm.org/citation.cfm?id=2297895. (accessed November 14, 2013).
5. Nick Robinson, "The Many Faces of IT Governance: Crafting an IT Governance Architecture," *ISACA Journal* 1 (2007), www.isaca.org/Journal/Past-Issues/2007/Volume-1/Pages/The-Many-Faces-of-IT-Governance-Crafting-an-IT-Governance-Architecture.aspx
6. Bryn Phillips, "IT Governance for CEOs and Members of the Board," 2012, p.18.
7. Ibid., p.26.
8. IBM Global Business Services/Public Sector, "Control Objectives for Information and related Technology (CobiT®) Internationally Accepted Gold Standard for IT Controls & Governance," http://www-304.ibm.com/industries/publicsector/fileserve?contentid=187551(accessed March 11, 2013).

9. Phillips, "IT Governance for CEOs and Members of the Board."
10. IBM Global Business Services/Public Sector, "Control Objectives for Information and related Technology (CobiT®) Internationally Accepted Gold Standard for IT Controls & Governance."
11. Ibid.
12. Ibid.
13. www.itil-officialsite.com/ (accessed March 12, 2013).
14. ITIL, "What Is ITIL?" www.itil-officialsite.com/AboutITIL/WhatisITIL.aspx(accessed March 12, 2013).
15. Ibid.
16. Ibid.
17. "ISO/IEC 38500:2008 "Corporate Governance of Information Technology" www.iso.org/iso/catalogue_detail?csnumber=51639(accessed November 14, 2013).
18. ISO 38500 www.38500.org/ (accessed March 12, 2013).
19. www.naa.gov.au/records-management/agency/digital/digital-continuity/principles/ (accessed November 14, 2013).
20. ARMA International, *Glossary of Records and Information Management Terms*, 4th ed. TR 22–2012 (from ARMA.org).
21. Arvind Krishna, "Three Steps to Trusting Your Data in 2011," *CTO Edge*, March 9, 2011, www.ctoedge.com/content/three-steps-trusting-your-data-2011

CHAPTER 3

Information Governance Principles*

Principles of information governance (IG) are evolving and expanding. Successful IG programs are characterized by ten key principles, which are the basis for best practices and should be designed into the IG approach. They include:

1. *Executive sponsorship.* No IG effort will survive and be successful if it does not have an accountable, responsible executive sponsor. The sponsor must drive the effort, clear obstacles for the IG team or committee, communicate the goals and business objectives that the IG program addresses, and keep upper management informed on progress.

2. *Information policy development and communication.* Clear policies must be established for the access and use of information, and those policies must be communicated regularly and crisply to employees. Policies for the use of e-mail, instant messaging, social media, cloud computing, mobile computing, and posting to blogs and internal sites must be developed in consultation with stakeholders and communicated clearly. This includes letting employees know what the consequences of violating IG policies are, as well as its value.

3. *Information integrity.* This area considers the consistency of methods used to create, retain, preserve, distribute, and track information. Adhering to good IG practices include **data governance** techniques and technologies to ensure quality data. Information integrity means there is the assurance that information is accurate, correct, and authentic. IG efforts to improve data quality and information integrity include de-duplicating (removing redundant data) and maintaining only unique data to reduce risk, storage costs, and information technology (IT) labor costs while providing accurate, trusted information for decision makers. Supporting technologies must enforce policies to meet legal standards of admissibility and preserve the integrity of information to guard against claims that it has been altered, tampered with, or deleted (called **"spoliation"**). Audit trails must be kept and monitored to ensure compliance with IG policies to assure information integrity.[1]

4. *Information organization and classification.* This means standardizing formats, categorizing all information, and semantically linking it to related information. It also means creating a retention and disposition schedule that spells out how

---

*Portions of this chapter are adapted from Chapter 3 of Robert F. Smallwood, *Managing Electronic Records: Methods, Best Practices, and Technologies*, © John Wiley & Sons, Inc., 2013. Reproduced with permission of John Wiley & Sons, Inc.

long the information (e.g. e-mail, e-documents, spreadsheets, reports) and records should be retained and how they are to be disposed of or archived. Information, and particularly documents, should be classified according to a global or corporate taxonomy that considers the business function and owner of the information, and semantically links related information. Information must be standardized in form and format. Tools such as **document labeling** can assist in identifying and classifying documents. Metadata associated with documents and records must be standardized and kept up-to-date. Good IG means good metadata management and utilizing metadata standards that are appropriate to the organization.

5. *Information security.* This means securing information in its three states: at rest, in motion, and in use. It means implementing measures to protect information from damage, theft, or alteration by malicious outsiders and insiders as well as nonmalicious (accidental) actions that may compromise information. For instance, an employee may lose a laptop with confidential information, but if proper IG policies are enforced using security-related information technologies, the information can be secured. This can be done by access control methods, data or document encryption, deploying information rights management software, using remote digital shredding capabilities, and implementing enhanced auditing procedures. Information privacy is closely related to information security and is critical when dealing with **personally identifiable information** (PII).

6. *Information accessibility.* Accessibility is vital not only in the short term but also over time using **long-term digital preservation** (LTDP) techniques when appropriate (generally if information is needed for over five years). Accessibility must be balanced with information security concerns. Information accessibility includes making the information as simple as possible to locate and access, which involves not only the user interface but also enterprise search principles, technologies, and tools. It also includes basic access controls, such as password management, **identity and access management**, and delivering information to a variety of hardware devices.

7. *Information control.* Document management and report management software must be deployed to control the access to, creation, updating, and printing of documents and reports. When documents or reports are declared records, they must be assigned to the proper retention and disposition schedule to be retained for as long as the records are needed to comply with legal retention periods and regulatory requirements. Also, information that may be needed or requested in legal proceedings is safeguarded through a **legal hold** process.

8. *Information governance monitoring and auditing.* To ensure that guidelines and policies are being followed and to measure employee compliance levels, information access and use must be monitored. To guard against claims of spoliation, use of e-mail, social media, cloud computing, and report generation should be logged in real time and maintained as an audit record. Technology tools such as **document analytics** can track how many documents or reports users access and print and how long they spend doing so.

9. *Stakeholder consultation.* Those who work most closely to information are the ones who best know why it is needed and how to manage it, so business units must be consulted in IG policy development. The IT department understands

Principles of successful IG programs are emerging. They include executive sponsorship, information classification, integrity, security, accessibility, control, monitoring, auditing, policy development, and continuous improvement.

its capabilities and technology plans and can best speak to those points. Legal issues must always be deferred to the in-house council or legal team. A cross-functional collaboration is needed for IG policies to hit the mark and be effective. The result is not only more secure information but also better information to base decisions on and closer adherence to regulatory and legal demands.[2]

10. *Continuous improvement.* IG programs are not one-time projects but rather ongoing programs that must be reviewed periodically and adjusted to account for gaps or shortcomings as well as changes in the business environment, technology usage, or business strategy.

Accountability Is Key

According to Debra Logan at Gartner Group, *none of the proffered definitions of IG includes "any notion of coercion, but rather ties governance to accountability* [emphasis added] that is designed to encourage the right behavior. . . . The word that matters most is *accountability.*" The root of many problems with managing information is the "fact that there is no accountability for information as such."[3]

Establishing policies, procedures, processes, and controls to ensure the quality, integrity, accuracy, and security of business records are the fundamental steps needed to reduce the organization's risk and cost structure for managing these records. Then it is essential that IG efforts are supported by IT. The auditing, testing, maintenance, and improvement of IG is enhanced by using electronic records management (ERM) software along with other complementary technology sets, such as workflow and business process management suite (BPMS) software and digital signatures.

Generally Accepted Recordkeeping Principles®

Contributed by Charmaine Brooks, CRM

A major part of an IG program is managing formal business records. Although they account for only about 7 to 9 percent of the total information that an organization holds, they are the most critically important subset to manage, as there are serious compliance and legal ramifications to not doing so.

Accountability is a key aspect of IG.

Records and recordkeeping are inextricably linked with any organized business activity. Through the information that an organization uses and records, creates, or receives in the normal course of business, it knows what has been done and by whom. This allows the organization to effectively demonstrate compliance with applicable standards, laws, and regulations as well as plan what it will do in the future to meet its mission and strategic objectives.

Standards and principles of recordkeeping have been developed by **records and information management** (RIM) practitioners to establish benchmarks for how organizations of all types and sizes can build and sustain compliant, defensible **records management** (RM) programs.

The Principles

In 2009 ARMA International published a set of eight Generally Accepted Recordkeeping Principles,® known as The Principles[4] (or sometimes GAR Principles), to foster awareness of good recordkeeping practices. These principles and associated metrics provide an IG framework that can support continuous improvement.

The eight Generally Accepted Recordkeeping Principles are:

1. *Accountability.* A senior executive (or person of comparable authority) oversees the recordkeeping program and delegates program responsibility to appropriate individuals. The organization adopts policies and procedures to guide personnel, and ensure the program can be audited.
2. *Transparency.* The processes and activities of an organization's recordkeeping program are documented in a manner that is open and verifiable and is available to all personnel and appropriate interested parties.
3. *Integrity.* A recordkeeping program shall be constructed so the records and information generated or managed by or for the organization have a reasonable and suitable guarantee of authenticity and reliability.
4. *Protection.* A recordkeeping program shall be constructed to ensure a reasonable level of protection to records and information that are private, confidential, privileged, secret, or essential to business continuity.
5. *Compliance.* The recordkeeping program shall be constructed to comply with applicable laws and other binding authorities, as well as the organization's policies.
6. *Availability.* An organization shall maintain records in a manner that ensures timely, efficient, and accurate retrieval of needed information.
7. *Retention.* An organization shall maintain its records and information for an appropriate time, taking into account legal, regulatory, fiscal, operational, and historical requirements.
8. *Disposition.* An organization shall provide secure and appropriate disposition for records that are no longer required to be maintained by applicable laws and the organization's policies.[5]

The Generally Accepted Recordkeeping Principles consist of eight principles that provide an IG framework that can support continuous improvement.

Table 3.1 Generally Accepted Recordkeeping Principles Levels

Level 1 Substandard	Characterized by an environment where recordkeeping concerns are either not addressed at all or are addressed in an ad hoc manner.
Level 2 In Development	Characterized by an environment where there is a developing recognition that recordkeeping has an impact on the organization, and the organization may benefit from a more defined information governance program.
Level 3 Essential	Characterized by an environment where defined policies and procedures exist that address the minimum or essential legal and regulatory requirements, but more specific actions need to be taken to improve recordkeeping.
Level 4 Proactive	Characterized by an environment where information governance issues and considerations are integrated into business decisions on a routine basis, and the organization consistently meets its legal and regulatory obligations.
Level 5 Transformational	Characterized by an environment that has integrated information governance into its corporate infrastructure and business processes to such an extent that compliance with program requirements is routine.

Source: Used with permission from ARMA.

The Principles apply to all sizes of organizations, in all types of industries, in both the private and public sectors, and can be used to establish consistent practices across business units. The Principles are an IG maturity model, and it is used as a preliminary evaluation of recordkeeping programs and practices.

Interest in and the application of The Principles for assessing an organization's recordkeeping practices have steadily increased since their establishment in 2009. The Principles form an accountability framework that includes the processes, roles, standards, and metrics that ensure the effective and efficient use of records and information in support of an organization's goals and business objectives.

As shown in Table 3.1, the Generally Accepted Recordkeeping Principles maturity model associates characteristics that are typical in five levels of recordkeeping capabilities ranging from 1 (substandard) to 5 (transformational). The levels are both descriptive and color coded for ease of understanding. The eight principles and levels (metrics) are applied to the current state of an organization's recordkeeping capabilities and can be cross-referenced to the policies and procedures. *While it is not unusual for an organization to be at different levels of maturity in the eight principles, the question "How good is good enough?" must be raised and answered*; a rating of less than "transformational" may be acceptable, depending on the organization's tolerance for risk and an analysis of the costs and benefits of moving up each level.

The maturity levels define the characteristics of evolving and maturing RM programs. The assessment should reflect the current RM environment and practices. The principles and maturity level definitions, along with improvement recommendations (roadmap), outline the tasks required to proactively approach addressing systematic RM practices and reach the next level of maturity for each principle. While the Generally Accepted

The Generally Accepted Recordkeeping Principles maturity model measures recordkeeping maturity in five levels.

Recordkeeping Principles are broad in focus, they illustrate the requirements of good RM practices. The Principles Assessment can also be a powerful communication tool to promote cross-functional dialogue and collaboration among business units and staff.

Accountability

The principle of **accountability** covers the assigned responsibility for RM at a senior level to ensure effective governance with the appropriate level of authority. A senior-level executive must be high enough in the organizational structure to have sufficient authority to operate the RM program effectively. The primary role of the senior executive is to develop and implement RM policies, procedures, and guidance and to provide advice on all recordkeeping issues. The direct responsibility for managing or operating facilities or services may be delegated.

The senior executive must possess an understanding of the business and legislative environment within which the organization operates, business functions and activities, and the required relationships with key external stakeholders to understand how RM contributes to achieving the corporate mission, aims, and objectives.

It is important for top-level executives to take ownership of the RM issues of the organization and to identify corrective actions required for mitigation or ensure resolution of problems and recordkeeping challenges. An executive sponsor should identify opportunities to raise awareness of the relevance and importance of RM and effectively communicate the benefits of good RM to staff and management.

The regulatory and legal framework for RM must be clearly identified and understood. The senior executive must have a sound knowledge of the organization's information and technological architecture and actively participate in strategic decisions for IT systems acquisition and implementation.

The senior executive is responsible for ensuring that the processes, procedures, governance structures, and related documentation are developed. The policies should identify the roles and responsibilities at all levels of the organization.

An audit process must be developed to cover all aspects of RM within the organization, including substantiating that sufficient levels of accountability have been assigned and accountability deficiencies are identified and remedied. Audit processes should include compliance with the organization policies and procedures for all records, regardless of format or media. Accountability audit requirements for electronic records include employing appropriate technology to audit the information architecture and systems. Accountability structures must be updated and maintained as changes occur in the technology infrastructure.

The audit process must reinforce compliance and hold individuals accountable. The results should be constructive, encourage continuous improvement, but not be used as a means of punishment. *The audit should contribute to records program improvements in risk mitigation, control, and governance issues and have the capacity to support sustainability.*

An audit process must be developed to cover all aspects of RM in the organization.

To be effective, policies must be formalized and integrated into business processes.

Transparency

Policies are broad guidelines for the operation of the organization and provide a basic guide to action that prescribes the boundaries within which business activities are to take place. They state the course of action to be followed by the organization, business unit, department, and employees.

Transparency of recordkeeping practices includes documenting processes and promoting an understanding of the roles and responsibilities of all stakeholders. *To be effective, policies must be formalized and integrated into business processes.* Business rules and recordkeeping requirements need to be communicated and installed at all levels of the organization.

Senior management must recognize that transparency is fundamental to IG and compliance. Documentation must be consistent, current, and complete. A review and approval process must be established to ensure that the introduction of new programs or changes can be implemented and integrated into business processes.

Employees must have ready access to RM policies and procedures. They must receive guidance and training to ensure they understand their roles and requirements for RM. Recordkeeping systems and business processes must be designed and developed to clearly define the records lifecycle.

In addition to policies and procedures, guidelines and operational instructions, diagrams and flowcharts, system documentation, and user manuals must include clear guidance on how records are to be created, retained, stored, and dispositioned. The documentation must be readily available and incorporated in communications and training provided to staff.

Integrity

Record generating systems and repositories must be assessed to determine record-keeping capabilities. *A formalized process must be in place for acquiring or developing new systems, including requirements for capturing the metadata required for lifecycle management of records in the systems.* In addition, the record must contain all the necessary elements of an official record, including structure, content, and context. **Records integrity**, reliability, and trustworthiness are confirmed by ensuring that a record was created by a competent authority according to established processes.

Maintaining the integrity of records means that they are complete and protected from being altered. The authenticity of a record is ascertained from internal and external evidence, including the characteristics, structure, content, and context of the records, to verify they are genuine and not corrupted or altered. In order to trust that a record is authentic, organizations must ensure that recordkeeping systems that create, **capture**, and manage electronic records are capable of protecting records from accidental or unauthorized alteration or deletion while the record has value.

Protection

*Organizations must ensure the **protection** of records and ensure they are unaltered through loss, tampering, or corruption.* This includes technological change or the failure of digital storage media and protecting records against damage or deterioration.

This principle applies equally to physical and electronic records, each of which has unique requirements and challenges.

Access and security controls need to be established, implemented, monitored, and reviewed to ensure business continuity and minimize business risk. Restrictions on access and disclosure include the methods for protecting personal privacy and proprietary information. Access and security requirements must be integrated into the business systems and processes for the creation, use, and storage of records.

LTDP is a series of managed activities required to ensure continued access to digital materials for as long as necessary. Electronic records requiring long-term retention may require conversion to a medium and format suitable to ensure long-term access and readability.

Compliance

RM programs include the development and training of the fundamental components, including **compliance monitoring** to ensure sustainability of the program.

Monitoring for compliance involves reviewing and inspecting the various facets of records management, including ensuring records are being properly created and captured, implementation of user permissions and security procedures, workflow processes through sampling to ensure adherence to policies and procedures, ensuring records are being retained following disposal authorization, and documentation of records destroyed or transferred to determine whether destruction/transfer was authorized in accordance with disposal instructions.

Compliance monitoring can be carried out by an internal audit, external organization, or RM and must be done on a regular basis.

Availability

Organizations should evaluate how effectively and efficiently records and information are stored and retrieved using present equipment, networks, and software. The evaluation should identify current and future requirements and recommend new systems as appropriate. Certain factors should be considered before upgrading or implementing new systems. These factors are practicality, cost, and effectiveness of new configurations.

A major challenge for organizations is ensuring timely and reliable access to and use of information and that records are accessible and usable for the entire length of the retention period. Rapid changes and enhancements to both hardware and software compound this challenge.

Retention

Retention *is the function of preserving and maintaining records for continuing use.* The retention schedule identifies the actions needed to fulfill the requirements for the retention and disposal of records and provides the authority for employees and systems to retain, destroy, or transfer records. The records retention schedule documents the record-keeping requirements and procedures, identifying how records are to be organized and maintained, what needs to happen to records and when, who is responsible for doing what, and whom to contact with questions or guidance.

Organizations must identify the scope of their recordkeeping requirements for documenting business activities based on regulated activities and jurisdictions that impose control over records. This includes business activities regulated by the government for every location or jurisdiction in which the company does business. Other considerations for determining retention requirements include operational, legal, fiscal, and historical ones.

Records appraisal is the process of assessing the value and risk of records to determine their retention and disposition requirements. Legal research is outlined in appraisal reports. This appraisal process may be accomplished as a part of the process of developing the records retention schedules as well as conducting a regular review to ensure that citations and requirements are current.

*The **records retention period** is the length of time that records should be retained and the actions taken for them to be destroyed or preserved.* The retention periods for different records should be based on legislative or regulatory requirements as well as on administrative and operational requirements.

It is important to document the legal research conducted and used to determine whether the law or regulation has been reasonably applied to the recordkeeping practices and provide evidence to regulatory officials or courts that due diligence has been conducted in good faith to comply with all applicable requirements.

Disposition

***Disposition** is the last stage in the life cycle of records.* When the retention requirements have been met and the records no longer serve a useful business purpose, records may be destroyed. Records requiring long-term or permanent retention should be transferred to an **archive** for preservation. The timing of the transfer of physical or electronic records should be determined through the records retention schedule process. Additional methods, including migration or conversion, are often required to preserve electronic records.

Records must be destroyed in a controlled and secure manner and in accordance with authorized disposal instructions. The destruction of records must be clearly documented to provide evidence of destruction according to an agreed-on program.

Destruction of records must be undertaken by methods appropriate to the confidentiality of the records and in accordance with disposal instructions in the records retention schedule. An audit trail documenting the destruction of records should be maintained, and certificates of destruction should be obtained for destruction undertaken by third parties. In the event disposal schedules are not in place, written authorization should be obtained prior to destruction. Procedures should specify who must supervise the destruction of records. Approved methods of destruction must be specified for each media type to ensure that information cannot be reconstructed.

Disposition is the last stage in the life cycle of records. Disposition is not synonymous with destruction, although destruction may be one disposal option.

Disposition is not synonymous with destruction, although destruction may be one disposal option. Destruction of records must be carried out under controlled, confidential conditions by shredding or permanent disposition. This includes the destruction of confidential microfilm, microfiche, computer cassettes, and computer tapes as well as paper.

Methods of Disposition

- *Discard.* The standard destruction method for nonconfidential records. If possible, all records should be shredded prior to recycling. Note that transitory records can also be shredded.
- *Shred.* Confidential and sensitive records should be processed under strict security. This may be accomplished internally or by secure on-site shredding by a third party vendor who provides certificates of secure destruction. The shredded material is then recycled.
- *Archive.* This designation is for records requiring long-term or permanent preservation. Records of enduring legal, fiscal, administrative, or historical value are retained.
- *Imaging.* Physical records converted to digital images, after which the original paper documents are destroyed.
- *Purge.* This special designation is for data, documents, or records sets that need to be purged by removing material based on specified criteria. This often applies to structure records in databases and applications.

Assessment and Improvement Roadmap

The Generally Accepted Recordkeeping Principles® maturity model can be leveraged to develop a current state assessment of an organization's recordkeeping practices and resources, identify gaps and assess risks, and develop priorities for desired improvements.

The Principles were developed by ARMA International to identify characteristics of an effective recordkeeping program. Each of the eight principles identifies issues and practices that, when evaluated against the unique needs and circumstances of an organization, can be applied to improvements for a recordkeeping program that meets recordkeeping requirements. The Principles identify requirements and can be used to guide incremental improvement in creation, organization, security, maintenance, and other activities over a period of one to five years. Fundamentally, RM and information governance are business disciplines that must be tightly integrated with operational policies, procedures, and infrastructure.

The Principles can be mapped to the four improvement areas in Table 3.2.

As an accepted industry guidance maturity model, the Principles provide a convenient and complete framework for assessing the current state of an organization's recordkeeping and developing a roadmap to identify improvements that will bring the organization into compliance. An assessment/analysis of the current RM practices, procedures, and capabilities together with current and future state practices provides two ways of looking at the future requirements of a complete RM (see Table 3.3).

Table 3.2   Improvement Areas for Generally Accepted Recordkeeping Principles

Improvement Area	Accountability	Transparency	Integrity	Protection	Compliance	Availability	Retention	Disposition
Roles and responsibilities	◊				◊		◊	
Policies and procedures	◊	◊	◊	◊	◊	◊	◊	◊
Communication and training	◊	◊		◊	◊		◊	
Systems and automation	◊			◊	◊	◊	◊	◊

Who Should Determine IG Policies?

When forming an IG steering committee or board, it is essential to include representatives from cross-functional groups and at different levels of the organization. The committee must be driven by an executive sponsor and include active members from key business units as well as other departments, including IT, finance, risk, compliance, RM, and legal. Then corporate training/education and communications must be involved to keep employees trained and current on IG policies. This function may be performed by an outside consulting firm if there is no corporate education staff.

Knowledge workers who work with records and sensitive information in any capacity best understand the nature and value of the records they work with as they perform their day-to-day functions. IG policies must be developed and communicated clearly and consistently. *Policies are worthless if people do not know or understand them or how to comply with them.* And training is a crucial element that will be examined in any compliance hearing or litigation that may arise. "Did senior management not only create the policies but provide adequate training on them on a consistent basis?" This will be a key question raised. So a training plan is a necessary piece of IG, and education should be heavily emphasized.[6]

The need for IG is increasing due to increased and tightened regulations, increased litigation, and the increased incidence of theft and misuse of internal documents and records. *Organizations that do not have active IG programs should reevaluate IG policies and their internal processes following any major loss of records, the inability to*

When forming an IG steering committee or board, it is essential to include representatives from cross-functional groups.

Knowledge workers who work with records in any capacity best understand the nature and value of the records they work with.

Table 3.3 Assessment Report and Road Map.

Principle	Level	Findings	Requirements to Move to the Next Step
Accountability	Level 1 Substandard	No senior executive (or person of comparable authority) is responsible for the RM program. The records manager role is largely nonexistent or is an administrative and/or clerical role distributed among general staff.	1. Assign RM responsibilities to senior executive. 2. Hire or promote records manager.
Transparency	Level 1 Substandard	It is difficult to obtain information about the organization or its records in a timely fashion. No clear documentation is readily available. There is no emphasis on transparency. Public requests for information, discovery for litigation, regulatory responses, or other requests (e.g., from potential business partners, investors, or buyers) cannot be readily accommodated. The organization has not established controls to ensure the consistency of information disclosure. Business processes are not well defined.	1. Develop policies and procedures. 2. Develop training for all levels of staff. 3. Identify requirements for records findability and accessibility. 4. Define business processes.
Integrity	Level 1 Substandard	There are no systematic audits or defined processes for showing the origin and authenticity of a record. Various organizational functions use ad hoc methods to demonstrate authenticity and chain of custody, as appropriate, but their trustworthiness cannot easily be guaranteed.	1. Develop audit process. 2. Identify business activities for creation and storage of records.
Protection	Level 1 Substandard	No consideration is given to record privacy. Records are stored haphazardly, with protection taken by various groups and departments with no centralized access controls. Access controls, if any, are assigned by the author.	1. Assess security and access controls. 2. Develop access and security control scheme.
Compliance	Level 3 Essential	The organization has identified all relevant compliance laws and regulations. Record creation and capture are systematically carried out in accordance with RM principles. The organization has a strong code of business conduct, which is integrated into its overall IG structure and record-keeping policies. Compliance and the records that demonstrate it are highly valued and measurable.	1. Implement systems to capture and protect records. 2. Develop metadata scheme. 3. Develop remediation plan and implement corrective actions.

Category	Level	Assessment	Recommendations
Availability	Level 2 In Development	The hold process is integrated into the organization's information management and discovery processes for the most critical systems. The organization has defined specific goals related to compliance. Record retrieval mechanisms have been implemented in certain areas of the organization. In those areas with retrieval mechanisms, it is possible to distinguish between official records, duplicates, and nonrecord materials. There are some policies on where and how to store official records, but a standard is not imposed across the organization. Legal discovery is complicated and costly due to the inconsistent treatment of information.	1. Develop enterprise classification scheme. 2. Identify user search and retrieval requirements. 3. Develop standards for managing the records lifecycle.
Retention	Level 2 In Development	A retention schedule is available but does not encompass all records, did not go through official review, and is not well known throughout the organization. The retention schedule is not regularly updated or maintained. Education and training about the retention policies are not available.	1. Develop enterprise-wide functional retention schedule. 2. Map retention schedule to classification scheme. 3. Implement an annual review process for record series and legal research. 4. Develop training for classification scheme and retention schedule.
Disposition	Level 2 In Development	Preliminary guidelines for disposition are established. There is a realization of the importance of suspending disposition in a consistent manner, repeatable by certain legal groupings. There may or may not be enforcement and auditing of disposition.	1. Develop procedures for records disposition. 2. Implement disposition processes. 3. Develop audit trails for records transfers and destruction.
Overall	Level 1 Substandard		

produce accurate records in a timely manner, or any document security breach or theft. If review boards include a broad section of critical players on the IG committee and leverage executive sponsorship, theywill better prepare the organization for legal and regulatory rigors.

CHAPTER SUMMARY: **KEY POINTS**

- Principles of successful IG programs are emerging. They include executive sponsorship, information classification, integrity, security, accessibility, control, monitoring, auditing, policy development, and continuous improvement.

- Accountability is a key aspect of IG.

- The Generally Accepted Recordkeeping Principles® ("The Principles") consist of eight principles that provide an IG framework that can support continuous improvement.

- An audit process must be developed to cover all aspects of RM in the organization.

- To be effective, policies must be formalized and integrated into business processes.

- Disposition is the last stage in the life cycle of records. Disposition is not synonymous with destruction, although destruction may be one disposal option.

- Knowledge workers who work with records in any capacity best understand the nature and value of the records they work with.

- When forming an information governance steering committee or board, it is essential to include representatives from cross-functional groups.

- Organizations without active IG programs should reevaluate IG policies and their internal processes following any major loss of records, the inability to produce accurate records in a timely manner, or any document security breach or theft.

Notes

1. Laura DuBois and Vivian Tero, "Practical Information Governance: Balancing Cost, Risk, and Productivity," IDC White Paper, August 2010, www.emc.com/collateral/analyst-reports/idc-practical-information-governance-ar.pdf
2. Ibid.
3. Debra Logan, "What Is Information Governance? And Why Is It So Hard?" January 11, 2010, http://blogs.gartner.com/debra_logan/2010/01/11/what-is-information-governance-and-why-is-it-so-hard/.

4. ARMA International, "Generally Accepted Recordkeeping Principles," www.arma.org/r2/generally-accepted-br-recordkeeping-principles/copyright (accessed November 14, 2013).
5. ARMA International,"Information Governance Maturity Model," www.arma.org/r2/generally-accepted-br-recordkeeping-principles (accessed November 14, 2013).
6. "Governance Overview (SharePoint Server 2010)," http://technet.microsoft.com/en-us/library/cc263356.aspx (accessed April 19, 2011).

PART TWO

Information Governance Risk Assessment and Strategic Planning

CHAPTER 4

Information Risk Planning and Management

Information risk planning involves a number of progressive steps: identifying potential risks to information, weighing those risks, creating strategic plans to mitigate the risks, and developing those plans into specific policies. Then it moves to developing metrics to measure compliance levels and identifying those who are accountable for executing the new risk mitigating processes. These processes must be audited and tested periodically not only to ensure compliance, but also to fine tune and improve the processes.

Depending on the jurisdiction, information is required by specific laws and regulations to be retained for specified periods, and to be produced in specified situations. To determine which laws and regulations apply to your organization's information, research into the legal and regulatory requirements for information in the jurisdictions in which your organization operates must be conducted.

Step 1: Survey and Determine Legal and Regulatory Applicability and Requirements

There are federal, provincial, state, and even municipal laws and regulations that may apply to the retention of information (data, documents, and records). Organizations operating in multiple jurisdictions must maintain compliance with laws and regulations that may cross national, state, or provincial boundaries. Legally required privacy requirements and retention periods must be researched for each jurisdiction (e.g. county, state, country) in which the business operates, so that it complies with all applicable laws.

IG, compliance, and records managers must conduct their own legislative research to apprise themselves of mandatory information retention requirements, as well as privacy considerations and requirements, especially in regard to **personally identifiable information** (PII). This information must be analyzed and structured and presented to legal staff for discussion. Then further legal and regulatory research must be conducted, and firm legal opinions must be rendered by legal counsel regarding information retention, privacy, and security requirements in accordance with laws and regulations. *This is an absolute requirement.* In order to arrive at a consensus on records that have legal value to the organization and to construct an appropriate retention

> In identifying information requirements and risks, legal requirements trump all others.

schedule, your legal staff or outside legal counsel should explain the legal hold process, provide opinions and interpretations of law that apply to your organization, and explain the value of formal records.

Legal requirements trump all others. The retention period for a particular type of document or PII data or records series must meet minimum retention, privacy, and security requirements as mandated by law. Business needs and other considerations are secondary. So, legal research is required before determining and implementing retention periods, privacy policies, and security measures.

In order to locate the regulations and citations relating to retention of records, there are two basic approaches. The first approach is to use a records retention citation service, which publishes in electronic form all of the retention-related citations. These services usually are purchased on a subscription basis, as the citations are updated on an annual or more frequent basis as legislation and regulations change.

Figure 4.1 is an excerpt from a Canadian records retention database product called FILELAW®.[1] In this case, the act, citation, and retention periods are clearly identified.

Another approach is to search the laws and regulations directly using online or print resources. Records retention requirements for corporations operating in the United States may be found in the **Code of Federal Regulations (CFR).**

```
Ontario
 Energy
  Electricity Act, 1998
   OE-Elect.-9 — Electricity Act Offence Prosecutions — Limitation Period
```

OE-Elect.-9 — *Electricity Act* Offence Prosecutions — Limitation Period

Date: 2011-4

Citation: *Electricity Act, 1998*, S. O. 2002, c. 1, Schedule A, s. 85.26; as am. S. O. 2000, c. 42, s. 27

Retention/Limitation:
  6 years

Description:
  85.26.(1) A proceeding to prosecute an offence under this Part must be commenced within six years after the date on which the matter of the offence arose.

Definition:
  155. An action or other proceeding shall not be commenced against a transferee in respect of any employee, asset, liability, right or obligation that has been transferred to the transferee if, had there been no transfer, the time for commencing the action or other proceeding would have expired.

  2.(1) In this Act, . . .

  "Minister" means the Minister of Energy or such other member of the Executive Council as may be assigned the administration of this Act under the *Executive Council Act*.

Figure 4.1   Excerpt from Canadian Records Retention Database
Source: Ontario, Electricity Act, FILELAW database, Thomson Publishers, May 2012.

> In the United States the Code of Federal Regulations lists retention require-
> ments for businesses, divided into 50 subject matter areas.

The Code of Federal Regulations (CFR) annual edition is the codification of
the general and permanent rules published in the Federal Register by the departments and agencies of the federal government. It is divided into 50 titles
that represent broad areas subject to federal regulation. The 50 subject matter
titles contain one or more individual volumes, which are updated once each
calendar year, on a staggered basis. The annual update cycle is as follows: titles
1 to 16 are revised as of January 1; titles 17 to 27 are revised as of April 1; titles
28 to 41 are revised as of July 1; and titles 42 to 50 are revised as of October 1.
Each title is divided into chapters, which usually bear the name of the issuing agency. Each chapter is further subdivided into parts that cover specific
regulatory areas. Large parts may be subdivided into subparts. All parts are
organized in sections, and most citations to the CFR refer to material at the
section level.[2]

There is an up-to-date version that is not yet a part of the official CFR but is
updated daily, the **Electronic Code of Federal Regulations (e-CFR)**. "It is not an
official legal edition of the CFR. The e-CFR is an editorial compilation of CFR material and Federal Register amendments produced by the National Archives and Records Administration's Office of the Federal Register . . . and the Government Printing
Office."[3] According to the gpoaccess.gov Web site:

> The Administrative Committee of the Federal Register (ACFR) has autho-
> rized the National Archives and Records Administration's (NARA) Office of
> the Federal Register (OFR) and the Government Printing Office (GPO) to
> develop and maintain the e-CFR as an informational resource pending ACFR
> action to grant the e-CFR official legal status. The OFR/GPO partnership is
> committed to presenting accurate and reliable regulatory information in the
> e-CFR editorial compilation with the objective of establishing it as an ACFR
> sanctioned publication in the future. While every effort has been made to en-
> sure that the e-CFR on GPO Access is accurate, those relying on it for legal
> research should verify their results against the official editions of the CFR,
> Federal Register and List of CFR Sections Affected (LSA), all available online
> at www.gpoaccess.gov. Until the ACFR grants it official status, the e-CFR
> editorial compilation does not provide legal notice to the public or judicial
> notice to the courts.
>   The OFR updates the material in the e-CFR on a daily basis. Generally,
> the e-CFR is current within two business days. The current update status is
> displayed at the top of all e-CFR web pages.

For governmental agencies, a key consideration is complying with requests for
information as a result of freedom of information laws like the U.S. Freedom of

Information Act, Freedom of Information Act 2000 (in the United Kingdom), and similar legislation in other countries. So the process of governing information is critical to meeting these requests by the public for governmental records.

Step 2: Specify IG Requirements to Achieve Compliance

Once the legal research has been conducted and a process for keeping updated on laws and regulations has been established, specific external compliance requirements can be listed and those data, document, and record sets that apply to those external compliance requirements can be mapped back to applicable holdings of data sets, document collections, and records series. The crucial task is keeping your legal and records management staff apprised of changes and updating the policies and processes appropriately.

Internal IG retention policies may be different from the legally mandated minimums. For instance, an organization that is not operating in a highly regulated industry that wants to balance defensible disposition with a need to retain corporate memory and develop **knowledge management** (KM) content or "knowledge bases" may have the option to dispose of e-mail that is not declared a record or cited for legal hold after 90 days, but may choose, based on corporate culture and other business factors, to retain e-mail messages for a year. Similarly, the organization may make legally defensible disposition decisions that reduce the total amount of information it must manage by using a "last accessed" rationale, whereby information that has not been accessed for over one year (or whatever the specified period is) may be destroyed and discarded, as a matter of policy.

Step 3: Create a Risk Profile

Creating a **risk profile** is a basic building block in **enterprise risk management** (yet *another* ERM acronym), which assists executives in understanding the risks associated with stated business objectives and allocating resources, within a structured evaluation approach or framework. There are multiple ways to create a risk profile, and how often it is done, the external sources consulted, and stakeholders who have input will vary from organization to organization.[4] *A key tenet to bear in mind is that simpler is better and that sophisticated tools and techniques should not make the process overly complex.* According to the ISO, risk is defined as "the effect of uncertainty on objectives," and a risk profile is "a description of a set of risks."[5] Creating a risk profile involves identifying, documenting, assessing, and prioritizing risks that an organization may face in pursuing its business objectives. It can be a simple table chart. Those associated risks can then be evaluated and delineated within a risk or IG framework.

The corporate risk profile should be an informative tool for executive management, the CEO, and the board of directors, so it should reflect that tone. In other

The risk profile is a high-level, executive decision input tool.

> A common risk profile method is to create a prioritized or ranked top-10 list of greatest risks to information.

words, it should be clear, succinct, and simplified. A risk profile may also serve to inform the head of a division or subsidiary, in which case it may contain more detail. The process can also be applied to public and nonprofit entities.

The time horizon for a risk profile varies, but looking out three to five years is a good rule of thumb.[6] The risk profile typically will be created annually, although semiannually would serve the organization better and account for changes in the business and legal environment. But if an organization is competing in a market sector with rapid business cycles or volatility, the risk profile should be generated more frequently, perhaps quarterly.

There are different types of risk profile methodologies; common methodologies are a **top-10** list, a **risk map**, and a **heat map**. The top-10 list is a simple identification and ranking of the 10 greatest risks in relation to business objectives. The risk map is a visual tool that is easy to grasp, with a grid depicting a likelihood axis and an impact axis, usually rated on a scale of 1 to 5. In a risk assessment meeting, stakeholders can weigh in on risks using voting technology to generate a consensus. A heat map is a color-coded matrix generated by stakeholders voting on risk level by color (e.g., red being highest).

Information gathering is a fundamental activity in building the risk profile. Surveys are good for gathering basic information, but for more detail, a good method to employ is direct, person-to-person interviews, beginning with executives and risk professionals.[7] Select a representative cross section of functional groups to gain a broad view. Depending on the size of the organization, you may need to conduct 20 to 40 interviews, with one person asking the questions and probing while another team member takes notes and asks occasionally for clarification or elaboration. Conduct the interviews in a compressed timeframe—knock them out within one to three weeks and do not drag the process out, as business conditions and personnel can change over the course of months.

Here are three helpful considerations to conducting successful interviews.

1. Prepare some questions for interviewees in advance and provide them to interviewees so they may prepare and do some of their own research.
2. Schedule the interview close to their offices, and at their convenience.
3. Keep the time as short as possible but long enough to get the answers you will need: approximately 20 to 45 minutes. Be sure to leave some open time between interviews to collect your thoughts and prepare for the next interview. And follow up with interviewees after analyzing and distilling your notes to confirm you have gained the correct insights.

The information you will be harvesting will vary depending on the interviewee's level and function. You will need to look for any hard data or reports that show performance and trends related to information risk. There may be benchmarking data

> Once a list of risks is developed, grouping them into basic categories helps stakeholders grasp them more easily and consider their likelihood and impact.

available as well. Delve into information access and security policies, policy development, policy adherence, and the like. Ask questions about retention of e-mail and legal hold processes. Ask about records retention and disposition policies. Ask about long-term preservation of digital records. Ask about data deletion policies. Ask for documentation regarding IG-related training and communications. Dig into policies for access to confidential data and securing vital records. Try to get a real sense of the way things are run, what is standard operating procedure, and also how workers might get around overly restrictive policies, or operate without clear policies. Learn enough so that you can grasp the management style and corporate culture, and then distill that information into your findings.

Key events and developments must also be included in the risk profile. For instance, a major data breach, the loss or potential loss of a major lawsuit, pending regulatory changes that could impact your IG policies, or a change in business ownership or structure must all be accounted for and factored into the information risk profile. Even changes in governmental leadership should be considered, if they might impact IG policies. These types of developments should be tracked on a regular basis and should continue to feed into the risk equation.[8] Key events should be monitored and incorporated in developing and subsequently updating the risk profile.

At this point, it should be possible to generate a list of specific potential risks. *It may be useful to group or categorize the potential risks into clusters, such as natural disaster, regulatory, safety, competitive, and so forth.* Armed with this list of risks, you should solicit input from stakeholders as to the likelihood and timing of the threats or risks. As the organization matures in its risk identification and handling capabilities, a good practice is to look at the risks and their ratings from previous years to attempt to gain insights into change and trends—both external and internal—that affected the risks.

Step 4: Perform Risk Analysis and Assessment

Once you have created a risk profile and identified key risks, you must conduct an assessment of the likelihood that these risks hold and their resultant impact.

There are five basic steps in conducting a risk assessment:[9]

1. *Identify the risks.* This should be an output of creating a risk profile, but if conducting an information risk assessment, first identify the major information-related risks.
2. *Determine potential impact.* If a calculation of a range of economic impact is possible (e.g., lose $5 to $10 million in legal damages), then include it. If not, be as specific as possible as to how a negative event related to an identified risk can impact business objectives.

Table 4.1 Risk Assessment

What Are the Risks?	How Might They Impact Business Objectives?	Actions and Processes Currently in Place	Additional Resources Needed to Manage This Risk	Action by Whom?	Action by When?	Done
Breach of confidential documents	Compromise confidential information	Utilizing ITIL and CobiT IT frameworks	Implement newer technologies including information rights management	IT staff, security officer	01/10/2016	01/10/2016
	Compromise competitive position	Published security policies	Implement quarterly audits			
	Compromise business negotiations	Semiannual security audits				

3. *Evaluate risk levels and probabilities and recommend action.* This may be in the form of recommending new procedures or processes, new investments in information technology (IT), or other actions to mitigate identified risks.
4. *Create a report with recommendations and implement.* You may want to include a risk assessment table (see Table 4.1) as well as written recommendations, then implement.
5. *Review periodically.* Review annually or semiannually, as appropriate for your organization.

A helpful exercise and visual tool is to draw up a table of top risks, their potential impacts, actions that have been taken to mitigate the risks, and suggested new risk countermeasures, as in Table 4.1.

Step 5: Develop an Information Risk Mitigation Plan

After setting out the risks, their potential impacts, and suggested countermeasures for mitigation, you must create the **information risk mitigation plan,** which means developing options and tasks to reduce the specified risks and improve the odds of achieving business objectives.[10] Basically, you are putting in writing the information you have collected and analyzed in creating the risk profile and risk assessment, and assigning specifics. The information risk mitigation plan should include a timetable and milestones for implementation of the recommended risk mitigation measures, including IT acquisition and implementation and assigning roles and responsibilities, such as executive sponsor, project manager (PM), and project team.

> The risk mitigation plan develops risk reduction options and tasks to reduce specified risks and improve the odds for achieving business objectives.

Step 6: Develop Metrics and Measure Results

How do you know how well you are doing? Have you made progress in reducing your organization's exposure to information risk? To measure conformance and performance of your IG program, you must have an objective way to measure how you are doing, which means numbers and metrics. Assigning some quantitative measures that are meaningful and do, in fact, measure progress may take some serious effort and consultation with stakeholders. Determining relevant ways of measuring progress will allow executives to see progress, as, realistically, reducing risk is not something anyone can see or feel—the painful realizations are made only when the risk comes home to roost. Also, valid metrics help to justify investment in the IG program.

Although the proper metrics will vary from organization to organization, some specific metrics include:

- Reduce the data lost on stolen or misplaced laptops by 50 percent over the previous fiscal year.
- Reduce the number of hacker intrusion events by 75 percent over the previous fiscal year.
- Reduce e-discovery costs by 25 percent over the previous fiscal year.
- Reduce the number of adverse findings in the risk and compliance audit by 50 percent over the previous fiscal year.
- Provide information risk training to 100 percent of the knowledge-level workforce this fiscal year.
- Roll out the implementation of information rights management software to protect confidential e-documents to 50 users this fiscal year.
- Provide confidential messaging services for the organization's 20 top executives this fiscal year.

Your organization's metrics should be tailored to address the primary goals of your IG program and should tie directly to stated business objectives.

Step 7: Execute Your Risk Mitigation Plan

Now that you have the risk mitigation plan, it must be executed. To do so, you must set up regular project/program team meetings, develop key reports on your information risk mitigation metrics, and manage the process. This is done using proven project and program management tools and techniques, which you may want to supplement with collaboration software tools, knowledge management software, or even internal social media.

But most important, execution of the risk mitigation plan involves communicating clearly and regularly with the IG team on the progress and status of the IG effort to reduce information risk.

Metrics are required to measure progress in the risk mitigation plan.

Step 8: Audit the Information Risk Mitigation Program

The metrics you have developed to measure risk mitigation effectiveness must also be used for audit purposes. Put a process in place to separately and independently audit compliance to risk mitigation measures, to see that they are being implemented. The result of the audit should be a useful input in improving and fine-tuning the program. It should not be viewed as an opportunity to cite shortfalls and implement punitive actions. It should be a periodic and regular feedback loop into the IG program.

CHAPTER SUMMARY: **KEY POINTS**

- In identifying information requirements and risks, legal requirements trump all others.

- In the United States, the Code of Federal Regulations lists information retention requirements for businesses, divided into 50 subject matter areas.

- The risk profile is a high-level, executive decision input tool.

- A common risk profile method is to create a prioritized or ranked top-10 list of greatest risks to information.

- Once a list of risks is developed, grouping them into basic categories helps stakeholders to grasp them more easily and consider their likelihood and impact.

- The risk mitigation plan develops risk reduction options and tasks to reduce specified risks and improve the odds for achieving business objectives.

- Metrics are required to measure progress in the risk mitigation plan.

- The risk mitigation plan must be reviewed and audited regularly and proper adjustments made.

Notes

1. Ontario, Electricity Act, FILELAW database, Thomson Publishers, May 2012.
2. U.S. Government Printing Office (GPO), "Code of Federal Regulations," www.gpo.gov/help/index .html#about_code_of_federal_regulations.htm (accessed April 22, 2012).
3. National Archives and Records Administration, "Electronic Code of Federal Regulations," http://ecfr .gpoaccess.gov/cgi/t/text/text-idx?c=ecfr&tpl=%2Findex.tpl (accessed October 2, 2012).
4. John Fraser and Betty Simkins, eds., *Enterprise Risk Management: Today's Leading Research and Best Practices for Tomorrow's Executives* (Hoboken, NJ: John Wiley & Sons, 2010), p. 171.
5. "ISO 31000 2009 Plain English, Risk Management Dictionary," www.praxiom.com/iso-31000-terms .htm (accessed March 25, 2013).
6. Fraser and Simkins, p. 172.
7. Ibid.
8. Ibid., p. 179.
9. Health and Safety Executive, "Five Steps to Risk Assessment," www.hse.gov.uk/risk/fivesteps.htm (accessed March 25, 2013).
10. Project Management Institute, *A Guide to the Project Management Body of Knowledge (PMBOK Guide)*, 4th ed. (Project Management Institute, 2008), ANSI/PMI 99-001-2008, pp. 273–312.

CHAPTER 5

Strategic Planning and Best Practices for Information Governance

Securing a sponsor at the executive management level is always crucial to projects and programs, and this is especially true of any **strategic planning** effort. An executive must be on board and supporting the effort in order to garner the resources needed to develop and execute the strategic plan, and that executive must be held accountable for the development and execution of the plan. These axioms apply to the development of an information governance (IG) strategic plan.

Also, resources are needed—time, human capital, and budget money. The first is a critical element: It is not possible to require managers to take time out of their other duties to participate in a project if there is no executive edict and consistent follow up, support, and communication. Executive sponsorship is a best practice and supports the key principle of accountability of the Generally Accepted Recordkeeping Principles® (The Principles)[1] (see Chapter 3 for more detail). And, of course, without an allocated budget, no program can proceed.

The higher your executive sponsor is in the organization, the better.[2] The implementation of an IG program may be driven by the chief compliance officer, chief information officer (CIO), or, ideally, the chief executive officer (CEO). With CEO sponsorship come many of the key elements needed to complete a successful project, including allocated management time, budget money, and management focus.

It is important to bear in mind that this IG effort is truly a *change management* effort, in that it aims to change the structure, guidelines, and rules within which employees operate. *The change must occur at the very core of the organization's culture.* It must be embedded permanently, and for it to be, the message must be constantly and consistently reinforced. Achieving this kind of change requires commitment from the very highest levels of the organization.

Executive sponsorship is critical to project success. There is no substitute. Without it, a project is at risk of failure.

If the CEO is not the sponsor, then another high-level executive must lead the effort and be accountable for meeting milestones as the program progresses. Programs with no executive sponsor can lose momentum and focus, especially as competing projects and programs are evaluated and implemented. Program failure is a great risk without an executive sponsor. Such a program likely will fade or fizzle out or be relegated to the back burner. Without strong high-level leadership, when things go awry, finger pointing and political games may take over, impeding progress and cooperation.

The executive sponsor must be actively involved, tracking program objectives and milestones on a regular, scheduled basis and ensuring they are aligned with business objectives. He or she must be aware of any obstacles or disputes that arise, take an active role in resolving them, and push the program forward.

Crucial Executive Sponsor Role

The role of an executive sponsor is high level, requiring periodic and regular attention to the status of the program, particularly with budget issues, staff resources, and milestone progress. The role of a program or project manager (PM) is more detailed and day to day, tracking specific tasks that must be executed to make progress toward milestones. Both roles are essential. The savvy PM brings in the executive sponsor to push things along when more authority is needed but reserves such project capital for those issues that absolutely cannot be resolved without executive intervention. It is best for the PM to keep the executive sponsor fully informed but to ask for assistance only when absolutely needed.

At the same time, the PM must manage the relationship with the executive sponsor, perhaps with some gentle reminders, coaxing, or prodding, to ensure that the role and tasks of executive sponsorship are being fulfilled. "[T]he successful Project Manager knows that if those duties are not being fulfilled, it's time to call a timeout and have a serious conversation with the Executive Sponsor about the viability of the project."[3]

The executive sponsor serves six key purposes on a project:

1. *Budget.* The executive sponsor ensures an adequate financial commitment is made to see the project through and lobbies for additional expenditures when change orders are made or cost overruns occur.
2. *Planning and control.* The executive sponsor sets direction and tracks accomplishment of specific, measureable business objectives.
3. *Decision making.* The executive sponsor makes or approves crucial decisions and resolves issues that are escalated for resolution.
4. *Expectation Management.* The executive sponsor must manage expectation, since success is quite often a stakeholder perception.
5. *Anticipation.* Every project that is competing for resources can run into unforeseen blockages and objections. Executive sponsors run interference and provide political might for the PM to lead the project to completion, through a series of milestones.
6. *Approval.* The executive sponsor signs off when all milestones and objectives have been met.

> While the executive sponsor role is high level, the PM's role and tasks are more detailed and involve day-to-day management.

An eager and effective executive sponsor makes all the difference to a project—if the role is properly managed by the PM. It is a tricky relationship, since the PM is always below the executive sponsor in the organization's hierarchy, yet the PM must coax the superior into tackling certain high-level tasks. Sometimes a third-party consultant who is an expert in the specific project can instigate and support requests made of the sponsor and provide a solid business rationale.

Evolving Role of the Executive Sponsor

The role of the executive sponsor necessarily evolves and changes over the life of the initial IG program launch, during the implementation phases, and on through the continued IG program.

To get the program off the ground, the executive sponsor must make the business case and get adequate budgetary funding. But an effort such as this takes more than money; it takes *time*—not just time to develop new policies and implement new technologies, but the time of the designated PM, program leaders, and needed program team members.

In order to get this time set aside, the IG program must be made a top priority of the organization. It must be recognized, formalized, and aligned with organizational objectives. All this up-front work is the responsibility of the executive sponsor.

Once the IG program team is formed, team members must clearly understand why the new program is important and how it will help the organization meet its business objectives. This message must be regularly reinforced by the executive sponsor; he or she must not only paint the vision of the future state of the organization but articulate the steps in the path to get there.

When the formal program effort commences, the executive sponsor must remain visible and accessible. He or she cannot disappear into everyday duties and expect the program team to carry the effort through. The executive sponsor must be there to help the team confront and overcome business obstacles as they arise and must praise the successes along the way. This requires active involvement and a willingness to spend the time to keep the program on track and focused.

The executive sponsor must be the lighthouse that shows the way even through cloudy skies and rough waters. This person is the captain who must steer the ship, even if the first mate (PM) is seasick and the deckhands (program team) are drenched and tired.

After the program is implemented, the executive sponsor is responsible for maintaining its effectiveness and relevance. This is done through periodic compliance audits, testing and sampling, and scheduled meetings with the ongoing PM.

> The role of the executive sponsor changes during the inception, planning, and execution of the IG program.

Building Your IG Team

Who should make up the IG team? Although there are no set requirements or formulas, the complex nature of IG and the fact that it touches upon a number of specialized disciplines and functional areas dictates that a cross-functional approach be taken. So you will need representatives from several departments. There are some absolutes: you must have a representative from your legal staff or outside counsel, your information technology (IT) department, a senior records officer (SRO) or the equivalent, a risk management specialist or manager, an executive sponsor, and the IG program manager. In addition, there may be a need for input from managers of human resources, company communications, and certain business units. Depending on the scope of the effort, other possible IG team members might include an IT security expert, the corporate or agency archivist, business analysts, chief knowledge officer or knowledge management (KM) professional, litigation support head, financial analyst, business process specialist, project management professional, and other professionals in functions related to these areas.

Assigning IG Team Roles and Responsibilities

The executive sponsor will need to designate an IG PM. Depending on the focus of the IG effort, that person could come from several areas, including legal, compliance, risk management, records management, or IT.

In terms of breaking down the roles and responsibilities of the remainder of the IG team, the easy decision is to have IG team representatives take responsibility for the functional areas of their expertise. But there will be overlap, and it is best to have some pairs or small work groups teamed up to gain the broadest amount of input and optimum results. This will also facilitate cross training. For instance, inside legal counsel may be responsible for rendering the final legal opinions, but because they are not expert in records, document management, or risk management, they could benefit from input of others in specialized functional areas, which will inform them and help narrow and focus their legal research. Basic research into which regulations and laws apply to the

> The risk mitigation plan develops risk reduction options and tasks to reduce specified risks and improve the odds for achieving business objectives.

The IG team must include a cross-functional group of stakeholders from various departments, including legal, records management, IT, and risk management.

organization regarding security, retention, and preservation of e-mail, e-records, and personally identifiable information (PII) could be conducted by the SRO or records management head, in consultation with the corporate archivist and CIO, with the results of their findings and recommendations drafted and sent to the legal counsel. The draft report may offer up several alternative approaches that need legal input and decisions. Then the legal team lead can conduct its own, focused research and make final recommendations regarding the organization's legal strategy, business objectives, financial position, and applicable laws and regulations.

The result of the research, consultation, and collaboration of the IG team should result in a final draft of the IG strategic plan. It will still need more input and development to align the plan with business objectives, an analysis of internal and external drivers, applicable best practices, competitive analysis, applicable IT trends, an analysis and inclusion of the organization's culture, and other factors.

Align Your IG Plan with Organizational Strategic Plans

The IG plan must support the achievement of the organization's business objectives and therefore must be melded into the organization's overall strategic plan. Integration with the strategic plan means that the business objectives in the IG plan are consistent with, and in support of, the enterprise strategic plan.

So, for example, if the corporate strategy includes plans for acquiring smaller competitors and folding them into the organization's structure as operating divisions, then the IG plan must assist and contribute to this effort. Plans for standardizing operating policies and procedures must include a consistent, systematized approach to the components of IG, including stakeholder consultation, user training and communications, and compliance audits. The IG plan should bring a standard approach across the spectrum of information use and management within the organization and it must be forged to accommodate the new technology acquisitions. This means that e-mail policies, e-discovery policies, mobile device policies, social media policies, cloud collaboration and storage use, and even nitty-gritty details like report formats, data structures, document taxonomies, and metadata must be consistent and aligned with the overall strategic plan. In other words, the goal is to get all employees on the same page and working to support the business objectives of the strategic plan in everyday small steps within the IG plan.

The IG strategic plan must be aligned and synchronized with the organization's overall strategic plans, goals, and business objectives.

The organization will also have an IT plan that must be aligned with the strategic plan to support overall business objectives. The IT strategy may be to convert new acquisitions to the internal financial and accounting systems of the organization and to train new employees to use the existing software applications under the umbrella of the IG plan. Again, the IG plan needs to be integrated with the IT strategy and must consider the organization's approach to IT.

The result of the process of aligning the IG effort with the IT strategy and the organization's overall strategic plan will mean, ideally, that employee efforts are more efficient and productive since they are *consistently moving toward the achievement of the organization's overall strategic goals.* The organization will be healthier and will have less dissent and confusion with clear IG policies that leverage the IT strategy and help employees pursue overall business objectives.

Further considerations must be folded into the IG plan. As every corporate culture is different and has a real impact on decision-making and operational approaches, corporate culture must be included in the plan. Corporate culture includes the organization's appetite for risk, its use of IT (e.g., forward-thinking first adopter), its capital investment strategies, and other management actions.

So, if the organization is conservative and risk averse, it may want to hold off on implementing some emerging e-discovery technologies that can cut costs but also induce greater risk. Or if it is an aggressive, progressive, risk-taking organization, it may opt to test and adopt newer e-discovery technologies under the IT strategy and umbrella of IG policies. An example may be the use of **predictive coding** technology in **early case assessment** (ECA). Predictive coding uses text auto-classification technology and neural technology with the assistance of human input to "learn" which e-documents might be relevant in a particular legal matter and which may not be. Through a series of steps of testing and checking subsets of the documents, humans can provide input to improve the document sorting and selection process. The software uses **machine learning** (artificial intelligence whereby the software can change and improve on a particular task, as its decision engine is shaped and "trained" by input) to improve its ability to cull through and sort documents.

Predictive coding can reduce e-discovery costs, yet there are risks that the approach can be challenged in court and could, in fact, affect the case adversely. Thus, a decision on a technology like predictive coding can involve and include elements of the IG plan, IT strategy, and overall organizational strategic plan.

And there are resource issues to consider: How much management time, or bandwidth, is available to pursue the IG plan development and execution? Is there a budget item to allow for software acquisitions and training and communications to support the execution of the IG plan? Obviously, without the allocated management time and budget money, the IG plan cannot be executed.

Survey and Evaluate External Factors

The IG plan is now harmonized and aligned with your organization's strategic plan and IT strategy, but you are not finished yet, because the plan cannot survive in a vacuum: Organizations must analyze and consider the external business, legal, and technological environment and fold their analysis into their plans.

The IG strategic plan must be informed with an assessment of relevant technology trends.

Analyze IT Trends

IG requires IT to support and monitor implementation of polices, so it *matters* what is developing and trending in the IT space. What new technologies are coming online? Why are they being developed and becoming popular? How do these changes in the business environment that created opportunities for new technologies to be developed affect your organization and its ability execute its IG plan? How can new technologies assist? Which ones are immature and too risky? These are some of the questions that must be addressed in regard to the changing IT landscape.

Some changes in **information and communications technology** (ICT) are rather obvious, such as the trends toward mobile computing, tablet and smartphone devices, cloud storage, and social media use. Each one of these major trends that may affect or assist in implementing IG needs to be considered within the framework of the organization's strategic plan and IT strategy. If the corporate culture is progressive and supportive of remote work and telecommuting, and if the organizational strategy aims to lower fixed costs by reducing the amount of office space for employees and moving to a more mobile workforce, then trends in tablet and smartphone computing that are relevant to your organization must be analyzed and considered. Is the organization going to provide mobile devices or support a bring-your-own-device (BYOD) environment? Which equipment will you support? Will you support iOS, Android, or both? What is your policy going to be on phone jacking? What is the IG policy regarding confidential documents on mobile devices? Will you use encryption? If so, which software? Is your enterprise moving to the cloud computing model? Utilizing social media? What about **Big Data and analytics**? Are you going to consider deploying auto-classification and predictive coding technologies? What are the trends that might affect your organization?

Many, many questions must be addressed, but the evaluation must be narrowed down to those technology trends that specifically might impact the execution of your IG plan and rollout of new technology.

On a more granular level, you must evaluate even supported file and document formats. It gets that detailed, when you are crafting IG policy. For instance, PDF/A is the standard format for archiving electronic documents. So your plans must include **long-term digital preservation** (LTDP) standards and best practices.

Survey Business Conditions and the Economic Environment

If the economy is on a down cycle, and particularly if your business sector has been negatively affected, resources may be scarcer than in better times. Hence, it may be more difficult to get budget approval for necessary program expenses, such as new technologies, staff, training materials, communications, and so forth. This means your IG plan may need to be scaled back or its scope reduced. Implementing the plan in a key division rather than attempting an enterprise rollout may be the best tactic in tough economic times.

Trends and conditions in the internal and external business environment must
be included in the IG strategic plan.

But if things are booming and the business is growing fast, budget money for investments in the IG program may be easier to secure, and the goals may be expanded.

IG should be an ongoing program, but it takes time to implement, and it takes resources to execute, audit, and continue to refine. So an executive looking for a quick and calculable payback on the investment may want to focus on narrower areas. For instance, the initial focus may be entirely on the legal hold and e-discovery process, with business objectives that include reducing pretrial costs and attorney fees by a certain percentage or amount. It is much easier to see concrete results when focusing on e-discovery, since legal costs are real, and always will be there. The business case may be more difficult to make if the IG effort is broader and improves the ability to organize and search for information faster and to execute more complete searches to improve the basis for management decision making. Improved management decision making will improve the organization's competitiveness long-term, but it may be difficult to cite specific examples where costs were saved or revenues were increased as a result of the "better decisions" that should come about through better IG.

Analyze Relevant Legal, Regulatory, and Political Factors

In consultation with your legal team or lead, the laws and regulations that affect your industry should be identified. Narrowing the scope of your analysis, those that specifically could impact your governance of information should be considered and analyzed. What absolute requirements do they impose? Where there is room for interpretation, where, legally, does your organization want to position itself? How much legal risk is acceptable? These are the types of questions you will have to look to your legal and risk management professionals to make. Again, *legal requirements trump all others.*

Your decision process must include considerations for the future and anticipated future changes. Changes in the legal and regulatory environment happen based on the political leaders who are in place and any pending legislation. So you must go further and analyze the current political environment and make some judgments based on the best information you can gather, the organization's culture and appetite for risk, management style, available resources, and other factors. Generally, a more conservative environment means less regulation, and this analysis must also be folded into your IG strategic plan.

Laws and regulations relevant to your organization's management and distribution of information in all jurisdictions must be considered and included in the IG strategic plan. Legal requirements trump all others.

Include a best practices review in your IG strategic plan. The most relevant best practices in IG are those in your industry proven by peers and competitors.

Survey and Determine Industry Best Practices

IG is a developing hybrid discipline. In a sense, it is a superset of records management and a subset of **governance, risk management, and compliance** (GRC), that emerged to help manage the explosion in the amount of records, documents, and data that must be managed in today's increasingly high-volume and velocity business environment and highly regulated compliance and litigation environment. As such, best practices are still being formed and added to. This process of testing, proving, and sharing best practices will continue for some time as the practices are expanded, revised, and refined.

The most relevant study of IG best practices is one that is conducted for your organization and surveys your industry and what some of your more progressive competitors are doing in regard to IG. Often the best way to accomplish such a study is by engaging a third-party consultant, who can more easily contact, study, and interview your competitors in regard to their practices. Business peer groups and trade associations also can provide some consensus as to emerging best practices.

Twenty-five IG best practices covering a number of areas in which IG has an impact or should be a major consideration are listed next.

1. *IG is a key underpinning for a successful RM program.* Practicing good IG is the essential foundation for building a legally defensible RM program; it provides the basis for consistent, reliable methods for managing documents and records. Having trusted and reliable records, reports, and databases allows managers to make key decisions with confidence.[4] And accessing that information and business intelligence in a timely fashion can yield a long-term sustainable competitive advantage, creating more agile enterprises.

   To implement a successful IG program, enterprises must standardize and systematize their handling of information, in particular their formal business records. They must analyze and optimize how information is accessed, controlled, managed, shared, stored, preserved, and audited. They must have complete, current, and relevant policies, processes, and technologies to manage and control information, including *who* is able to access *what* information, and *when*, to meet external legal and regulatory demands and internal governance requirements. This, in short, is IG.

2. *IG is not a project but rather an ongoing program* that provides an umbrella of rules and policies, monitored and enforced with the support of IT to manage and control information output and communications. Since technologies change so quickly, it is necessary to have overarching technology-agnostic policies that can manage the various IT platforms that an organization may use.

   Compare the IG program to a workplace safety program; every time a new location, team member, piece of equipment, or toxic substance is acquired by the organization, the workplace safety program should dictate how that is handled. If it does not, the workplace safety policies/procedures/training that are part of the workplace safety program need to be updated. Regular reviews are conducted to ensure the program is being followed, and adjustments are made based on the findings. *The effort never ends.*[5]

3. *Using an IG framework or maturity model is helpful in assessing and guiding IG programs.* Various models are offered, such as The Principles from ARMA International; the Information Governance Reference Model, which grew out of the Electronic Discovery Reference Model (found at EDRM.net);[6] or MIKE2.0, which was developed by the consulting firm Bearing Point and released to the public domain. Another tool that is particularly used in the Australian market for records management projects is Designing and Implementing Recordkeeping Systems (DIRKS).

4. *Defensible deletion of data debris and information that no longer has value is critical in the era of Big Data.* You must have IG polices in place and be able to prove that you follow them consistently and systematically in order to justify, to the courts and regulators, deletion of information. With a smaller information footprint, organizations can more easily find what they need and derive business value from it.[7] Data debris must be eliminated regularly and consistently, and to do this, processes and systems must be in place to cull out valuable information and discard the data debris. An IG program sets the framework to accomplish this.

5. *IG policies must be developed before enabling technologies are deployed to assist in enforcement.* After the policy-making effort, seek out the proper technology tools to assist in monitoring, auditing, and enforcement.

6. *To provide comprehensive e-document security throughout a document's life cycle, documents must be secured upon creation using highly sophisticated technologies, such as information rights management (IRM) technology.* IRM acts as a sort of "security wrapper" that denies access without proper credentials. Document access and use by individuals having proper and current credentials is also tightly monitored IRM software controls the access, copying, editing, forwarding, and printing of documents using a policy engine that manages the rights to view and work on an e-document. Access rights are set by levels or "roles" that employees are responsible for within an organization.

7. *A records retention schedule and legal hold notification (LHN) process are the two primary elements of a fundamental IG program.* These are the basics. Implementation will require records inventorying, taxonomy development, metadata normalization and standardization, and a survey of LHN best practices.

8. *A cross-functional team is required to implement IG.* Since IG contains and requires elements of a number of established disciplines, representatives from the key areas must be included in the planning and implantation effort. At a minimum, you will need team leaders from legal, IT, records management, compliance and risk management, human resources, and executive management. Members from corporate communications, knowledge management, systems security, finance and accounting, and other functional areas also may be needed. Depending on the circumstances, you may need representatives from major business units within the organization.

9. *The first step in information risk planning is to consider the applicable laws and regulations that apply to your organization in the jurisdictions in which it conducts*

business. Federal, provincial, state, and even municipal laws and regulations may apply to the retention of data, documents, and records. Organizations operating in multiple jurisdictions must be compliant with laws and regulations that may cross national, state, or provincial boundaries. Legally required privacy requirements and retention periods must be researched for each jurisdiction (state, country) in which the business operates, so that all applicable laws are complied with.

10. *Developing a risk profile is a basic building block in enterprise risk management, which assists executives in understanding the risks associated with stated business objectives and in allocating resources within a structured evaluation approach or framework.* There are multiple ways to create a risk profile, and the frequency with which it is created, the external sources consulted, and stakeholders who have input will vary from organization to organization.[8] A key tenet to bear in mind is that simpler is better and that sophisticated tools and techniques should not make the process overly complex.

11. *An information risk mitigation plan is a critical part of the IG planning process.* An information risk mitigation plan helps in developing risk mitigation options and tasks to reduce the specified risks and improve the odds of achieving business objectives.[9]

12. *Proper metrics are required to measure the conformance and performance of your IG program.* You must have an objective way to measure how you are doing, which means numbers and metrics. Assigning some quantitative measures that are meaningful before rolling out the IG program is essential.

13. *IG programs must be audited for effectiveness.* Periodic audits will tell you how your organization is doing and where to fine-tune your efforts. To keep an IG program healthy, relevant, and effective, changes and fine-tuning will always be required.

14. *An enterprise wide retention schedule is preferable because it eliminates the possibility that different business units will have conflicting records retention periods.* For example, if one business unit discards a group of records after 5 years, it would not make sense for another business unit to keep the same records for 10 years. Where enterprise-wide retention schedules are not possible, smaller business units, such as divisions or regions, should operate under a consistent retention schedule.

15. *Senior management must set the tone and lead sponsorship for vital records program governance and compliance.* Although e-records are easier to protect and backup, most vital records today are e-records. These are an organization's most essential records. Without them, an organization cannot continue operations.

16. *Business processes must be redesigned to improve and optimize the management and security of information and especially the most critical of information, electronic records,* before *implementing enabling technologies.* For instance, using electronic records management (ERM) software fundamentally changes the way people work, and greater efficiencies can be gained with business process redesign (versus simply using ERM systems as electronic filing cabinets to speed up poor processes).

17. *E-mail messages, both inbound and outbound, should be archived automatically and (preferably) in real time.* This ensures that spoliation (i.e., the loss of proven authenticity of an e-mail) does not occur. Archiving preserves legal validity

and forensic compliance. By policy, most messages will be deleted in a short timeframe. Additionally, e-mail should be indexed to facilitate the searching process, and all messages should be secured in a single location (with backups). With these measures, the authenticity and reliability of e-mail records can be ensured.

18. *Personal archiving of e-mail messages should be disallowed.* Although users will want to save certain e-mail messages for their own reasons, control and management of e-mail archiving must be at the organization level or as high of a level as is practical, such as division or region.

19. *Destructive retention of e-mail helps to reduce storage costs and legal risk while improving "findability" of critical records.* It makes good business sense to have a policy to, say, destroy all e-mail messages after 90 or 120 days that are not flagged as potential records (which, e.g., help document a transaction or a situation that may come into dispute in the future) or those that have a legal hold.

20. *Take a practical approach and limit cloud use to documents that do not have long retention periods and carry a low litigation risk.* Doing this will reduce the risk of compromising or losing critical documents and e-records. Some duplicate copies of vital records may be stored securely in the cloud to help the organization recover in the event of a disaster.

21. *Manage social media content by IG policies and monitor it with controls that ensure protection of critical information assets and preservation of business records.* Your organization must state clearly what content and tone is acceptable in social media use, and it must retain records of that use, which should be captured in real time.

22. *International and national standards provide effective guidance for implementing IG.* Although there are no absolutes, researching and referencing International Organization for Standardization (ISO) and other standards must be a part of any IG effort.

23. *Creating standardized metadata terms should be part of an IG effort that enables faster, more complete, and more accurate searches and retrieval of records.* This is important not only in everyday business operations but also when delving through potentially millions of records during the discovery phase of litigation. Good metadata management also assists in the maintenance of corporate memory and in improving accountability in business operations.[10] Using a standardized format and controlled vocabulary provides a "precise and comprehensible description of content, location, and value."[11] Using a controlled vocabulary means your organization has standardized a set of terms used for metadata elements that describe records. This ensures consistency across a collection and helps with optimizing search and retrieval functions and records research as well as with meeting e-discovery requests, compliance demands, and other legal and regulatory requirements.

24. *Some digital information assets must be preserved permanently as part of an organization's documentary heritage.*[12] It is critical to identify records that must be kept long term as early in the process as possible; ideally, these records should be identified prior to or upon creation. LTDP applies to content that is born digital as well as content that is converted to digital form. Digital preservation is defined as long-term, error-free storage of digital information, with means for retrieval and interpretation, for the entire time span that the information

is required to be retained. Dedicated repositories for historical and cultural memory, such as libraries, archives, and museums, need to move forward to put in place trustworthy digital repositories that can match the security, environmental controls, and wealth of descriptive metadata that these institutions have created for analog assets (such as books and paper records). Digital challenges associated with records management affect all sectors of society—academic, government, private, and not-for-profit enterprises—and ultimately citizens of all developed nations.

25. *Executive sponsorship is crucial.* Securing an executive sponsor at the senior management level is key to successful IG programs. It is not possible to require managers to take time out of their other duties to participate in a project if there is no executive edict. It is a best practice across industry sectors and technology sets and supports the Accountability principle of The Principles.[13]

Formulating the IG Strategic Plan

Now comes the time to make sense of all the data and input your IG team has gathered and hammer it into a workable IG strategic plan. Doing this will involve some give-and-take among IG team members, each having their own perspective and priorities. Everyone will be lobbying for the view of their functional groups. It is the job of the executive sponsor to set the tone and to emphasize organizational business objectives so that the effort does not drag out or turn into a competition but is a well-informed consensus development process that results in a clear, workable IG strategic plan.

Synthesize Gathered Information and Fuse It into IG Strategy

Your IG team will have gathered a great deal of information, which needs to be analyzed and distilled into actionable strategies. This process will depend on the expertise and input of the specialized knowledge your team brings to the table within your organizational culture. Team members must be able to make decisions and establish priorities that reflect organizational business objectives and consider a number of influencing factors.

Do not prolong the strategy development process. The longer it lasts, the more key factors influencing it can change. You want to develop a strategic plan that is durable enough to withstand changes in technology, legislation, and other key influencing factors, but it should be relevant to that snapshot of information that was collected early on. When all the parts and pieces start changing and require reconsideration, a dated IG plan does not serve the organization well.

Develop IG strategies for each of the critical areas, including the legal hold process, e-discovery action plans, e-mail policy, mobile computing policy, IT acquisition strategy, confidential document handling, vital records and disaster planning, social media policy, and other areas that are important to your organization. To maintain focus, do this first without regard to the prioritization of these areas.

Fuse the findings of all your analyses of external and internal factors into your IG strategic plan. Develop strategies and then prioritize them.

Then you must go through the hard process of prioritizing your strategies and aligning them to your organizational goal and objectives. This may not be difficult in the beginning—for instance, your IG strategies for legal holds and e-discovery readiness are likely going to take higher priority than your social media policy, and protecting vital records is paramount to any organization. As the process progresses, it will become more challenging to make trade-offs and establish priorities. Then you must tie these strategies to overall organizational goals and business objectives.

A good technique to keep goals and objectives in mind may be to post them prominently in the meeting room where these strategy sessions take place. This will help to keep the IG team focused.

Develop Actionable Plans to Support Organizational Goals and Objectives

Plans and policies to support your IG efforts must be developed that identify specific tasks and steps and define roles and responsibilities for those who will be held accountable for their implementation. This is where the rubber meets the road. But you cannot simply create the plan and marching orders: You must build in periodic checks and audits to test that new IG policies are being followed and that they have hit their mark. Invariably, there will be adjustments made continually to craft the policies for maximum effectiveness and continued relevance in the face of changes in external factors, such as legislation and business competition, and internal changes in management style and structure.

Create New IG Driving Programs to Support Business Goals and Objectives

You have to get things moving and get employees motivated, and launching new subprograms within the overall IG program is a good way to start. For instance, a new "e-discovery readiness" initiative can show almost immediate results if implemented properly, with the support of key legal and records management team members, driven by the executive sponsor. You may want to revamp the legal hold process to make it more complete and verifiable, assigning specific employees accountability for specific tasks. Part of that effort may be evaluating and implementing new technology-assisted review (TAR) processes and predictive coding technology. So you will need to bring in the IG team members responsible for IT and perhaps business analysis. Working cooperatively on smaller parts of the overall IG program is a way to show real results within defined time frames. Piecing together a series of program components is the best way to get started, and it breaks the overall IG program

Create supporting subprograms to jump-start your IG program effort. Smaller programs should be able to measure real results based on metrics that are agreed on in advance.

down into digestible, doable chunks. A small win early on is crucial to maintain momentum and executive sponsorship. And e-discovery has real costs: yet progress can be measured objectively in terms of reducing the cost of activities such as early case assessment (ECA). Benefits can be measured in terms of reduced attorney review hours, reduced costs, and reduced time to accomplish pretrial tasks.

To be clear, you will need to negotiate and agree on the success metrics the program will be measured on in advance.

There are other examples of supporting IG subprograms, such as e-mail management and archiving, where storage costs, search times, and information breaches can be measured in objective terms. Or you may choose to roll out new policies for the use of mobile devices within your organization, where adherence to policy can be measured by scanning mobile devices and monitoring their use.

Draft the IG Strategic Plan and Gain Input from a Broader Group of Stakeholders

Once you have the pieces of the plan drafted and the IG team is in agreement that it has been harmonized and aligned with overall organizational goals and objectives, you must test the waters to see if you have hit the mark. It is a good practice to expose a broader group of stakeholders to the plan to gain their input. Perhaps your IG team has become myopic or has passed over some points that are important to the broader stakeholder audience. Solicit and discuss their input, and to the degree that there is a consensus, refine the IG strategic plan one last time before finalizing it. But remember, it is a living document, a work in progress, which will require revisiting and updating to ensure it is in step with changing external and internal factors. Periodic auditing and review of the plan will reveal areas that need to be adjusted and revised to keep it relevant and effective.

Get Buy-in and Sign-off and Execute the Plan

Take the finalized plan to executive management, preferably including the CEO, and present the plan and its intended benefits to them. Field their questions and address any concerns to gain their buy-in and the appropriate signatures. You may have to make some minor adjustments if there are significant objections, but, if you have executed the stakeholder consultation process properly, you should be very close to the mark. Then begin the process of implementing your IG strategic plan, including regular status meetings and updates, steady communication and reassurance of your executive sponsor, and planned audits of activities.

CHAPTER SUMMARY: **KEY POINTS**

- Engaged and vested executive sponsors are necessary for IG program success. It is not possible to require managers to take time out of their other duties to participate in a project if there is no executive edict or allocated budget.

- The executive sponsor must be: (1) directly tied to the success of the program, (2) fully engaged in and aware of the program, and (3) actively eliminating barriers and resolving issues.

- The role of the executive sponsor evolves over the life of the IG program and IG program effort. Initially, the focus is on garnering the necessary resources, but as the program commences, the emphasis is more on supporting the IG program team and clearing obstacles. Once the program is implemented, the responsibilities shift to maintaining the effectiveness of the program through testing and audits.

- While the executive sponsor role is high level, the project manager's role and tasks involve more detailed and day-to-day management.

- The risk mitigation plan develops risk reduction options and tasks to reduce specified risks and improve the odds for achieving business objectives.

- The IG team must include a cross-functional group of stakeholders from various departments, including legal, records management, IT, and risk management.

- The IG strategic plan must be aligned and synchronized with the organization's overall strategic plans, goals, and business objectives.

- The IG strategic plan must include an assessment of relevant technology trends.

- Trends and conditions in the internal and external business environment must be included in the IG strategic plan.

- Laws and regulations relevant to your organization's management and distribution of information in all jurisdictions must be considered and included in the IG strategic plan. Legal requirements trump all others.

- Include a best practices review in your IG strategic plan. The most relevant best practices in IG are those in your industry proven by peers and competitors. (Twenty-five IG best practices are listed in this chapter for the first time in print.)

- Fuse the findings of all your analysis of external and internal factors into your IG strategic plan. Develop strategies and then prioritize them.

- Creating supporting subprograms to jump-start your IG program effort. Smaller programs should be able to measure real results based on metrics that are agreed on in advance.

- Make sure to get executive sign-off on your IG strategic plan before moving to execute it.

Notes

1. ARMA International, "How to Cite GARP," www.arma.org/garp/copyright.cfm (accessed October 9, 2013).
2. Roger Kastner, "Why Projects Succeed—Executive Sponsorship," February 15, 2011, http://blog .slalom.com/2011/02/15/why-projects-succeed-%E2%80%93-executive-sponsorship/
3. Ibid.
4. Economist Intelligence Unit, "The Future of Information Governance," www.emc.com/leadership /business-view/future-information-governance.htm (accessed October 9, 2013).
5. Monica Crocker, e-mail to author, June 21, 2012.
6. EDRM, "Information Governance Reference Model (IGRM) Guide," www.edrm.net/resources /guides/igrm (accessed November 30, 2012).
7. Randolph A. Kahn, https://twitter.com/InfoParkingLot/status/273791612172259329, Nov. 28, 2012.
8. John Fraser and Betty Simkins, eds., *Enterprise Risk Management: Today's Leading Research and Best Practices for Tomorrow's Executives* (Hoboken, NJ: John Wiley & Sons, 2010), p. 171.
9. Project Management Institute, *A Guide to the Project Management Body of Knowledge* (*PMBOK Guide*), 4th ed. (Newtown Square, PA Project Management Institute, 2008), ANSI/PMI 99–001–2008, pp. 273–312.
10. Kate Cumming, "Metadata Matters," in Julie McLeod and Catherine Hare, eds., *Managing Electronic Records*, p. 34 (London: Facet, 2005).
11. Minnesota State Archives, Electronic Records Management Guidelines, "Metadata," March 12, 2012, www.mnhs.org/preserve/records/electronicrecords/ermetadata.html .
12. Charles Dollar and Lori Ashley, e-mail to author, August 10, 2012.
13. ARMA International, "How to Cite GARP."

CHAPTER 6

Information Governance Policy Development

To develop an **information governance** (IG) policy, you must inform and frame the policy with internal and external frameworks, models, best practices, and standards—those that apply to your organization and the scope of its planned IG program. In this chapter, we first present and discuss major IG frameworks and models and then identify key standards for consideration.

A Brief Review of Generally Accepted Recordkeeping Principles®

In Chapter 3 we introduced and discussed ARMA International's eight Generally Accepted Recordkeeping Principles®, known as The Principles[1] (or sometimes GAR Principles). These Principles and associated metrics provide an IG framework that can support continuous improvement.

To review, the eight Principles are:

1. Accountability
2. Transparency
3. Integrity
4. Protection
5. Compliance
6. Availability
7. Retention
8. Disposition[2]

The Principles establish benchmarks for how organizations of all types and sizes can build and sustain compliant, legally defensible **records management** (RM) programs. Using the maturity model (also presented in Chapter 3), organizations can assess where they are in terms of IG, identify gaps, and take steps to improve across the eight areas The Principles cover.

IG Reference Model

In late 2012, with the support and collaboration of ARMA International and the Compliance, Governance and Oversight Council (CGOC), the Electronic Discovery Reference Model (EDRM) Project released version 3.0 of its Information Governance Reference Model (IGRM), which added **information privacy and security** "as primary functions and stakeholders in the effective governance of information."[3] The model is depicted in Figure 6.1.

The IGRM is aimed at fostering IG adoption by facilitating communication and collaboration between disparate (but overlapping) IG stakeholder functions, including information technology (IT), legal, RM, risk management, and business unit

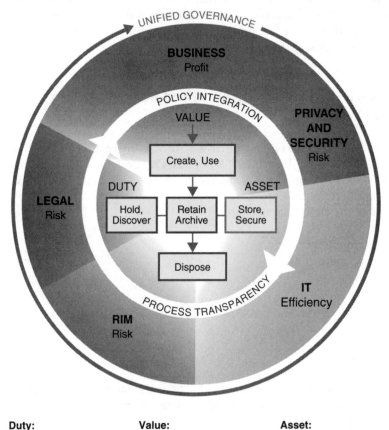

Linking duty + value to information asset = efficient, effective management

Duty:	Value:	Asset:
Legal obligation for specific information	Utility or business purpose of specific information	Specific container of information

Information Governance Reference Model / © 2012 / v3.0 / edrm.net

Figure 6.1   Information Governance Reference Model
Source: EDRM.net

You must inform and frame IG policy with internal and external frameworks, models, best practices, and standards.

stakeholders.[4] It also aims to provide a common, practical framework for IG that will foster adoption of IG in the face of new Big Data challenges and increased legal and regulatory demands. It is a clear snapshot of where IG touches and shows critical interrelationships and unified governance.[5] It can help organizations forge policy in an orchestrated way and embed critical elements of IG policy across functional groups. Ultimately, implementation of IG helps organizations leverage information value, reduce risk, and address legal demands.

The growing CGOC community (2,000+ members and rising) has widely adopted the IGRM and developed a process maturity model that accompanies and leverages IGRM v3.0.[6]

Interpreting the IGRM Diagram*

Outer Ring

Starting from the outside of the diagram, successful information management is about conceiving a complex set of interoperable processes and implementing the procedures and structural elements to put them into practice. It requires:

- An understanding of the business imperatives of the enterprise,
- Knowledge of the appropriate tools and infrastructure for managing information, and
- Sensitivity to the legal and regulatory obligations with which the enterprise must comply.

For any piece of information you hope to manage, the primary stakeholder is the business user of that information [emphasis added]. We use the term "business" broadly; the same ideas apply to end users of information in organizations whose ultimate goal might not be to generate a profit.

Once the business value is established, you must also understand the legal duty attached to a piece of information. The term "legal" should also be read broadly to refer to a wide range of legal and regulatory constraints and obligations, from e-discovery and government regulation to contractual obligations such as payment card industry requirements.

Finally, IT organizations must manage the information accordingly, ensuring privacy and security as well as appropriate retention as dictated by both business and legal or regulatory requirements.

---

*This section is adapted with permission by EDRM.net, http://www.edrm.net/resources/guides/igrm (accessed January 24, 2014).

The business user is the primary stakeholder of managed information.

Center

In the center of the diagram is a work-flow or life-cycle diagram. We include this component in the diagram to illustrate the fact that *information management is important at all stages of the information life cycle—from its creation through its ultimate disposition*. This part of the diagram, once further developed, along with other secondary-level diagrams, will outline concrete, actionable steps that organizations can take in implementing information management programs.

Even the most primitive business creates information in the course of daily operations, and IT departments spring up to manage the logistics; indeed, one of the biggest challenges in modern organizations is trying to stop individuals from excess storing and securing of information. Legal stakeholders can usually mandate the preservation of what is most critical, though often at great cost. However, it takes the coordinated effort of all three groups to defensibly dispose of a piece of information that has outlived its usefulness and retain what *is* useful in a way that enables accessibility and usability for the business user.

How the IGRM Complements the Generally Accepted Recordkeeping Principles*

The IGRM supports ARMA International's "Principles" by identifying the cross-functional groups of key information governance stakeholders and by depicting their intersecting objectives for the organization. This illustration of the relationship among duty, value, and the information asset demonstrates cooperation among stakeholder groups to achieve the desired level of maturity of effective information governance.

Effective IG requires a continuous and comprehensive focus. The IGRM will be used by proactive organizations as an introspective lens to facilitate visualization and discussion about how best to apply The Principles. The IGRM puts into sharp focus The Principles and provides essential context for the maturity model.

Information management is important at all stages of the life cycle.

Legal stakeholders can usually mandate the preservation of what is most critical, though often at great cost.

---

* This section is adapted with permission by EDRM.net, http://www.edrm.net/resources/guides/igrm (accessed January 24, 2014).

The IGRM was developed by the EDRM Project to foster communication among stakeholders and adoption of IG. It complements ARMA's Generally Accepted Recordkeeping Principles.

Best Practices Considerations

IG best practices should also be considered in policy formulation. Best practices in IG are evolving and expanding, and those that apply to organizational scenarios may vary. A best practices review should be conducted, customized for each particular organization.

In Chapter 5, we provided a list of 25 IG best practices, with some detail. The IG world is maturing, and more best practices will evolve. The 25 best practices, summarized next, are fairly generic and widely applicable.

1. IG is a key underpinning for a successful ERM program.
2. IG is not a project but rather an ongoing program.
3. Using an IG framework or maturity model is helpful in assessing and guiding IG programs.
4. Defensible deletion of data debris and information that no longer has value is critical in the era of Big Data.
5. IG policies must be developed before enabling technologies are added to assist in enforcement.
6. To provide comprehensive e-document security throughout a document's life cycle, documents must be secured upon creation using highly sophisticated technologies, such as information rights management (IRM) technology.
7. A records retention schedule and legal hold notification process (LHN) are the two primary elements of a fundamental IG program.
8. A cross-functional team is required to implement IG.
9. The first step in information risk planning is to consider the applicable laws and regulations that apply to your organization in the jurisdictions in which it conducts business.
10. A risk profile is a basic building block in enterprise risk management, assisting executives in understanding the risks associated with stated business objectives and in allocating resources within a structured evaluation approach or framework.
11. An information risk mitigation plan is a critical part of the IG planning process. An information risk mitigation plan involves developing risk mitigation options and tasks to reduce the specified risks and improve the odds of achieving business objectives.[7]
12. Proper metrics are required to measure the conformance and performance of your IG program.
13. IG programs must be audited for effectiveness.
14. An enterprise-wide retention schedule is preferable because it eliminates the possibility that different business units will have different records retention periods.

15. Senior management must set the tone and lead sponsorship for vital records program governance and compliance.
16. Business processes must be redesigned to improve the management of electronic records or implement an **electronic records management** (ERM) system.
17. E-mail messages, both inbound and outbound, should be archived automatically and (preferably) in real time.
18. Personal archiving of e-mail messages should be disallowed.
19. Destructive retention of e-mail helps to reduce storage costs and legal risk while improving "findability" of critical records.
20. Take a practical approach and limit cloud use to documents that do not have long retention periods and carry a low litigation risk.
21. Manage social media content by IG policies and monitor it with controls that ensure protection of critical information assets and preservation of business records.
22. International and national standards provide effective guidance for implementing IG.
23. Creating standardized metadata terms should be part of an IG effort that enables faster, more complete, and more accurate searches and retrieval of records.[8]
24. Some digital information assets must be preserved permanently as part of an organization's documentary heritage.
25. Executive sponsorship is crucial.

Standards Considerations

Standards must also be considered in policy development. *There are two general types of standards: de jure and de facto.* De jure ("the law") standards are those published by recognized standards-setting bodies, such as the International Organization for Standardization (ISO), American National Standards Institute (ANSI), National Institute of Standards and Technology (NIST—this is how most people refer to it, as they do not know what the acronym stands for), British Standards Institute (BSI), Standards Council of Canada, and Standards Australia. Standards promulgated by authorities such as these have the formal status of standards.

De facto ("the fact") standards are not formal standards but are regarded by many as if they were. They may arise though popular use (e.g., Windows at the business desktop in the 2001–2010 decade) or may be published by other bodies, such as the U.S. National Archives and Records Administration (NARA) or Department of Defense (DoD) for the U.S. military sector. They may also be published by formal standards-setting bodies without having the formal status of a "standard" (such as some technical reports published by ISO).[9]

Benefits and Risks of Standards

Some benefits of developing and promoting standards are:

- *Quality assurance support.* If a product meets a standard, you can be confident of a certain level of quality.

- *Interoperability support.* Some standards are detailed and mature enough to allow for system interoperability between different vendor platforms.
- *Implementation frameworks and certification checklists.* These help to provide guides for projects and programs to ensure all necessary steps are taken.
- *Cost reduction*, due to supporting uniformity of systems. Users have lower maintenance requirements and training and support costs when systems are more uniform.
- *International consensus.* Standards can represent "best practice" recommendations based on global experiences.[10]

Some *downside* considerations are:

- *Possible decreased flexibility* in development or implementation. Standards can, at times, act as a constraint when they are tied to older technologies or methods, which can reduce innovation.
- *"Standards confusion"* from competing and overlapping standards. For instance, an ISO standard may be theory-based and use different terminology, whereas regional or national standards are more specific, applicable, and understandable than broad international ones.
- *Real-world shortcomings due to theoretical basis.* Standards often are guides based on theory rather than practice.
- *Changing and updating requires cost and maintenance.* There are costs to developing, maintaining, and publishing standards.[11]

Key Standards Relevant to IG Efforts

Below we introduce and discuss some established standards that should be researched and considered as a foundation for developing IG policy.

Risk Management

ISO 31000:2009 is a broad, industry-agnostic (not specific to vertical markets) risk management standard. It states "principles and generic guidelines" of risk management that can be applied to not only IG but also to a wide range of organizational activities and processes throughout the life of an organization.[12] It provides a structured framework within which to develop and implement risk management strategies and programs.

ISO 31000 defines a **risk management framework** as a set of two basic components that "support and sustain risk management throughout an organization."[13] The stated components are: foundations, which are high level and include risk management policy, objectives, and executive edicts; and organizational arrangements, which are more specific and actionable, including strategic plans, roles and responsibilities, allocated budget, and business processes that are directed toward managing an organization's risk.

Additional risk management standards may be relevant to your organization's IG policy development efforts, depending on your focus, scope, corporate culture, and demands of your IG program executive sponsor.

ISO 31000 is a broad risk management standard that applies to all types of businesses.

Information Security and Governance

ISO/IEC 27001:2005 is an information security management system (ISMS) standard that provides guidance in the development of security controls to safeguard information assets. Like ISO 31000, the standard is applicable to all types of organizations, irrespective of vertical industry.[14] It "specifies the requirements for establishing, implementing, operating, monitoring, reviewing, maintaining and improving a documented information security management system within the context of the organization's overall business risks."

ISO/IEC 27001 is flexible enough to be applied to a variety of activities and processes when evaluating and managing information security risks, requirements, and objectives, and compliance with applicable legal and regulatory requirements. *This includes use of the standards guidance by internal and external auditors as well as internal and external stakeholders (including customers and potential customers).*

ISO/IEC 27002:2005, "Information Technology—Security Techniques—Code of Practice for Information Security,"[15]

> establishes guidelines and general principles for initiating, implementing, maintaining, and improving information security management in an organization and is identical to the previous published standard, ISO 17799. The objectives outlined provide general guidance on the commonly accepted goals of information security management. ISO/IEC 27002:2005 contains best practices of control objectives and controls in the following areas of information security management:
>
> - security policy;
> - organization of information security;
> - asset management;
> - human resources security;
> - physical and environmental security;
> - communications and operations management;
> - access control;
> - information systems acquisition, development, and maintenance;
> - information security incident management;
> - business continuity management; and
> - compliance.
>
> The control objectives and controls in ISO/IEC 27002:2005 are intended to be implemented to meet the requirements identified by a risk assessment. ISO/IEC 27002:2005 is intended as a common basis and practical guideline for developing organizational security standards and effective security management practices, and to help build confidence in inter-organizational activities.

ISO/IEC 27001 and ISO/IEC 27002 are information security management systems standards that provide guidance in the development of security controls.

ISO/IEC 38500:2008 is an international standard that provides high-level principles and guidance for senior executives and directors, and those advising them, for the effective and efficient use of IT.[16] Based primarily on AS 8015, the Australian IT governance standard, it "applies to the governance of management processes" that are performed at the IT service level, but the guidance assists executives in monitoring IT and ethically discharging their duties with respect to legal and regulatory compliance of IT activities.

The ISO 38500 standard comprises three main sections:

1. Scope, Application and Objectives
2. Framework for Good Corporate Governance of IT
3. Guidance for Corporate Governance of IT

It is largely derived from AS 8015, the guiding principles of which were:

- Establish responsibilities
- Plan to best support the organization
- Acquire validly
- Ensure performance when required
- Ensure conformance with rules
- Ensure respect for human factors

The standard also has relationships with other major ISO standards, and embraces the same methods and approaches. It is certain to have a major impact upon the IT governance landscape.[17]

Records and E-Records Management

ISO 15489–1:2001 is the international standard for RM. It identifies the elements of RM and provides a framework and high-level overview of RM core principles. RM is defined as the "field of management responsible for the efficient and systematic control of the creation, receipt, maintenance, use and disposition of records, including the processes for capturing and maintaining evidence of and information about business activities and transactions in the form of records."[18]

ISO 38500 is an international standard that provides high-level principles and guidance for senior executives and directors responsible for IT governance.

The second part of the standard, ISO 15489–2:2001, contains the technical specifications and a methodology for implementing the standard, originally based on early standards work in Australia (**Design and Implementation of Recordkeeping Systems—DIRKS**). Note: Although still actively used in Australian states, the National Archives of Australia has not recommended use of DIRKS by Australian national agencies since 2007 and has removed DIRKS from its Web site.)[19]

The ISO 15489 standard makes little mention of electronic records, as it is written to address all kinds of records; nonetheless it was widely viewed as the definitive framework of what RM means.

In 2008, the **International Council on Archives** (ICA) formed a multinational team of experts to develop "Principles and Functional Requirements for Records in Electronic Office Environments," commonly referred to as **ICA-Req**.[20] The project was cosponsored by the Australasian Digital Recordkeeping Initiative (ADRI), which was undertaken by the Council of Australasian Archives and Records Authorities, which "comprises the heads of the government archives authorities of the Commonwealth of Australia, New Zealand, and each of the Australian States and Territories."[21] The National Archives of Australia presented a training and guidance manual to assist in implementing the principles at the 2012 International Congress on Archives Congress in Brisbane, Australia.

In Module 1 of ICA-Req, principles are presented in a high-level overview; Module 2 contains specifications for electronic document and records management systems (EDRMS) that are "globally harmonized"; and Module 3 contains a requirements set and "implementation advice for managing records in business systems."[22] Module 3 recognizes that digital recordkeeping does not have to be limited to the EDRMS paradigm—the insight that has now been picked up by "Modular Requirements for Records Systems" (MoReq2010, the European standard released in 2011).[23]

Parts 1 to 3 of **ISO 16175** were fully adopted in 2010–2011 based on the ICA-Req standard. The standard may be purchased at www.ISO.org, and additional information on the Australian initiative may be found at www.adri.gov.au.

ISO 16175 is guidance, not a standard that can be tested and certified against. This is the criticism by advocates of testable, certifiable standards like U.S. DoD 5015.2 and the European standard, MoReq2010.

In November 2011, ISO issued new standards for ERM, the first two in the ISO 30300 series, which are based on a *managerial* point of view and targeted at a management-level audience rather than at records managers or technical staff:

- **ISO 30300:2011**, "Information and Documentation—Management Systems for Records—Fundamentals and Vocabulary"
- **ISO 30301:2011**, "Information and Documentation—Management Systems for Records—Requirements"

ISO 15489 is the international RM standard.

The ICA-Req standard was adopted as ISO 16175. It does not contain a testing regime for certification.

The standards apply to "**management systems for records**" (MSR), a term that, as of this printing, is not typically used to refer to ERM or RM application [RMA] software in the United States or Europe and is not commonly found in ERM research or literature.

The ISO 30300 series is a systematic approach to the creation and management of records that is "*aligned with organizational objectives and strategies.*" [italics added][24]

"ISO 30300 MSR 'Fundamentals and Vocabulary' explains the rationale behind the creation of an MSR and the guiding principles for its successful implementation. and it provides the terminology that ensures that it is compatible with other management systems standards.

ISO 30301 MSR 'Requirements' specifies the requirements necessary to develop a records policy. It also sets objectives and targets for an organization to implement systemic improvements. This is achieved through designing records processes and systems; estimating the appropriate allocation of resources; and establishing benchmarks to monitor, measure, and evaluate outcomes. These steps help to ensure that corrective action can be taken and continuous improvements are built into the system in order to support an organization in achieving its mandate, mission, strategy, and goals."[25]

Major National and Regional ERM Standards

For *great detail* on national and regional standards related to ERM, see the book *Managing Electronic Records: Methods, Best Practices, and Technologies* (Wiley 2013) by Robert F. Smallwood. Below is a short summary:

United States E-Records Standard

The U.S. Department of Defense 5015.2 *Design Criteria Standard for Electronic Records Management Software Applications*, standard was established in 1997 and is endorsed by the leading archival authority, the U.S. National Archives and Records Administration (NARA). There is a testing regime that certifies software vendors that is administered by JITC. JITC "builds test case procedures, writes detailed and summary final reports on 5015.2-certified products, and performs on-site inspection of software."[26] The DoD standard was built for the defense sector, and logically "reflects its government and archives roots."

Since its endorsement by NARA, the standard has been the key requirement for ERM system vendors to meet, not only in U.S. public sector bids, but also in the commercial sector.

The 5015.2 standard has since been updated and expanded, in 2002 and 2007, to include requirements for metadata, e-signatures and Privacy and Freedom of Information Act requirements, and, as previously stated, was scheduled for update by 2013.

> The U.S. DoD 5015.2-STD has been the most influential worldwide since it was first introduced in 1997. It best suits military applications.

The 5015.2 standard has been updated to include specifications such as those for e-signatures and FOI requirements.

Canadian Standards and Legal Considerations for Electronic Records Management*

The National Standards of Canada for electronic records management are: (1) *Electronic Records as Documentary Evidence* CAN/CGSB-72.34–2005 ("72.34"), published in December 2005; and, (2) *Microfilm and Electronic Images as Documentary Evidence* CAN/CGSB-72.11–93, first published in 1979 and updated to 2000 ("72.11").[27] 72.34 incorporates all that 72.11 deals with and is therefore the more important of the two. Because of its age, 72.11 should not be relied upon for its "legal" content. However, 72.11 has remained the industry standard for "imaging" procedures—converting original paper records to electronic storage. The Canada Revenue Agency has adopted these standards as applicable to records concerning taxation.[28]

72.34 deals with these topics: (1) management authorization and accountability; (2) documentation of procedures used to manage records; (3) "reliability testing" of electronic records according to existing legal rules; (4) the procedures manual and the chief records officer; (5) readiness to produce (the "prime directive"); (6) records recorded and stored in accordance with "the usual and ordinary course of business" and "system integrity," being key phrases from the Evidence Acts in Canada; (7) retention and disposal of electronic records; (8) backup and records system recovery; and, (9) security and protection. From these standards practitioners have derived many specific tests for auditing, establishing, and revising electronic records management systems.[29]

The "prime directive" of these standards states: "An organization shall always be prepared to produce its records as evidence."[30] *The duty to establish the "prime directive" falls upon senior management:*[31]

5.4.3 Senior management, the organization's own internal law-making authority, proclaims throughout the organization the integrity of the organization's records system (and, therefore, the integrity of its electronic records) by establishing and declaring:

a. the system's role in the usual and ordinary course of business;
b. the circumstances under which its records are made; and
c. its prime directive for all RMS [records management system] purposes, i.e., an organization shall always be prepared to produce its records as evidence. This dominant principle applies to all of the organization's business records, including electronic, optical, original paper source records, microfilm, and other records of equivalent form and content.

---

* This section was contributed by Ken Chasse J.D., LL.M., a records management attorney and consultant, and member of the Law Society of Upper Canada (Ontario) and of the Law Society of British Columbia, Canada.

Being the "dominant principle" of an organization's electronic records management system, the duty to maintain compliance with the "prime directive" should fall upon its senior management.

Legal Considerations

Because an electronic record is completely dependent upon its ERM system for everything, compliance with these National Standards and their "prime directive" should be part of the determination of the "admissibility" (acceptability) of evidence and of electronic discovery in court proceedings (litigation) and in regulatory tribunal proceedings.[32]

There are 14 legal jurisdictions in Canada: 10 provinces, 3 territories, and the federal jurisdiction of the Government of Canada. Each has an Evidence Act (the Civil Code in the province of Quebec[33]), which applies to legal proceedings within its legislative jurisdiction. For example, criminal law and patents and copyrights are within federal legislative jurisdiction, and most civil litigation comes within provincial legislative jurisdiction.[34]

The admissibility of records as evidence is determined under the "business record" provisions of the Evidence Acts.[35] They require proof that a record was made "in the usual and ordinary course of business," and of "the circumstances of the making of the record." In addition, to obtain admissibility for electronic records, most of the Evidence Acts contain electronic record provisions, which state that an electronic record is admissible as evidence on proof of the "integrity of the electronic record system in which the data was recorded or stored."[36] This is the "system integrity" test for the admissibility of electronic records. The word "integrity" has yet to be defined by the courts.[37]

However, by way of sections such as the following, the electronic record provisions of the Evidence Acts make reference to the use of standards such as the National Standards of Canada:

> For the purpose of determining under any rule of law whether an electronic record is admissible, evidence may be presented in respect of any standard, procedure, usage or practice on how electronic records are to be recorded or stored, having regard to the type of business or endeavor that used, recorded, or stored the electronic record and the nature and purpose of the electronic record.[38]

U.K. and European Standards

In the United Kingdom, The National Archives (TNA) (formerly the Public Record Office, or PRO) "has published two sets of functional requirements to promote the development of the electronic records management software market (1999 and 2002)." It ran a program to evaluate products against the 2002 requirements.[39] Initially these requirements were established in collaboration with the central government, and they later were utilized by the public sector in general, and also in other nations. The National Archives 2002 requirements remain somewhat relevant, although no additional development has been underway for years. It is clear that the second version of Model Requirements for Management of Electronic Records, MoReq2, largely supplanted the UK standard, and subsequently the newer MoReq2010 may further supplant the UK standard.

MoReq2010 "unbundles" some of the core requirements in MoReq2, and sets out functional requirements in modules. The approach seeks to permit the later creation of e-records software standards in various vertical industries such as defense, health care, financial services, and legal services.

MoReq2010 is available free—all 525 pages of it (by comparison, the U.S. DoD 5015.2 standard is less than 120 pages long). For more information on MoReq2010, visit www.moreq2010.eu. The entire specification may be downloaded at: http://moreq2010.eu/pdf/moreq2010_vol1_v1_1_en.pdf.

MoReq2010

In November 2010, the DLM Forum, a European Commission–supported body, announced the availability of the final draft of the MoReq2010 specification for electronic records management systems (ERMS), following extensive public consultation. The final specification was published in mid-2011.[40]

The DLM Forum explains that "With the growing demand for [electronic] records management, across a broad spectrum of commercial, not-for-profit, and government organizations, MoReq2010 provides the first practical specification against which all organizations can take control of their corporate information. IT software and services vendors are also able to have their products tested and certified that they meet the MoReq2010 specification."[41]

MoReq2010 supersedes its predecessor MoReq2 and has the continued support and backing of the European Commission.

Australian ERM and Records Management Standards

Australia has adopted all three parts of ISO 16175 as its e-records management standard.[42] (For more detail on this standard go to ISO.org.)

Australia has long led the introduction of highly automated electronic document management systems and records management standards. Following the approval and release of the AS 4390 standard in 1996, the international records management community began work on the development of an International standard. This work used AS 4390–1996 Records Management as its starting point.

Development of Australian Records Standards

In 2002 Standards Australia published a new Australian Standard on records management, AS ISO 15489, based on the ISO 15489 international records management standard. It differs only in its preface verbiage.[43] AS ISO 15489 carries through all these main components of AS 4390, but internationalizes the concepts and brings them up to date. The standards thereby codify Australian best practice but are also progressive in their recommendations.

Additional Relevant Australian Standards

The **Australian Government Recordkeeping Metadata Standard Version 2.0** provides guidance on metadata elements and subelements for records management. It is a baseline tool that "describes information about records and the context in which they are captured and used in Australian Government agencies." This standard is intended to help Australian agencies "meet business, accountability and archival requirements in a systematic and consistent way by maintaining reliable, meaningful and accessible records." The standard is written in two parts, the first describing its purpose and features and the second outlining the specific metadata elements and subelements.[44]

The **Australian Government Locator Service**, AGLS, is published as AS 5044–2010, the metadata standard to help find and exchange information online. It updates the 2002 version, and includes changes made by the Dublin Core Metadata Initiative (DCMI).

Another standard, **AS 5090:2003, "Work Process Analysis for Recordkeeping,"** complements AS ISO 15489 and provides guidance on understanding business processes and workflow so that recordkeeping requirements may be determined.[45]

Long-Term Digital Preservation

Although many organizations shuffle dealing with digital preservation issues to the back burner, **long-term digital preservation (LTDP)** is a key area in which IG policy should be applied. LTDP methods, best practices, and standards should be applied to preserve an organization's historical and **vital records** (those without which it cannot operate or restart operations) and to maintain its corporate or organizational memory. The key standards that apply to LTDP are listed next.

The official standard format for preserving electronic documents is PDF/A-1, based on PDF 1.4 originally developed by Adobe. **ISO 19005–1:2005**, "Document Management—Electronic Document File Format for Long-Term Preservation—Part 1: Use of PDF 1.4 (PDF/A-1)," is the published specification for using PDF 1.4 for LTDP, which is applicable to e-documents that may contain not only text characters but also graphics (either raster or vector).[46]

ISO 14721:2012, "Space Data and Information Transfer Systems—Open Archival Information Systems—Reference Model (OAIS)," is applicable to LTDP.[47] ISO 14271 "specifies a reference model for an open archival information system (OAIS). The purpose of ISO 14721 is to establish a system for archiving information, both digitalized and physical, with an organizational scheme composed of people who accept the responsibility to preserve information and make it available to a designated community."[48] The fragility of digital storage media combined with ongoing and sometimes rapid changes in computer software and hardware poses a fundamental challenge to ensuring access to trustworthy and reliable digital content over time. Eventually, every digital repository committed to long-term preservation of digital content must have a strategy to mitigate computer technology obsolescence. Toward this end, the

The ISO 30300 series of e-records standards are written for a managerial audience and encourage ERM that is aligned to organizational objectives.

LTDP is a key area to which IG policy should be applied.

Consultative Committee for Space Data Systems developed the OAIS reference model to support formal standards for the long-term preservation of space science data and information assets. OAIS was not designed as an implementation model.

OAIS is the lingua franca of digital preservation, as the international digital preservation community has embraced it as the framework for viable and technologically sustainable digital preservation repositories. *An LTDP strategy that is OAIS compliant offers the best means available today for preserving the digital heritage of all organizations, private and public.* (See Chapter 17.)

ISO TR 18492 (2005), "Long-Term Preservation of Electronic Document Based Information," provides practical methodological guidance for the long-term preservation and retrieval of authentic electronic document-based information, when the retention period exceeds the expected life of the technology (hardware and software) used to create and maintain the information assets. ISO 18492 takes note of the role of ISO 15489 but does not cover processes for the capture, classification, and disposition of authentic electronic document-based information.

ISO 16363:2012, "Space Data and Information Transfer Systems—Audit and Certification of Trustworthy Digital Repositories," "defines a recommended practice for assessing the trustworthiness of digital repositories. It is applicable to the entire range of digital repositories."[49] It is an audit and certification standard organized into three broad categories: Organization Infrastructure, Digital Object Management, and Technical Infrastructure and Security Risk Management. *ISO 16363 represents the gold standard of audit and certification for trustworthy digital repositories.* (See Chapter 17.)

Business Continuity Management

ISO 22301:2012, "Societal Security—Business Continuity Management Systems—Requirements," spells out the requirements for creating and implementing a standardized approach to business continuity management (BCM, also known as disaster recovery [DR]), in the event an organization is hit with a disaster or major business interruption.[50] The guidelines can be applied to any organization regardless of vertical industry or size. The specification includes the "requirements to plan, establish, implement, operate, monitor, review, maintain and continually improve a documented management system to protect against, reduce the likelihood

An LTDP strategy that is OAIS compliant (based on ISO 14721) offers the best means available today for preserving the digital heritage of all organizations.

ISO 16363 represents the gold standard of audit and certification for trustworthy digital repositories.

ISO 22301 spells out requirements for creating and implementing a standardized approach to business continuity management.

of occurrence, prepare for, respond to, and recover from disruptive incidents when they arise."

The UK business continuity standard, BS25999-2, which heavily influenced the newer ISO standard, was withdrawn when ISO 22301 was released.[51] The business rationale is that, with the increasing globalization of business, ISO 22301 will allow and support more consistency worldwide not only in business continuity planning and practices but also will promote common terms and help to embed various ISO management systems standards within organizations. U.S.-based ANSI, Standards Australia, Standards Singapore, and other standards bodies also contributed to the development of ISO 22301.

Benefits of ISO 22301

- *Threat identification and assessment.* Discover, name, and evaluate potential serious threats to the viability of the business.
- *Threat and recovery planning.* so the impact and resultant downtime and recovery from real threats that do become incidents is minimized
- *Mission-critical process protection.* Identifying key processes and taking steps to ensure they continue to operate even during a business interruption.
- *Stakeholder confidence.* Shows prudent management planning and business resilience to internal and external stakeholders, including employees, business units, customers, and suppliers.[52]

Making Your Best Practices and Standards Selections to Inform Your IG Framework

You must take into account your organization's corporate culture, management style, and organizational goals when determining which best practices and standards should receive priority in your IG framework. However, you must step through your business rationale in discussions with your cross-functional IG team and fully document the reasons for your approach. Then you must present this approach and your draft IG

You must take into account your organization's corporate culture, management style, and organizational goals when determining which best practice and standards should be selected for your IG framework.

framework to your key stakeholders and be able to defend your determinations while allowing for input and adjustments. Perhaps you have overlooked some key factors that your larger stakeholder group uncovers, and their input should be folded into a final draft of your IG framework.

Next, you are ready to begin developing IG policies that apply to various aspects of information use and management, in specific terms. You must detail the policies you expect employees to follow when handling information on various information delivery platforms (e.g., e-mail, blogs, social media, mobile computing, cloud computing). It is helpful at this stage to collect and review all your current policies that apply and to gather some examples of published IG policies, particularly from peer organizations and competitors (where possible). Of note: You should not just adopt another organization's polices and believe that you are done with policy making. Rather, you must enter into a deliberative process, using your IG framework for guiding principles and considering the views and needs of your cross-functional IG team. Of paramount importance is to be sure to incorporate the alignment of your organizational goals and business objectives when crafting policy.

With each policy area, be sure that you have considered the input of your stakeholders, so that they will be more willing to buy into and comply with the new policies and so that the policies do not run counter to their business needs and required business processes. Otherwise, stakeholders will skirt, avoid, or halfheartedly follow the new IG policies, and the IG program risks failure.

Once you have finalized your policies, be sure to obtain necessary approvals from your executive sponsor and key senior managers.

Roles and Responsibilities

Policies will do nothing without people to advocate, support, and enforce them. So *clear lines of authority and accountability must be drawn*, and responsibilities must be assigned.

Overall IG program responsibility resides at the executive sponsor level, but beneath that, an IG program manager should drive team members toward milestones and business objectives and should shoulder the responsibility for day-to-day program activities, including implementing and monitoring key IG policy tasks. These tasks should be approved by executive stakeholders and assigned as appropriate to an employee's functional area of expertise. For instance, the IG team member from legal may be assigned the responsibility for researching and determining legal requirements for retention of business records, perhaps working in conjunction with the IG team member from RM, who can provide additional input based on interviews with representatives from business units and additional RM research into best practices.

Lines of authority, accountability, and responsibility must be clearly drawn for the IG program to succeed.

Program Communications and Training

Your IG program must contain a communications and training component, as a standard function. Your stakeholder audience must be made aware of the new policies and practices that are to be followed and how this new approach contributes toward the organization's goals and business objectives.

The first step in your communications plan is to identify and segment your stakeholder audiences and to customize or modify your message to the degree that is necessary to be effective. Communications to your IT team can have a more technical slant, and communications to your legal team can have some legal jargon and emphasize legal issues. The more forethought you put into crafting your communications strategy, the more effective it will be.

That is not to say that *all* messages must have several versions: Some core concepts and goals should be emphasized in communications to all employees.

How should you communicate? The more ways you can get your IG message to your core stakeholder audiences, the more effective and lasting the message will be. So posters, newsletters, e-mail, text messages, internal blog or intranet posts, and company meetings should all be a part of the communications mix. Remember, the IG program requires not only training but *re*training, and the aim should be to create a compliance culture that is so prominent and expected that employees adopt the new practices and policies and integrate them into their daily activities. Ideally, employees will provide valuable input to help fine-tune and improve the IG program.

Training should take multiple avenues as well. Some can be classroom instruction, some online learning, and you may want to create a series of training videos. But the training effort must be consistent and ongoing to maintain high levels of IG effectiveness. Certainly, this means you will need to add to your new hire training program for employees joining or transferring to your organization.

Program Controls, Monitoring, Auditing, and Enforcement

How do you know how well you are doing? You will need to develop metrics to determine the level of employee compliance, its impact on key operational areas, and progress made toward established business objectives.

Testing and auditing the program provides an opportunity to give feedback to employees on how well they are doing and to recommend changes they may make. But having objective feedback on key metrics also will allow for your executive sponsor to see where progress has been made and where improvements need to focus.

Communications regarding your IG program should be consistent and clear and somewhat customized for various stakeholder groups.

Clear penalties for policy violations must be communicated to employees so they know the seriousness of the IG program and how important it is in helping the organization pursue its business goals and accomplish stated business objectives.

CHAPTER SUMMARY: **KEY POINTS**

- You must inform and frame IG policy with internal and external frameworks, models, best practices, and standards

- The business user is the primary stakeholder of managed information.

- Information management is important at all stages of the life cycle.

- Legal stakeholders usually can mandate the preservation of what is most critical, though often at great cost.

- The IGRM was developed by the EDRM Project to foster communication among stakeholders and adoption of IG. It complements ARMA's The Principles.

- ISO 31000 is a broad risk management standard that applies to all types of businesses.

- ISO/IEC 27001 and ISO/IEC 27002 are ISMS standards that provide guidance in the development of security controls.

- ISO 15489 is the international RM standard.

- The ICA-Req standard was adopted as ISO 16175. It does not contain a testing regime for certification.

- The ISO 30300 series of e-records standards are written for a managerial audience and encourage ERM that is aligned to organizational objectives.

- DoD 5015.2 is the U.S. ERM standard; the European ERM standard is MoReq2010. Australia has adopted all three parts of ISO 16175 as its e-records management standard.

- LTDP is a key area to which IG policy should be applied.

- An LTDP strategy that is OAIS compliant (based on ISO 14721) offers the best means available today for preserving the digital heritage of all organizations.

- ISO 16363 represents the gold standard of audit and certification for trustworthy digital repositories.

- ISO 38500 is an international standard that provides high-level principles and guidance for senior executives and directors responsible for IT governance.

- ISO 22301 spells out requirements for creating and implementing a standardized approach to business continuity management.

CHAPTER SUMMARY: **KEY POINTS** (*Continued*)

- You must take into account your organization's corporate culture, management style, and organizational goals when determining which best practices and standards should be selected for your IG framework.

- Lines of authority, accountability, and responsibility must be clearly drawn for the IG program to succeed.

- Communications regarding your IG program should be consistent and clear and somewhat customized for various stakeholder groups.

- IG program audits are an opportunity to improve training and compliance, not to punish employees.

Notes

1. ARMA International, "Generally Accepted Recordkeeping Principles," www.arma.org/r2/generally-accepted-br-recordkeeping-principles/copyright (accessed November 25, 2013).
2. ARMA International, "Information Governance Maturity Model," www.arma.org/r2/generally-accepted-br-recordkeeping-principles/metrics (accessed November 25, 2013).
3. Electronic Discovery, "IGRM v3.0 Update: Privacy & Security Officers As Stakeholders – Electronic Discovery," http://electronicdiscovery.info/igrm-v3-0-update-privacy-security-officers-as-stakeholders-electronic-discovery/ (accessed April 24, 2013).
4. EDRM, "Information Governance Reference Model (IGRM)," www.edrm.net/projects/igrm (accessed October 9, 2013).
5. Ibid.
6. Ibid.
7. Project Management Institute, *A Guide to the Project Management Body of Knowledge* (*PMBOK Guide*), 4th ed. (Newtown Square, PA, Project Management Institute, 2008), ANSI/PMI 99-001-2008, pp. 273–312.
8. Kate Cumming, "Metadata Matters," in Julie McLeod and Catherine Hare, eds., *Managing Electronic Records*, p. 34 (London: Facet, 2005).
9. Marc Fresko, e-mail to author, May 13, 2012.
10. Hofman, "The Use of Standards and Models," in Julie McLeod and Catherine Hare, eds., *Managing Electronic Records*, p. 34 (London: Facet, 2005) pp. 20–21.
11. Ibid.
12. International Organization for Standardization, "ISO 31000:2009 Risk Management—Principles and Guidelines," www.iso.org/iso/home/store/catalogue_tc/catalogue_detail.htm?csnumber=43170 (accessed April 22, 2013).
13. Ibid.
14. International Organization for Standardization, ISO/IEC 27001:2005, "Information Technology—Security Techniques—Information Security Management Systems—Requirements," www.iso.org/iso/catalogue_detail?csnumber=42103 (accessed April 22, 2013).
15. International Organization for Standardization, ISO/IEC 27002:2005, "Information Technology—Security Techniques—Code of Practice for Information Security Management," www.iso.org/iso/catalogue_detail?csnumber=50297 (accessed July 23, 2012).
16. International Organization for Standardization, ISO/IEC 38500:2008, www.iso.org/iso/catalogue_detail?csnumber=51639 (accessed March 12, 2013).
17. ISO 38500 IT Governance Standard, www.38500.org/ (accessed March 12, 2013).
18. International Organization for Standardization, *ISO 15489-1: 2001 Information and Documentation—Records Management. Part 1: General* (Geneva: ISO, 2001), section 3.16.

19. National Archives of Australia, www.naa.gov.au/records-management/publications/DIRKS-manual .aspx (accessed October 15, 2012).

20. International Council on Archives, "ICA-Req: Principles and Functional Requirements for Records in Electronic Office Environments: Guidelines and Training Material," November 29, 2011, www .ica.org/11696/activities-and-projects/icareq-principles-and-functional-requirements-for-records-in-electronic-office-environments-guidelines-and-training-material.html.

21. Council of Australasian Archives and Records Authorities, www.caara.org.au/ (accessed May 3, 2012).

22. Adrian Cunningham, blog post comment, May 11, 2011. http://thinkingrecords.co.uk/2011/05/06/how-moreq-2010-differs-from-previous-electronic-records-management-erm-system-specifications/.

23. Ibid.

24. "Relationship between the ISO 30300 Series of Standards and Other Products of ISO/TC 46/SC 11: Records Processes and Controls," White Paper, ISO TC46/SC11- Archives/Records Management (March 2012), www.iso30300.es/wp-content/uploads/2012/03/ISOTC46SC11_White_paper_rela-tionship_30300_technical_standards12032012v6.pdf

25. Ibid.

26. Julie Gable, *Information Management Journal*, November 1, 2002, www.thefreelibrary.com/Everything-+you+wanted+to+know+about+DoD+5015.2:+the+standard+is+not+a...-a095630076.

27. These standards were developed by the CGSB (Canadian General Standards Board), which is a stan-dards-writing agency within Public Works and Government Services Canada (a department of the federal government). It is accredited by the Standards Council of Canada as a standards development agency. The Council must certify that standards have been developed by the required procedures be-fore it will designate them as being National Standards of Canada. *72.34* incorporates by reference as "normative references": (1) many of the standards of the International Organization for Standardiza-tion (ISO) in Geneva, Switzerland. ("ISO," derived from the Greek word *isos* (equal) so as to provide a common acronym for all languages); and (2) several of the standards of the Canadian Standards Association (CSA). The "Normative references" section of 72.34 (p. 2) states that these "referenced documents are indispensable for the application of this document." 72.11 cites (p. 2, "Applicable Pub-lications") several standards of the American National Standards Institute/Association for Information and Image Management (ANSI/AIIM) as publications "applicable to this standard." The process by which the National Standards of Canada are created and maintained is described within the standards themselves (reverse side of the front cover), and on the CGSB's Web site (see, "Standards Develop-ment"), from which Web site these standards may be obtained; http://www.ongc-cgsb.gc.ca.

28. The Canada Revenue Agency (CRA) informs the public of its policies and procedures by means, among others, of its *Information Circulars* (IC's), and *GST/HST Memoranda*. (GST: goods and services tax; HST: harmonized sales tax, *i.e.*, the harmonization of federal and provincial sales taxes into one retail sales tax.) In particular, see: *IC05-1*, dated June 2010, entitled, *Electronic Record Keeping*, paragraphs 24, 26 and 28. Note that use of the National Standard cited in paragraph 26, *Microfilm and Electronic Images as Documen-tary Evidence* CAN/CGSB-72.11-93 is mandatory for, "Imaging and microfilm (including microfiche) reproductions of books of original entry and source documents . . ." Paragraph 24 recommends the use of the newer national standard, *Electronic Records as Documentary Evidence* CAN/CGSB-72.34-2005, "To ensure the reliability, integrity and authenticity of electronic records." However, if this newer standard is given the same treatment by CRA as the older standard, it will be made mandatory as well. And similar statements appear in the GST Memoranda, *Computerized Records* 500-1-2, *Books and Records* 500-1. IC05-1. *Electronic Record Keeping*, concludes with the note, "Most Canada Revenue Agency publications are available on the CRA Web site www.cra.gc.ca under the heading 'Forms and Publications.'"

29. There are more than 200 specific compliance tests that can be applied to determine if the principles of 72.34 are being complied with. The analysts—a combined team of records management and legal expertise—analyze: (1) the nature of the business involved; (2) the uses and value of its records for its various functions; (3) the likelihood and risk of the various types of its records being the subject of legal proceedings, or of their being challenged by some regulating authority; and (4) the consequences of the unavailability of acceptable records—for example, the consequences of its records not being accepted in legal proceedings. Similarly, in regard to the older National Standard of Canada, 72.11, there is a comparable series of more than 50 tests that can be applied to determine the state of compliance with its principles.

30. *Electronic Records as Documentary Evidence* CAN/CGSB-72.34-2005 ("72.34"), clause 5.4.3 c) at p. 17; and *Microfilm and Electronic Images as Documentary Evidence* CAN/CGSB-72.11-93 ("72.11"), paragraph 4.1.2 at p. 2, *supra* note 49.

31. 72.34, Clause 5.4.3, ibid.

32. "Admissibility" refers to the procedure by which a presiding judge determines if a record or other proffered evidence is acceptable as evidence according the rules of evidence. "Electronic discovery"

is the compulsory exchange of relevant records by the parties to legal proceedings prior to trial." As to the admissibility of records as evidence see: Ken Chasse, "The Admissibility of Electronic Business Records" (2010), 8 Canadian Journal of Law and Technology 105; and Ken Chasse, "Electronic Records for Evidence and Disclosure and Discovery" (2011) 57 The Criminal Law Quarterly 284. For the electronic discovery of records see: Ken Chasse, "Electronic Discovery—*Sedona Canada* is Inadequate on Records Management—Here's *Sedona Canada* in Amended Form," *Canadian Journal of Law and Technology* 9 (2011): 135; and Ken Chasse, "Electronic Discovery in the Criminal Court System," *Canadian Criminal Law Review* 14 (2010): 111. See also note 18 *infra*, and accompanying text.

33. For the province of Quebec, comparable provisions are contained in Articles 2831-2842, 2859-2862, 2869-2874 of Book 7 "Evidence" of the Civil Code of Quebec, S.Q. 1991, c. C-64, to be read in conjunction with, An Act to Establish a Legal Framework for Information Technology, R.S.Q. 2001, c. C-1.1, ss. 2, 5-8, and 68.

34. For the legislative jurisdiction of the federal and provincial governments in Canada, see The Constitution Act, 1867 (U.K.) 30 & 31 Victoria, c. 3, s. 91 (federal), and s. 92 (provincial), www.canlii.org/en/ca/laws/stat/30—31-vict-c-3/latest/30—31-vict-c-3.html.

35. The two provinces of Alberta and Newfoundland and Labrador do not have business record provisions in their Evidence Acts. Therefore "admissibility" would be determined in those jurisdictions by way of the court decisions that define the applicable common law rules; such decisions as, *Ares v. Venner* [1970] S.C.R. 608, 14 D.L.R. (3d) 4 (S.C.C.), and decisions that have applied it.

36. See for example, the Canada Evidence Act, R.S.C. 1985, c. C-5, ss. 31.1-31.8; Alberta Evidence Act, R.S.A. 2000, c. A-18, ss. 41.1-41.8; (Ontario) Evidence Act, R.S.O. 1990, c. E.23, s. 34.1; and the (Nova Scotia) Evidence Act, R.S.N.S. 1989, c. 154, ss. 23A-23G. The Evidence Acts of the two provinces of British Columbia and Newfoundland and Labrador do not contain electronic record provisions. However, because an electronic record is no better than the quality of the record system in which it is recorded or stored, its "integrity" (reliability, credibility) will have to be determined under the other provincial laws that determine the admissibility of records as evidence.

37. The electronic record provisions have been in the Evidence Acts in Canada since 2000. They have been applied to admit electronic records into evidence, but they have not yet received any detailed analysis by the courts.

38. This is the wording used in, for example, s. 41.6 of the Alberta Evidence Act, s. 34.1(8) of the (Ontario) Evidence Act; and s. 23F of the (Nova Scotia) Evidence Act, *supra* note 10. Section 31.5 of the Canada Evidence Act, *supra* note 58, uses the same wording, the only significant difference being that the word "document" is used instead of "record." For the province of Quebec, see sections 12 and 68 of, An Act to Establish a Legal Framework for Information Technology, R.S.Q., chapter C-1.1.

39. "Giving Value: Funding Priorities for UK Archives 2005–2010, a key new report launched by the National Council on Archives (NCA) in November 2005," www.nationalarchives.gov.uk/documents/standards_guidance.pdf (accessed October 15, 2012).

40. DLM Forum Foundation, *MoReq2010®: Modular Requirements for Records Systems—Volume 1: Core Services & Plug-in Modules*, 2011, http://moreq2010.eu/ (accessed May 7, 2012, published in paper form as ISBN 978-92-79-18519-9 by the Publications Office of the European Communities, Luxembourg.

41. DLM Forum, Information Governance across Europe, www.dlmforum.eu/ (accessed December 14, 2010).

42. National Archives of Australia, "Australian and International Standards," 2012, www.naa.gov.au /records-management/strategic-information/standards/ASISOstandards.aspx (accessed July 16, 2012).

43. E-mail to author from Marc Fresko, May 13, 2012.

44. National Archives of Australia, "Australian Government Recordkeeping Metadata Standard," 2012, www.naa.gov.au/records-management/publications/agrk-metadata-standard.aspx (accessed July 16, 2012).

45. National Archives of Australia, "Australian and International Standards," 2012, www.naa.gov.au /records-management/strategic-information/standards/ASISOstandards.aspx (accessed July 16, 2012).

46. International Organization for Standardization, ISO 19005-1:2005, "Document Management— Electronic Document File Format for Long-Term Preservation—Part 1: Use of PDF 1.4 (PDF/A-1)," www.iso.org/iso/catalogue_detail?csnumber=38920 (accessed July 23, 2012).

47. International Organization for Standardization, ISO 14721:2012, "Space Data and Information Transfer Systems Open Archival Information System—Reference Model," www.iso.org/iso/iso_catalogue/catalogue_ics/catalogue_detail_ics.htm?csnumber=57284 (accessed November 25, 2013).

48. Ibid.

49. International Organization for Standardization, ISO 16363:2012, "Space Data and Information Transfer Systems—Audit and Certification of Trustworthy Digital Repositories," www.iso.org/iso/iso_catalogue/catalogue_tc/catalogue_detail.htm?csnumber=56510 (accessed July 23, 2012).

50. International Organization for Standardization, ISO 22301:2012 "Societal Security—Business Continuity Management Systems—Requirements," www.iso.org/iso/catalogue_detail?csnumber=50038 (accessed April 21, 2013).
51. International Organization for Standardization, "ISO Business Continuity Standard 22301 to Replace BS 25999-2," www.continuityforum.org/content/news/165318/iso-business-continuity-standard-22301-replace-bs-25999-2 (accessed April 21, 2013).
52. BSI, "ISO 22301 Business Continuity Management," www.bsigroup.com/en-GB/iso-22301-business-continuity (accessed April 21, 2013).

PART THREE

Information Governance Key Impact Areas Based on the IG Reference Model

CHAPTER 7

Business Considerations for a Successful IG Program

By Barclay T. Blair

The business case for **information governance** (IG) programs has historically been difficult to justify. It is hard to apply a strict, short-term return on investment (ROI) calculation. A lot of time, effort, and expense is involved before true economic benefits can be realized. So a commitment to the long view and an understanding of the many areas where an organization will improve as a result of a successful IG program are needed. But the bottom line is that reducing exposure to business risk, improving the quality and security of data and e-documents, cutting out unneeded stored information, and streamlining information technology (IT) development while focusing on business results add up to better organizational health and viability and, ultimately, an improved bottom line.

Let us take a step back and examine the major issues affecting information costing and calculating the real cost of holding information, consider Big Data and e-discovery ramifications, and introduce some new concepts that may help frame information costing issues differently for business managers. Getting a good handle on the true cost of information is essential to governing it properly, shifting resources to higher-value information, and discarding information that has no discernible business value and carries inherent, avoidable risks.

Changing Information Environment

The information environment is changing. Data volumes are growing, but **unstructured information** (such as e-mail, word processing documents, social media posts) is growing faster than our ability to manage it. Some unstructured information has more structure than others containing some identifiable metadata (e.g., e-mail messages all have a header, subject line, time/date stamp, and message body). This is often termed as *semistructured* information, but for purposes of this book, we use the term "unstructured information" to include semistructured information as well.

The volume of unstructured information is growing dramatically. Analysts estimate that, over the next decade, the amount of data worldwide will grow by 44 times (from .8 zettabytes to 35 zettabytes: 1 zettabyte = 1 trillion gigabytes).[1] However, the volume

> The problem of unstructured IG is growing faster than the problem of data volume itself.

of *unstructured information* will actually grow 50 percent faster than structured data. Analysts also estimate that fully 90 percent of unstructured information will require formal governance and management by 2020. In other words, the problem of unstructured IG is growing faster than the problem of data volume itself.

What makes unstructured information so challenging? There are several factors, including

- *Horizontal versus vertical.* Unstructured information is typically not clearly attached to a department or a business function. Unlike the vertical focus of an enterprise resource planning (ERP) database, for example, an e-mail system serves multiple business functions—from employee communication to filing with regulators—for all parts of the business. Unstructured information is much more horizontal, making it difficult to develop and apply business rules.
- *Formality.* The tools and applications used to create unstructured information often engender informality and the sharing of opinions that can be problematic in litigation, investigations, and audits—as has been repeatedly demonstrated in front-page stories over the past decade. This problem is not likely to get any easier as social media technologies and mobile devices become more common in the enterprise.
- *Management location.* Unstructured information does not have a single, obvious home. Although e-mail systems rely on central messaging servers, e-mail is just as likely to be found on a file share, mobile device, or laptop hard drive. This makes the application of management rules more difficult than the application of the same rules in structured systems, where there is a close marriage between the application and the database.
- *"Ownership" issues.* Employees do not think that they "own" data in an accounts receivable system like they "own" their e-mail or documents stored on their hard drive. Although such information generally has a single owner (i.e., the organization itself), this non-ownership mind-set can make the imposition of management rules for unstructured information more challenging than for structured data.
- *Classification.* The business purpose of a database is generally determined prior to its design. Unlike structured information, the business purpose of unstructured information is difficult to infer from the application that created or stores the information. A word processing file stored in a collaboration environment could be a multimillion-dollar contract or a lunch menu. As such, classification of unstructured content is more complex and expensive than structured information.

Taken together, these factors reveal a simple truth: *Managing unstructured information is a separate and distinct discipline from managing databases.* It requires different methods and tools. Moreover, determining the costs and benefits of owning and managing unstructured information is a unique—but critical—challenge.

The governance of unstructured information creates enormous complexity and risk for business managers to consider while making it difficult for organizations to generate *real value* from all this information. Despite the looming crisis, most organizations have limited ability to quantify the real cost of owning and managing unstructured information. Determining the total cost of owning unstructured information is an essential precursor to managing and monetizing that information while cutting information costs—key steps in driving profit for the enterprise.

> Storing things is cheap . . . I've tended to take the attitude, "Don't throw electronic things away."
> —*Data scientist quoted in Anne Eisenberg, "What 23 Years of E-Mail May Say About You," New York Times, April 7, 2012*

> The company spent $900,000 to produce an amount of data that would consume less than one-quarter of the available capacity of an ordinary DVD.
> — *Nicholas M. Pace and Laura Zakaras, "Where the Money Goes: Understanding Litigant Expenditures for Producing Electronic Discovery," RAND Institute for Civil Justice, 2012*

Calculating Information Costs

We are not very good at figuring out what information costs—*truly* costs. Many organizations act as if storage is an infinitely renewable resource and the only cost of information. But, somehow, enterprise storage spending rises each year and IT support costs rise, even as the root commodity (disk drives) grows ever cheaper and denser. Obviously, they are not considering labor and overhead costs incurred with managing information, and the additional knowledge worker time wasted sifting through mountains of information to find what they need.

Some of this myopic focus on disk storage cost is simple ignorance. The executive who concludes that a terabyte costs less than a nice meal at a restaurant after browsing storage drives on the shelves of a favorite big-box retailer on the weekend is of little help.

Rising information storage costs cannot be dismissed. Each year the billions that organizations worldwide spend on storage grows, even though the cost of a hard drive is less than 1 percent of what it was about a decade ago. We have treated storage as a resource that has no cost to the organization outside of the initial capital outlay and basic operational costs. This is shortsighted and outdated.

Some of the reason that managers and executives have difficulty comprehending the true cost of information is old-fashioned miscommunication. IT departments do not see (or pay for) the full cost of e-discovery and litigation. Even when IT "partners" with litigators, what IT learn rarely drives strategic IT decisions. Conversely, law departments (and outside firms) rarely own and pay for the IT consequences of their litigation strategies. It is as if when the litigation fire needs to be put out, nobody calculates the cost of gasoline and water for the fire trucks.

But calculating the cost of information—especially information that does not sit neatly in the rows and columns of enterprise database "systems of record"—is complex. It is more art than science. And it is more politics than art. There is no Aristotelian Golden Mean for information.

The true cost of mismanaging information is much more profound than simply calculating storage unit costs. It is the cost of *opportunity* lost—the lost benefit of information that is disorganized, created and then forgotten, cast aside and left to rot. It is the cost of *information that cannot be brought to market.* Organizations that realize this, and invest in managing and leveraging their unstructured information, will be the winners of the next decade.

Most organizations own vast pools of information that is effectively "dark": They do not know what it is, where it is, who is responsible for managing it, or whether it is an asset or a liability. It is not classified, indexed, or managed according to the organization's own policies. It sits in shared drives, mobile devices, abandoned content systems, single-purpose cloud repositories, legacy systems, and outdated archives.

And when the light is finally flicked on for the first time by an intensive hunt for information during e-discovery, this dark information can turn out to be a liability. An e-mail message about "paying off fat people who are a little afraid of some silly lung problem" might seem innocent—until it is placed in front of a jury as evidence that a drug company did not care that its diet drug was allegedly killing people.[2]

The importance of understanding the total cost of owning unstructured information is growing. We are at the beginning of a "seismic economic shift" in the information landscape, one that promises to not only "reinvent society," (according to an MIT data scientist) but also to create "the new oil . . . a new asset class touching all aspects of society."[3]

Big Data Opportunities and Challenges

We are entering the epoch of Big Data—an era of Internet-scale enterprise infrastructure, powerful analytical tools, and massive data sets from which we can potentially wring profound new insights about business, society, and ourselves. It is an epoch that, according to the consulting firm McKinsey, promises to save the European Union public sector billions of euros, increase retailer margins by 60 percent, and reduce U.S. national health care spending by 8 percent, while creating hundreds of thousands of jobs.[4] Sounds great, right?

However, the early days of this epoch are unfolding in almost total ignorance of the true cost of information. In the near nirvana contemplated by some Big Data

Smart leaders across industries will see using big data for what it is: a management revolution.

—*Andrew McAfee and Erik Brynjolfsson, "Big Data: The Management Revolution,"* Harvard Business Review (October 2012)

proponents, *all data is good, and more data is better.* Yet it would be an exaggeration to say that there is no awareness of potential Big Data downsides. A recent study by the Pew Research Center was positive overall but did note concerns about privacy, social control, misinformation, civil rights abuses, and the possibility of simply being overwhelmed by the deluge of information.[5]

But the real-world burdens of managing, protecting, searching, classifying, retaining, producing, and migrating unstructured information are foreign to many Big Data cheerleaders. This may be because the Big Data hype cycle[6] is not yet in the "trough of disillusionment" where the reality of corporate culture and complex legal requirements sets in. But set in it will, and when it does, the demand for intelligent analysis of costs and benefits will be high.

IG professionals must be ready for these new challenges and opportunities—ready with new models for thinking about unstructured information. Models that calculate the *risks* of keeping too much of the wrong information as well as the *benefits* of clean, reliable, and accessible pools of the right information. Models that drive desirable behavior in the enterprise, and position organizations to succeed on the "next frontier for innovation, competition, and productivity."[7]

Full Cost Accounting for Information

It is difficult for organizations to make educated decisions about unstructured information without knowing its full cost. Models like total cost of ownership (TCO) and ROI are designed for this purpose and have much in common with **full cost accounting** (FCA) models. FCA seeks to create a complete picture of costs that includes past, future, direct, and indirect costs rather than direct cash outlays alone.

FCA has been used for many purposes, including the decidedly earthbound task of determining what it costs to take out the garbage and the loftier task of calculating how much the International Space Station really costs. A closely related concept, often called triple bottom line, has gained traction in the world of environmental accounting, positing that organizations must take into account societal and environmental costs as well as monetary costs.

The U.S. Environmental Protection Agency promotes the use of FCA for municipal waste management, and several states have adopted laws requiring its use. It is fascinating—and no accident—that this accounting model has been widely used to calculate the full cost of managing an unwanted by-product of modern life. The analogy to outdated, duplicate, and unmanaged unstructured information is clear.

Applying the principles of FCA to information can increase cost transparency and drive better management decisions. In municipal garbage systems where citizens do not see a separate bill for taking out the garbage, it is more difficult to get new

IG professionals must be ready with new models that calculate the risks of storing too much of the wrong information and also the benefits of clean, reliable, accessible information.

Organizations can learn from accounting models used by cities to calculate the total cost of managing municipal waste and apply them to the IG problem.

spending on waste management approved.[8] Without visibility into the true cost, how can citizens—or CEOs—make informed decisions?

Responsible, innovative managers and executives should investigate FCA models for calculating the total cost of owning unstructured information. Consider costs such as:

- *General and administrative costs*, such as cost of IT operations and personnel, facilities, and technical support.
- *Productivity gains or losses* related to the information.
- *Legal and e-discovery* costs associated with the information and information systems.
- *Indirect costs*, such as the accounting, billing, clerical support, contract management, insurance, payroll, purchasing, and so on.
- *Up-front costs*, such as the acquisition of the system, integration and configuration, and training. This should include the depreciation of capital outlays.
- *Future costs*, such as maintenance, migration, and decommissioning of information systems. Future outlays should be amortized.

Calculating the Cost of Owning Unstructured Information

Any system designed to calculate the cost or benefit of a business strategy is inherently political. That is, it is an *argument* designed to convince an *audience*. Well-known models like TCO and ROI are primarily decision tools designed to help organizations predict the economic consequences of a decision. While there are certainly objective truths about the information environment, human decision making is a complex and imperfect process. There are plenty of excellent guides on how to create a standard TCO or ROI. That is not our purpose here. Rather, we want to inspire creative thinking about how to calculate the cost of owning unstructured information and help organizations minimize the risk—and maximize the value—of unstructured information.

Any economic model for calculating the cost of unstructured information depends on reliable facts. But facts can be hard to come by. A client recently went in search of an accurate number for the annual cost per terabyte of Tier 1 storage in her company. The company's storage environment was completely outsourced, leading her to believe that the number would be transparent and easy to find. However, after days spent poring over the massive contract, she was no closer to the truth. Although there was a line item for storage costs, the true costs were buried in "complexity fees" and other opaque terms.

Organizations need tools that help them establish facts about their unstructured information environment. The business case for better management depends on these facts. Look for tools that can help you:

- *Find unstructured information wherever it resides* across the enterprise, including e-mail systems, shared network drives, legacy content management systems, and archives.

Identifying and building consensus on the sources of cost for unstructured information is critical to any TCO or ROI calculation. It is critical that all stakeholders agree on these sources, or they will not incorporate the output of the calculation in their strategy and planning.

- Enable fast and intuitive access to *basic metrics*, such as size, date of last access, and file type.
- Provide *sophisticated analysis* of the nature of the content itself to drive classification and information life cycle decisions.
- Deliver visibility into the environment through *dashboards* that are easy to for nonspecialists to configure and use.

Sources of Cost

Unstructured information is ubiquitous. It is typically not the product of a single-purpose business application. It often has no clearly defined owner. It is endlessly duplicated and transmitted across the organization. Determining where and how unstructured information generates cost is difficult.

However, doing so *is* possible. Our research shows that at least 10 key factors that drive the total cost of owning unstructured information. These 10 factors identify where organizations typically spend money throughout the life cycle of managing unstructured information. These factors are listed in Figure 7.1, along with examples of elements that typically *increase* cost ("Cost Drivers," on the left side) and elements that typically *reduce* costs ("Cost Reducers," on the right side).

1. *E-discovery:* finding, processing, and producing information to support lawsuits, investigations, and audits. Unstructured information is typically the most common target in e-discovery, and a poorly managed information environment can add millions of dollars in cost to large lawsuits. Simply reviewing a gigabyte of information for litigation can cost $14,000 or more.[9]
2. *Disposition:* getting rid of information that no longer has value because it is duplicate, out of date, or has no value to the business. In poorly managed information environments, separating the wheat from the chaff can cost large organizations millions of dollars. For enterprises with frequent litigation, the risk of throwing away the wrong piece of information only increases risk and cost. Better management and smart IG tools drive costs down.
3. *Classification and organization:* keeping unstructured information organized so that employees can use it. It also is necessary so management rules supporting privacy, privilege, confidentiality, retention, and other requirements can be applied.
4. *Digitization and automation.* Many business processes continue to be a combination of digital, automated steps and paper-based, manual steps. Automating

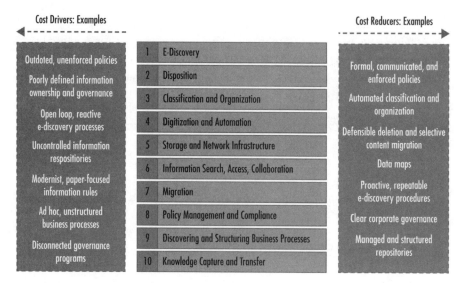

Figure 7.1   Key Factors Driving Cost
Source: Barclay T. Blair

and digitizing these processes requires investment but also can drive significant returns. For example, studies have shown that automating accounts payable "can reduce invoice processing costs by 90 percent."[10]

5. *Storage and network infrastructure:* the cost of the devices, networks, software, and labor required to store unstructured information. Although the cost of the baseline commodity (i.e., a gigabyte of storage space) continues to fall, for most organizations overall volume growth and complexity means that storage budgets go up each year. For example, between 2000 and 2010, organization more than doubled the amount they spent on storage-related software even though the cost of raw hard drive space dropped by almost 100 times.[11]

6. *Information search, access, and collaboration:* the cost of hardware, software, and services designed to ensure that information is available to those who need it, when they need it. This typically includes enterprise content management systems, enterprise search, case management, and the infrastructure necessary to support employee access and use of these systems.

7. *Migration:* the cost of moving unstructured information from outdated systems to current systems. In poorly managed information environments, the cost of migration can be very high—so high that some organizations maintain legacy systems long after they are no longer supported by the vendor just to avoid (more likely, simply to *defer*) the migration cost and complexity.

8. *Policy management and compliance:* the cost of developing, implementing, enforcing, and maintaining IG policies on unstructured information. Good policies, consistently enforced, will drive down the total cost of owning unstructured information.

9. *Discovering and structuring business processes:* the cost of identifying, improving, and systematizing or "routinizing" business processes that are currently ad hoc and disorganized. Typical examples include contract management and

accounts receivable as well as revenue-related activities, such as sales and customer support. Moving from informal e-mail and document-based processes to fixed work flows drives down cost.

10. *Knowledge capture and transfer:* the cost of capturing critical business knowledge held at the department and employee level and putting that information in a form that enables other employees and parts of the organization to benefit from it. Examples include intranets and their more contemporary cousins such as wikis, blogs, and enterprise social media platforms.

The Path to Information Value

At its peak during World War II, the Brooklyn Navy Yard had 70,000 people coming to work every day. The site was once America's premier shipbuilding facility, building the steam-powered *Ohio* in 1820 and the aircraft carrier USS *Independence* in the 1950s. But the site fell apart after it was decommissioned in the 1960s. Today, an "Admiral's Row" of Second Empire–style mansions once occupied by naval officers are an extraordinary sight, with gnarled oak trees pushing through the rotting mansard roofs.[12]

> Seventy percent of managers and executives say data are "extremely important" for creating competitive advantage. "The key, of course, is knowing which data matter, who within a company needs them, and finding ways to get that data into users' hands."
> — *The Economist Intelligence Unit, "Levelling the Playing Field: How Companies Use Data to Create Advantage" (January 2011)*

However, after decades of decay, the Navy Yard is being reborn as the home of hundreds of businesses—from major movie studios to artisanal whisky makers—taking advantage of abundant space and a desirable location. There were three phases in the yard's rebirth:

1. *Clean.* Survey the site to determine what had value and what did not. Dispose of toxic waste and rotting buildings, and modernize the infrastructure.
2. *Build and maintain.* Implement a plan to continuously improve, upgrade, and maintain the facility.
3. *Monetize.* Lease the space.

Most organizations face a similar problem. However, our Navy Yards are the vast piles of unstructured information that were created with little thought to how and when the pile might go away. They are records management programs built for a different era—like an automobile with a metal dashboard, six ashtrays, and no seat belts. Our Navy Yards are information environments no longer fit for purpose in the Big Data era, overwhelmed by volume and complexity.

We are doing a bad job at managing information. McKinsey estimates that in some circumstances, companies are using up to 80 percent of their infrastructure to store *duplicate* data.[13] Nearly half of respondents in a survey ViaLumina recently conducted said that at least 50 percent of the information in their organization is duplicate, out-dated, or unnecessary.[14] We can do better.

1. Clean

We should put the Navy Yard's blueprint to work, first by identifying our piles of rot-ting unstructured information. Duplicate information. Information that has not been accessed in years. Information that no longer supports a business process and has little value. Information that we have no legal obligation to keep. The economics of such "defensible deletion" projects can be compelling simply on the basis of recovering the storage space and thus *reallocating capital that would have been spent on the annual storage purchase.*

2. Build and Maintain

Cleaning up the Navy Yard is only the first step. We cannot repeat the past mistakes. We avoid this by building and maintaining an IG program that establishes our infor-mation constitution (why), laws (what), and regulations (how). We need a corporate governance, compliance, and audit plan that gives the program teeth, and a technology infrastructure that makes it real. It must be a defensible program to ensure we comply with the law and manage regulatory risk.

3. Monetize

IG is a means to an end, and that end is value creation. IG also mitigates risk and drives down cost. But extracting value is the key. Although monetization and value creation often are associated with structured data, new tools and techniques create exciting new opportunities for value creation from unstructured information.

For example, what if an organization could use sophisticated analytics on the e-mail account of their top salesperson (the more years of e-mail the better), look for markers of success, then train and hire salespeople based on that template? What is the pattern of a salesperson's communications with customers and prospects in her territory? What is the substance of the communications? What is the tone? When do successful salespeople communicate? How are the patterns different between suc-cessful deals and failed deals? What knowledge and insight resides in the thousands of messages and gigabytes of content? The tools and techniques of Big Data applied to e-mail can bring powerful business insights. However, we have to know what questions to ask. According to *Computerworld*, "the hardest part of using big data is trying to get business people to sit down and define what they want out of the huge amount of unstructured and semi-structured data that is available to enterprises these days."[15]

Key steps in driving information value are: (1) clean; (2) build and maintain; and (3) monetize.

Table 7.1   Key Steps in the IG Process

1. Clean	2. Build and Maintain	3. Monetize
Information inventory	IG policies and procedures	Create value through information, e.g., drive sales and improve customer satisfaction
Defensible deletion	Corporate governance, compliance and audit	Business insights
Records retention and legal hold	Technology	Increase margins

Source: Barclay T. Blair

The analytics challenges of Big Data create opportunities. For example, McKinsey predicts that demand for "deep analytical talent in the United States could be 50 to 60 percent greater than its projected supply by 2018." A chief reason for this gap is that "this type of talent is difficult to produce, taking years of training in the case of someone with intrinsic mathematical abilities." However, the more profound opportunity is for the "1.5 million extra additional managers and analysts in the United States who can ask the right questions and consume the results of the analysis of big data effectively."[16]

Some companies are using analytics to set prices. For example, the largest distributor of heating oil in the United States sets prices on the fly, based on commodity prices and customer retention risks.[17] In a case that caught the attention of morning news shows, with breathless headlines like "Are Mac Users Paying More?" an online travel company revealed that "Mac users are 40 percent more likely to book four or five-star hotels . . . compared to PC users."[18] Despite the headlines, the company was not charging Mac users more. Rather, computer brand was a variable used to determine which products were highlighted.

The path to information value is not necessarily linear. Different parts of your business may achieve maturity at different rates, driven by the unique risks and opportunities of the information they possess.

Challenging the Culture

The best models for calculating the total cost of owning unstructured are those that information professionals can use to challenge and change organizational culture. Much of the unstructured information that represents the greatest cost and risk to organizations is created, communicated, and managed directly by employees—that is, by human beings. As such, better IG relies in part on improving the way those human beings use and manage information.

New Information Models

The "information calorie" and "information cap-and-trade," explored next, are two new models designed to help with the challenge of governing information.

Information Calorie

The Western world is suffering from an embarrassment of riches when it comes to calories. The calorie has been weaponized in the form of tasty, cheap, and fast food loaded with sugar and fat. Even a cup of "coffee" can contain as much as 800 calories.[19] We have gotten very, very good at maximizing available calories, at a staggering cost: $190 billion per year in additional medical spending as a result of obesity in the United States, greater than the cost of smoking.[20]

Governments are taking action. A new national health care law in the United States requires restaurant chains to disclose calorie counts for the food they sell by 2013, building on similar state laws.[21] Calories are not inherently bad. We would literally die without them. But too many calories make us sick.

The analogy to information is clear. Information is the "lifeblood" of our organizations and is central to our survival. But too much unmanaged unstructured information leaves us fat, slow, and coughing and wheezing at the back of the pack.

In 2012, New York City initially passed a controversial law limiting the size of soft drinks that can be sold at movie theaters and convenience stores (later challenged in court). The "Bloomberg soda ban" was based on the premise that humans need help making good choices. There is some basis for this approach, with studies showing that, for example, the size of the candy scoop determines how much free candy we eat.[22] Under the new law, it was still possible in New York to buy two smaller cups of soda, but it was hoped that inconvenience (and cost) will reduce overconsumption.

> A new study . . . examined consumer behavior before and after calorie counts were posted, and determined that when restaurants post calories on menu boards, there is a reduction in calories per transaction.
>
> —*Bryan Bollinger, Phillip Leslie, Alan Sorensen, "Calorie Posting in Chain Restaurants," Stanford University, January 2010*

Thinking about information as calories at your organization can improve awareness of its costs and drive change. The goal is not to add friction to desirable behaviors, like collaboration and mobile work, but rather to make it more difficult to create and consume empty information calories.

Here are some tips to get started:

- *Educate executives and employees* about the cost of information mismanagement through anecdotes, case studies, and facts.
- *Show employees their information footprint* by regularly exposing them to the amount of data storage they are using in e-mail, shared drives, content management systems, and other environments they work with. With a little creative programming, you can post "information calories" on your menus.
- *Design systems to minimize information calories.* Examples include: preventing employees from exporting e-mail to .pst files; turning off the ability to store documents on desktop hard drives to encourage the use of managed collaboration environment; and requiring employees to send links to shared content rather than creating yet another e-mail attachment. Clever technology *and* social engineering, like the soda ban, can drive healthy information behavior.

Information Cap-and-Trade

Originally designed as a regulatory approach for fighting acid rain in the 1980s, cap-and-trade has gained new attention as a method of curbing carbon emissions. Cap-and-trade systems differ from command-and-control regulatory approaches that mandate, rather than economically encourage, a course of action. In other words, rather than forcing companies to install scrubbers on power plant exhausts (command and control), cap-and-trade provides companies with an emissions quota, which they can hit as they see fit, and even profit from. Companies with unused room on their quota can sell those "credits" on specialized markets.

Consider a cap-and-trade system for information. Do not limit the creation and storage of *useful* information—that defeats the purpose of investing in IT in the first place. Rather, design a cap-and-trade system that controls the amount of *information pollution* and rewards innovation and management discipline.

While there is no objective "right amount" of information for every organization or department, we can certainly do better than "as much as you want, junk or not." After all, "nearly all sectors in the US economy had at least an average of 200 terabytes of stored data . . . and many sectors had more than 1 petabyte in mean stored data per company."[23] Moreover, up to 50 percent of that information is easily identifiable as data pollution.[24] So, we have a reasonable starting point.

Here are some tips for creating an information cap-and-trade system:

- *Baseline the desired amount* of information per system, department, and/or type of user. How much information do you currently have? How much has value? How much should you have? These are not easy questions to answer, but even rough calculations can make a big difference.
- Create information volume targets or quotas, and *allocate them by business unit,* system, or user. This is the "cap" part of the system.
- Calculate the fully loaded cost of a *unit of information*, and adopt it as a baseline metric for the "trade" part of the system. Consider whether annual e-discovery costs can be allocated to this unit in a reasonable way.
- Create an internal accounting system for tracking and *trading information units,* or credits within the organization. Innovative departments will be rewarded, laggards will be motivated.
- Get *creative* in what the credits can purchase. New revenue-generating software? Headcount?

"There's not a person in a business anywhere who gets up in the morning and says, 'Gee, I want to race into the office to follow some regulation.' On the other hand, if you say, 'There's an upside potential here, you're going to make money,' people do get up early and do drive hard around the possibility of finding themselves winners on this."
—*Dan Etsy, environmental policy professor at Yale University, quoted in Richard Conniff, "The Political History of Cap and Trade,"* Smithsonian Magazine *(August 2009)*

Future State: What Will the IG-Enabled Organization Look Like?

When an organization is IG enabled, or "IG mature"—meaning IG is infused into operations throughout the enterprise and coordinated on an organization-wide level—it will look significantly different from most organizations today. Not only will the organization have a solid handle on the total cost of information; not only will it have shifted resources to capitalize on the opportunities of Big Data; not only will it be managing the deluge in a systematic, business-oriented way by cutting out data debris and leveraging information value; it will also look significantly different in key operational areas including legal, records and information management (RIM), and IT.

In legal matters, the mature IG-enabled organization will be better suited to address litigation in a more efficient way through a standardized legal hold notification (LHN) process. Legal risk is reduced through improved IG, which will manage information privacy in accordance with applicable laws and regulations. During litigation, your legal team will be able to sort through information more rapidly and efficiently, improving your legal posture, cutting e-discovery costs, and allowing for attorney time to be focused on strategy and to zero in on key issues. This means attorneys should have the technology tools to be more effective. Adherence to retention schedules means that records and documents can be discarded at the earliest possible time, which reduces the chances that some information could pose a legal risk. Hard costs can be saved by eliminating that approximately 69 percent of stored information that no longer has business value. That cost savings may be the primary rationale for the initial IG program effort. By leveraging advanced technologies such as predictive coding, the organization can reduce the costs of e-discovery and better utilize attorney time.

Your RIM functions will operate with more efficiency and in compliance with laws and regulations. Appropriate retention periods will be applied and enforced, and authentic, original copies of business records will be easily identifiable, so that managers are using current and accurate information on which to base their decisions. Over the long term, valuable information from projects, product development, marketing programs, and strategic initiatives will be retained in corporate memory, reducing the impact of turnover and providing distilled information and knowledge to contribute to a **knowledge management** (KM) program. KM programs can facilitate innovation in organizations, as a knowledge base is built, retained, expanded, and leveraged.

In your IT operations, a focus on how IT can contribute to business objectives will bring about a new perspective. Using more of a business lens to view IT projects will help IT to contribute toward the achievement of business objectives. IT will be working more closely with legal, RIM, risk, and other business units, which should help these groups to have their needs and issues better addressed by IT solutions. Having a standardized data governance program in place means cleaning up corrupted or duplicated data and providing users with clean, accurate data as a basis for line-of-business software applications and for decision support analytics in **business intelligence** (BI) applications. Better data is the basis for improved insights, which can be gained by leveraging BI and will improve management decision-making capabilities and help to provide better customer service, which can impact customer retention. It costs a lot more to gain a new customer than to retain an existing one, and with better data quality, the opportunities to cross-sell and upsell customers are improved. This can provide a sustainable competitive advantage. Standardizing the use of business terms will facilitate improved communications between IT and other business units, which should lead to improved software applications that address user needs. Adhering to information life cycle management principles will help the organization to apply the proper level of IT resources to its high-value information while decreasing costs by managing information of declining value appropriately. IT effectiveness and efficiency will be improved by using IT frameworks and standards, such as CobiT 5 and ISO/IEC 38500:2008, the international standard that provides high-level principles and guidance for senior executives and directors, and those advising them, for the effective and efficient governance of IT.[25] Implementing a master data management program will help larger organizations with complex IT operations to ensure that they are working with consistent data from a single source. Improved database security through data masking, database activity monitoring, database auditing, and other tools will help guard the organization's critical databases against the risk of rogue attacks by hackers. Deploying document life cycle security tools such as data loss prevention and information rights management will help secure your confidential information assets and keep them from prying eyes. This helps to secure the organization's competitive position and protect its valuable intellectual property.

By securing your electronic documents and data, not only within the organization but also for mobile use, and by monitoring and complying with applicable privacy laws, your confidential information assets will be safeguarded, your brand will be better protected, and your employees will be able to be productive without sacrificing the security of your information assets.

Moving Forward

We are not very good at figuring out what unstructured information costs. The Big Data deluge is upon us. If we hope to manage—and, more important, to monetize—this deluge, we must form cross-functional teams and challenge the way our organizations think about unstructured information. The first and most important step is developing the ability to convincingly calculate what unstructured information really costs and then to discover ways we can recue those costs and drive value. These are foundational skills for information professionals in the new era of Big Data. In this era, information is currency—but a currency that has value only when IG professionals drive innovation and management rigor in the unstructured information environment.

CHAPTER SUMMARY: **KEY POINTS**

- The business case for IG programs has historically been difficult to justify.
- It takes a commitment to the long view to develop a successful IG program.
- The problem of unstructured IG is growing faster than the problem of data volume itself.
- IG professionals must be ready with new models that calculate the risks of storing too much of the wrong information and also the benefits of clean, reliable, accessible information.

(continued)

CHAPTER SUMMARY: **KEY POINTS** (*Continued*)

■ Key steps in driving information value are: (1) clean; (2) build and maintain; and (3) monetize.

■ The information calorie approach and information cap-and-trade are two new models for assisting in IG.

■ Legal risk is reduced through improved IG, and legal costs are reduced.

■ Leveraging newer technologies like predictive coding can improve the efficiency of legal teams.

■ Adherence to retention schedules means that records and documents can be discarded at the earliest possible time, which reduces costs by eliminating unneeded information that no longer has business value.

■ RIM functions will operate with more efficiency and in compliance with laws and regulations under a successful IG program.

■ A compliant RIM program helps to build the organization's corporate memory of essential "lessons learned," which can foster a KM program.

■ KM programs can facilitate innovation in organizations.

■ Focusing on business impact and customizing your IG approach to meet business objectives are key best practices for IG in the IT department.

■ Effective data governance can yield bottom-line benefits derived from new insights, especially with the use of business intelligence software.

■ IT governance seeks to align business objectives with IT strategy to deliver business value.

■ Using IT frameworks like CobiT 5 can improve the ability of senior management to monitor IT value and processes.

■ Identifying sensitive information in your databases and implementing database security best practices help reduce organizational risk and the cost of compliance.

■ By securing your electronic documents and data, your information assets will be safeguarded and your organization can more easily comply with privacy laws and regulations.

■ We are not very good at figuring out what unstructured information costs. To thrive in the era of Big Data requires challenging the way we think about the cost of managing unstructured information.

Notes

1. International Data Corporation, "The 2011 Digital Universe Study," June 2011. www.emc.com/leadership/programs/digital-universe.htm (accessed November 25, 2013).
2. Richard B. Schmidt, "The Cyber Suit: How Computers Aided Lawyers In Diet-Pill Case," *Wall Street Journal*, October 8, 1999. http://webreprints.djreprints.com/0000000000000000000012559001.html
3. Nick Bilton, "At Davos, Discussions of a Global Data Deluge," *New York Times*, January 25, 2012, http://bits.blogs.nytimes.com/2012/01/25/at-davos-discussions-of-a-global-data-deluge/; Alex Pentland, quoted by Edge.org in "Reinventing Society in the Wake of Big Data," August 8, 2012, www.edge.org/conversation/reinventing-society-in-the-wake-of-big-data; World Economic Forum, "Personal Data: The Emergence of a New Asset Class" (January 2011), http://www3.weforum.org/docs/WEF_ITTC_PersonalDataNewAsset_Report_2011.pdf
4. James Manyika et al., "Big Data: The Next Frontier for Innovation, Competitions, and Productivity," McKinsey Global Institute, May 2011, www.mckinsey.com/insights/business_technology/big_data_the_next_frontier_for_innovation
5. Janna Quitney Anderson and Lee Ranie, "Future of the Internet: Big Data," Pew Internet and American Life Project, July 20, 2012, http://pewinternet.org/~/media//Files/Reports/2012/PIP_Future_of_Internet_2012_Big_Data.pdf
6. Louis Columbus, "Roundup of Big Data Forecasts and Market Estimates, 2012," *Forbes*, August 16, 2012, www.forbes.com/sites/louiscolumbus/2012/08/16/roundup-of-big-data-forecasts-and-market-estimates-2012/
7. McKinsey Global Institute, "Big Data: The Next Frontier for Innovation, Competitions, and productivity," May 2011.
8. U.S. EPA, "Making Solid Waste Decisions with Full Cost Accounting," n.d., www.epa.gov/osw/conserve/tools/fca/docs/primer.pdf (accessed November 25, 2013).
9. Nicholas M. Pace and Laura Zakaras, "Where the Money Goes: Understanding Litigant Expenditures for Producing Electronic Discovery," RAND Institute for Civil Justice, 2012. www.rand.org/content/dam/rand/pubs/monographs/2012/RAND_MG1208.pdf (accessed November 25, 2013).
10. Accounts Payable Network, "A Detailed Guide to Imaging and Workflow ROI," 2010.
11. Various sources. See, for example: Barclay T. Blair, "Today's PowerPoint Slide: The Origins of Information Governance by the Numbers," October 28, 2010. http://barclaytblair.com/origins-of-information-governance-powerpoint/ (accessed November 25, 2013).
12. Brooklyn Navy Yard Development Corporation, "The History of Brooklyn Navy Yard," www.brooklynnavyyard.org/history.html (accessed November 25, 2013).
13. James Manyika et al., "Big Data."
14. Barclay Blair and Barry Murphy, "Defining Information Governance: Theory or Action? Results of the 2011 Information Governance Survey," ViaLumina, *eDiscovery Journal* (September 2011).
15. Jaikumar Vijayan, "Finding the Business Value in Big Data Is a Big Problem," *Computerworld*, September 12, 2012, www.computerworld.com/s/article/9231224/Finding_the_business_value_in_big_data_is_a_big_problem
16. James Manyika et al., "Big Data."
17. Economist Intelligence Unit, "Leveling the Playing Field: How Companies Use Data to Create Advantage" (January 2011), http://blogs.sap.com/wp-content/blogs.dir/15/files/2012/02/EIU_Levelling_The_Playing_Field_1.pdf
18. Genevieve Shaw Brown, "Mac Users My See Pricier Options on Orbitz," *ABC Good Morning America*, June 25, 2012, http://abcnews.go.com/Travel/mac-users-higher-hotel-prices-orbitz/story?id=16650014#.UDlkVBqe7oV
19. "Health Care Bill Requires Calories on Menus at Chain Restaurants," *USA Today*, March 23, 2010, http://usatoday30.usatoday.com/news/health/weightloss/2010-03-23-calories-menus_N.htm
20. Sharon Beley, "As America's Waistline Expands, Cost Soar," Reuters, April 30, 2012, www.reuters.com/article/2012/04/30/us-obesity-idUSBRE83T0C820120430
21. Stephanie Rosenbloom, "Calorie Data to Be Posted at Most Chains," *New York Times*, March 23, 2010, www.nytimes.com/2010/03/24/business/24menu.html
22. James Surowiecki, "Downsizing Supersize," *New Yorker*, August 13, 2012, www.newyorker.com/talk/financial/2012/08/13/120813ta_talk_surowiecki
23. Manyika et al., "Big Data."
24. Blair and Murphy, "Defining Information Governance."
25. International Organization for Standardization, ISO/IEC 38500:2008, Corporate governance of information technology. www.iso.org/iso/catalogue_detail?csnumber=51639 (accessed November 25, 2013).

CHAPTER 8

Information Governance and Legal Functions

By Robert Smallwood with Randy Kahn, Esq., and Barry Murphy

Perhaps the key functional area that **information governance** (IG) impacts most is legal functions, since legal requirements are paramount. Failure to meet them can literally put an organization out of business or land executives in prison. Privacy, security, records management, information technology (IT), and business management functions are important—very important—but the most significant aspect of all of these functions relates to legality and regulatory compliance.

Key legal processes include electronic discovery (**e-discovery**) readiness and associated business processes, information and record retention policies, the **legal hold notification** (LHN) process, and legally **defensible disposition** practices.

Some newer technologies have become viable to assist organizations in implementing their IG efforts, namely, **predictive coding** and **technology-assisted review** (TAR; also known as **computer-assisted review**). In this chapter we explore the need for leveraging IT in IG efforts aimed at defensible disposition, the intersection between IG processes and legal functions, policy implications, and some key enabling technologies.

Introduction to e-Discovery: The Revised 2006 Federal Rules of Civil Procedure Changed Everything

Since 1938, the **Federal Rules of Civil Procedure** (FRCP) "have governed the discovery of evidence in lawsuits and other civil cases."[1] In law, **discovery** is an early phase of civil litigation where plaintiffs and defendants investigate and exchange evidence and testimony to better understand the facts of a case and to make early determinations of the strength of arguments on either side. Each side must produce evidence requested by the opposition or show the court why it is unreasonable to produce the information.

The FRCP apply to U.S. district courts, which are the trial courts of the federal court system. The district courts have jurisdiction (within limits set by Congress and the Constitution) to hear nearly all categories of federal cases, including civil and criminal matters.[2]

Legal functions are the most important area of IG impact.

The FRCP were amended in 2006, and some of the revisions apply specifically to the preservation and discovery of electronic records in the litigation process.[3] These changes were a long time coming, reflecting the lag between the state of technology and the courts' ability to catch up to the realities of electronically generated and stored information.

After years of applying traditional paper-based discovery rules to e-discovery, amendments to the FRCP were made to accommodate the modern practice of discovery of **electronically stored information** (ESI). *ESI is any information that is created or stored in electronic format.* The goal of the 2006 FRCP amendments was to recognize the importance of ESI and to respond to the increasingly prohibitive costs of document review and protection of privileged documents. These amendments reinforced the importance of IG policies, processes, and controls in the handling of ESI.[4] Organizations must produce requested ESI reasonably quickly, and failure to do so, or failure to do so within the prescribed time frame, can result in sanctions. This requirement dictates that organizations put in place IG policies and procedures to be able to produce ESI accurately and in a timely fashion.[5]

All types of litigation are covered under the FRCP, and all types of e-documents—most especially e-mail—are included, which can be created, accessed, or stored in a wide variety of methods, and on a wide variety of devices beyond hard drives. The FRCP apply to ESI held on all types of storage and communications devices: thumb drives, CDs/DVDs, smartphones, tablets, personal digital assistants (PDAs), personal computers, servers, zip drives, floppy disks, backup tapes, and other storage media. ESI content can include information from e-mail, reports, blogs, social media posts (e.g., Twitter posts), voicemails, wikis, websites (internal and external), word processing documents, and spreadsheets, and includes the **metadata** associated with the content itself, which provides descriptive information.[6]

Under the FRCP amendments, corporations must proactively manage the e-discovery process to avoid sanctions, unfavorable rulings, and a loss of public trust. Corporations must be prepared for early discussions on e-discovery with all departments. Topics should include the form of production of ESI and the methods for preservation of information. Records management and IT departments must have made available all relevant ESI for attorney review.[7]

This new era of ESI preservation and production demands the need for cross-functional collaboration: records management, IT, and legal teams particularly need to work closely together. Legal teams, with assistance and input of records management staff, must identify relevant ESI, and IT teams must be mindful of preserving and protecting the ESI to maintain its legal integrity and prove its authenticity.

ESI is any information that is created or stored in electronic format.

The goal of the FRCP amendments is to recognize the importance of ESI and to respond to the increasingly prohibitive costs of document review and protection of privileged documents.

Big Data Impact

Now throw in the Big Data effect: The average employee creates roughly one gigabyte of data annually (and growing), and data volumes are expected to increase over the next decade not 10-fold, or even 20-fold, but as much as 40 to 50 times what it is today![8] This underscores the fact that organizations must meet legal requirements while paring down the mountain of data debris they are holding to reduce costs and potential liabilities hidden in that monstrous amount of information. There are also costs associated with **dark data**—unknown or useless data, such as old log files, that takes up space and continues to grow and needs to be cleaned up.

Some data is important and relevant, but distinctions must be made by IG policy to classify, prioritize, and schedule data for disposition *and to dispose of the majority of it in a systematic, legally defensible way.* If organizations do not accomplish these critical IG tasks they will be overburdened with storage and data handling costs and will be unable to meet legal obligations.

According to a recent survey, approximately 25 percent of information stored in organizations has real business value, while 5 percent must be kept as business records and about 1 percent is retained due to a litigation hold.[9] *"This means that [about] 69 percent of information in most companies has no business, legal, or regulatory value.* Companies that are able to [identify and] dispose of this debris return more profit to shareholders, can use more of their IT budgets for strategic investments, and can avoid excess expense in legal and regulatory response" (emphasis added).

If organizations are not able to draw clear distinctions between that roughly 30 percent of "high-value" business data, records, and that which is on legal hold, their IT department are tasked with the impossible job of managing all data as if it is high value. This "overmanaging" of information is a significant waste of IT resources.[10]

More Details on the Revised FRCP Rules

Here we present a synopsis of the key points in FRCP rules that apply to e-discovery.

> *FRCP 1—Scope and Purpose.* This rule is simple and clear; its aim is to "secure the just, speedy, and inexpensive determination of every action."[11] Your discovery effort and responses must be executed in a timely manner.

The amended FRCP reinforce the importance of IG. Only about 25 percent of business information has real value, and 5 percent are business records.

FRCP 16—Pretrial Conferences; Scheduling; Management. This rule provides guide-lines for preparing for and managing the e-discovery process; the court expects IT and network literacy on both sides, so that pretrial conferences regarding discoverable evidence are productive.

FRCP 26—Duty to Disclose; General Provisions Governing Discovery. This rule pro-tects litigants from costly and burdensome discovery requests, given certain guidelines.

FRCP 26(a)(1)(C): Requires that you make initial disclosures no later than 14 days after the Rule 26(f) meet and confer, unless an objection or another time is set by stipulation or court order. If you have an objection, now is the time to voice it.

Rule 26(b)(2)(B): Introduced the concept of *not reasonably accessible* ESI. The concept of *not reasonably accessible paper* had not existed. This rule pro-vides procedures for shifting the cost of accessing not reasonably accessible ESI to the requesting party.

FRCP 26(b)(5)(B): Gives courts a clear procedure for settling claims when you hand over ESI to the requesting party that you shouldn't have.

Rule 26(f): This is the meet and confer rule. This rule requires all par-ties to meet within 99 days of the lawsuit's filing and at least 21 days before a scheduled conference.

Rule 26(g): Requires an attorney to sign every e-discovery request, re-sponse, or objection.

FRCP 33—Interrogatories to Parties. This rule provides a definition of business e-records that are discoverable and the right of opposing parties to request and access them.

FRCP 34—Producing Documents, Electronically Stored Information, and Tangible Things, or Entering onto Land, for Inspection and Other Purposes. In disputes over document production, this rule outlines ways to resolve and move forward. Specifically, FRCP 34(b) addresses the format for requests and requires that e-records be accessible without undue difficulty (i.e., the records must be orga-nized and identified). The requesting party chooses the preferred format, which are usually native files (which also should contain metadata). The key point is that electronic files must be accessible, readable, and in a standard format.

FRCP 37—Sanctions. Rule 37(e) is known as the safe harbor rule. In principle, it keeps the court from imposing sanctions when ESI is damaged or lost through routine, "good faith" operations, although this has proven to be a high standard to meet. This rule underscores the need for a legally defensible document man-agement program under the umbrella of clear IG policies.

The Big Data trend underscores the need for defensible deletion of data debris.

Landmark E-Discovery Case: *Zubulake v. UBS Warburg*

A landmark case in e-discovery arose from the opinions rendered in *Zubulake v. U.B.S. Warburg*, an employment discrimination case where the plaintiff, Laura Zubulake, sought access to e-mail messages involving or naming her. Although UBS produced over 100 pages of evidence, it was shown that employees intentionally deleted some relevant e-mail messages.[12] The plaintiffs requested copies of e-mail from backup tapes, and the defendants refused to provide them, claiming it would be too expensive and burdensome to do so.

The judge ruled that U.B.S. had not taken proper care in preserving the e-mail evidence, and the judge ordered an **adverse inference** (assumption that the evidence was damaging) instruction against U.B.S. Ultimately, the jury awarded Zubulake over $29 million in total compensatory and punitive damages. "The court looked at the proportionality test of Rule 26(b)(2) of the Federal Rules of Civil Procedure and applied it to the electronic communication at issue. Any electronic data that is as accessible as other documentation should have traditional discovery rules applied."[13] Although Zubulake's award was later overturned on appeal, it is clear the stakes are huge in e-discovery and preservation of ESI.

E-Discovery Techniques

Current e-discovery techniques include online review, e-mail message archive review, and cyberforensics. Any and all other methods of seeking or searching for ESI may be employed in e-discovery. Expect capabilities for searching, retrieving, and translating ESI to improve, expanding the types of ESI that are discoverable. Consider this potential when evaluating and developing ESI management practices and policies.[14]

E-Discovery Reference Model

The **E-Discovery Reference Model** is a visual planning tool created by EDRM.net to assist in identifying and clarifying the stages of the e-discovery process. Figure 8.1 is the graphic depiction with accompanying detail on the process steps.

> *Information Management.* Getting your electronic house in order to mitigate risk and expenses should e-discovery become an issue, from initial creation of electronically stored information through its final disposition
>
> *Identification.* Locating potential sources of ESI and determining their scope, breadth, and depth

In the landmark case *Zubulake v. U.B.S. Warburg*, the defendants were severely punished by an adverse inference for deleting key e-mails and not producing copies on backup tapes.

SEVEN STEPS OF THE E-DISCOVERY PROCESS

In the e-discovery process, you must perform certain functions for identifying and preserving electronically stored (ESI), and meet requirements regarding conditions such as relevancy and privilege. Typically, you follow this e-discovery process:

1. Create and retain ESI according to an enforceable electronic records retention policy and electronic records management (ERM) program. Enforce the policy, and monitor compliance with it and the ERM program.

2. Identify the relevant ESI, preserve any so it cannot be altered or destroyed, and collect all ESI for further review.

3. Process and filter the ESI to remove the excess and duplicates. You reduce costs by reducing the volume of ESI that moves to the next stage in the e-discovery process.

4. Review and analyze the filtered ESI for privilege because privileged ESI is not discoverable, unless some exception kicks in.

5. Produce the remaining ESI, after filtering out what's irrelevant, duplicated, or privileged. Producing ESI in native format is common.

6. Clawback the ESI that you disclosed to the opposing party that you should have filtered out, but did not. Clawback is not unusual, but you have to work at getting clawback approved, and the court may deny it.

7. Present at trial if your case hasn't settled. Judges have little to no patience with lawyers who appear before them not understanding e-discovery and the ESI of their clients or the opposing side.

Source: Linda Volonino and Ian Redpath, e-*Discovery for Dummies* (Hoboken, NJ: John Wiley & Sons, 2010), http://www.dummies.com/how-to/content/ediscovery-for-dummies-cheat-sheet.html (accessed May 22, 2013). Used with permission.

Preservation. Ensuring that ESI is protected against inappropriate alteration or destruction

Collection. Gathering ESI for further use in the e-discovery process (processing, review, etc.)

Processing. Reducing the volume of ESI and converting it, if necessary, to forms more suitable for review and analysis

Review. Evaluating ESI for relevance and privilege

Analysis. Evaluating ESI for content and context, including key patterns, topics, people, and discussion

Production. Delivering ESI to others in appropriate forms, and using appropriate delivery mechanisms

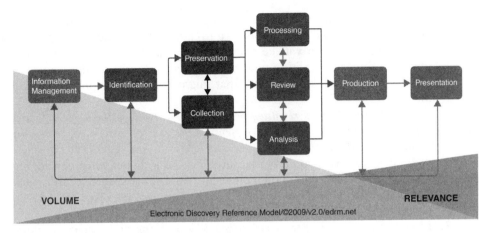

Figure 8.1   Electronic Discovery Reference Model
Source: EDRM (edrm.net)

Presentation. Displaying ESI before audiences (at depositions, hearings, trials, etc.), especially in native and near-native forms, to elicit further information, validate existing facts or positions, or persuade an audience[15]

The Electronic Discovery Reference Model can assist organizations in focusing and segmenting their efforts when planning e-discovery initiatives.

Guidelines for E-Discovery Planning

1. *Implement an IG program.* The highest impact area to focus are your legal processes, particularly e-discovery. From risk assessment to processes, communications, training, controls, and auditing, fully implement IG to improve and measure compliance capabilities.
2. *Inventory your ESI.* File scanning and e-mail archiving software can assist you. You also will want to observe files and data flows by doing a walk-through beginning with centralized servers in the computer room and moving out into business areas. Then, using a prepared inventory form, you should interview users to find out more detail. Be sure to inventory ESI based on computer systems or applications, and diagram it out.
3. *Create and implement a comprehensive records retention policy, and also include an e-mail retention policy and retention schedules for major ESI areas.* This is required since all things are potentially discoverable. You must devise a comprehensive retention and disposition policy that is legally defensible.

The E-Discovery Reference Model is in a planning tool that presents key e-discovery process steps.

So, for instance, if your policy is to destroy all e-mail messages that do not have a legal hold (or are expected to) after 90 days and you apply that policy uniformly, you will be able to defend the practice in court. Also, implementing the retention policy reduces your storage burden and costs while cutting the risk of liability that might be buried in obscure e-mail messages.

4. *As an extension of your retention policy, implement a legal hold policy that is enforceable, auditable, and legally defensible. Be sure to include all potentially discoverable ESI XE "litigation:e-discovery"*. We discuss legal holds in more depth later in this chapter, but be sure to cast a wide net when developing retention policies so that you include all relevant electronic records, such as e-mail, e-documents and scanned documents, storage discs, and backup tapes.

5. *Leverage technology.* Bolster your e-discovery planning and execution efforts by deploying enabling technologies, such as e-mail archiving, advanced enterprise search, TAR, and predictive coding.

6. *Develop and execute your e-discovery plan.* You may want to begin from this point forward with new cases, and bear in mind that starting small and piloting is usually the best course of action.

The Intersection of IG and E-Discovery

By Barry Murphy

Effective IG programs can alleviate e-discovery headaches by reducing the amount of information to process and review, allowing legal teams to get to the facts of a case quickly and efficiently, and can even result in better case outcomes. Table 8.1 shows the impact of IG on e-discovery, by function.

Legal Hold Process

The legal hold process is a foundational element of IG.[16] The way the legal hold process is supposed to work is that a formal system of polices, processes, and controls is put in place to notify key employees of a civil lawsuit (or impending one) and the set of documents that must put on legal hold. These documents, e-mail messages, and other relevant ESI must be preserved in place and no longer edited or altered so that they may be reviewed by attorneys during the discovery phase of the litigation. But, in practice, this is not always what takes place. In fact, *the opposite can take place*—employees can quickly edit or even delete relevant e-documents that may raise questions or even

Implementing IG, inventorying ESI, and leveraging technology to implement records retention and LHN policies are key steps in e-discovery planning.

Table 8.1   IG Impact on E-Discovery

Impact	Function
Cost reduction	Reduce downstream costs of processing and review by defensibly disposing of data according to corporate retention policies
	Reduce cost of collection by centralizing collection interface to save time
	Keep review costs down by prioritizing documents and assigning to the right level associates (better resource utilization)
	Reduce cost of review by culling information with advanced analytics
Risk management	Reduce risk of sanctions by managing the process of LHN and the collection and preservation of potentially responsive information
Better litigation win rates	Optimize decision making (e.g., settling cases that can't be won) quickly with advanced analytics that prioritize hot documents
	Quickly find the necessary information to win cases with advanced searches and prioritized review
Strategic planning for matters based on merit	Determine the merits of a matter quickly and decide if it is a winnable case
	Quickly route prioritized documents to the right reviewers via advanced analytics (e.g., clustering)
Strategic planning for matters based on cost	Quickly determine how much litigation will cost via early access to amount of potentially responsive information and prioritized review to make decisions based on the economics of the matter (e.g., settle for less than the cost of litigation)
Litigation budget optimization	Minimize litigation budget by only pursuing winnable cases
	Minimize litigation budget by utilizing the lowest cost resources possible while putting high-cost resource on only the necessary documents

Source: Barry Murphy, *eDiscovery Journal* http://ediscoveryjournal.com/

implicate them. This is possible only if proper IG controls are not in place, monitored, enforced, and audited.

Many organizations start with Legal Hold Notification (LHN) management as a very discrete IG project. *LHN management is arguably the absolute minimum an organization should be doing* in order to meet the guidelines provided by court rules, common law, and case law precedent. It is worth noting, though, that the expectation is that organizations should connect the notification process to the actual collection and preservation of information in the long term.

> LHN management is the absolute minimum an organization should implement to meet the guidelines, rules, and precedents.

How to Kick-Start Legal Hold Notification

Implementing an LHN program attacks some of the lower-hanging fruit within an organization's overall IG position. *This part of the e-discovery life cycle must not be outsourced.* Retained counsel provides input, but the mechanics of LHN are managed and owned by internal corporate resources.

In preparing for a LHN implementation project, it is important to first lose the perception that LHN tools are expensive and difficult to deploy. It is true that some of these tools cost considerably more than others and can be complex to deploy; however, that is because the tools in question go far beyond simple LHN and reach into enterprise systems and also handle data mapping, collection, and workflow processes. Other options include Web-based hosted solutions, custom-developed solutions, or processes using tools already in the toolbox (e.g., e-mail, spreadsheets, word processing).

The most effective approach involves three basic steps:

1. Define requirements.
2. Define the ideal process.
3. Select the technology.

Defining both LHN requirements and processes should include input from key stakeholders—at a minimum—in legal, records management, and IT. Be sure to take into consideration the organization's litigation profile, corporate culture, and available resources as part of the requirements and process defining exercise. Managing steps 1 and 2 thoroughly makes tool selection easier because defining requirements and processes creates the confidence of knowing exactly what the tool must accomplish.

IG and E-Discovery Readiness

Having a solid IG underpinning means that your organization will be better prepared to respond and execute key tasks when litigation and the e-discovery process proceed. Your policies will have supporting business processes, and clear lines of responsibility and accountability are drawn. The policies must be reviewed and fine-tuned periodically, and business processes must be streamlined and continue to aim for improvement over time.

In order for legal hold or **defensible deletion** (discussed in detail in the next section—disposing of unneeded data, e-documents, and reports based on set policy) projects to deliver the promised benefit to e-discovery, it is important to avoid the very real roadblocks that exist in most organization. To get the light to turn green at the intersection of e-discovery and IG, it is critical to:

- *Establish a culture that both values information and recognizes the risks inherent in it.* Every organization must evolve its culture from one of keeping everything to one of information compliance. This kind of change requires high-level executive support. It also requires constant training of employees about how to create, classify, and store information. While this advice may seem trite, many managers in leading organizations say that without this kind of culture change, IG projects tend to be dead on arrival.
- *Create a truly cross-functional IG team.* Culture change is not easy, but it can be even harder if the organization does not bring all stakeholders together when setting requirements for IG. Stakeholders include: legal; security and ethics; IT;

records management; internal audit; corporate governance; human resources; compliance; and business units and employees. That is a lot of stakeholders. In organizations that are successfully launching and executing IG projects, many have dedicated IG teams. Some of those IG teams are the next generation of records management departments, while others are newly formed. The stakeholders can be categorized into three areas: legal/risk, IT, and the business. The IG team can bring those areas together to ensure that any projects meet requirements of all stakeholders.

- *Use e-discovery as an IG proof of concept.* Targeted programs like e-discovery, compliance, and archiving have a history of return on investment (ROI) and an ability to get budget. These projects are also challenging, but more straightforward to implement and can address sub-sets of information in early phases (e.g., only those information assets that are reasonable to account for). The lessons learned from these targeted projects can then be applied to other IG initiatives.
- *Measure ROI on more than just cost savings.* Yes, one of the primary benefits of addressing e-discovery via IG is cost reduction, but it is wise to begin measuring all e-discovery initiatives on how they impact the life cycle of legal matters. The efficiencies gained in collecting information, for example, have benefits that go way beyond reduced cost; the IT time not wasted on reactive collection is more time available for innovative projects that drive revenue for companies. And a better litigation win rate will make any legal team happier.

Building on Legal Hold Programs to Launch Defensible Disposition

By Barry Murphy

Defensible deletion programs can build on legal hold programs, because legal hold management is a necessary first step before defensibly deleting anything. The standard is "reasonable effort" rather than "perfection." Third-party consultants or auditors can support the diligence and reasonableness of these efforts.

Next, prioritize what information to delete and what information the organization is capably able to delete in a defensible manner. *Very few organizations are deleting information across all systems.* It can be overly daunting to try to apply deletion to all enterprise information. Choosing the most important information sources—e-mail, for example—and attacking those first may make for a reasonable and tenable approach. *For most organizations, e-mail is the most common information source to begin deleting.* Why e-mail? It is fairly easy for companies to put systematic rules on e-mail because the technology is already available to manage e-mail in a sophisticated manner. Because e-mail is such a critical data system, e-mail providers and e-mail archiving providers early on provided for systematic deletion or application of retention rules. However, in

IG serves as the underpinning for efficient e-discovery processes.

For most organizations, e-mail is the most common information source to begin deleting according to established retention policies.

non–e-mail systems, the retention and deletion features are less sophisticated; therefore, organizations do not systematically delete across all systems.

Once e-mail is under control, the organization can begin to apply lessons learned to other information sources and eventually have better IG policies and processes that treat information consistently based on content rather than on the repository.

Destructive Retention of E-mail

A **destructive retention program** is an approach to e-mail archiving where e-mail messages are retained for a limited time (say, 90 days), followed by the permanent manual or automatic deletion of the messages from the organization network, so long as there is no litigation hold or the e-mail has not been declared a record.

E-mail retention periods can vary from 90 days to as long as seven years:

- Osterman Research reports that "nearly one-quarter of companies delete e-mail after 90 days."[17]
- Heavily regulated industries, including energy, technology, communications, and real estate, favor archiving for one year or more, according to Fulbright and Jaworski research.
- The most common e-mail retention period traditionally has been seven years; however, some organizations are taking a hard-line approach and stating that e-mails will be kept for only 90 days or six months, unless it is declared as a record, classified, and identified with a classification/retention category and tagged or moved to a repository where the integrity of the record is protected (i.e., the record cannot be altered and an audit trail on the history of the record's usage is maintained).

Newer Technologies That Can Assist in E-Discovery

Few newer technologies are viable for speeding the document review process and improving the ability to be responsive to court-mandated requests. Here we introduce predictive coding and technology-assisted review (also known as computer-assisted review), the most significant of new technology developments that can assist in e-discovery.

Destructive retention of e-mail is a method whereby e-mail messages are retained for a limited period and then destroyed.

Predictive Coding

During the **early case assessment** (ECA) phase of e-discovery, **predictive coding** is a "court-endorsed process"[18] utilized to perform document review. It uses human expertise and IT to facilitate analysis and sorting of documents. Predictive coding software leverages human analysis when experts review a subset of documents to "teach" the software what to look for, so it can apply this logic to the full set of documents,[19] making the sorting and culling process faster and more accurate than solely using human review or automated review.

Predictive coding uses a blend of several technologies that work in concert:[20] software that performs **machine learning** (a type of **artificial intelligence** software that "learns" and improves its accuracy, fostered by guidance from human input and progressive ingestion of data sets—in this case documents);[21] **workflow** software, which routes the documents through a series of work steps to be processed; and **text analytics** software, used to perform functions such as searching for keywords (e.g., "asbestos" in a case involving asbestos exposure). Then using **keyword search** capabilities, or *concepts* using **pattern search** or **meaning-based** search, and sifting through and sorting documents into basic groups using **filtering** technologies, based on document content, and **sampling** a portion of documents to find patterns and to review the accuracy of filtering and keyword search functions.

The goal of using predictive coding technology is to reduce the total group of documents a legal team needs to review manually (viewing and analyzing them one by one) by finding that gross set of documents that is most likely to be relevant or **responsive** (in legalese) to the case at hand. It does this by automating, speeding up, and improving the accuracy of the document review process to locate and "digitally categorize" documents that are responsive to a discovery request.[22] Predictive coding, when deployed properly, also reduces billable attorney and paralegal time and therefore the costs of ECA. Faster and more accurate completion of ECA can provide valuable time for legal teams to develop insights and strategies, improving their odds for success. Skeptics claim that the technology is not yet mature enough to render more accurate results than human review.

The first state court ruling allowing the use of predictive coding technology instead of human review to cull through approximately 2 million documents to "execute a first-pass review" was made in April 2012 by a Virginia state judge.[23] This was the first time a judge was asked to grant permission without the two opposing sides first coming to an agreement. The case, *Global Aerospace, Inc., et al. v. Landow Aviation, LP, et al.*, stemmed from an accident at Dulles Jet Center.

In an exhaustive 156-page memorandum, which included dozens of pages of legal analysis, the defendants made their case for the reliability, cost-effectiveness, and legal merits of predictive coding. At the core of the memo

Predictive coding software leverages human analysis when experts review a subset of documents to "teach" the software what to look for, so it can apply this logic to the full set of documents.

was the argument that predictive coding "is capable of locating upwards of seventy-five percent of the potentially relevant documents and can be effectively implemented at a fraction of the cost and in a fraction of the time of linear review and keyword searching."[24]

This was the first big legal win for predictive coding use in e-discovery.

Basic Components of Predictive Coding

Here is a summary of the main foundational components of predictive coding.

- *Human review.* Human review is used to determine which types of document content will be legally responsive based on a case expert's review of a sampling of documents. These sample documents are fed into the system to provide a seed set of examples.[25]
- *Text analytics.* This involves the ability to apply "keyword-agnostic" (through a thesaurus capability based on contextual meaning, not just keywords) to locate responsive documents and build create seed document sets.
- *Workflow.* Software to route e-documents through the processing steps automatically to improve statistical reliability and streamlined processing.
- *Machine learning.* The software "learns" what it is looking for and improves its capabilities along the way through multiple, iterative passes.
- *Sampling.* Sampling is best applied if it is integrated so that testing for accuracy is an ongoing process. This improves statistical reliability and therefore defensibility of the process in court.

Predictive Coding Is the Engine; Humans Are the Fuel

Predictive coding sounds wonderful, but it does not replace the expertise of an attorney; it merely helps leverage that knowledge and speed the review process. It "takes all the documents related to an issue, ranks and tags them so that a human reviewer can look over the documents to confirm relevance." So it cannot work without human input to let the software know what documents to keep and which ones to discard, but it is an emerging technology tool that will play an increasingly important role in e-discovery.[26]

Technology-Assisted Review

TAR, also known as computer-assisted review, is *not* predictive coding. TAR includes aspects of the nonlinear review process, such as culling, clustering and de-duplication, but it does not meet the requirements for comprehensive predictive coding.

Many technologies can help in making incremental reductions in e-discovery costs. *Only fully integrated predictive coding, however, can completely transform the economics of e-discovery.*

Mechanisms of Technology-Assisted Review

There are three main mechanisms, or methods, for using technology to make legal review faster, less costly, and generally smarter.[27]

1. *Rules driven.* "I know what I am looking for and how to profile it." In this scenario, a case team creates a set of criteria, or rules, for document review and

builds what is essentially a coding manual. The rules are fed into the tool for execution on the document set. For example, one rule might be to "redact for privilege any time XYZ term appears and add the term 'redacted' where the data was removed." This rule-driven approach requires iteration to truly be effective. The case team will likely have rules changes and improvements as the case goes on and more is learned about strategy and merit. This approach assumes that the case team knows the document set well and can apply very specific rules to the corpus in a reasonable fashion.

2. *Facet driven.* "I let the system show me the profile groups first." In this scenario, a tool analyzes documents for potential items of interest or groups potentially similar items together so that reviewers can begin applying decisions. Reviewers typically utilize visual analytics that guide them through the process and take them to prioritized documents. This mechanism can also be called present and direct.

3. *Propagation based.* "I start making decisions and the system looks for similar-related items." This type of TAR is about passing along, or propagating, what is known based on a sample set of documents to the rest of the documents in a corpus. In the market, this is often referred to as predictive coding because the system predicts whether documents will be responsive or privileged based on how other documents were coded by the review team. Propagation-based TAR comes in different flavors, but all involve an element of machine learning. In some scenarios, a review team will have access to a seed set of documents that the team codes and then feeds into the system. The system then mimics the action of the review team as it codes the remainder of the corpus. In other scenarios, there is not a seed set; rather, the systems give reviewers random documents for coding and then create a model for relevance and nonrelevance. It is important to note that propagation-based TAR goes beyond simple mimicry; it is about creating a linguistic mathematical model for what relevance looks like.

These TAR mechanisms are not mutually exclusive. In fact, combining the mechanisms can help overcome the limitations of individual approaches. *For example, if a document corpus is not rich (e.g., does not have a high enough percentage of relevant documents), it can be hard to create a seed set that will be a good training set for the propagation-based system.* However, it is possible to use facet-based TAR—for example, concept searching—to more quickly find the documents that are relevant so as to create a model for relevance that the propagation-based system can leverage.[28]

It is important to be aware that these approaches require more than just technology. It is critical to have the right people in place to support the technology and the workflow required to conduct TAR. Organizations looking to exercise these mechanisms of TAR will need:

- *Experts in the right tools and information retrieval.* Software is an important part of TAR. The team executing TAR will need someone that can program the tool set with the rules necessary for the system to intelligently mark documents. Furthermore, information retrieval is a science unto itself, blending linguistics, statistics, and computer science. Anyone practicing TAR will need the right team of experts to ensure a defensible and measurable process.

- *Legal review team.* While much of the chatter around TAR centers on its ability to cut lawyers out of the review process, the reality is that the legal review team will become more important than ever. The quality and consistency of the decisions this team makes will determine the effectiveness that any tool can have in applying those decisions to a document set.
- *Auditor.* Much of the defensibility and acceptability of TAR mechanisms will rely on the statistics behind how certain the organization can be that the output of the TAR system matches the input specification. Accurate measures of performance are important not only at the end of the TAR process, but also throughout the process in order to understand where efforts need to be focused in the next cycle or iteration. Anyone involved in setting or performing measurements should be trained in statistics.

For an organization to use a propagated approach, in addition to people it may need a "seed" set of known documents. Some systems use random samples to create seed sets while others enable users to supply small sets from the early case investigations. These documents are reviewed by the legal review team and marked as relevant, privileged, and the like. Then, the solution can learn from the seed set and apply what it learns to a larger collection of documents. Often this seed set is not available, or the seed set does not have enough positive data to be statistically useful.

Professionals using TAR state that the practice has value, but it requires a sophisticated team of users (with expertise in information retrieval, statistics, and law) who understand the potential limitations and danger of false confidence that can arise from improper use. For example, using a propagation-based approach with a seed set of documents can have issues when less than 10 percent of the seed set documents are positive for relevance. In contrast, rules driven and other systems can result in false negative decisions when based on narrow custodian example sets.

However TAR approaches and tools are used, they will only be effective if usage is anchored in a thought out, methodically sound process. This requires a definition of what to look for, searching for items that meet that definition, measuring results, and then refining those results on the basis of the measured results. Such an end-to-end plan will help to decide what methods and tools should be used in a given case.[29]

Defensible Disposal: The Only Real Way To Manage Terabytes and Petabytes

By Randy Kahn, Esq.

Records and information management (RIM) is not working. At least, it is *not working well.* Information growth and management complexity has meant that the old records retention rules and the ways businesses apply them are no longer able to address the lifecycle of information. So the mountains of information grow and grow and grow, often unfettered.

Too much data has outlived its usefulness, and no one seems to know how or is willing to get rid of it. While most organizations need to right-size their information footprint by cleaning out the digital data debris, they are stymied by the complexity and enormity of the challenge.

Growth of Information

According to International Data Corporation (IDC), from now until 2020, the digital universe is expected by expand to more than 14 times its current size.[30] One exabyte is the data equivalent of about 50,000 years of DVD movies running continuously. With about 1,800 exabytes of new data created in 2011, 2840 exabytes in 2012, and a predicted 6,120 exabytes in 2014, the volumes are truly staggering. While the data footprint grows significantly each year, that says nothing of what has already been created and stored.

Contrary to what many say (especially hardware salespeople) storage is *not* cheap. In fact, it is really becomes quite expensive when you add up not only the hardware costs but also maintenance, air conditioning and space overhead, and the highly skilled labor needed to keep it running. Many large companies spend tens if not hundreds of millions of dollars per year just to store data. This is money that could go straight to the bottom line if the unneeded data could be discarded. When you consider that most organizations' information footprints are growing at between 20 and 50 percent per year and the cost of storage is declining by a few percentage points per year, in real terms they are spending way more this year than last to simply house information.

Volumes Now Impact Effectiveness

The law of diminishing returns applies to information growth. Assuming information is an asset, at some point when there is so much data, its value starts to decline. That is not because the intrinsic value goes down (although many would argue there is a lot of idle chatter in the various communications technologies). Rather the decline is related to the inability to expeditiously find or have access to needed business information. According the Council of Information Auto-Classification "Information Explosion" Survey, there is now so much information that nearly 50 percent of companies need to re-create business records to run their business and protect their legal interests because they cannot find the original retained record.[31] It is a poor business practice to spend resources to retain information and then, when it cannot be found, to spend more to reconstitute it.

There is increasing regulatory pressure, enforcement, and public scrutiny on all of an organization's data storage activities. Record sanctions and fines, new regulations, and stunning court decisions have converged to mandate heightened controls and accountability from government regulators, industry and standards groups as well as the public. When combined with the volume of data, information privacy, security, protection of trade secrets, and records compliance become complex and critical, high-risk business issues that only executive management can truly fix. However, executives typical view records and information management (RIM) as a low-importance cost center activity, which means that the real problem does not get solved.

In most companies, there is no clear path to classify electronic records, to formally manage official records, or to ensure the ultimate destruction of these records. Vast stores of legacy data are unclassified, and most data is never touched again shortly after creation. Further, traditional records retention rules are too voluminous, too complex, and too granular and do not work well with the technology needed to manage records.

Finally, it is clear that employees can no longer be expected to pull the oars to cut through the information ocean, let alone boil it down into meaningful chunks of good information. Increasingly, technology has to play a more central role in managing information. Better use of technology will create business value by reducing risk, driving improvements in productivity, and facilitating the exploitation and protection of ungoverned corporate knowledge.

How Did This Happen?

Over the past several years, organizations have come to realize that the exposure posed by uncontrolled data growth requires emergency, reactive action, as seemingly no other viable approach exists. Faced with massive amounts of unknown unstructured data, many organizations have chosen to adopt a risk-averse save-everything policy. This approach has brought with it immediate repercussions:

- Inability to quickly locate needed business content buried in ill-managed file systems.
- Sharply increased storage costs, with some companies refusing to allocate any more storage to the business. The users' reaction, out of necessity, is to store data wherever they can find a place for it. (Do *not* buy the argument that storage is cheap—everyone is spending more on storing unnecessary data, even if the per-gigabyte media cost has gone down).
- Soaring litigation and discovery costs, as organizations have lost track of what is where, who owns it, and how to collect, sort, and process it.
- Buried intellectual property, trade secrets, personally identifiable information, and regulated content, which are subject to leakage and unauthorized deletion, and are a clear target for opposing counsel—or anyone who can access them.
- Lack of centralized policies and systems for the storage of records, which results in hard-to-manage record sites spread throughout the organization.
- The lack of a clear strategy for managing records that have long-term, rather than short-term, business, legal, and research value.

Information Glut in Organizations

- 71 percent of organizations surveyed have no idea of the content in their stored data.
- 58 percent of organizations are keeping information indefinitely.
- 79 percent of organizations say too much time and effort is spent manually searching and disposing information.
- 58 percent of organizations still rely on employees to decide how to apply corporate policies.[32]

What Is Defensible Disposition, and How Will It Help?

A solution to the unmitigated data sprawl is to defensibly dispose of the business content that no longer has business or legal value to the organization. In the old days of records management, it was clear that courts and regulators alike understood that records came into being and eventually were destroyed in the ordinary course of business. It is good business practice to destroy unneeded content, provided that the rules on which those decisions are made consider legal requirements and business needs. Today, however, the good business practice of cleaning house of old records has somehow become taboo for some businesses. Now it needs to start again.

An understanding of how technology can help defensibly dispose and how methodology and process help an organization achieve a thinner information footprint is critical for all companies overrun with outdated records that do not know where to start to address the issue. While no single approach is right for every organization, records and legal teams need to take an informed approach, looking at corporate culture, risk tolerance, and litigation profile.

A defensible disposition framework is an ecosystem of technology, policies, procedures, and management controls designed to ensure that records are created, managed, and disposed at the end of their life cycle.

New Technologies—New Information Custodians

Responsibility for records management and IG have changed dramatically over time. In the past, the responsibility rested primarily with the records manager. However, the nature of electronic information is such that its governance today requires the participation of IT, which frequently has custody, control, or access to such data, along with guidance from the legal department. As a result, IT personnel with no real connection or ownership of the data may be responsible for the accuracy and completeness of the business-critical information being managed. *See the problem?*

For many organizations, advances in technology mixed with an explosive growth of data forced a reevaluation of core records management processes. Many organizations have deployed archiving, litigation, and e-discovery point solutions with the intent of providing record retention compliance and responsiveness to litigation. Such systems may be tactically useful but fail to strategically address the heart of the matter: too much information, poorly managed over years and years—if not decades.

A better approach is for organizations to move away from a reactive keep-everything strategy to a proactive strategy that allows the reasonable and reliable identification and deletion of records when retention requirements are reached, absent a preservation obligation. Companies develop retention schedules and processes precisely for this reason; it is not misguided to apply them.

Why Users Cannot, Will Not—and Should Not—Make the Hard Choices

Employees usually are not sufficiently trained on records management principles and methods and have little incentive (or downside) to properly manage or dispose of records. Further, many companies today see that requiring users to properly declare or manage records places an undue burden on them. The employees not only do not provide a

A defensible disposition framework is an ecosystem of technology, policies, procedures, and management controls designed to ensure that records are created, managed, and disposed at the end of their life cycle.

reasonable solution to the huge data pile (which for some companies may be petabytes of data) but contribute to its growth by using more unsanctioned technologies and parking company information in unsanctioned locations. So the digital landfill continues to grow.

Most organizations have programs that address paper records, but these same organizations commonly fail to develop similar programs for electronic records and other digital content.

Technology Is Essential to Manage Digital Records Properly

Having it all—but not being able to find it—is like *not* having it at all.

While the content of a paper document is obvious, viewing the content of an electronic document depends on software and hardware. Further, the content of electronic storage media cannot be easily accessed without some clue as to its structure and format. Consequently, *the proper indexing of digital content is fundamental to its utility.* Without an index, retrieving electronic content is expensive and time consuming, if it can be retrieved at all.

Search tools have become more robust, but they do not provide a panacea for finding electronic records when needed because there is too much information spread out across way too many information parking lots. Without **taxonomies** and common business terminology, accessing the one needed business record may be akin to finding the needle in a stadium-size haystack.

Technological advances can help solve the challenges corporations face and address the issues and burdens for legal, compliance, and information governance. When faced with hundreds of terabytes to petabytes of information, no amount of user intervention will begin to make sense of the information tsunami.

Auto-Classification and Analytics Technologies

Increasingly companies are turning to new analytics and classification technologies that can analyze information faster, better, and cheaper. These technologies should be considered essential for helping with defensible disposition, but do not make the mistake of underestimating their expense or complexity.

As discussed in the previous section by Barry Murphy, machine learning technologies mean that software can "learn" and improve at the tasks of clustering files and assigning information (e.g., records, documents) to different preselected topical categories based on a statistical analysis of the data characteristics. In essence, classification technology evaluates a set of data with known classification mappings and attempts to map newly encountered data within the existing classifications. This type of technology should be on the list of considerations when approaching defensible disposition in large, uncontrolled data environments.

Can Technology Classify Information?

What is clear is that IT is better and faster than people in classifying information. Period.

A better approach is for organizations to move away from a reactive keep-everything strategy to a proactive strategy of defensible deletion.

Increasingly studies and court decisions make clear that, when appropriate, companies should not fear using enabling technologies to help manage information.

For example, in the recent *Da Silva Moore v. Publicis Groupe* case, Judge Andrew Peck stated:

> Computer-assisted review appears to be better than the available alternatives, and thus should be used in appropriate cases. While this Court recognizes that computer-assisted review is not perfect, the Federal Rules of Civil Procedure do not require perfection. . . . Counsel no longer have to worry about being the "first" or "guinea pig" for judicial acceptance of computer assisted review.
>
> This work presents evidence supporting the contrary position: that a technology-assisted process, in which only a small fraction of the document collection is ever examined by humans, can yield higher recall and/or precision than an exhaustive manual review process, in which the entire document collection is examined and coded by humans.[33]

Moving Ahead by Cleaning Up the Past

Organizations can improve disposition and IG programs with a systemized, repeatable, and defensible approach that enables them to retain and dispose of all data types in compliance with the business and statutory rules governing the business's operations.

Generally, an organization is under no legal obligation to retain every piece of information it generates in the course of its business. Its records management process is there to clean up the information junk in a consistent, reasonable way. That said, what should companies do if they have not been following disposal rules, so information has piled up and continues unabated? They need to clean up old data. *But how?*

Manual intervention (by employees) will likely not work, due to the sheer volumes of data involved. Executives will not and should not have employees abdicate their regular jobs in favor of classifying and disposing of hundreds of millions of old stored files. (Many companies have billions of old files.) *This buildup necessitates leveraging technology, specifically, technologies that can discern the meaning of stored unstructured content, in a variety of formats, regardless of where it is stored.*

Here is a starting point: Most likely, file shares, legacy e-mail systems, and other large repositories will prove the most target-rich environments, while better-managed document management, records management, or archival systems will be in less need of remediation. A good time to undertake a cleanup exercise is when litigation will not prevent action or when migrating to a new IT platform. (Trying to conduct a comprehensive, document-level inventory and disposition is neither reasonable nor practical. In most cases, it will create limited results and even further frustration.)

Technology choices should be able to withstand legal challenges in court. Sophisticated technologies available today should also look beyond mere keyword searches (as their defensibility may be called into question) and should look to

Organizations can improve disposition and IG programs with a systemized, repeatable, and defensible approach.

advanced techniques such as automatic text classification (auto-classification), concept search, contextual analysis, and automated clustering. While technology is imperfect, it is better than what employees can do and will never be able to accomplish—to manage terabytes of stored information and clean up big piles of dead data.

Defensibility Is the Desired End State; Perfection Is Not

Defensible disposition is a way to take on huge piles of information without personally cracking each one open and evaluating it. Perhaps it is, in essence, operationalizing a retention schedule that is no longer viable in the electronic age. Defensible disposition is a must because most big companies have hundreds of millions or billions of files, which makes their individualized management all but impossible.

As the list of eight steps to defensible disposition makes clear, different chunks of data will require different diligence and analysis levels. If you have 100,000 backup tapes from 20 years ago, minimal or cursory review may be required before the whole lot of tapes can be comfortably discarded. If, however, you have an active shared drive with records and information that is needed for ongoing litigation, there will need to be deeper analysis with analytics and/or classification technologies that have become much more powerful and useful. In other words, the facts surrounding the information will help inform if the information can be properly disposed with minimal analysis or if it requires deep diligence.

Kahn's Eight Essential Steps to Defensible Disposition

1. Define a reasonable diligence process to assess the business needs and legal requirements for continued information retention and/or preservation, based on the information at issue.
2. Select a practical information assessment and/or classification approach, given information volumes, available resources, and risk profile.
3. Develop and document the essential aspects of the disposition program to ensure quality, efficacy, repeatability, auditability, and integrity.
4. Develop a mechanism to modify, alter, or terminate components of the disposition process when required for business or legal reasons.
5. Assess content for eligibility for disposition, based on business need, record retention requirements, and/or legal preservation obligations.
6. Test, validate, and refine as necessary the efficacy of content assessment and disposition capability methods with actual data until desired results have been attained.
7. Apply disposition methodology to content as necessary, understanding that some content can be disposed with sufficient diligence without classification.
8. On an ongoing basis, verify and document the efficacy and results of the disposition program and modify and/or augment the process as necessary.

Source: "Chucking Daises: Ten Rules for Taking Control of Your Organization's Digital Debris," Randy Kahn, Esq., and Galena Datskovsky Ph.D., CRM (ARMA International, 2013), Overland Park, KS.

Business Case around Defensible Disposition

What is clear is that defensible disposition can have significant ROI impact to a company's financial picture. This author has clients for whom we have built the defensible disposition business case, which saves them tens of millions of dollars on a net basis but also makes them a more efficient business, reduces litigation cost and risks, mitigates the information security and privacy risk profiles, and makes their work force more productive, and so on.

However, remember auto-classification technology is neither simple nor inexpensive, so be realistic and conservative when building the business case. Often it is easiest to simply use only hardware storage cost savings to make the case because it is a hard number and provides a conservative approach to justifying the activities. Then you can add on the additional benefits, which are more difficult to calculate, and also the intangible benefits of giving your employees a cleaner information stack to search and base decisions on.

Defensible Disposition Summary

Defensible disposition is a way to bring your records management program into today's business reality—information growth makes management at the record level all but impossible. Defensible disposition should be about taking simplified retention rules and applying them to both structured and unstructured content with the least amount of human involvement possible. While it can be a daunting challenge, it is also an opportunity to establish and promote operational excellence through better IG and to significantly enhance an organization's business performance and competitive advantage.

Retention Policies and Schedules

By Robert Smallwood, edited by Paula Lederman, MLS

With limited resources, today's legal counsel, compliance managers, and records manager are faced with an onslaught of increasingly pressing and complex compliance and legal demands. At the core of these demands is the ability of the organization to demonstrate that it has *legally defensible* records management practices that can hold up in court.

Organizations can legally destroy records—but will have a greater legal defensibility if:

- The authority to destroy the records is identified on a retention schedule.
- The retention requirements have been met.
- The records are slated for destruction in the normal course of business.
- There are no existing legal or financial holds.
- Al records of the same type are treated consistently and systematically.

The foundation of legally defensible records management practices is a solid IG underpinning, where policies and processes, supported and enforced by IT, help the organization meet its externally mandated legal requirements and internally mandated IG requirements for handling and controlling information.

A complete, current, and documented records retention program reduces storage and handling costs and improves searchability for records by making records easier and faster to find. This reduced search time and more complete search capability improves knowledge worker productivity. It also reduces legal risk by improving the ability to meet compliance demands while also reducing e-discovery costs and improving the ability to more efficiently respond to discovery requests during litigation.

Most large organizations maintain records retention schedules by business unit, department, or functional area. Some organizations, particularly smaller ones, may establish organization-wide IG programs that call for the developing, updating, and improvement of an enterprise or master retention schedule. This is a tall order and is almost never accomplished—but it is possible with a determined, sustained effort. Developing enterprise-wide records retention schedules requires consultation with stakeholder groups that have valuable input to contribute to the overall development of the IG effort and to specific schedules for retaining record collections and their planned disposition. Consultation by the records management department, **senior records officer**, or records team must take place with representatives from the business units that create and own the records as well as with legal, compliance, risk management, IT, and other relevant stakeholder groups.

Meeting Legal Limitation Periods

A key consideration in developing retention schedules is researching and determining the minimum time required to keep records that may be demanded in legal actions. "A **limitation period** is the length of time after which a legal action cannot be brought before the courts. Limitation periods are important because they determine the length of time records must be kept to support court action [including subsequent appeal periods]. It is important to be familiar with the purpose, principles, and special circumstances that affect limitation periods and therefore records retention."[34]

Legal Requirements and Compliance Research

As stated at the beginning of this chapter, *legal requirements trump all others.* The retention period for a particular records series must meet minimum retention requirements as mandated by law. Business needs and other considerations are secondary. So, legal research is required before determining retention periods. Legally required retention periods must be researched for each jurisdiction (state, country) in which the business operates, so that it complies with all applicable laws.

A **limitation period** is the length of time after which a legal action cannot be brought before the courts. Such a period must be factored into retention policies.

In order to locate the regulations and citations relating to retention of records, there are two basic approaches. The first approach is to use a records retention citation service, which publishes in electronic form all of the retention-related citations. These services usually are bought on a subscription basis, as citations are updated on an annual or more frequent basis as legislation and regulations change.

Another approach is to search the laws and regulations directly using online or print resources. Records retention requirements for corporations operating in the United States may be found in the **Code of Federal Regulations (CFR),** the annual edition of which:

> is the codification of the general and permanent rules published in the Federal Register by the departments and agencies of the federal government. It is divided into 50 titles that represent broad areas subject to federal regulation. The 50 subject matter titles contain one or more individual volumes, which are updated once each calendar year, on a staggered basis. The annual update cycle is as follows: titles 1 to 16 are revised as of January 1; titles 17 to 27 are revised as of April 1; titles 28 to 41 are revised as of July 1, and titles 42 to 50 are revised as of October 1. Each title is divided into chapters, which usually bear the name of the issuing agency. Each chapter is further subdivided into parts that cover specific regulatory areas. Large parts may be subdivided into subparts. All parts are organized in sections, and most citations to the CFR refer to material at the section level.[35]

There is an up-to-date version that is not yet a part of the official CFR but is updated daily, the **Electronic Code of Federal Regulations (e-CFR).** "It is not an official legal edition of the CFR. The e-CFR is an editorial compilation of CFR material and Federal Register amendments produced by the National Archives and Records Administration's Office of the Federal Register (OFR) and the Government Printing Office."[36] According to the gpoaccess.gov Web site:

> The Administrative Committee of the Federal Register (ACFR) has authorized the National Archives and Records Administration's (NARA) Office of the Federal Register (OFR) and the Government Printing Office (GPO) to develop and maintain the e-CFR as an informational resource pending ACFR action to grant the e-CFR official legal status. The OFR/GPO partnership is committed to presenting accurate and reliable regulatory information in the e-CFR editorial compilation with the objective of establishing it as an ACFR sanctioned publication in the future. While every effort has been made to ensure that the e-CFR on GPO Access is accurate, those relying on it for legal research should verify their results against the official editions of the CFR, Federal Register and List of CFR Sections Affected (LSA), all available online at www.gpoaccess.gov. Until the ACFR grants it official status, the e-CFR editorial compilation does not provide legal notice to the public or judicial notice to the courts.
>
> The OFR updates the material in the e-CFR on a daily basis. Generally, the e-CFR is current within two business days. The current update status is displayed at the top of all e-CFR web pages.

A complete, current, and documented records retention program reduces storage and handling costs and improves searchability for records by making records easier and faster to find.

What Is a Records Retention Schedule?

A **records retention schedule** delineates how long a (business) record series is to be retained, and its disposition after its life cycle is complete (e.g., destruction, transfer, archiving); the schedule also contains "lists of records by name or type that authorize the disposition of records."[37] Retention schedules apply to all records regardless of their format or media (e.g., physical or electronic). *Retention schedules are developed for records not individually but rather by records series, categories, functions, or systems.* Ideally, they include all of the record series in an organization, although they may be broken down into smaller subset schedules, such as by business unit.

Retention schedules may be maintained separately for electronic records, or they may be included in a combined schedule that includes both e-records and paper or other physical records.

Corporate records retention schedules are increasingly being maintained online, where users and also IT, legal, risk, and records management personnel can view and reference them. Electronic data and documents can easily reference these schedules and initiate a process based on a trigger event so that the life cycle of the electronic document can be automated and managed in a consistent manner. Retention schedules are basic tools that allow an organization to prove that it has a legally defensible basis on which to dispose records.

Retention schedules in large organizations typically are broken down and by business function. A **functional retention schedule** groups record series based on business functions, such as financial, legal, product management, or sales. Each function or grouping also is used for classification. Rather than detail every sequence of records, these larger functional groups are less numerous and are easier for users to understand.

Some organizations are able to reach the ultimate retention goal: to keep an enterprise-wide **master retention schedule**, which includes the retention and

Retention schedules are developed by records series, category, function, or system—not for individual records.

Retention schedules are basic tools that allow an organization to prove that it has a legally defensible basis on which to dispose records.

disposition requirements for records series that cross business unit boundaries. The master retention schedule contains all records series in the entire enterprise. An enterprise-wide retention schedule is preferable because it eliminates the possibility that different business units will follow conflicting records retention periods. For example, if one business unit is discarding a group of records after 5 years, it would not make sense for another business unit to keep the same records for 10 years.

Benefits of a Retention Schedule

According to the U.S. National Archives and Records Administration, developing and maintaining a records retention schedule provides the following benefits. The retention schedule:[38]

1. Reduces legal risk and legal liability exposure.
2. Supports a legally defensible records management program.
3. Improves IG by enforcing uniformity and standardization.
4. Improves search quality and reduces search time.
5. Provides higher-quality records information to improve decision support for knowledge workers.
6. Prevents inadvertent, malicious, or premature destruction of records.
7. Improves accountability for life cycle management of records on an enterprise-wide basis.
8. Improves security for confidential records assets.[39]
9. Reduces and minimizes costs for maintaining records.
10. Determines which records have historic value.
11. Saves hardware, utility, and labor costs by deleting records after their life span.
12. Optimizes use of online storage and access resources.

A formal approach to records management has been around since the mid-1900s, so a great deal of guidance is available before embarking on developing or updating your records retention program. Models and guides can be used to assist in the development of records retention schedules for your organization, including the international standard for records management, ISO 15489—Part 1 and 2:2001, "Information and Documentation—Records Management"; the ISO 15489 standard was written to address all kinds of records. Additional guidance may be obtained by referencing national standards, such as those in Canada, Europe, Australia, and other countries.[40] Often, in the public sector, retention guidelines are published by an authority such as the office of the national, state, or provincial archivist. Some additional insights may be gleaned from ISO 16175–1:2010, "Information and Documentation—Principles and Functional Requirements for Records in Electronic Office Environments—Part 1: Overview and Statement of Principles," which establishes fundamental principles and functional requirements for software used to create and manage digital records in office environments.[41]

A records retention schedule is an essential part of an overall IG program. Due to the fact that a concerted IG program standardizes and enforces uniformity and

> The master retention schedule contains all records series in the entire enterprise.

control, the entire organization benefits in terms of productivity, reduced risk, and improved compliance and e-discovery processes. These overarching goals and benefits should be championed by senior management in words and deeds. This means making the IG effort visible and providing the proper budgetary resources in terms of money and employee time to achieve its aims.

More detail on retention schedules can be found in Chapter 9 on IG and RIM functions.

CHAPTER SUMMARY: **KEY POINTS**

- Legal functions are the most important area of IG impact.

- IG serves as the underpinning for efficient e-discovery processes.

- ESI is any information that is created or stored in electronic format.

- The goal of the FRCP amendments is to recognize the importance of ESI and to respond to the increasingly prohibitive costs of document review and protection of privileged documents.

- The amended FRCP reinforce the importance of IG. Only about 25 percent of business information has real value and 5 percent are business records.

- The Big Data trend underscores the need for defensible deletion of data debris.

- In the landmark case *Zubulake v. U.B.S. Warburg*, the defendants were severely punished by an adverse inference for deleting key e-mails and not producing copies on backup tapes.

- The E-Discovery Reference Model is a planning tool that depicts key e-discovery process steps.

- Implementing IG, inventorying ESI, and leveraging technology to implement records retention and LHN policies are key steps in e-discovery planning.

- LHN management is the absolute minimum an organization should implement to meet the guidelines, rules, and precedents.

- Predictive coding software leverages human analysis when experts review a subset of documents to "teach" the software what to look for, so it can apply this logic to the full set of documents.

CHAPTER SUMMARY: **KEY POINTS** (*Continued*)

- Many technologies assist in making incremental reductions in e-discovery costs, but only fully integrated predictive coding is able to completely transform the economics of e-discovery.

- TAR, also known as computer-assisted review, speeds the review process by leveraging IT tools.

- In TAR, there are three main ways to use technology to make legal review faster, less costly, and generally smarter: rules driven, facet driven, and propagation based.

- It is important to have the right people in place to support the technology and the work flow required to conduct TAR.

- A defensible disposition framework is an ecosystem of technology, policies, procedures, and management controls designed to ensure that records are created, managed, and disposed of at the end of their life cycle.

- A better approach is for organizations to move away from a reactive "keep-everything" strategy to a *proactive strategy* of defensible deletion.

- Organizations can improve disposition and IG programs with a systemized, repeatable, and defensible approach.

- A limitation period—the length of time after which a legal action cannot be brought before the courts—must be factored into retention policies.

- A complete, current, and documented records retention program reduces storage and handling costs and improves searchability for records by making records easier and faster to find.

- Retention schedules are developed by records series, not for individual records.

- Retention schedules are basic tools that allow an organization to prove that it has a legally defensible basis on which to dispose of records.

- The master retention schedule contains all records series in the entire enterprise.

- "Records retention" defines the length of time that records are to be kept and considers legal, regulatory, operational, and historical requirements.

- Disposition means not just destruction but can also mean archiving and a change in ownership and responsibility for the records.

- For most organizations, e-mail is the most common information source to begin deleting according to established retention policies.

Notes

1. Linda Volonino and Ian Redpath, *e-Discovery for Dummies* (Hoboken, NJ: John Wiley & Sons, 2010), p. 9. This material is reproduced with permission from John Wiley & Sons, Inc.
2. "New Fed. Rules to Civil Procedure," www.uscourts.gov/FederalCourts/UnderstandingtheFederalCourts/DistrictCourts.aspx; (accessed November 26, 2013).
3. Ibid.
4. Ibid.
5. Volonino and Redpath, *e-Discovery for Dummies*, p. 13.
6. Ibid., p. 11.
7. "New Fed. Rules to Civil Procedure." www.uscourts.gov/FederalCourts/UnderstandingtheFederalCourts/DistrictCourts.aspx; (accessed November 26, 2013).
8. "The Digital Universe Decade—Are You Ready?" IDC iView (May 2010).
9. Deidra Paknad, "Defensible Disposal: You Can't Keep All Your Data Forever," July 17, 2012, www.forbes.com/sites/ciocentral/2012/07/17/defensible-disposal-you-cant-keep-all-your-data-forever/
10. Sunil Soares, *Selling Information Governance to the Business* (MC Press Online, Ketchum, ID, 2011), p. 229.
11. All quotations from the FRCP are from Volonino and Redpath, *e-Discovery for Dummies*, www.dummies.com/how-to/content/ediscovery-for-dummies-cheat-sheet.html (accessed May 22, 2013).
12. Linda Volonino and Ian Redpath, *e-Discovery for Dummies* (Hoboken, NJ: John Wiley & Sons, 2010), p. 13.
13. Case Briefs, LLC, "Zubulake v. UBS Warburg LLC," www.casebriefs.com/blog/law/civil-procedure/civil-procedure-keyed-to-friedenthal/pretrial-devices-of-obtaining-information-depositions-and-discovery-civil-procedure-keyed-to-friedenthal-civil-procedure-law/zubulake-v-ubs-warburg-llc/2/ (accessed May 21, 2013).
14. Amy Girst, "E-discovery for Lawyers," IMERGE Consulting Report, 2008.
15. ECM², "15-Minute Guide to eDiscovery and Early Case Assessment," www.emc.com/collateral/15-min-guide/h9781-15-min-guide-ediscovery-eca-gde.pdf (accessed May 21, 2013
16. Barry Murphy, telephone interview with author, April 12, 2013.
17. Email to author August 16, 2012.
18. Recommind, "What Is Predictive Coding?" www.recommind.com/predictive-coding (accessed May 7, 2013).
19. Michael LoPresti, "What Is Predictive Coding?: Including eDiscovery Applications," *KMWorld*, January 14, 2013, www.kmworld.com/Articles/Editorial/What-Is-.../What-is-Predictive-Coding-Including-eDiscovery-Applications-87108.aspx
20. "Predictive Coding," TechTarget.com, http://searchcompliance.techtarget.com/definition/predictive-coding, August 31, 2012 (accessed May 7, 2013).
21. "Machine Learning," TechTarget.com http://whatis.techtarget.com/definition/machine-learning, accessed May 7, 2013.
22. "Predictive Coding."
23. LoPresti, "What Is Predictive Coding?"
24. Ibid.
25. "What Does Predictive Coding Require?" Recommind Corp., www.recommind.com/predictive-coding (accessed May 24, 2013).
26. Ibid.
27. Barry Murphy, e-mail to author, May 10, 2013.
28. Ibid.
29. Ibid.
30. "The digital universe in 2020: Big Data, Bigger Digital Shadows, and Biggest Grow in the Far East," www.emc.com/collateral/analyst-reports/idc-the-digital-universe-in-2020.pdf (accessed November 26, 2013).
31. Council of Information Auto-Classification, "Information Explosion" survey, http://infoautoclassification.org/survey.php (accessed November 26, 2013).
32. Ibid.
33. Maura R. Grossman and Gordon V. Cormack, "Technology-Assisted Review in E-Discovery Can Be More Effective and More Efficient Than Exhaustive Manual Review." http://delve.us/downloads/Technology-Assisted-Review-In-Ediscovery.pdf (accesssed November 26, 2013).
34. Government of Alberta, "Developing Retention and Disposition Schedules," July 2004, p. 122, www.rimp.gov.ab.ca/publications/pdf/SchedulingGuide.pdf
35. U.S. Government Printing Office (GPO), "Code of Federal Regulations," www.gpo.gov/help/index.html#about_code_of_federal_regulations.htm (accessed April 22, 2012).

36. National Archives and Records Administration, "Electronic Code of Federal Regulations," October 2, 2012 http://ecfr.gpoaccess.gov/cgi/t/text/text-idx?c=ecfr&tpl=%2Findex.tpl

37. U.S. Department of Energy, Records Retention Schedule Definition, https://commons.lbl.gov/display/aro/Records+Retention+Schedule+Definition (accessed July 30, 2012).

38. National Archives, "Frequently Asked Questions about Records Scheduling and Disposition," updated June 6, 2005, www.archives.gov/records-mgmt/faqs/scheduling.html#whysched

39. Government of Alberta, "Developing Retention and Disposition Schedules."

40. National Archives, "Frequently Asked Questions about Records Scheduling and Disposition."

41. International Organization for Standardization, ISO 16175-1:2010, "Information and Documentation—Principles and Functional Requirements for Records in Electronic Office Environments—Part 1: Overview and Statement of Principles," www.iso.org/iso/catalogue_detail.htm?csnumber=55790 (accessed July 30, 2012).

CHAPTER 9

Information Governance and Records and Information Management Functions

Records management (RM) is a key impact area of **information governance** (IG)—so much so that in the RM space, IG is often thought of as synonymous with or a simple superset of RM. But IG is much more than that. We delve into the details of RM here—a sort of crash course on how to identify and inventory records, conduct the necessary legal research, develop retention and disposition schedules, and more. Also, we identify the relationship and impact of IG on the RM function in an organization in this chapter.

The International Organization for Standardization (ISO) defines (business) **records** as "information created, received, and maintained as evidence and information by an organization or person, in pursuance of legal obligations or in the transaction of business."[1] It further defines RM as "[the] field of management responsible for the efficient and systematic control of the creation, receipt, maintenance, use, and disposition of records, including the processes for capturing and maintaining evidence of and information about business activities and transactions in the form of records."[2]

The U.S.-based Association of Records Managers and Administrators (ARMA) defines records as "evidence of what an organization does. They capture its business activities and transactions, such as contract negotiations, business correspondence, personnel files, and financial statements."[3]

Records and information management (RIM) extends beyond RM (although the terms are often used interchangeably) to include information—that is, information such as data, electronic documents, and reports. For this reason, RIM professionals must expand their reach and responsibilities to include policies for retention and disposition of all legally discoverable forms of information, such as e-mail, social media posts, mobile data and documents held on portable devices, cloud storage and applications, and other enterprise data and information.

Electronic records management (ERM) has moved to the forefront of business issues with the increasing automation of business processes and the vast growth in the volume of electronic documents and records that organizations create. These

Portions of this chapter are adapted from Chapters 1, 5, and 7 of Robert F. Smallwood, *Managing Electronic Records: Methods, Best Practices, and Technologies,* © John Wiley & Sons, Inc., 2013. Reproduced with permission of John Wiley & Sons, Inc.

> E-records management has become much more critical to enterprises with increased compliance legislation and massively increasing volumes of electronic information.

factors, coupled with expanded and tightened reporting laws and compliance regulations, have made ERM essential for most enterprises—especially highly regulated and public ones.

ERM follows generally the same principles as traditional paper-based records management: There are **classification** and **taxonomy** needs to group and organize the records, and there are **retention** and **disposition** schedules to govern the length of time a record is kept and its ultimate disposition (destruction, transfer, or long-term archiving) destruction or long-term archiving. Yet e-records must be handled differently, and they contain more detailed data about their contents and characteristics, known as **metadata.** (For more detail on these topics see Appendix A.)

E-records are also subject to changes in **information technology** (IT) that may make them difficult to retrieve and view and therefore render them obsolete. These issues can be addressed through a sound ERM program that includes **long-term digital preservation (LTDP)** methods and technologies.

ERM is primarily the organization, management, control, monitoring, and auditing of formal business records that exist in electronic form. But automated ERM systems also track paper-based and other physical records. So ERM goes beyond simply managing electronic records; it is *the management of electronic records and the electronic management of non-electronic records (e.g., paper, CD/DVDs, magnetic tape, audio-visual, and other physical records).*

Most electronic records, or e-records, originally had an equivalent in paper form, such as memos (now e-mail), accounting documents (e.g., purchase orders, invoices), personnel documents (e.g., job applications, resumes, tax documents), contractual documents, line-of-business documents (e.g., loan applications, insurance claim forms, health records), and required regulatory documents (e.g., material safety data sheets). Before e-document and e-record software began to mature in the 1990s, many of these documents were first archived to microfilm or microform/microfiche.

Not all documents rise to the level of being declared a formal business record that needs to be retained; that definition depends on the specific regulatory and legal requirements imposed on the organization and the internal definitions and requirements the organization imposes on itself, through internal IG measures and business policies. IG *is the policies, processes, and technologies used to manage and control information throughout the enterprise to meet internal business requirements and external legal and compliance demands.*

> ERM follows the same basic principles as paper-based records management.

> ERM includes the management of electronic and nonelectronic records, such as paper and other physical records.

ERM is a component of enterprise content management (ECM), just as document management, Web content management, digital asset management, enterprise report management, and several other technology sets are components. ECM encompasses *all* an organization's unstructured digital content, which means it excludes structured data (i.e., databases). ECM includes the vast majority—over 90 percent—of an organization's overall information that must be governed and managed.

ERM extends ECM to provide control and to manage records through their life cycle—from creation to destruction. ERM is used to complete the life cycle management of information, documents, and records.

ERM adds the functionality to complete the management of information and records by applying business rules to manage the maintenance, preservation, and disposition of records. Both ERM and ECM systems aid in locating and managing the records and information needed to conduct business efficiently, to comply with legal and regulatory requirements, and to effectively destroy (paper) and delete (digital) records that have met their retention policy time frame requirement, freeing up valuable physical and digital space and eliminating records that could be a liability if kept.

Records Management Business Rationale

Historically, highly regulated industries, such as banking, energy, and pharmaceuticals, have had the greatest need to implement RM programs, due to their compliance and reporting requirements.[4] However, over the past decade or so, increased regulation and changes to legal statutes and rules have made RM a business necessity for nearly every enterprise (beyond very small businesses).

Notable industry drivers include:

- *Increased government oversight and industry regulation.* Government regulations that require enhanced reporting and accountability were early business drivers that fueled the implementation of formal RM programs. This is true at the federal and state or provincial level. In the United States, the Sarbanes–Oxley Act of 2002 (SOX) created and enhanced standards of financial reporting and transparency for the boards and executive management of public corporations and accounting firms. It also addressed auditor independence and corporate governance concerns. SOX imposes fines or imprisonment penalties for noncompliance and requires that senior officers sign off on the veracity of financial statements. It states clearly that pertinent business records cannot be destroyed during litigation or compliance investigations. Since SOX was enacted, Japan, Australia, Germany, France, and India also have adopted stricter "SOX-like" governance and financial reporting standards.

A number of factors provide the business rationale for ERM, including facilitating compliance, supporting IG, and providing backup capabilities in the event of a disaster.

- *Changes in legal procedures and requirements during civil litigation.* In 2006, the need to amend the U.S. Federal Rules of Civil Procedure (FRCP) to contain specific rules for handling electronically generated evidence was addressed. The changes included processes and requirements for legal discovery of electronically stored information (ESI) during civil litigation. *Today, e-mail is the leading form of evidence requested in civil trials.* The changes to the U.S. FRCP had a pervasive impact on American enterprises and required them to gain control over their ESI and implement formal RM and electronic discovery (e-discovery) programs to meet new requirements. Although they have been ahead of the United States in their development and maturity of RM practices, Canadian, British, and Australian law is closely tracking that of the United States in legal discovery. The United States is a more litigious society, so this is not unexpected.
- *IG awareness.* IG, in short, is the set of rules, policies, and business processes used to manage and control the totality of an organization's information. Monitoring technologies are required to enforce and audit IG compliance. Beginning with SOX in 2002 and continuing with the massive U.S. FRCP changes in 2006, enterprises have become more IG aware and have ramped up efforts to control, manage, and secure their information. *A significant component of any IG program is implementing an RM program that specifies the retention periods and disposition (e.g., destruction, transfer, archive) of formal business records.* This program, for instance, allows enterprises to destroy records once their required retention period (based on external regulations, legal requirements, and internal IG policies) has been met and allows them to legally destroy records with no negative impact or lingering liability.
- *Business continuity concerns.* In the face of real disasters, such as the 9/11 terrorist attacks, Hurricane Katrina, and Superstorm Sandy, executives now realize that disaster recovery and business resumption must be planned and prepared for. Disasters really happen, and businesses that are not well prepared really go under. The focus is on **vital records** that are necessary to resume operations in the event of a disaster, and managing those records is part of an overall RM program.

Why Is Records Management So Challenging?

With these changes in the business environment and in regulatory, legal, and IG influences comes increased attention to RM as a driver for **corporate compliance.** For most organizations, a lack of defined policies and the enormous and growing volumes of documents (e.g., e-mail messages) make implementing a formal RM program challenging and costly. Some reasons for this include:

- *Changing and increasing regulations.* Just when records and compliance managers have sorted through the compliance requirements of federal regulations, new ones at the state or provincial level are created or tightened down.
- *Maturing IG requirements within the organization.* As senior managers become increasingly aware of IG—the rules, policies, and processes that control and manage information—they promulgate more reporting and auditing requirements for the management of formal business records.
- *Managing multiple retention and disposition schedules.* Depending on the type of record, retention requirements vary, and they may vary for the same type of record based on state and federal regulations. Further, internal information governance policies may extend retention periods and may fluctuate with management changes.[5]
- *Compliance costs and requirements with limited staff.* RM and compliance departments are notoriously understaffed, since they do not generate revenue. Departments responsible for executing and proving compliance with new and increasing regulatory requirements must do so expediently, often with only skeletal staffs. This leads to expensive outsourcing solutions or staff increases. The cost of compliance must be balanced with the risk of maintaining a minimum level of compliance.
- *Changing information delivery platforms.* With cloud computing, mobile computing, Web 2.0, social media, and other changes to information delivery and storage platforms, records and compliance managers must stay apprised of the latest IT trends and provide records on multiple platforms all while maintaining the security and integrity of organizational records.
- *Security concerns.* Protecting and preserving corporate records is of paramount importance, yet users must have reasonable access to official records to conduct everyday business. "Organizations are struggling to balance the need to provide accessibility to critical corporate information with the need to protect the integrity of corporate records."[6]
- *Dependence on the IT department or provider.* Since tracking and auditing use of formal business records requires IT, and records and compliance departments typically are understaffed, those departments must rely on assistance from the IT department or outsourced IT provider—which often does not have the same perspective and priorities as the departments they serve.
- *User assistance and compliance.* Users often go their own way with regard to records, ignoring directives from records managers to stop storing shadow files of records on their desktop (for their own convenience) and inconsistently following directives to classify records as they are created. Getting users across a range of departments in the enterprise to adhere uniformly with records and compliance requirements is a daunting and unending task that requires constant attention and reinforcement.[7]

Implementing ERM is challenging because it requires user support and compliance, adherence to changing laws, and support for new information delivery platforms, such as mobile and cloud computing.

> An investment in ERM is an investment in business process automation and yields document control, document integrity, and security benefits.

Benefits of Electronic Records Management

A number of business drivers and benefits combine to create a strong case for implementing an enterprise ERM program. Most are tactical, such as cost savings, time savings, and building space savings. *But some drivers can be thought of as strategic,* in that they proactively give the enterprise an advantage. One example may be the advantages gained in litigation by having more control and ready access to complete business records, which yields more accurate results and more time for corporate attorneys to develop strategies while the opposition is wading through reams of information, never knowing if it has found the complete set of records it needs. Another example is more complete and better information for managers to base decisions on.

Implementing ERM represents a significant investment. *An investment in ERM is an investment in business process automation and yields document control, document integrity, and security benefits.* The volume of records in organizations often exceeds employees' ability to manage them. ERM systems do for the information age what the assembly line did for the industrial age. The cost/benefit justification for ERM is sometimes difficult to determine, although there are real labor and cost savings. Also, many of the benefits are intangible or difficult to calculate but help to justify the capital investment. There are many ways in which an organization can gain significant business benefits with ERM.

More detail on business benefits is provided in Chapter 7, but hard, calculable benefits (when compared to storing paper files) include office space savings, office supplies savings, cutting wasted search time, and reduced office automation costs (e.g., fewer printers, copiers, cutting automated filing cabinets).

In addition, implementing ERM will provide the organization with:

- Improved capabilities for enforcing IG over business documents and records
- Improved, more complete, and more accurate searches
- Improved knowledge worker productivity
- Reduced risk of compliance actions or legal consequences
- Improved records security
- Improved ability to demonstrate legally defensible RM practices
- Increased working confidence in making searches, which should improve decision making

> ERM benefits are both tangible and intangible or difficult to calculate.

Additional Intangible Benefits

The U.S. Environmental Protection Agency (EPA), a pioneer and leader in e-records implementation in the federal sector, lists some additional benefits of implementing ERM:

1. *To control the creation and growth of records.* Despite decades of using various nonpaper storage media, the amount of paper in our offices continues to escalate. An effective records management program addresses both creation control (limits the generation of records or copies not required to operate the business) and records retention (a system for destroying useless records or retiring inactive records), thus stabilizing the growth of records in all formats.

2. *To assimilate new records management technologies.* A good records management program provides an organization with the capability to assimilate new technologies and take advantage of their many benefits. Investments in new computer systems don't solve filing problems unless current manual record-keeping systems are analyzed (and occasionally, overhauled) before automation is applied.

3. *To safeguard vital information.* Every organization, public or private, needs a comprehensive program for protecting its vital records and information from catastrophe or disaster, because every organization is vulnerable to loss. Operated as part of the overall records management program, vital records programs preserve the integrity and confidentiality of the most important records and safeguard the vital information assets according to a "plan" to protect the records.

4. *To preserve the corporate memory.* An organization's files contain its institutional memory, an irreplaceable asset that is often overlooked. Every business day, you create the records that could become background data for future management decisions and planning. These records document the activities of the agency that future scholars may use to research the workings of the Environmental Protection Agency.

5. *To foster professionalism in running the business.* A business office with files askew, stacked on top of file cabinets and in boxes everywhere, creates a poor working environment. The perceptions of customers and the public, and "image" and "morale" of the staff, though hard to quantify in cost-benefit terms, may be among the best reasons to establish a good records management program.[8]

Thus, there are a variety of tangible and intangible benefits derived from ERM programs, and the business rationale that fits for your organization depends on its specific needs and business objectives.

Improved professionalism, preserving corporate memory, and support for better decision making are key intangible benefits of ERM.

Inventorying E-Records

According to the U.S. National Archives and Records Administration (NARA), "In **records management**, an **inventory** is a descriptive listing of each record series or system, together with an indication of location and other pertinent data. *It is not a list of each document or each folder but rather of each series or system*"[9] (emphasis added).

Conducting an inventory of electronic records is more challenging than performing a physical records inventory, but the purposes are the same: to ferret out RM problems and to use the inventory as the basis for developing the retention schedule. Some of the RM problems that may be uncovered

> include inadequate documentation of official actions, improper applications of record-keeping technology, deficient filing systems and maintenance practices, poor management of nonrecord materials, insufficient identification of vital records, and inadequate records security practices. When completed, the inventory should include all offices, all records, and all nonrecord materials. An inventory that is incomplete or haphazard can only result in an inadequate schedule and loss of control over records.[10]

The first step in gaining control over an organization's records and implementing IG measures to control and manage them is to complete an inventory of all groupings of business records, including electronic records,[11] *at the system or file series level.*

The focus of this book is on IG and more granually e-records, and when it comes to e-records, NARA has a specific recommendation: Inventory *at the computer systems level.* This differs from advice given by experts in the past.

The records inventory is the basis for developing a **records retention schedule** that spells out how long different types of records are to be held and how they will be archived or disposed of at the end of their life cycle. But first you must determine where business records reside, how they are stored, how many exist, and how they are used in the normal course of business.

There are a few things to keep in mind when approaching the e-records inventorying process:

- Those who create and work with the records themselves are the best source of information about how the records are used. They are your most critical resource in the inventorying process.
- RM is something that everyone wants done but no one wants to do (although everyone will have an opinion on how to do it).
- The people working in business units are touchy about their records. It will take some work to get them to trust a new RM approach.[12]

> NARA recommends that electronic records are inventoried by information system, not by record series.

These knowledge workers are your best resource and can be your greatest allies or worst enemies when it comes to gathering accurate inventory data; developing a workable file plan; and keeping the records declaration, retention, and disposition process operating efficiently. A sound RM program will keep the records inventory accurate and up to date.

Generally Accepted Recordkeeping Principles®

See Chapter 3 for more detail on applicable principles in IG. To summarize: It may be useful to use a model or framework to guide your records inventorying efforts. Such frameworks could be the D.I.R.K.S. (Designing and Implementing Recordkeeping Systems) used in Australia or the Generally Accepted Recordkeeping Principles® (or "the Principles") that originated in the United States at **ARMA International.** The Principles are a *"framework for managing records in a way that supports an organization's immediate and future regulatory, legal, risk mitigation, environmental, and operational requirements."*[13]

Special attention should be given to creating an accountable, open inventorying process that can demonstrate integrity. The result of the inventory should help the organization adhere to records retention, disposition, availability, protection, and compliance aspects of The Principles.

> The Generally Accepted Recordkeeping Principles were created with the assistance of ARMA International and legal and IT professionals who reviewed and distilled global best practice resources. These included the international records management standard ISO15489–1 from the American National Standards Institute and court case law. The principles were vetted through a public call-for-comment process involving the professional records information management . . . community.[14]

E-Records Inventory Challenges

If your organization has received a legal summons for e-records, and you do not have an accurate inventory, the organization is already in a compromising position: You do not know where the requested records might be, how many copies there might be, or the process and cost of producing them. Inventorying must be done sooner rather than later and proactively rather than reactively.

E-records present challenges beyond those of paper of microfilmed records due to their (electronic) nature:

1. You cannot see or touch them without searching online, as opposed to simply thumbing through a filing cabinet or scrolling through a roll of microfilm.

> What are The Principles? They are guidelines for information management and governance of record creation, organization, security, maintenance, and other activities used to effectively support the recordkeeping of an organization.

2. They are not sitting in a central file room but rather may be scattered about on servers, shared network drives, or on storage attached to mainframe or minicomputers.
3. They have metadata attached to them that may distinguish very similar-looking records.
4. Additional "shadow" copies of the e-records may exist, and it is difficult to determine the true or original copy.[15]

Records Inventory Purposes

The completed records inventory contributes toward the pursuit of an organization's IG objectives in a number of ways: It supports the ownership, management, and control of records; helps to organize and prepare for the discovery process in litigation; reduces exposure to business risk; and provides the foundation for a disaster recovery/business continuity plan.

Completing the records inventory offers at least eight additional benefits:

1. It identifies records ownership and sharing relationships, both internal and external.
2. It determines which records are physical, electronic, or a combination of both.
3. It provides the basis for retention and disposition schedule development.
4. It improves compliance capabilities.
5. It supports training objectives for those handling records.
6. It identifies vital and sensitive records needing added security and backup measures.
7. It assesses the state of records storage, its quality and appropriateness.
8. It supports the release of information for Freedom of Information Act (FOIA), Data Protection Act, and other mandated information release requirements for governmental agencies.[16]

With respect to e-records, the purpose of the records inventory should include the following objectives:

- Provide a survey of the existing electronic records situation.
- Locate and describe the organization's electronic record holdings.
- Identify obsolete electronic records.
- Determine storage needs for active and inactive electronic records.
- Identify vital and archival electronic records, indicating need for their ongoing care.
- Raise awareness within the organization of the importance of electronic records management.
- Lead to electronic record keeping improvements that increase efficiency.
- Lead to the development of a needs assessment for future actions.
- Provide the foundation of a written records management plan with a determination of priorities and stages of actions, ensuring the continuing improvement of records management practices.[17]

The completed records inventory contributes toward the pursuit of an organization's IG objectives in a number of ways.

Records Inventorying Steps

NARA's guidance on how to approach a records inventory applies to both physical and e-records.

The steps in the records inventory process are:

1. *Define the inventory's goals.* While the main goal is gathering information for scheduling purposes, other goals may include preparing for conversion to other media, or identifying particular records management problems.
2. *Define the scope of the inventory;* it should include all records and other materials.
3. *Obtain top management's support,* preferably in the form of a directive, and keep management and staff informed at every stage of the inventory.
4. *Decide on the information to be collected* (the elements of the inventory). Materials should be located, described, and evaluated in terms of use.
5. *Prepare an inventory form,* or use an existing one.
6. *Decide who will conduct the inventory,* and train them properly.
7. *Learn where the agency's* [or business's] *files are located,* both physically and organizationally.
8. *Conduct the inventory.*
9. *Verify and analyze the results.*[18]

Goals of the Inventory Project

The goals of the inventorying project must be set and conveyed to all stakeholders. At a basic level, the primary goal can be simply to generate a complete inventory for compliance and reporting purposes. It may focus on a certain business area or functional group or on the enterprise as a whole. An enterprise approach requires segmenting the effort into smaller, logically sequenced work efforts, such as by business unit. *Perhaps the organization has a handle on its paper and microfilmed records but e-records have been growing exponentially and spiraling out of control, without good policy guidelines or IG controls.* So a complete inventory of records and e-records by system is needed, which may include e-records generated by application systems, residing in e-mail, created in office documents and spreadsheets, or other potential business records. This is a tactical approach that is limited in scope.

The goal of the inventorying process may be more ambitious: to lay the groundwork for the acquisition and implementation of an ERM system that will manage the retention, disposition, search, and retrieval of records. It requires more business

Whatever the business goals for the inventorying effort are, they must be conveyed to all stakeholders, and that message must be reinforced periodically and consistently, and through multiple means.

process analysis and redesign, some rethinking of business classification schemes or file plans, and development of an enterprise-wide taxonomy. This redesign will allow for more sharing of information and records; faster, easier, and more complete retrievals; and a common language and approach for knowledge professionals across the enterprise to declare, capture, and retrieve business records.

The plan may be still much greater in scope and involve more challenging goals: That is, the inventorying of records may be the first step in the process of implementing an organization-wide IG program to manage and control information by rolling out ERM and IG systems and new processes; to improve litigation readiness and stand ready for e-discovery requests; and to demonstrate compliance adherence with business agility and confidence. Doing this involves an entire cultural shift in the organization and a long-term approach.

Whatever the business goals for the inventorying effort, they must be conveyed to all stakeholders, and that message must be reinforced periodically and consistently, and through multiple means. It must be clearly spelled out in communications and presented in meetings as the overarching goal that will help the organization meet its business objectives. The scope of the inventory must be appropriate for the business goals and objectives it targets.

Scoping the Inventory

"With senior-level support, the records manager must decide on the scope of the records inventory. A single inventory could not describe every electronic record in an organization; *an appropriate scope might enumerate the records of a single program or division, several functional series across divisions, or records that fall within a certain time frame.*" [emphasis added.][19] Most organizations have not deployed an enterprise-wide records management system, which makes the e-records inventorying process arduous and time-consuming. It is not easy to find where all the electronic records reside—they are scattered all over the place, and on different media. But impending (and inevitable) litigation and compliance demands require that it be done. And, again, sooner has been proven to be better than later. Since courts have ruled that if lawsuits have been filed against your competitors over a certain (industry-specific) issue, your organization should anticipate and prepare for litigation—which means conducting records inventories and placing a litigation hold on documents that might be relevant. Simply doing nothing and waiting on a subpoena is an avoidable business risk.

An appropriate scope might enumerate the records of a single program or division, several functional series across divisions, or records that fall within a certain time frame.

A methodical, step-by-step approach must be taken—it is the only way to accomplish the task. A plan that divides up the inventorying tasks into smaller, accomplishable pieces is the only one that will work. It has been said, "How do you eat an elephant?" And the answer is "One bite at a time." So scope the inventorying process into segments, such as a business unit, division, or information system/application.

Management Support: Executive Sponsor

It is crucial to have management support to drive the inventory process to completion. There is no substitute for an executive sponsor. Asking employees to take time out for yet another survey or administrative task without having an executive sponsor will likely not work. Employees are more time-pressed than ever, and they will need a clear directive from above, along with an understanding of what role the inventorying process plays in achieving a business goal for the enterprise, if they are to take the time to properly participate and contribute meaningfully to the effort.

Information/Elements for Collection

During the inventory you should collect the following information at a minimum:

- What kind of record it is—contracts, financial reports, memoranda, etc.
- What department owns it
- What departments access it
- What application created the record (e-mail, MS Word, Acrobat PDF)
- Where it is stored, both physically (tape, server) and logically (network share, folder)
- Date created
- Date last changed
- Whether it is a vital record (mission-critical to the organization)
- Whether there are other forms of the record (for example, a document stored as a Word document, a PDF, and a paper copy) and which of them is considered the official record

Removable media should have a unique identifier and the inventory should include a list of records on the particular volume as well as the characteristics of the volume, e.g., the brand, the recording format, the capacity and volume used, and the date of manufacture and date of last update.[20] (Emphasis added.)

Additional information not included in inventories of physical records must be collected in any inventory of e-records.

IT Network Diagram

Laying out the overall topology of the IT infrastructure in the form of a network diagram is an exercise that is helpful in understanding where to target efforts and to map information flows. Creating this map of the IT infrastructure is a crucial step in inventorying e-records. It graphically depicts how and where computers are connected to each other and the software operating environments of various applications that are in use. This high-level diagram does not need to include every device; rather, it should indicate each *type* of device and how it is used.

The IT staff usually has a network diagram that can be used as a reference; perhaps after some simplification it can be put into use as the underpinning for inventorying e-records. It does not need great detail, such as where network bridges and routers are located, but it should show which applications are utilizing the cloud or hosted applications to store and/or process documents and records.

In diagramming the IT infrastructure for purposes of the inventory, it is easiest to start in the central computer room where any mainframe or other centralized servers are located and then follow the connections out into the departments and business unit areas, where there may be multiple shared servers and drives supported a network of desktop personal computers or workstations.

Microsoft's SharePoint® is a prevalent document and RM portal platform, and many organizations have SharePoint servers to house and process e-documents and records. Some utilities and tools may be available to assist in the inventorying process on SharePoint systems.

Mobile devices (e.g., tablets, smartphones, and other portable devices) that are processing documents and records should also be represented. And any e-records residing in cloud storage should also be included.

Creating a Records Inventory Survey Form

The record inventory survey form must suit its purpose. Do not collect data that is irrelevant, but, in conducting the survey, be sure to collect all the needed data elements. You can use a standard form, but some customization is recommended. The sample records survey form in Figure 9.1 is wide ranging yet succinct and has been used successfully in practice.

If conducting the e-records portion of the inventory, the sample form may be somewhat modified, as shown in Figure 9.2.

Who Should Conduct the Inventory?

Typically, a RM project team is formed to conduct the survey, often assisted by resources outside of the business units. These may be RM and IT staff members, business analysts, members of the legal staff, outside specialized consultants, or a combination of these groups. The greater the cross-section from the organization, the better, and the more expertise brought to bear on the project, the more likely it will be completed thoroughly and on time.

Critical to the effort is that those conducting the inventory are trained in the survey methods and analysis, so that when challenging issues arise, they will have the resources and know-how to continue the effort and get the job done.

Figure 9.1   Records Inventory Survey Form

Department Information

1. What is the reporting structure of the department?
2. Who is the department liaison for the records inventory?
3. Who is the IT or business analyst liaison?

Record Requirements

4. Are there any external agencies that impose guidelines, standards or other requirements?
5. Are there specific legislative requirements for creating or maintaining records? Please provide a copy.
6. Is there a departmental records retention schedule?
7. What are the business considerations that drive recordkeeping? Regulatory requirements? Legal requirements?
8. Does the department have an existing records management policy? Guidelines? Procedures? Please provide a copy.
9. Does the department provide guidance to employees on what records are to be created?
10. How are policies, procedures and guidance disseminated to the employees?
11. What is the current level of employees' awareness of their responsibilities for records management?
12. How are nonrecords managed?
13. What is the process for ensuring compliance with policies, procedures, and guidelines?

    When an employee changes jobs/roles or is terminated?
14. Does the department have a classification or file plans?
15. Are any records in the department confidential or sensitive?
16. What information security controls does the department have for confidential or sensitive records?
17. Does the department have records in sizes other than letter (8½×11)?
18. What is the cutoff date for the records?

    ☐ Fiscal Year   ☐ Calendar Year   ☐ Other
19. Have department vital records been identified?
20. Is there an existing business or disaster recovery policy?
21. Is the department subject to audits? Internal? External? Who conducts the audits?
22. Where and how are records stored?

    Online? Near Line? Offline? On-site? Off-site? One location? Multiple locations?
23. How does the department ensure that records will remain accessible, readable, and useable throughout their scheduled retention period?

Technology and Tools

24. Are any tools used to track active records? Spreadsheets, word documents, databases, and so forth?
25. Are any tools used to track inactive records? Spreadsheets, word documents, databases, and so forth?
26. Does the department use imaging, document management, and so forth?

Disposition

27. Are there guidelines for destroying obsolete records?

(continued)

Figure 9.1   (*continued*)

28. What disposition methods are authorized or required?

29. How does disposition occur? Paper? Electronic? Other?

30. What extent does the department rely on each individual to destroy records? Paper? Electronic? Other?

Records Holds

31. What principles govern decisions for determining the scope of records that must be held or frozen for an audit or investigations?

32. How is the hold or freeze communicated to employees?

33. How are records placed on hold protected?

Source: Charmain Brooks, IMERGE Consulting, e-mail to author, March 20, 2012.

Figure 9.2   Electronic Records Inventory Survey Form

Identifying Information

1. Name of system.

2. Program or legal authority for system.

3. System identification or control number.

4. Person responsible for administering the system. Include e-mail, office address, and phone contact info.

5. Date system put in service.

6. Business unit or agency supported by system.

7. Description of system (what does the application software do?).

8. Purpose of system.

System Inputs/Outputs

9. Primary sources of data inputs.

10. Major outputs of system (e.g., specific reports).

11. Informational content (all applicable): Description of data; applicability of data (people, places, things); geographic information; time span; update cycle; applications the system supports; how data are manipulated; key unit analysis for each file; public use or not?

12. Hardware configuration.

13. Software environment, including revision levels, operating system, database, and so forth.

14. Indices or any classification scheme/file plan that is in place?

15. Duplicate records? Location and volume of any other records containing the same information.

Record Requirements

16. Are there any external agencies that impose guidelines, standards, or other requirements?

17. Are their specific legislative requirements for creating or maintaining records? Please provide a copy.

18. Is there a departmental records retention schedule?

19. What are the business considerations that drive recordkeeping? Regulatory requirements? Legal requirements?

20. Does the department have an existing records management policy? Guidelines? Procedures? If so, please provide a copy.

Figure 9.2   (*continued*)

21. How are nonrecords managed?

22. Are any records in the department confidential or sensitive? How are they indicated or set apart?

23. What information security controls does the department have for confidential or sensitive records?

24. What is the cutoff date for the records?

☐ Fiscal Year   ☐ Calendar Year   ☐ Other

25. Have department vital records been identified?

26. Is there an existing business or disaster recovery policy?

27. Is the department subject to audits? Internal? External? Who conducts the audits?

28. Where and how are records stored?

Online? Near line? Offline? On-site? Off-site? One location? Multiple locations?

29. How does the department ensure that records will remain accessible, readable, and useable throughout their scheduled retention period?

Disposition

30. Are there guidelines for destroying obsolete records?

31. What disposition methods are authorized or required?

32. How does disposition occur? Are electronic deletions verified?

33. What extent does the department rely on each individual to destroy e-records?

Records Holds

34. What principles govern decisions for determining the scope of records that must be held or frozen for an audit or investigations?

35. How is the hold or freeze communicated to employees?

36. How are records placed on hold protected?

Source: Adapted from: www.archives.gov/records-mgmt/faqs/inventories.html and Charmaine Brooks, IMERGE Consulting.

Determine Where Records Are Located

The inventory process is, in fact, a surveying process, and it involves going physically out into the units where the records are created, used, and stored. Mapping out where the records are *geographically* is a basic necessity. Which buildings are they located in? Which office locations? Computer rooms?

Also, the inventory team must look *organizationally* at where the records reside (i.e., determine which departments and business units to target and prioritize in the survey process).

Conduct the Inventory

Several approaches can be taken to conduct the inventory, including three basic methods:

1. Distributing and collecting surveys
2. Conducting in-person interviews
3. Direct observation

There are three ways to conduct the inventory: surveys, interviews, and observation. Combining these methods yields the best results.

Creating and distributing a survey form is traditional and proven way to collect e-records inventory data. This is a relatively fast and inexpensive way to gather the inventory data. The challenge is getting the surveys completed in a consistent fashion. This is where a strong executive sponsor can assist. The sponsor can make the survey a priority and tie it to business objectives, making the survey completion compulsory. The survey is a good tool, and it can be used to cover more ground in the data collection process. If following up with interviews, the survey form is a good starting point; responses can be verified and clarified, and more detail can be gathered.

Some issues may not be entirely clear initially, so following up with scheduled in-person interviews can dig deeper into the business processes where formal records are create and used. A good approach is to have users walk you through their typical day and how they access, use, and create records—but be sure to interview managers too, as managers and users have differing needs and uses for records.[21]

You will need some direction to conduct formal observation, likely from IT staff or business analysts familiar with the recordkeeping systems and associated business processes. They will need to show you where business documents and records are created and stored. If there is an existing ERM system or other automated search and retrieval tools available, you may use them to speed the inventorying process.

When observing and inventorying e-records, starting in the server room and working outward toward the end user is a logical approach. Begin by enumerating the e-records created by enterprise software applications (such as accounting, enterprise resource planning, or customer relationship management systems), and work your way to the departmental or business unit applications, on to shared network servers, then finally out to individual desktop and laptop PCs and other mobile devices. With today's smartphones, this can be a tricky area, due to the variety of platforms, operating systems, and capabilities. In a bring-your-own-device environment, records should not be stored on personal devices, but if they must be, they should be protected with technologies like encryption or information rights management.

There are always going to be thorny areas when attempting to inventory e-records to determine what files series exist in the organization. Mobile devices and removable media may contain business records. These must be identified and isolated, and any records on these media must be recorded for the inventory. Particularly troublesome are thumb or flash drives, which are compact yet can store 20 gigabytes of data or more. If your IG measures call for excluding these types of media, the ports they use can be blocked on PCs, tablets, smartphones, and other mobile computing devices. A sound IG program will consider the proper use of removable media and the potential impact on your RM program.[22]

The best approach for conducting the inventory is to combine the available inventorying methods, where possible. Begin by observing, distribute surveys, collect and analyze them, and then target key personnel for follow-up interviews and walk-throughs. Utilize whatever automated tools are available along the way. This approach is the most complete. *Bear in mind that the focus is not on individual electronic files but rather, the file series level for physical records and the file series or system level for e-records (preferably the latter).*

Interviewing Programs/Service Staff

Interviews are a very good source of records inventory information. Talking with actual users will help the records lead or inventory team to better understand how documents and records are created and used in everyday operations. Users can also report why they are needed—an exercise that can uncover some obsolete or unnecessary processes and practices. This is helpful in determining where e-records reside and how they are grouped in records series or by system and ultimately, the proper length of their retention period and whether they should be archived or destroyed at the end of their useful life.[23]

Since interviewing is a time-intensive task, it is crucial that some time is spent in determining the key people to interview: Interviews not only take your time but others' as well, and the surest way to lose momentum on an inventorying project is to have stakeholders believe you are wasting their time.

> You need to interview representatives from all functional areas and levels of the program or service, including:
>
> - managers
> - supervisors
> - professional/technical staff
> - clerical/support staff
>
> The people who work with the records can best describe to you their use. They will likely know where the records came from, whether copies exist, who needs the records, any computer systems that are used, how long the records are needed and other important information that you need to know to schedule the records.

Selecting Interviewees

As stated earlier, it is wise to include a cross-section of staff, managers and frontline employees to get a rounded view of how records are created and used. Managers have a different perspective and may not know how workers utilize electronic records in their everyday operations.

A good lens to use is to focus on those who make decisions based on information contained in the electronic records and to follow those decision-based processes through to completion, observing and interviewing at each level.

> For example, an application is received (mail room logs date and time), checked (clerk checks the application for completeness and enters into a computer system), verified (clerk verifies that the information on the application is correct), and approved (supervisor makes the decision to accept the application). These staff members may only be looking at specific pieces of the record and making decisions on those pieces.

Interview Scheduling and Tips

One rule to consider is this: Be considerate of other people's work time. Since they are probably not getting compensated for participating in the records inventory, the time you take to interview them is time taken away from compensated tasks they are evaluated on. So, once the interviewees are identified, provide as much advance notice as possible, follow up to confirm appointments, and stay within the scheduled time. Interviews should be kept to 20 to 60 minutes. Most of all—*never be late!*

Before starting any interviews, be sure to restate the goals and objectives of the inventorying process and how the resulting output will benefit people in their jobs.

In some cases, it may be advisable to conduct interviews in small groups, not only to save time but to generate a discussion of how records are created, used, and stored. Some new insights may be gained.

Try to schedule interviews that are as convenient as possible for participants. That means providing participants with questions in advance and holding the interviews as close to their work area as possible. Do not schedule interviews back to back with no time for a break between. You will need time to consolidate your thoughts and notes, and, at times, interviews may exceed their planned time if a particularly enlightening line of questioning takes place.

If you have some analysis from the initial collection of surveys, share that with the interviewees so they can validate or help clarify the preliminary results. Provide it in advance, so they have some time to think about it and discuss it with their peers.

Sample Interview Questionnaire

You'll need a guide to structure the interview process. A good starting point is the sample questions presented in the questionnaire shown in Figure 9.3. It is a useful tool that has been used successfully in actual records inventory projects.

Analyze and Verify the Results

Once collected, some follow-up will be required to verify and clarify responses. Often this can be done over the telephone. For particularly complex and important areas, a follow-up in person visit can clarify the responses and gather insights.

Once the inventory draft is completed, a good practice is to go out into the business units and/or system areas and verify what the findings of the survey are. Once presented with findings in black and white, key stakeholders may have additional insights that are relevant to consider before finalizing the report. Do not miss out on the opportunity to allow power users and other key parties to provide valuable input.

Be sure to tie the findings in the final report of the records inventory to the business goals that launched the effort. This helps to underscore the purpose and importance of the effort, and will help in getting that final signoff from the executive sponsor that states the project is complete and there is no more work to do.

Depending on the magnitude of the project, it may (and *should*) turn into a formal IG program that methodically manages records in a consistent fashion in accordance with internal governance guidelines and external compliance and legal demands.

Be sure to tie the findings in the final report of the records inventory to the business goals that launched the effort.

Figure 9.3   Sample Interview Questionnaire

What is the mandate of the office?

What is the reporting structure of the department?

Who is the department liaison for the records inventory?

Are there any external agencies that impose guidelines, standards, or other requirements?

Is there a departmental records retention schedule?

Are there specific legislative requirements for creating or maintaining records? Please provide a copy.

What are the business considerations that drives record keeping? Regulatory requirements? Legal requirements?

Does the department have an existing records management policy? Guidelines? Procedures?

Please provide a copy.

Does the department provide guidance to employees on what records are to be created?

What is the current level of awareness of employees their responsibilities for records management?

How are nonrecords managed?

Does the department have a classification or file plans?

What are the business drivers for creating and maintaining records?

Where are records stored? Onsite? Offsite? One location? Multiple locations?

Does the department have records in sizes other than letter (8 ½×11)?

What is the cutoff date for the records?

☐ Fiscal Year   ☐ Calendar Year   ☐ Other

Are any tools used to track active records? Excel, Access, and so forth?

Does the department use imaging, document management, and so forth?

Is the department subject to audits? Internal? External? Who conducts the audits?

Are any records in the department confidential or sensitive?

Are their guidelines for destroying obsolete records?

What disposition methods are authorized or required?

How does disposition occur? Paper? Electronic? Other?

What extent does the department rely on each individual to destroy records?

☐ Paper   ☐ Electronic   ☐ Other

What principles govern decisions for determining the scope of records that must be held or frozen for an audit or investigations?

How is the hold or freeze communicated to employees?

Source: Charmaine Brooks, IMERGE Consulting, e-mail to author, March 20, 2012.

Appraising the Value of Records

Part of the process of determining the retention and disposition schedule of records is to appraise their value. Records can have value in different ways, which affects retention decisions.

> **Records appraisal** is an analysis of all records within an agency [or business] to determine their administrative, fiscal, historical, legal, or other archival value. The purpose of this process is to determine for how long, in what format, and

> Records appraisal is based on the information contained in the records inventory.

under what conditions a record series ought to be preserved. *Records appraisal is based upon the information contained in the records inventory.* Records series shall be either preserved permanently or disposed of when no longer required for the current operations of an agency or department, depending upon:

- *Historical value* or the usefulness of the records for historical research, including records that show an agency [or business] origin, administrative development, and present organizational structure.
- *Administrative value* or the usefulness of the records for carrying on [a business or] an agency's current and future work, and to document the development and operation of that agency over time.
- *Regulatory and statutory* [value to meet] requirements.
- *Legal value* or the usefulness of the records to document and define legally enforceable rights or obligations of [business owners, shareholders, or a] government and/or citizens.
- *Fiscal value* or the usefulness of the records to the administration of [a business or] an agency's current financial obligations, and to document the development and operation of that agency over time
- Other archival value as determined by the State [or corporate] Archivist.[24] (Emphasis added.)

Ensuring Adoption and Compliance of RM Policy

The inventorying process in not a one-shot deal: It is useful only if the records inventory is kept up to date, so it should be reviewed, at least annually. A process should be put in place so that business unit or agency heads notify the RM head/lead if a new file series or system has been put in place and new records collections are created.[25]

[Five] tips can help ensure that a records management program achieves its goals:

1. *Records management is everyone's role.* The volume and diversity of business records, from e-mails to reports to tweets, means that the person who creates or receives a record is in the best [position] to classify it. Everyone in the organization needs to adopt the records management program.
2. *Don't micro-classify.* Having hundreds, or possibly thousands, of records classification categories may seem like a logical way to organize the multitude of different records in a company. However, the average information worker, whose available resources are already under pressure, does not want to spend any more time than necessary classifying records. Having a few broad classifications makes the decision process simpler and faster.

3. *Talk the talk from the top on down.* A culture of compliance starts at the top. Businesses should establish a senior-level steering committee comprised of executives from legal, compliance, and information technology (IT). A committee like this signals the company's commitment to compliant records management and ensures enterprise adoption.

4. *Walk the walk, consistently.* For compliance to become second nature, it needs to be clearly communicated to everyone in the organization, and policies and procedures must be accessible. Training should be rigorous and easily available, and organizations may consider rewarding compliance through financial incentives, promotions and corporate-wide recognition.

5. *Measure the measurable.* The ability to measure adherence to policy and adoption of procedures should be included in core business operations and audits. Conduct a compliance assessment, including a gap analysis, at least once a year, and prepare an action plan to close any identified holes.

The growth of data challenges a company's ability to use and store its records in a compliant and cost-effective manner. Contrary to current practices, the solution is not to hire more vendors or to adopt multiple technologies. The key to compliance is consistency, with a unified enterprise-wide approach for managing all records, regardless of their format or location.[26]

So a steady and consistent IG approach that includes controls, audits, and clear communication is key to maintaining an accurate and current records inventory.

General Principles of a Retention Scheduling

We discussed records retention briefly in Chapter 8, mostly as it relates to legal research and determining retention and limitation periods. In this section we go more in depth. A series of principles is common to all retention schedules:[27]

- The retention schedule must include all records.
- Records scheduling includes all records, regardless of media or location.[28]
- All legal and regulatory requirements for records must be reflected in the records scheduling process. For public entities, retention scheduling fosters and enables the agency to comply with information requests (e.g., FOIA in the United States, Freedom of Information Act 2000 in the United Kingdom, Freedom of Information and Protection of Privacy Act and the Health Information Act in Canada, and Freedom of Information Amendment [Reform] Act 2010 in Australia).
- Records scheduling is a "proactive" planning process, where schedules are set in place and standardized in advance.
- Periodic review of the retention schedule must take place when significant legislation, technology acquisitions, or other changes are being considered; but in any case this should be at least annually or biannually.
- Records scheduling is a continuous process that needs updating and amending, based on legal, technology, or business changes over time.
- Classification and records scheduling are inextricably linked.

- File series with similar characteristics or value should be assigned consistent and appropriate retention periods.
- Records of historical value must be preserved.
- Records retention periods should reflect the business needs of users, the value of the records, and any legal or compliance requirements. The best way to make these determinations is with a team that includes cross-functional representatives from RM, legal, risk, compliance, IT and business unit representatives, headed by an executive sponsor.
- RM resource use is optimized, and costs are minimized by keeping records a minimum amount of time under a planned and controlled set of processes.
- Records must be retained in a repository (file room or software system) where the record is protected (e.g., made read-only and monitored with an audit trail) so that the integrity of the record is maintained in a manner that meets all evidence and legal admissibility standards if or when litigation is encountered.
- Senior management must approve of and sign off on the retention schedule and will be legally accountable for compliance with the schedule.
- Senior management must be able to readily review retention schedules, policy documentation, and audit information to ensure users are in compliance with the retention schedule.
- Complete documentation of scheduling requirements and activities must take place so that future users and archivists can view and track changes to the retention schedule.[29]

Developing a Records Retention Schedule

A **records retention schedule** *defines the length of time that records are to be kept and considers legal, regulatory, operational, and historical requirements.*[30] The retention schedule also includes direction as to how the length of time is calculated (i.e., the event or trigger that starts the clock [e.g., two years from completion of contract]). Legal research and opinions are required, along with consultation with owners and users of the records. Users typically overestimate the time they need to keep records, as they confuse the legal requirements with their own personal wishes. Some hard questioning has to take place, since having these records or copies of records lying around the organization on hard drives, thumb drives, or in file cabinets may create liabilities for the organization.

Disposition means not just destruction but also can mean archiving and transfer and a change in ownership and responsibility for the records. The processes of archiving and preserving are an example where records may be handed over to a historical recordkeeping unit. At this time, the records may be sampled and only selective parts of the group of records may be retained.

Records retention defines the length of time that records are to be kept and considers legal, regulatory, operational, and historical requirements.[31]

Disposition means not just destruction but can also mean archiving and a change in ownership and responsibility for the records.

Why Are Retention Schedules Needed?

A retention schedule allows for uniformity in the retention and disposition process, regardless of the media or location of the records. Further, it tracks, enforces, and audits the retention and disposition of records while optimizing the amount of records kept to legal minimums, which saves on capital and labor costs, and reduces liability (by discarding unneeded records that carry legal risk).[32] The **Generally Accepted Recordkeeping Principles**® state the critical importance of having a retention schedule (see the section "Generally Accepted Recordkeeping Principles" in Chapter 3 for more details) and provide guidelines for open collaboration in developing one. In the public sector, holding records that have passed their legally required retention period also can have negative ramifications and liabilities in meeting information service requests made during litigation, compliance actions, or, for example, under the U.S. FOIA, or similar acts in other countries.

Information Included on Retention Schedules

A retention schedule consists of these components:

- *Title* of the record series
- *Descriptions* of the records series
- *Office responsible* for the retention of the record (default is usually the office of origin)
- *Disposal decision*—destroy, transfer to the archives, or, in exceptional circumstances, reconsider at a later (specified) date
- *Timing of disposal*—a minimum period for which the records should be retained in the office or in an off-site store before disposal action is undertaken
- *Event that triggers* the disposal action
- *Dates on which the schedule was agreed*, signed, or modified
- *Legal citations or a link to a citation* that reference the retention requirements of that group of records

A sample of a simple records retention schedule is shown in Figure 9.4.

Steps in Developing a Records Retention Schedule

If you already have existing retention schedules but are revising and updating them, there may be useful information in those schedules that can serve as a good reference

A retention schedule allows for uniformity in the retention and disposition process, regardless of the media or location of the records.

Records Retention Schedule	ENVIRONMENTAL HEALTH AND SAFETY		
December 10, 2015			

Record Type	Responsible Department	Event	Retention Period
Accident/Injury Reports *Includes:* *Accidents* *Diagnosis (Accident or Injury)* *First aid reports* *Injuries* *Medical reviews* *Occupational Health Incident* *Treatment and Progress (Accident or Injury)* *Work related accidents* *Workers health information* *Workers Compensation Claims*	HR	Date of Incident	E+30
Employee Medical Files *Includes:* *Audiology* *Lung Function* *Return to Work Authorization* *Related to:* *Employee Files (Active)*	HR	Termination	E+30
Health and Safety Programs *Includes:* *Health and Safety Committee* *Health and Safety Reports*	Health and Safety		CY+10

Figure 9.4   Sample Records Retention Schedule
Source: IMERGE Consulting, Inc.

point—but be wary, as they may be out of date and may not consider current legal requirements and business needs.

According to the U.S. National Archives, some key steps are involved in developing retention schedules:

1. Review the functions and recordkeeping requirements for the [business unit or] agency or the organizational component of the agency whose records will be included on the schedule
2. Inventory the records.
3. Determine the period of time the records are needed for conducting [business or] agency operations and meeting legal obligations
4. Draft disposition instructions including:
   - File cutoffs or file breaks (convenient points within a filing plan/system (end of a letter of the alphabet, end of year or month, etc.) at which files are separated for purposes of storage and/or disposition)
   - Retention periods for temporary records
   - Instructions for transferring permanent records to the National Archives of the United States [or corporate archive for businesses]
   - Instructions for sending inactive records to off-site storage
   - Organize the schedule and clear it internally
   - Obtain approval from [your corporate archivist or] NARA [for federal agencies], as well as from GAO if required by Title 8 of the GAO, "*Policy and Procedures Manual for the Guidance of Federal Agencies.*"[33]

> An information map is a critical first step in developing a records retention schedule. It shows where information is created, where it resides, and who uses it.

What Records Do You Have to Schedule? Inventory and Classification

Inventory and classification are prerequisites for compiling a retention schedule. Before starting work, develop an **information map** that shows where information is created, where it resides, and the path it takes. What records are created, who uses them, and how is their disposition handled? Questions like these will provide key insights in the development of the retention schedule.[34] Confirm that the information map covers all the uses of the records by all parts of the organization, including use for accountability, audit, and reference purposes.

In the absence of a formal information map, at a minimum *you must compile a list of all the different types of records in each business area.* This list should include information about who created them and what they are used for (or record **provenance**), which parts of the organization have used them subsequently and for what purpose (its **usage**), and the actual **content**.

In the absence of any existing documentation or records inventory, you will need to conduct a records inventory or survey to find out what records the business unit (or organization) holds. Tools are available to scan e-records folders to expedite the inventory process. A retention schedule developed in this way will have a shorter serviceable life than one based on an information map because it will be based on existing structures rather than functions and will remain usable only as long as the organizational structure remains unchanged.

Once a records inventory or survey is complete, building a records retention schedule begins with **classification** of records.[35]

This basic classification can be grouped into three areas:

1. Business functions and activities
2. Records series
3. Document types

Business functions are basic business units such as accounting, legal, human resources, and purchasing. (See Appendix A, Information Organization and Classification: Taxonomies and Metadata, for details on the process of developing classifications.) It basically answers this question: *What were you doing when you created the record?*

> Tools are available to scan e-records folders to expedite the inventory process.

Business activities are the tasks *performed* to accomplish the business function. Several activities may be associated with each function.

A **records series** *is a group or unit of identical or related records that are normally used and filed as a unit* and that can be evaluated as a unit or business function for scheduling purposes.[36]

A **document type** is a term used by many software systems to refer to a grouping of related records. When the records are all created by similar processes, then the document type is equivalent to the business functions or activities mentioned previously. However, "document type" often refers to the format of the record (e.g., presentation, meeting minutes). In this case, there is not enough information to determine a retention period because it is ambiguous regarding what type of work was being done when that document was created. Retention schedules require that record series be defined by business function and activity, not by record format or display type.

Rationale for Records Groupings

Records are grouped together for fundamental reasons to improve information organization and access. These reasons include:

- Grouping by "similar theme" for improved completeness
- Improving information search speed and completeness
- Increasing organizational knowledge and memory by providing the "context" within which individual documents were grouped
- Clearly identifying who the record owner or creator is and assigning and tracking responsibility for a group of records
- Grouping records with the same retention requirements for consistent application of disposition processes to records

Records Series Identification and Classification

After completing a records inventory including characterizing, descriptive information about the records such as their contents, use, file size, and projected growth volumes, you will need to interview staff in those target areas you are working with to determine more information about the specific organizational structure, its business functions, services, programs, and plans.[37]

In the course of business, there are several different types of records series. There are **case records**, for example, which are characterized as having a beginning and

After completing an inventory, developing a retention schedule begins with records classification.

an end but are added to over time. Case records generally have titles that include names, dates, numbers, or places. These titles do not provide insight into the nature of the function of the record series. Examples of case records include personnel files, mortgage loan folders, contract and amendment/addendum records, accident reports, insurance claims, and other records that accumulate and expand over time. Although the contents of case files may be similar, you should break out each type of case record under a unique title.

Subject records (also referred to as **topic** or **function records**) "contain information relating to specific or general topics and that are arranged according to their informational content or by the function/activity/transaction they pertain to."[38] These types of records accumulate information on a particular topic or function to be added to the organization's memory and make it easier for knowledge workers to find information based on subject matter, topics, or business functions. Records such as those on the progression of relevant laws and statutes, policies, standard operating procedures, education and training have long-term reference value and should be kept until they are no longer relevant or are displaced by more current and relevant records. In a record retention schedule, the trigger event often is defined as "*superseded or obsolete.*" Records of this type that relate to "routine operations of a [project], program or service" do not have as much enduring value and should be scheduled to be kept for a shorter period.

Retention of E-Mail Records

Are e-mail messages records? This question has been debated for years. *The short answer is no, not all e-mail messages constitute a record.* But how do you determine whether certain messages are a business record or not? The general answer is that a record documents a transaction or business-related event that may have legal ramifications or historic value. Most important are business activities that may relate to compliance requirements or those that could possibly come into dispute in litigation. Particular consideration should be given to financial transactions of any type.

Certainly evidence that required governance oversight or compliance activities have been completed needs to be documented and becomes a business record. Also, business transactions, where there is an exchange of money or the equivalent in goods or services is documented are also business records. Today, these transactions are often documented by a quick e-mail. And, of course, any contracts (and any progressively developed or edited versions) that are exchanged through e-mail become business records.

The form or format of a potential record is irrelevant in determining whether it should be classified as a business record. For instance, if a meeting of the board of directors is recorded by a digital video recorder and saved to DVD, it constitutes a

Not all e-mail messages are records; those that document a business transaction or progress toward it are clearly records and require retention.

E-mail messages that document business activities, especially those that may be disputed in the future, should be retained as records.

record. If photographs are taken of a ground-breaking ceremony for a new manufacturing plant, the photos are records too. If the company's founders tape-recorded a message to future generations of management on reel-to-reel tape, it is a record also, since it has historical value. But most records are going to be in the form of paper, microfilm, or an electronic document.

Here are three guidelines for determining whether an e-mail message should be considered a business record:

1. *The e-mail documents a transaction or the progress toward an ultimate transaction where anything of value is exchanged between two or more parties.* All parts or characteristics of the transaction, including who (the parties to it), what, when, how much, and the composition of its components are parts of the transaction. Often seemingly minor parts of a transaction are found buried within an e-mail message. One example would be a last-minute discount offered by a supplier based on an order being placed or delivery being made within a specified time frame.

2. *The e-mail documents or provides support of a business activity occurring that pertains to internal corporate governance policies or compliance* to externally mandated regulations.

3. *The e-mail message documents other business activities that may possibly be disputed in the future,* whether it ultimately involves litigation or not. (Most business disputes actually are resolved without litigation, provided that proof of your organization's position can be shown.) For instance, your supplier may dispute the discount you take that was offered in an e-mail message and, once you forward the e-mail thread to the supplier, it acquiesces.

Managing e-mail business records is challenging, even for technology professionals. According to an AIIM and ARMA survey, *fully two-thirds of records managers doubt that their IT departments really understand the concept of electronic records life cycle management.* That is despite the fact that *70 percent of companies rely on IT professionals alone to manage their electronic records.*

Although the significance of e-mail in civil litigation cannot be overstated (it is the leading piece of evidence requested at civil trials today), *one-third of IT managers state that they would be incapable of locating and retrieving e-mails that are more than one year old,* according to Osterman Research.[39]

How Long Should You Keep Old E-Mails?

There are different schools of thought on e-mail retention periods and retention schedules. The retention and deletion of your electronic business records may be governed by laws or regulations. *Unless your organization's e-mail and ESI records are governed by law or regulations,*

Destructive retention of e-mail is a method whereby e-mail messages are retained for a limited period and then destroyed.

your organization is free to determine the retention periods and deletion schedules that are most appropriate for your organization.[40] If your organization's e-mail retention periods are not specified by law or regulation, consider keeping them for at least as long as you retain paper records. Many software providers provide automated software that allows e-mail messages to be moved to controlled repositories as they are declared to be records.

Destructive Retention of E-Mail

(We repeat this short section from Chapter 8 for those who are more focused on RIM than on legal functions.)

A destructive retention program is an approach to e-mail archiving where e-mail messages are retained for a limited time (say, 90 days), followed by the permanent manual or automatic deletion of the messages from the organization network, so long as there is no litigation hold or the e-mail has not been declared a record.

E-mail retention periods can vary from 90 days to as long as seven years:

- Osterman Research reports that "nearly one-quarter of companies delete e-mail after 90 days."[41]
- Heavily regulated industries, including energy, technology, communications, and real estate, favor archiving for one year or more, according to Fulbright and Jaworski research.[42]
- The most common e-mail retention period traditionally has been seven years; however, some organizations are taking a hard-line approach and stating that e-mails will be kept for only 90 days or six months, unless it is declared as a record, classified, and identified with a classification/retention category and tagged or moved to a repository where the integrity of the record is protected (i.e., the record cannot be altered and an audit trail on the history of the record's usage is maintained)

Long-Term Archival Records

Inactive records that are have historical value or are essential for maintaining corporate memory must be kept the longest. Although they are not needed for present operations, they still have some value to the organization and must be preserved. When it comes to preserving electronic records, this process can be complex and technical. (See Chapter 17 for details.) If you have a corporate or agency archivist, his or her input is critical.[43]

Meeting Legal Limitation Periods

(This short section is repeated from Chapter 8 for those who are more focused on RIM than on legal functions.)

A key consideration in developing retention schedules is researching and determining the minimum time required to keep records that may be demanded in legal actions. "A **limitation period** is the length of time after which a legal action cannot be brought before the courts. Limitation periods are important because they determine the length of time records must be kept to support court action [including subsequent appeal periods]. It is important to be familiar with the purpose, principles, and special circumstances that affect limitation periods and therefore records retention."[44]

Legal Requirements and Compliance Research

(Note: This section also appears in Chapter 8 but is included here for completeness.)

Legal requirements trump all others. The retention period for a particular records series must meet minimum retention requirements as mandated by law. Business needs and other considerations are secondary. So, legal research is required before determining retention periods. Legally required retention periods must be researched for each jurisdiction (state, country) in which the business operates, so that it complies with all applicable laws.

In order to locate the regulations and citations relating to retention of records, there are two basic approaches. The first approach is to use a records retention citation service, which publishes in electronic form all of the retention-related citations. These services usually are bought on a subscription basis, as citations are updated on an annual or more frequent basis as legislation and regulations change.

Figure 9.5 is an excerpt from a Canadian records retention database product called FILELAW®. In this case, the act, citation, and retention periods are clearly identified.

Another approach is to search the laws and regulations directly using online or print resources. Records retention requirements for corporations operating in the United States may be found in the **Code of Federal Regulations (CFR)**, the annual edition of which

> is the codification of the general and permanent rules published in the Federal Register by the departments and agencies of the federal government. It is divided into 50 titles that represent broad areas subject to federal regulation. The 50 subject matter titles contain one or more individual volumes, which are updated once each calendar year, on a staggered basis. The annual update cycle is as follows: titles 1 to 16 are revised as of January 1; titles 17 to 27 are revised as of April 1; titles 28 to 41 are revised as of July 1, and titles 42 to 50 are revised as of October 1. Each title is divided into chapters, which usually bear the name of the issuing agency. Each chapter is further subdivided into parts that cover specific regulatory areas. Large parts may be subdivided into subparts. All parts are organized in sections, and most citations to the CFR refer to material at the section level.[45]

There is an up-to-date version that is not yet a part of the official CFR but is updated daily, the **Electronic Code of Federal Regulations (e-CFR)**. "It is not an official legal edition of the CFR. The e-CFR is an editorial compilation of CFR material and Federal Register amendments produced by the National Archives and Records Administration's Office of the Federal Register (OFR) and the Government Printing Office."[46]

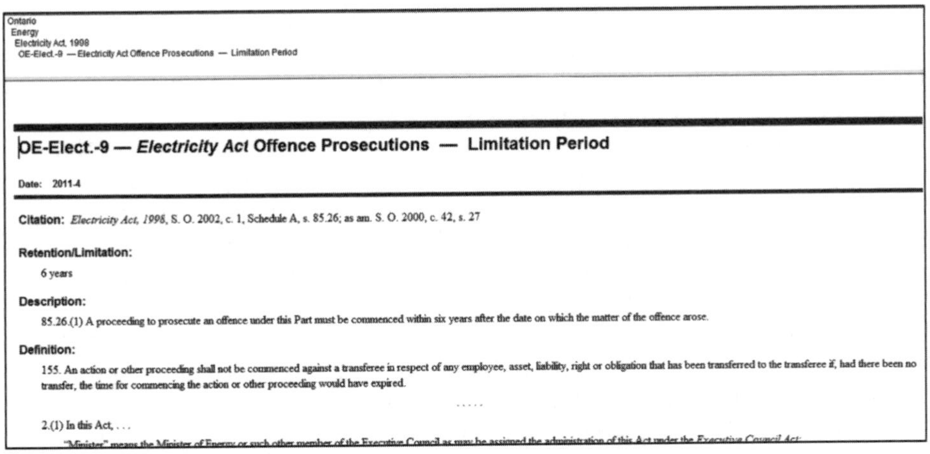

Ontario
Energy
Electricity Act, 1998
OE-Elect.-9 — Electricity Act Offence Prosecutions — Limitation Period

OE-Elect.-9 — *Electricity Act* Offence Prosecutions — Limitation Period

Date: 2011-4

Citation: *Electricity Act, 1998*, S. O. 2002, c. 1, Schedule A, s. 85.26; as am. S. O. 2000, c. 42, s. 27

Retention/Limitation:

6 years

Description:

85.26.(1) A proceeding to prosecute an offence under this Part must be commenced within six years after the date on which the matter of the offence arose.

Definition:

155. An action or other proceeding shall not be commenced against a transferee in respect of any employee, asset, liability, right or obligation that has been transferred to the transferee if, had there been no transfer, the time for commencing the action or other proceeding would have expired.

.....

2.(1) In this Act, . . .

"Minister" means the Minister of Energy or such other member of the Executive Council as may be assigned the administration of this Act under the *Executive Council Act*;

Figure 9.5 Excerpt from Canadian Records Retention Database
Source: Ontario, Electricity Act, FILELAW database, Thomson Publishers, May 2012.

Event-Based Retention Scheduling for Disposition of E-Records

Event-based disposition is kicked off with the passage of an event, such as hiring or firing an employee, the end of a project, or the initiation of a lawsuit.

Event-based disposition can have an associated retention schedule, and the clock starts running once the event occurs. The required retention period begins only after the triggering event occurs. The length of the retention period may be regulated by law, or it may be determined by IG guidelines set internally by the organization. So, when an employee is terminated, and personnel files are destroyed after (say) five years, the retention schedule entry would be "Termination + 5 years."

One other definition of event-based disposition comes from the U.S. e-records standard, Department of Defense 5015.2, which states that a disposition instruction in which a record is eligible for the specified disposition (transfer or destroy) upon or immediately after the specified event occurs. No retention period is applied and there is no fixed waiting period, as with "timed" or combination "timed-event" dispositions. Example: "Destroy when no longer needed for current operations."[47]

Some hardware vendors, such as IBM and EMC, provide solutions that assist in executing event-based disposition with assistance from firmware (fixed instructions on a microchip). The firmware-assisted solution should be considered if your RM or IG team aims to perform a complete and thorough retention solution analysis. These hardware-based solutions can potentially streamline the event-based disposition process.[48]

> Event-based disposition begins with the passage of a triggering event.

Triggering events may be record-related, "such as supersession or obsolescence." This is common to a policy statement. For example, if a group of policies are to be destroyed five years after superseded or obsolete, the old policy would be held for five years after the new policy has been created.

Sounds simple. But in an attempt to meet retention requirements, organizations handle event-based triggers in different ways, ways that often are problematic. For instance, the trigger events often are not captured electronically and fed directly into the retention scheduling software or records repository to start the clock running, or the event itself is not well documented in the retention schedule so it is not consistently being applied and tracked. In other cases, the organization simply does not have the ERM functionality it needs to manage event-based triggers.

This causes many organizations to simply over-retain and keep the records indefinitely, or until disk storage is full, which means that those records are retained for an incorrect—and indefensible—time. The period is either too long or possibly too short, but it always is *always* inconsistent. *And inconsistent means legally indefensible.*

The only prudent and defensible approach is to implement the proper IG policies to manage and control the implementation of event-based disposition.

Prerequisites for Event-Based Disposition

Three key prerequisite tasks must be completed before event-based disposition can be implemented:

1. *Clarify trigger events.* Not all of the events that can trigger the beginning of a retention period are as clear as the date an employee is terminated. For instance, "contract completion date" could be the day a vendor finishes work, when a final invoice is rendered, when the invoice is paid, or some other period, such as 30 days following the payment of the final invoice. These definitions, depending on the record series in question, may be regulated by law or governed by IG policies.

   What is needed is an agreement as to what the definition is, so that the retention period will be uniform among the record series in question, providing a defensible policy.

   To gain this agreement on these blurry areas, the RM lead/manager or team will need to work with the relevant business unit representatives, IT, compliance, risk management, and any other stakeholders.

   The event triggers must be clear and agreed on so that they may kick off a retention period and disposition process.

   In a number of cases, the answer to these questions will rely on trigger points, such as one year after completion or four months after the board of directors' meeting. *It is important to choose a* trigger point *that you can implement.* For example, there is no point in saying that records should be kept until an individual dies, if you have no reliable way of knowing the person is alive. Instead, choose a trigger point based on the information you have about the individual; in this case, the 100th birthday might be a suitable trigger point.

2. *Automated capture of agreed-on trigger events must be performed and sent to the ERM.* It is easy to know an employee's termination date—most human resources management systems or payroll systems can supply it—but other

types of events are not so easily captured and may require some customization in order that this information is fed into an ERM. The metadata about the event must be seamlessly entered into the ERM so that it may launch the beginning of the retention period. If systems external to the ERM need to be interfaced, a common locator (e.g., contract number) can link the two.

3. *The ERM systems must have complete retention and disposition capabilities.* In order for the retention to start properly and run to final disposition, this tracking capability must be an inherent feature of the software. (In some cases, organizations may use specialized retention and disposition software that can perform this task minimally without complete ERM functionality, but it falls short of the type of richness that a robust ERM system provides. What is needed is the ability to include the details or retention rules beyond simple date calculations (i.e., to store descriptive data or scope notes, and records series code in addition to retention requirements, which are automatically associated with the retention rule, and to have a records hold and release capability). If destruction is the final disposition, then the system must be able to perform a deletion of the record (so long as there is no preservation or legal hold) with no traces that can allow reconstruction of it, and this process must be verifiable.

To accomplish clarity and agreement on event-based triggers requires close consultation and collaboration among RM staff, business units, IT, legal, compliance, risk management, and other stakeholders, as relevant.

Final Disposition and Closure Criteria

After completing the records values analysis and legislative and legal research, you must determine the closure criteria and final disposition (e.g., destroy, transfer, archive) for each records series. To minimize costs and litigation risk, retention periods should be kept as short as possible while meeting all applicable regulatory, legal, and business requirements.[49]

Retention Periods: Online versus Offline

For e-records, retention periods may be segmented into active and inactive, or online and offline. Offline may be segmented further into on-site and off-site or archival storage.

Going back and combing through records retrieval requests and usage logs may provide helpful insights as to the needs of records users—but bear in mind that these logs may be misleading as users may have (in the past, before a formal IG program was implemented) kept shadow copies of files on their local hard drives or backed up to flash drives or other storage devices.

Closure Dates

A clear closure start date is required to kick off a retention period for any record, whether the retention is scheduled for on- or off-site. Calendar or fiscal year-ends are typical and practical closure dates for subject or topical records. The date used to indicate the start year is usually the date the file closed or the date of last use or update. In a university setting, school year-end may be more logical. Still, a reasoned analysis is required to determine the best closure start date for subject records in your organization.

Case records are different; logically, their closure date is set when a case record is completed (e.g., the date when an employee resigns, retires, or is terminated).

Future dates may be used, such as an employee promotion date, student graduation, or project completion. After consulting those who create and handle the records series you are analyzing, apply good business judgment and common sense when determining closure dates.[50]

Retaining Records Indefinitely

There may be some vital, historical, or other critical records that, in the best interests of the organization, need to be retained permanently. This is rare, and storing records long term must be scrutinized heavily. If certain electronic records are to be retained indefinitely or permanently, then LTDP policies and techniques must be used. (See Chapter 17 for more details.)

Retaining Transitory Records

Transitory documents usually do not rise to the level of becoming a record; they are temporary and are useful only in the short term, such as direct mail or e-mail advertising (brochures, price lists, etc.), draft documents (although not all are transitory, and some may need longer retention periods, such as draft contracts) and work in progress, duplicates, external publications (e.g., magazines, journals, newspapers, etc.), and temporary notices (e.g., company picnic, holiday party, or football pool). You must consider transitory records in your master records retention schedule.

Implementation of the Retention Schedule and Disposal of Records

Automated programs that interpret these retention periods are the best way to ensure that records are disposed of at the correct time and that an audit trail of the disposition is maintained.

Getting Acceptance and Formal Sign-off of the Retention Schedule

Upon completion of the records retention schedule, project management best practices dictate that it be signed off by an executive or project sponsor, to indicate it has been completed and there is no more work to be done on that phase of the project. In addition, you may want to gain the sign-off and acceptance by other key stakeholders, such as senior representatives from legal, IT, the board of directors or executive committee, and perhaps audit and information governance. The schedule should be updated when new record types are introduced and, in any case, at least annually.

Disposition Timing: Records Disposal

It is much easier to time or schedule the disposal of e-records than of paper or physical records, but true and complete destruction of all traces of a record cannot be done by hitting a simple "delete" key. There must be a process in place to verify the total destruction of all copies of the record. (See Chapter 17 for more details.) Records destruction can occur daily, routinely, or be scheduled at intervals (i.e., monthly or quarterly).

Automating Retention/Disposal Actions

ERM systems typically are capable of automatically executing a record deletion when a record has reached the end of its life cycle. Often these systems have a safety feature that allows an operator who has the authority to review deletions before they are performed.

Disposal Date Changes

To make a retention schedule change, such as extending the life of a record series, IG controls must be in place. So, usually, ERM systems require that a person of higher authority than the system operator make these approvals. Every subsequent delay in destroying the records often requires an escalation in approval period to extend the time that records are kept past the destruction date.

Proving Record Destruction

In some environments, especially in the public sector, a certificate of destruction or other documentation is required to prove that a record and all its copies have been completely deleted (including its metadata—although at times it is beneficial to retain metadata longer than the record itself; see Appendix A, "Information Organization and Classification," for more details). ERM systems can be configured to keep an audit trail and prove that destruction has occurred.

Ongoing Maintenance of the Retention Schedule

Records series are not static; they change, are added to, and are amended. New record functions emerge, based on changes in business, acquisitions, and divestitures. So it is necessary for organizations to review and update—at least annually—their records retention schedule.

In addition, retention requirements change as legislation changes, lawsuits are filed, and the organization refines and improves its IG policies. Development of a records retention schedule is not a one-time project; it requires attention, maintenance, and updating on a regular schedule, and using a controlled change process.

Audit to Manage Compliance with the Retention Schedule

Once your organization establishes records retention schedules for business units, or a master retention schedule, there must be IG policies in place to audit and ensure that policies are being followed. *This is a key requirement of maintaining a legally defensible retention schedule that will hold up to legal challenges.*

CHAPTER SUMMARY: **KEY POINTS**

- According to ISO, a record is "information created, received, and maintained as evidence and information by an organization or person, in pursuance of legal obligations or in the transaction of business."

- RM is "[the] field of management responsible for the efficient and systematic control of the creation, receipt, maintenance, use, and disposition of records, including the processes for capturing and maintaining evidence of and information about business activities and transactions in the form of records."

- ERM includes the management of electronic and nonelectronic records, such as paper and other physical records.

- ERM has become much more critical to enterprises with increased compliance legislation and massively increasing volumes of electronic information.

- ERM follows the same basic principles as paper-based records management.

- A number of factors provide the business rationale for ERM, including facilitating compliance, supporting IG, and providing backup capabilities in the event of a disaster.

- Implementing ERM is challenging since it requires user support and compliance, adherence to changing laws, and support for new information delivery platforms like mobile and cloud computing.

- ERM benefits are both tangible and intangible or difficult to calculate.

- Improved professionalism, preserving corporate memory, support for better decision making, and safeguarding vital records are key intangible benefits of ERM.

- NARA recommends that e-records are inventoried by information system rather than file series, which is the traditional approach for physical records.

- Generally Accepted Recordkeeping Principles® are "information management and governance of record creation, organization, security, maintenance and other activities used to effectively support recordkeeping of an organization."

- It may be helpful to use a record-keeping methodology such as the Principles or D.I.R.K.S. to guide inventorying efforts.

- Perhaps the organization has a handle on their paper and microfilmed records, but e-records have been growing exponentially and spiraling out of control.

- Whatever the business goals for the inventorying effort are, they must be conveyed to all stakeholders, and that message must be reinforced periodically and consistently, and through multiple means.

CHAPTER SUMMARY: **KEY POINTS** (*Continued*)

- An appropriate scope might enumerate the records of a single program or division, several functional series across divisions, or records that fall within a certain time frame versus an entire enterprise.

- The completed records inventory contributes toward the pursuit of an organization's IG objectives in a number of ways.

- There are basic three ways to conduct the inventory: surveys, interviews, and observation. Combining these methods yields the best results.

- Additional information not included in inventories of physical records must be collected in any inventory of e-records.

- Be sure to tie the findings in the final report of the records inventory to the business goals that launched the effort.

- Records appraisal is based on the information contained in the records inventory.

- Records can have different types of value to organizations: historical, administrative, regulatory and statutory, legal, fiscal, or other archival value as determined by an archivist.

- Consistency in managing records across an enterprise, regardless of media, format, or location, is the key to compliance.

- A complete, current, and documented records retention program reduces storage and handling costs and improves searchability for records by making records easier and faster to find.

- Retention schedules are developed by records series—not for individual records.

- Retention schedules are basic tools that allow an organization to prove that it has a legally defensible basis on which to dispose records.

- The master retention schedule contains all records series in the entire enterprise.

- Records retention defines the length of time that records are to be kept and considers legal, regulatory, operational, and historical requirements.

- "Disposition" means not just destruction but can also mean archiving and a change in ownership and responsibility for the records.

- An information map is a critical first step in developing a records retention schedule. It shows where information is created, where it resides, and who uses it.

- After inventorying, developing a retention schedule begins with records classification.

- All e-mail messages are not records; those that document a business transaction, or progress toward it, are clearly records and require retention.

- E-mail messages that document business activities, especially those that may be disputed in the future, should be retained as records.

(continued)

CHAPTER SUMMARY: **KEY POINTS** *(Continued)*

- Destructive retention of e-mail is a method whereby e-mail messages are retained for a limited period and then destroyed.

- Tools are available to scan e-records folders to expedite the inventorying process.

- Assessing the relative value of records is key to determining their retention periods and disposition path.

- Records have different types of value, such as financial, legal, technical, and administrative/operational.

- Event-based disposition begins with a triggering event.

- Retention schedules, once established, must be maintained and updated to add new records series, as appropriate, and to comply with new or changed legislation and regulatory requirements.

- Auditing to ensure compliance with established retention policies is key to maintaining a legally defensible records retention program.

Notes

1. International Organization for Standardization, *ISO 15489-1: 2001 Information and Documentation—Records Management. Part 1: General* (Geneva: ISO, 2001), section 3.15.
2. Ibid., section 3.16
3. ARMA.org, "What Is Records Management?" 2009, www.arma.org/pdf/WhatIsRIM.pdf. (accessed December 2, 2013).
4. Microsoft White Paper, "Records Management with Office SharePoint Server," 2007, www.microsoft .com/en-us/download/details.aspx?id=15932, Used with permission from Microsoft. (accessed December 2, 2013).
5. Ibid.
6. Ibid.
7. Ibid.
8. U.S. Environmental Protection Agency, "Why Records Management? Ten Business Reasons," updated March 8, 2012, www.epa.gov/records/what/quest1.htm.
9. U.S. National Archives and Records Administration,*Disposition of Federal Records: A Records Management Handbook*, 2000, Web edition, www.archives.gov/records-mgmt/publications/disposition-of-federal-records/chapter-3.html.
10. Ibid.
11. State and Consumer Services Agency Department of General Services, *Electronic Records Management Handbook*, State of California Records Management Program (February 2002), www.documents.dgs .ca.gov/osp/recs/ermhbkall.pdf .
12. U.S. Environmental Protection Agency, "Six Steps to Better Files," updated March 8, 2012, www.epa .gov/records/tools/toolkits/6step/6step-02.htm .
13. Margaret Rouse, "Generally Accepted Recordkeeping Principles," updated March 2011, http:// searchcompliance.techtarget.com/definition/Generally-Accepted-Recordkeeping-Principles-GARP (accessed March 19, 2012).

14. Ibid.
15. Ibid.
16. Public Record Office, "Guidance for an Inventory of Electronic Record Collections: A Toolkit," September 2000, www.humanrightsinitiative.org/programs/ai/rti/implementation/general/guidance_for_inventory_elect_rec_collection.pdf, pp. 5–6.
17. Ibid. (accessed December 2, 2013).
18. National Archives, "Frequently Asked Questions about Records Inventories," updated October 27, 2000, www.archives.gov/records-mgmt/faqs/inventories.html .
19. William Saffady, "Managing Electronic Records, 4th ed.," *Journal of the Medical Library Association*, 2009, www.ncbi.nlm.nih.gov/pmc/articles/PMC2947138/ .
20. Jesse Wilkins, "The First Step: Inventory Your Electronic Records," http://pr1vacy.blogspot.mx/2005/11/first-step-inventory-your-electronic.html (accessed October 11, 2012).
21. Ibid.
22. Ibid.
23. Quotes in this section are from Government of Alberta, Records and Information Management, www.im.gov.ab.ca/index.cfm?page=imtopics/Records.html. (accessed December 2, 2013).
24. Maryland State Archives, "Retention Schedule Preparation," June 1, 2012, www.msa.md.gov/msa/intromsa/html/record_mgmt/retention_schedule.html .
25. National Health Service, "Connecting for Health," www.connectingforhealth.nhs.uk/ (accessed April 10, 2012).
26. Wortzman Nickle Professional Corporation, "Effective Records Management—Part 4—Ensuring Adoption and Compliance of RM Policy," 2009, www.wortzmannickle.com/ediscovery-blog/2011/12/14/rmpart4/ (accessed April 12, 2012).
27. Government of Alberta, "Developing Retention and Disposition Schedules."
28. National Archives, "Disposition of Federal Records."
29. Government of Alberta, "Developing Retention and Disposition Schedules."
30. National Archives, "Frequently Asked Questions about Records Scheduling and Disposition."
31. Ibid.
32. University of Edinburgh, Records Management Section, July 5, 2012, www.recordsmanagement.ed.ac.uk/InfoStaff/RMstaff/Retention/Retention.htm.
33. National Archives, "Frequently Asked Questions about Records Scheduling and Disposition." http://www.archives.gov/records-mgmt/faqs/scheduling.html#steps accessed December 2, 2013.
34. University of Edinburgh, Records Management Section.
35. National Archives, "Frequently Asked Questions about Records Scheduling and Disposition."
36. University of Toronto Archives, "Glossary," www.library.utoronto.ca/utarms/info/glossary.html (accessed September 10, 2012).
37. Government of Alberta, "Developing Retention and Disposition Schedules."
38. Ibid.
39. Marty Foltyn, "Getting Up to Speed on FRCP," June 29, 2007, www.enterprisestorageforum.com/continuity/features/article.php/3686491/Getting-Up-To-Speed-On-FRCP.htm.
40. Nancy Flynn, *The E-Policy Handbook* (New York: AMACOM, 2009), pp. 24–25.
41. ArcMail Blog http://arcmail.com/blog/archiving-rules-the-dangers-of-destructive-retention/ (accessed Dec. 2, 2013).
42. Mary Flood, "Survey: They see a more litigious future," October 18, 2010, http://blog.chron.com/houstonlegal/2010/10/survey-they-see-a-more-litigious-future/ (accessed Dec. 2, 2013).
43. Ibid., pp. 127.
44. Government of Alberta, "Developing Retention and Disposition Schedules," p. 122.
45. U.S. Government Printing Office, *Code of Federal Regulations*, www.gpo.gov/help/index.html#about_code_of_federal_regulations.htm (accessed April 22, 2012).
46. U.S. National Archives and Records Administration, "Electronic Code of Federal Regulations," October 2, 2012, http://ecfr.gpoaccess.gov/cgi/t/text/text-idx?c=ecfr&tpl=%2Findex.tpl.
47. Department of Defense, "Design Criteria Standard for Electronic Records Management Software Applications," July 19, 2002, http://jitc.fhu.disa.mil/cgi/rma/downloads/p50152s2.doc.
48. Craig Rhinehart, IBM, e-mail to author, July 30, 2012.
49. Government of Alberta, "Records and Information Management."
50. Ibid., p. 125.

CHAPTER 10

Information Governance and Information Technology Functions

Information technology (IT) is a core function impacted by information governance (IG) efforts. IT departments typically have been charged with keeping the "plumbing" of IT intact—the network, servers, applications, and data—but although the output of IT is in their custody, they have not been held to account for it; that is, the information, reports, and databases they generate have long been held to be owned by users in business units. This has left a gap of responsibility for governing the information that is being generated and managing it in accordance with legal and regulatory requirements, standards, and best practices.

Certainly, on the IT side, shared responsibility for IG means the IT department itself must take a closer look at IT processes and activities with an eye to IG. A focus on improving IT efficiency, software development processes, and data quality will help contribute to the overall IG program effort. IT is an integral piece of the program.

Debra Logan, vice president and distinguished analyst at Gartner, states:

> Information governance is the only way to comply with regulations, both current and future, and responsibility for it lies with the CIO and the chief legal officer. When organizations suffer high-profile data losses, especially involving violations of the privacy of citizens or consumers, they suffer serious reputational damage and often incur fines or other sanctions. IT leaders will have to take at least part of the blame for these incidents.[1]

Gartner predicts that the need to implement IG is so critical that, by 2016, fully one in five chief information officers (CIOs) will be terminated for their inability to implement IG successfully.

Aaron Zornes, chief research officer at the MDM (Master Data Management) Institute, stated: "While most organizations' information governance efforts have focused on IT metrics and mechanics such as duplicate merge/purge rates, they tend to ignore the industry- and business-metrics orientation that is required to ensure the economic success of their programs."[2]

Four IG best practices in this area can help CIOs and IT leaders to be successful in delivering business value as a result of IG efforts:

1. *Don't focus on technology, focus on business impact*

   Technology often enthralls those in IT—to the point of obfuscating the reason that technologies are leveraged in the first place: to deliver business benefit. So IT needs to reorient its language, its vernacular, its very focus when implementing IG programs. IT needs to become more business savvy, more businesslike, more focused on delivering business benefits that can help the organization to meet its business goals and achieve its business objectives. "Business leaders want to know why they should invest in an information governance program based on the potential resulting business outcomes, which manifest as increased revenues, lower costs and reduced risk."[3]

2. *Customize your IG approach for your specific business, folding in any industry-specific best practices possible.*

   You cannot simply take a boilerplate IG plan, implement it in your organization, and expect it to be successful. Sure, there are components that are common to all industries, but tailoring your approach to your organization is the only way to deliver real business value and results. That means embarking on an earnest effort to develop and sharpen your business goals, establishing business objectives that consider your current state and capabilities and external business environment and legal factors unique to your organization. It also means developing a communications and training plan that fits with your corporate culture. And it means developing meaningful metrics to measure your progress and the impact of the IG program, to allow for continued refinement and improvement.

3. *Make the business case for IG by tying it to business objectives*

   To garner the resources and time needed to implement an IG program, you must develop a business case in real, measureable terms. The business case must be presented in order to gain executive sponsorship, which is an essential component of any IG effort. Without executive sponsorship, the IG effort will fail. Making the business case and having metrics to measure progress and success toward meeting business objectives are absolute musts.

4. *Standardize use of business terms*

   IG requires a cross-functional effort, so you must be speaking the same language, which means the business terms you use in your organization must be standardized. This is the very minimum to get the conversation started. But IG efforts will delve much more deeply into information organization and seek to standardize the taxonomy for organizing documents and records and even the metadata fields that describe in detail those document and records across the enterprise.

Overall, being able to articulate the business benefits of your planned IG program will help you recruit an executive sponsor, help the program gain traction and support, and help you implement the program successfully.[4]

Several key foundational programs should support your IG effort in IT, including data governance, master data management (MDM), and implementing accepted IT standards and best practices. We will now delve into these concepts in more detail.

Focusing on business impact and customizing your IG approach to meet business objectives are key best practices for IG in the IT department.

Data Governance

We touched on **data governance** in Chapter 2. Data is big, data is growing, data is valuable, and the insights that can be gained by analyzing clean, reliable data with the latest analytic tools are a sort of new currency. There are nuggets of gold in those mountains of data. And leveraging those discoveries can provide a sustainable competitive advantage in areas such as customer acquisition, customer retention, and customer service.

The challenge is largely in garnering control over data and in cleaning, securing and protecting it; doing so requires effective data governance strategies. But data governance is not only about cleaning and securing data; it is also about delivering it to the right people at the right time (sometimes this means in realtime) to provide strategic insights and opportunities. If a data governance program is successful, it can add profits directly to the bottom line.[5]

Data governance involves processes and controls to ensure that information at the *data* level—raw data that the organization is gathering and inputting—is true and accurate, and unique (not redundant). It involves **data cleansing (or data scrubbing)** to strip out corrupted, inaccurate, or extraneous data and **de-duplication** to eliminate redundant occurrences of data.

Data governance focuses on **information quality** from the ground up (at the lowest or root level), so that subsequent reports, analyses and conclusions are based on clean, reliable, trusted data (or records) in database tables. Data governance is the most fundamental level at which to implement IG. Data governance efforts seek to ensure that formal management controls—systems, processes, and accountable employees who are stewards and custodians of the data—are implemented to govern critical data assets to improve data quality and to avoid negative downstream effects of poor data.

Data governance is a newer, hybrid *quality control discipline* that includes elements of data quality, data management, IG policy development, business process improvement, and compliance and risk management.

Good data governance programs should extend beyond the enterprise to include external stakeholders (suppliers, customers) so an organization has its finger on the pulse of its extended operations. In other words, enforcing data governance at the earliest possible point of entry—even external to the organization—can yield significant efficiencies and business benefits downstream. And combining data governance with real-time analytics and **business intelligence** (BI) software not only can yield insights into significant and emerging trends but also can provide solid information for decision makers to use in times of crisis—or opportunity.

Effective data governance can yield bottom-line benefits derived from new insights.

Steps to Governing Data Effectively

Nine key steps you can take to govern data effectively are listed next. The first five are based on recommendations by Steven Adler in *CIO Magazine:*

1. *Recruit a strong executive sponsor.* As in broader IG efforts, data governance requires cross-functional collaboration with a variety of stakeholders. To drive and facilitate this sometimes contentious conversation, a strong executive sponsor is required. This is not an easy task since executives generally do not want to deal with the minutia at the data level. You must focus on the realizable business benefits of improved data governance (i.e., specific applications that can assist in customer retention, revenue generation, and cost cutting).

2. *Assess your current state.* Survey the organization to see where the data repositories or silos of data are, what problems related to data exist, and where some opportunities to improve lie. Document where your data governance program stands today and then map out your road to improvement in fundamental steps.

3. *Set the ideal state vision and strategy.* Create a realistic vision of where your organization wants to go in its data governance efforts, and clearly articulate the business benefits of getting there. Articulate a measureable impact. Track your progress with metrics and milestones.

4. *Compute the value of your data.* Try to put some hard numbers to it. Calculate some internal numbers on how much value data—good data—can add to specific business units. Data is unlike other assets that you can see or touch (cash, buildings, equipment, etc.), and it changes daily, but it has real value.

5. *Assess risks.* What is the likelihood and potential cost of a data breach? A major breach? What factors come into play and how might you combat these potential threats? Perform a risk assessment to rank and prioritize threats and assign probabilities to those threats so you may fashion appropriate strategies to counter them.

6. *Implement a going-forward strategy.* It is a significantly greater task to try to improve data governance across the enterprise for existing data, versus a smaller business unit.[6] Remember, you may be trying to fix years if not decades of bad behavior, mismanagement, and lack of governance. Taking an "incremental approach with an eye to the future" provides for a clean starting point and can substantially reduce the pain required to implement. A strategy where new data governance policies for handling data are implemented beginning on a certain future date is a proven best practice.

7. *Assign accountability for data quality to business units, not IT.* Typically, IT has had responsibility for data quality, yet the data generation is mostly not under that department's control, since most is created out in the business units. A pointed effort must be made to push responsibility and ownership for data to the business units that create and use the data.

8. *Manage the change.* Educate, educate, educate. People must be trained to understand why the data governance program is being implemented and how it will benefit the business. The new policies represent a cultural change, and supportive program messages and training are required to make the shift.

9. *Monitor your data governance program.* See where shortfalls might be, and continue to fine-tune the program.[7]

Good data governance ensures that downstream negative effects of poor data are avoided and that subsequent reports, analyses, and conclusions are based on reliable, trusted data.

From a risk management perspective, data governance is a critical activity that supports decision makers and can mean the difference between retaining a customer and losing one. Protecting your data is protecting the lifeblood of your business, and improving the quality of the data will improve decision making, foster compliance efforts, and yield competitive advantages.

Data Governance Framework

The Data Governance Institute has created a **data governance framework,** a visual model to help guide planning efforts and a "logical structure for classifying, organizing, and communicating complex activities involved in making decisions about and taking action on enterprise data."[8] (See Figure 10.1.) The framework applies more to

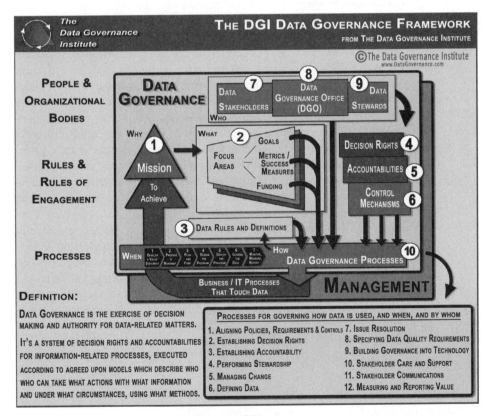

Figure 10.1   DGI Data Governance Framework™
Source: The Data Governance Institute (datagovernance.com).

larger organizations, which have greater complexity, greater internal requirements, and greater, more complex regulatory demands. It allows for a conceptual look at data governance processes, rules, and people requirements.

Information Management

Information management is a principal function of IT. It is complex and spans a number of subdisciplines but can be defined as the "application of management techniques to collect information, communicate it within and outside the organization, and process it to enable managers to make quicker and better decisions."[9] It is about managing information, which is more than just collecting and processing data from varying sources and distributing it to various user audiences. It includes a number of subcomponent tasks, including these four:

1. *Master data management* (MDM) is a key process for IG success in the IT department, which extends to involved business units. An emerging discipline, MDM came into prominence around 2010 to 2012, coinciding with the Big Data trend. The goal of MDM is to ensure that reliable, accurate data from a *single source* is leveraged across business units. That is, a key aim is to establish a "single version of the truth"[10] and eliminate multiple, inconsistent versions of data sets, which are more common than most might think, especially in larger organizations with physically distributed operations and large numbers of servers and databases.[11] MDM gets to the core of **data integrity** issues, essentially asking "Is this data true and accurate? Is this the best and only, final version?" MDM grew from the need to create a standardized, "discrete discipline" to ensure there was a single version to base BI analyses on and to base decisions on.[12] According to Gartner, MDM is a technology-enabled discipline in which business and IT work together to ensure the uniformity, accuracy, stewardship, semantic consistency and accountability of the enterprise's official shared master data assets. Master data is the consistent and uniform set of identifiers and extended attributes that describes the core entities of the enterprise, including customers, prospects, citizens, suppliers, sites, hierarchies and chart of accounts.[13]

   What is the business impact? How are operations enhanced and how does that contribute to business goals? One set of reliable, clean data is critical to delivering quality customer service, reducing redundant efforts and therefore operational costs, improving decision making, and even potentially lowering product and marketing costs. "A unified view of customers, products, or other data elements is critical to turning these business goals into reality."[14]

   Again, the larger the organization, the greater the need for MDM.

Master data management is a key IG process in IT.

2. *Information lifecycle management* (ILM) is managing information appropriately and optimally at different stages of its useful life, from creation through distribution and use, including meeting legal and regulatory requirements, and through its final disposition, which can be destruction, archiving, or transfer to another entity. Organizations historically over-retain information; however, studies show that information quickly loses its value and that once data has aged 10 to 15 days, the likelihood it will be used again is around 1 percent.[15] Based on its use characteristics, differing storage management strategies are appropriate. It defies business logic to manage information that has little value with as much IT resource as information that is high value. *Doing so is a misuse of resources.* To execute ILM properly, the value of certain data sets and records must be appraised and policies must be formed to manage it, recognizing that information value changes over the life cycle, which requires varying strategies and resource levels.[16] ILM conceptually includes and can begin with MDM and is linked to compliance requirements and capabilities.

3. *Data architecture* refers to the "design of structured and unstructured information systems"[17] in an effort to optimize data flow between applications and systems so that they are able to process data efficiently. Further, data architecture uses data modeling, standards, IG policies, and rules for governing data and how it populates databases and how those databases and applications are structured.[18] Some key issues to uncover when researching data architecture and design include data structure, or **schema**, which databases are used (e.g., Oracle Database 11g, DB2, SQL Server), methods of query and access (e.g., SQL), the operating systems the databases operate on, and even their hardware (which can affect data architecture features and capabilities).

4. *Data modeling* can be complex, yet it is an important step in overall IG for the IT department. It "illustrates the relationships between data." Data modeling is an application software design process whereby data processes and flows between applications are diagrammed graphically in a type of flowchart that formally depicts where data is stored, which applications share it, where it moves, and the interactions regarding data movement between applications. "Data modeling techniques and tools capture and translate complex system designs into easily understood representations of the data flows and processes, creating a blueprint for construction and/ or re-engineering."[19] Good data models allow for troubleshooting *before* applications are written and implemented.

   The importance of data modeling as a foundation for the application development process is depicted in Figure 10.2.

   Once the data model is developed, business rules and logic can be applied through application development. A user interface is constructed for the application, followed by movement of data or e-documents through work steps using work flow capabilities, and then integration with existing applications (e.g., enterprise resource planning or customer relationship management systems). Typically this is accomplished through an **application programming interface,** a sort of connector that allows interaction with other applications and databases.

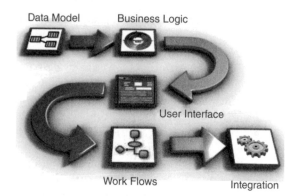

Figure 10.2   Key Steps from Data Modeling to Integration
Source: Reproduced from Orangescape.com (www.orangescape.com/wp-content/uploads/2010/10/Application-Development-Lifecycle-OrangeScape.png).

There are six approaches to data modeling:

1. *Conceptual.* The conceptual approach merely diagrams data relationships at the "highest level"[20] showing the storage, warehousing, and movement of data between applications.
2. *Enterprise.* The enterprise approach is a more business-oriented version of conceptual data modeling that includes specific requirements for an enterprise or business unit.
3. *Logical.* Pertinent to the design and architecture of physical storage, logical data modeling "illustrates the specific entities, attributes and relationships involved in a business function."
4. *Physical.* The physical approach depicts the "implementation of a logical data model" relative to a specific application and database system.
5. *Data integration.* This approach is just what it says; it involves merging data from two or more sources, processing the data, and moving it into a database. "This category includes Extract, Transform, and Load (ETL) capabilities."[21]
6. *Reference data management.* This approach often is confused with MDM, although they do have interdependencies. Reference data is a way to refer to data in categories (e.g., having lookup tables— standard industry classification or SIC codes) to insert values,[22] and is used only to "categorize other data found in a database, or solely for relating data in a database to information beyond the boundaries of the enterprise."[23] So reference data is not your actual data itself but a reference to categorize data.

Figure 10.3 shows different categories of data.

IT Governance

As introduced in Chapter 2, IT governance is about efficiency and value creation. *IT governance is the primary way that stakeholders can ensure that investments in IT create*

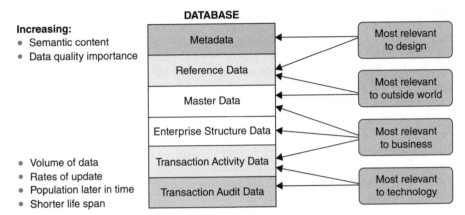

Figure 10.3   Categories of Data
Source: http://www.information-management.com/issues/20060401/1051002-1.html?zkPrintable =1&nopagination=1

business value and contribute toward meeting business objectives.[24] This strategic alignment of IT with the business is challenging yet essential. IT governance programs go further and aim to "improve IT performance, deliver optimum business value and ensure regulatory compliance."[25]

Although the CIO typically has line responsibility for implementing IT governance, the chief executive officer and board of directors must receive reports and updates to discharge their responsibilities for IT governance and to see that the program is functioning well and providing business benefits.

The focus of governance in IT is on the actual software development and maintenance activities of the IT department or function, and IT governance efforts focus on making IT efficient and effective. That means minimizing costs by following proven software development methodologies and best practices, principles of data governance and information quality, and project management best practices while aligning IT efforts with the business objectives of the organization.

IT Governance Frameworks

Several IT governance frameworks can be used as a guide to implementing an IT governance program.

Although frameworks and guidance like **CobiT®** and **ITIL** have been widely adopted, there is no absolute standard IT governance framework; the combination that works best for your organization depends on business factors, corporate culture, IT maturity, and staffing capability. The level of implementation of these frameworks will also vary by organization.

IT governance seeks to align business objectives with IT strategy to deliver business value.

CobiT®

CobiT (Control Objectives for Information and related Technology) is a process-based IT governance framework that represents a consensus of experts worldwide. It was codeveloped by the IT Governance Institute and ISACA. CobiT addresses business risks, control requirements, compliance, and technical issues.[26]

CobiT offers IT controls that:

- Cut IT risks while gaining business value from IT under an umbrella of a globally accepted framework.
- Assist in meeting regulatory compliance requirements.
- Utilize a structured approach for improved reporting and management decision making.
- Provide solutions to control assessments and project implementations to improve IT and information asset control.[27]

CobiT consists of detailed descriptions of processes required in IT and tools to measure progress toward maturity of the IT governance program. It is industry agnostic and can be applied across all vertical industry sectors, and it continues to be revised and refined.[28]

CobiT is broken into three basic organizational levels and their responsibilities: (1) board of directors and executive management; (2) IT and business management; and (3) line-level governance, security, and control knowledge workers.[29]

The CobiT model draws on the traditional "plan, build, run, monitor" paradigm of traditional IT management, only with variations in semantics. There are four IT domains in the COBIT framework, which contain 34 IT processes and 210 control objectives that map to the four specific IT processes of:

1. Plan and organize.
2. Acquire and implement.
3. Deliver and support.
4. Monitor and evaluate.

Specific goals and metrics are assigned, and responsibilities and accountabilities are delineated.

The CobiT framework maps to ISO 17799 of the International Organization for Standardization and is compatible with **Information Technology Infrastructure Library (ITIL)** and other accepted practices in IT development and operations.[30]

COBIT 5

Released in 2012, CobiT 5 is the latest version of the business framework for the governance of IT from ISACA. CobiT 5

builds and expands on COBIT 4.1 by integrating other major frameworks, standards and resources, including ISACA's Val IT and Risk IT, Information Technology Infrastructure Library (ITIL®) and related standards from the International Organization for Standardization (ISO). [31]

Key Principles and Enablers

"CobiT 5 is based on five key principles for governance and management of enterprise IT:

- Principle 1: Meeting Stakeholder Needs
- Principle 2: Covering the Enterprise End-to- End
- Principle 3: Applying a Single, Integrated Framework
- Principle 4: Enabling a Holistic Approach
- Principle 5: Separating Governance From Management

The CobiT 5 framework describes seven categories of enablers:

- **Principles, policies and frameworks** are the vehicle to translate the desired behavior into practical guidance for day-to-day management.
- **Processes** describe an organized set of practices and activities to achieve certain objectives and produce a set of outputs in support of achieving overall IT-related goals.
- **Organizational structures** are the key decision-making entities in an enterprise.
- **Culture, ethics and behavior** of individuals and of the enterprise are very often underestimated as a success factor in governance and management activities.
- **Information** is required for keeping the organization running and well governed, but at the operational level, information is very often the key product of the enterprise itself.
- **Services, infrastructure and applications** include the infrastructure, technology and applications that provide the enterprise with information technology processing and services.

People, skills and competencies are required for successful completion of all activities, and for making correct decisions and taking corrective actions."[32]

VallT®

VallT is a newer value-oriented framework that is compatible with and complementary to CobiT. Its principles and best practices focus is on leveraging IT investments to gain maximum value. Forty key VallT essential management practices (analogous to CobiT's control objectives) support three main processes: value governance, portfolio management, and investment management. VallT and CobiT "provide a full framework and supporting tool set to help managers develop policies to manage

> CobiT 5 is the latest version of the business framework for the governance of IT. It has just five principles and seven enablers.

CobiT is process-oriented and has been widely adopted as an IT governance framework. VallT is value-oriented and compatible and complementary with CobiT yet focuses on value delivery.

business risks and deliver business value while addressing technical issues and meeting control objectives in a structured, methodic way."[33]

VallT Integrated with CobiT 5

The VallT framework has been folded into the CobiT 5 framework.[34] For more details, you may download free or acquire publications and operational tools on this and related topics at isaca.org.

Key functions of VallT include:

- Define the relationship between IT and the business and those functions in the organization with governance responsibilities;
- Manage an organization's portfolio of IT-enabled business investments;
- Maximize the quality of business cases for IT-enabled business investments with particular emphasis on the definition of key financial indicators, the quantification of "soft" benefits and the comprehensive appraisal of the downside risk.

Val IT addresses assumptions, costs, risks and outcomes related to a balanced portfolio of IT-enabled business investments. It also provides benchmarking capability and allows enterprises to exchange experiences on best practices for value management.[35]

ITIL

ITIL is a set of process-oriented best practices and guidance originally developed in the United Kingdom to standardize delivery of IT service management. ITIL is applicable to both the private and public sectors and is the "most widely accepted approach to IT service management in the world."[36] As with other IT governance frameworks, ITIL provides essential guidance for delivering business value through IT, and it "provides guidance to organizations on how to use IT as a tool to facilitate business change, transformation and growth."[37]

ITIL best practices form the foundation for ISO/IEC 20000 (previously BS 15000), the International Service Management Standard for organizational certification and compliance.[38] ITIL 2011 is the latest revision (as of this writing).

The Val IT framework has been folded into the COBIT 5 framework.

CobiT is process oriented and has been widely adopted as an IT governance framework. ValIT is value oriented and compatible and complementary with CobiT yet focuses on value delivery.

It consists of five core published volumes that map the IT service cycle in a systematic way:

1. ITIL Service Strategy
2. ITIL Service Design
3. ITIL Service Transition
4. ITIL Service Operation
5. ITIL Continual Service Improvement

ISO 38500

ISO/IEC 38500:2008 is an international standard that provides high-level principles and guidance for senior executives and directors, and those advising them, for the effective and efficient use of IT.[39] Based primarily on AS 8015, the Australian IT governance standard, it "applies to the governance of management processes" performed at the IT service level, but the guidance assists executives in monitoring IT and ethically discharging their duties with respect to legal and regulatory compliance of IT activities.

The ISO 38500 standard comprises three main sections:

1. Scope, Application and Objectives
2. Framework for Good Corporate Governance of IT
3. Guidance for Corporate Governance of IT

It is largely derived from AS 8015, the guiding principles of which were:

- Establish responsibilities
- Plan to best support the organization
- Acquire validly
- Ensure performance when required
- Ensure conformance with rules
- Ensure respect for human factors

The standard also has relationships with other major ISO standards, and embraces the same methods and approaches.[40]

ITIL is the "most widely accepted approach to IT service management in the world."

ISO 38500 is an international standard that provides high-level principles and guidance for senior executives and directors responsible for IT governance.

IG Best Practices for Database Security and Compliance

Although security is a topic primarily for Chapter 11, it is a technical topic that we address here as well. Best practices have been developed over the past few years and can prevent leakage of structured data from databases and Web services due to SQL injections (where hackers attack SQL databases) and other types of attacks.

An organization and its data needs to be connected to its stakeholders—employees, customers, suppliers, and strategic partners. In this interconnected world that keeps expanding (e.g., cloud, mobile devices) proprietary data is exposed to a variety of threats. It is critical to protect the sensitive information assets that reside in your databases.[41]

Perimeter security often is easily penetrated. Web apps are vulnerable to attacks such as SQL injection (a favorite among malicious approaches). Hackers also can gain access by spear phishing (very specific phishing attacks that include personal information) to glean employee login credentials in order to get access to databases.

Streamlining your approach to database security by implementing a uniform set of policies and processes helps in compliance efforts and reduces costs. Here are some proven database security best practices:

- *Inventory and document.* You must first identify where your sensitive data and databases reside in order to secure them. So a discovery and mapping process must take place. You can begin with staff interviews but also use tools such as **data loss prevention** to map out data flows. Include all locations, including legacy applications, and intellectual property such as price lists, marketing and strategic plans, product designs, and the like. This inventorying/discovery process must be done on a regular basis with the assistance of automated tools, since the location of data can migrate and change.
- *Assess exposure/weaknesses.* Look for security holes, missing updates and patches, and any irregularities on a regular basis, using

  standard checklists such as the CIS Database Server Benchmarks and the DISA Security Technical Implementation Guides (STIGs). Do not forget to check OS-level parameters such as file privileges for database configuration files and database configuration options such as roles and permissions, or how many failed logins result in a locked account (these types of database-specific checks are typically not performed by network vulnerability assessment scanners).

- *Shore up the database.* Based on your evaluation of potential vulnerabilities, take proper steps and also be sure to that used database functions are disabled.
- *Monitor.* On a regular basis, monitor and document any configuration changes, and make sure the "gold" configuration is stable and unchanged. "Use change auditing tools that compare configuration snapshots and immediately alert whenever a change is made that affects your security posture."[42]

■ *Deploy monitoring/auditing tools.* Deploy these tools to immediately detect intrusions or suspicious activity, use your database's **database activity monitoring (DAM)** and **database auditing tools** continuously and in real time. Note any anomalies, such as usually large numbers of records being downloaded even by authorized users—this could indicate, for instance, a rogue employee gathering information. But also higher-level "privileged users—such as database administrators (DBAs), developers and outsourced personnel" must be monitored to comply with certain regulations. Watch for attackers who have gained access through authorized credentials. DAM creates an audit trail generated in real time that can be the forensic smoking gun in investigations after attacks have occurred. Also, monitor the application layer, as

> well-designed DAM solutions associate specific database transactions performed by the application with specific end-user IDs, in order to deterministically identify individuals violating corporate policies. In addition, combining database auditing information with OS [operating system] and network logs via a security information and event management . . . system to see everything that a user has done can also provide critical information for forensic investigations.

■ *Verify privileged access.* In your audit process, periodically review the list of privileged users and entitlement reports to ensure that superusers and those with access to sensitive information are still authorized.
■ *Protect sensitive data.* Known sensitive data should be encrypted, so that even if attackers gain access, it is unreadable. "File-level encryption at the OS layer, combined with granular real-time monitoring and access control at the database layer, is typically accepted as a practical alternative to column-level encryption and a compensating control for Requirement 3.3 of PCI-DSS."[43]
■ *Deploy masking.* Hide your live production data by masking test data. "Masking is a key database security technology that de-identifies live production data, replacing it with realistic but fictional data that can then be used for testing, training and development purposes, because it is contextually appropriate to the production data it has replaced."
■ *Integrate and automate standardized security processes.* To pass compliance audits, you need to show that processes and system are in place to reduce risks and detect potential intrusions, attacks, and unauthorized use. Standardizing and automating these tasks as much as possible helps minimize compliance costs while protecting the organization's data.

Implementing these best practices will help keep sensitive data in your databases secure.

> Identifying sensitive information in your databases and implementing database security best practices help reduce organizational risk and the cost of compliance.

Tying It All Together

Multiple frameworks and standards can be applied to the IT process to more effectively govern it and focus the processes on business impact. Beginning with a robust data governance program, organizations can ensure, at the more fundamental level, that the information they are using to base decisions on is clean, reliable, and accurate. Implementing an MDM program will help larger organizations with complex IT operations ensure that they are working with consistent data from a single source. Implementing the CobiT 5 business framework for delivering IT results will help support a more efficient IT operation and include other major frameworks, standards, and best practices. Leveraging the use of the ISO 38500 standard will help senior executives to better manage and govern IT operations, and employing database security best practices will help guard against outside threats.

CHAPTER SUMMARY: **KEY POINTS**

- Focusing on business impact and customizing your IG approach to meet business objectives are key best practices for IG in the IT department.

- Effective data governance can yield bottom-line benefits derived from new insights.

- Good data governance ensures that downstream negative effects of poor data are avoided and that subsequent reports, analyses, and conclusions are based on reliable, trusted data.

- Master data management is a key IG process in IT.

- IT governance seeks to align business objectives with IT strategy to deliver business value.

- CobiT 5 is the latest version of the business framework for the governance of IT. It has just five principles and seven enablers.

- CobiT is process oriented and has been widely adopted as an IT governance framework. ValIT is value oriented and compatible and complementary with CobiT yet focuses on value delivery.

- ValIT is a framework that focuses on delivering IT vale. It is folded into CobiT 5.

- ITIL is the "most widely accepted approach to IT service management in the world."

- ISO 38500 is an international standard that provides high-level principles and guidance for senior executives and directors responsible for IT governance

- Identifying sensitive information in your databases and implementing database security best practices help reduce organizational risk and the cost of compliance.

Notes

1. Ibid. Gartner Says Master Data Management Is Critical to Achieving Effective Information Governance, www.gartner.com/newsroom/id/1898914 (accessed on January 19, 2012).
2. IBM, "Selling Information Governance to Business Leaders," www.information-management.com/newsletters/governance-ROI-BI-business-rules-GRC-10021663-1.html (accessed June 3, 2013).
3. Ibid.
4. Ibid.
5. Steven Adler, "Six Steps to Data Governance Success," May 31, 2007, www.cio.com/article/114750/Six_Steps_to_Data_Governance_Success .
6. "New Trends and Best Practices for Data Governance Success," SeachDataManagement.com e-book, http://viewer.media.bitpipe.com/1216309501_94/1288990195_946/Talend_sDM_SO_32247_EB-ook_1104.pdf (accessed March 11, 2013).
7. Ibid.
8. "The DGI Data Governance Framework," DataGovernance.com, www.datagovernance.com/fw_the_DGI_data_governance_framework.html (accessed June 4, 2013).
9. "Information Management," BusinessDictionary.com, www.businessdictionary.com/definition/information-management.html (accessed June 4, 2013).
10. Sunil Soares, *Selling Information Governance to the Business* (Ketcham, ID: MC Press, 2011), p. 4.
11. Daniel Teachey, "The Year of Master Data Management," May 1, 2012, http://tdwi.org/articles/2012/05/01/lesson-2012-the-year-of-master-data-management.aspx.
12. Andrew White, "We Are Only Half Pregnant with MDM," April 17, 2013, http://blogs.gartner.com/andrew_white/2013/04/17/we-are-only-half-pregnant-with-master-data-management/
13. Gartner IT Glossary, "Master Data Management," www.gartner.com/it-glossary/master-data-management-mdm/ (accessed June 11, 2013).
14. Teachey, "Year of Master Data Management."
15. Bill Tolson, "Information Governance 101," May 21, 2013, http://informationgovernance101.com/2013/05/21/the-lifecycle-of-information/.
16. Gartner IT Glossary, "Information Lifecycle Management," www.gartner.com/it-glossary/information-life-cycle-management-ilm (accessed June 11, 2013).
17. Soares, *Selling Information Governance to the Business.*
18. "Data Architecture," BusinessDictionary.com, www.businessdictionary.com/definition/data-architecture.html (accessed June 11, 2013).
19. "Data Modeling," TechTarget, http://searchdatamanagement.techtarget.com/definition/data-modeling (accessed June 11, 2013).Ibid.
20. Ibid.
21. Soares, *Selling Information Governance to the Business.*
22. Ibid.
23. Malcolm Chisholm, "Master Data Versus Reference Data," *Information Management*, April 1, 2006, www.information-management.com/issues/20060401/1051002-1.html .
24. M. N. Kooper, R. Maes, and E.E.O. Roos Lindgreen, "On the Governance of Information: Introducing a New Concept of Governance to Support the Management of Information," *International Journal of Information Management* 31 (2011): 195–20, www.sciencedirect.com/science/article/pii/S0268401210000708.
25. Nick Robinson, "The Many Faces of IT Governance: Crafting an IT Governance Architecture," *ISACA Journal* 1 (2007), www.isaca.org/Journal/Past-Issues/2007/Volume-1/Pages/The-Many-Faces-of-IT-Governance-Crafting-an-IT-Governance-Architecture.aspx.
26. Bryn Phillips, "IT Governance for CEOs and Members of the Board," 2012, p. 26.
27. IBM Global Business Services—Public Sector, "Control Objectives for Information and related Technology (CobiT®) Internationally Accepted Gold Standard for IT Controls and Governance," 2008, http://www-304.ibm.com/industries/publicsector/fileserve?contentid=187551 (accessed March 11, 2013).
28. Phillips, "IT Governance for CEOs and Members of the Board."
29. IBM Global Business Services—Public Sector, "CobiT®."
30. Ibid.
31. "COBIT 5: A Business Framework for the Governance and Management of Enterprise IT," www.isaca.org/COBIT/Pages/default.aspx (accessed December 8, 2013).
32. Ibid.
33. IBM Global Business Services—Public Sector, "CobiT®."
34. IASCA, "Val IT Framework for Business Technology Management," www.isaca.org/Knowledge-Center/Val-IT-IT-Value-Delivery-/Pages/Val-IT1.aspx?utm_source=multiple&utm_medium=multiple&utm_content=friendly&utm_campaign=valit (accessed June 12, 2013).

35. Ibid.
36. ITIL, "Welcome to the Official ITIL® Website," www.itil-officialsite.com/ (accessed March 12, 2013).
37. ITIL, "What Is ITIL?" www.itil-officialsite.com/AboutITIL/WhatisITIL.aspx (accessed March 12, 2013).
38. Ibid.
39. ISO, "ISO/IEC 38500:2008: Corporate Governance of Information Technology," www.iso.org/iso/catalogue_detail?csnumber=51639 (accessed March 12, 2013).
40. "ISO 38500 IT Governance Standard" (2008), www.38500.org/ (accessed March 12, 2013).
41. The following discussion and quotes are from Phil Neray, "Beating the Breach: 10 Best Practices for Database Security and Compliance," November 3, 2011, http://datasafestorage.wordpress.com/2011/11/15/beating-the-breach-10-best-practices-for-database-security-and-compliance/.
42. Ibid
43. Ibid

CHAPTER 11

Information Governance and Privacy and Security Functions

Privacy and security go hand in hand. Privacy cannot be protected without implementing proper security controls and technologies. Organization must make not only reasonable efforts to protect privacy of data, but they must go much further as privacy breaches are damaging to its customers, reputation, and potentially, could put the company out of business.

Breaches are increasingly being carried out by malicious attacks, but also a significant source of breaches is internal mistakes caused by poor information governance (IG) practices, software bugs, and carelessness. The average cost of a data breach in 2013 was over $5 million dollars, according to the Ponemon Institute,[1] but some spectacular breaches have occurred, such as the $45 million in fraudulent automated teller machine cash withdrawals in New York City within hours in early 2013, and the 110 million customer records breached at giant retailer Target in late 2013. Millions of breaches occur each year: There were an estimated 354 million privacy breaches between 2005 and 2010 in the United States alone.

Cyberattacks Proliferate

Online attacks and snooping continue at an increasing rate. Organizations must be vigilant about securing their internal, confidential documents and e-mail messages. In 2011, security experts at Intel/McAfee "discovered an unprecedented series of cyber attacks on the networks of 72 organizations globally, including the United Nations, governments and corporations, over a five-year period."[2] Dmitri Alperovitch of McAfee described the incident as "the biggest transfer of wealth in terms of intellectual property in history."[3] The level of intrusion is ominous.

The targeted victims included governments, including the United States, Canada, India, and others; corporations, including high-tech companies and defense contractors; the International Olympic Committee; and the United Nations. "In the case of the United Nations, the hackers broke into the computer system of its secretariat in

---

Portions of this chapter are adapted from Chapters 11 and 12, Robert F. Smallwood, *Safeguarding Critical E-Documents: Implementing a Program for Securing Confidential Information Assets,* © John Wiley & Sons, Inc., 2012. Reproduced with permission of John Wiley & Sons, Inc.

The average cost of a data breach in 2013 was over $5 million.

Geneva in 2008, hid there for nearly two years, and quietly combed through reams of secret data, according to McAfee."[4] *Attacks can be occurring in organizations for years before they are uncovered—if they are discovered at all.* This means that an organization may be covertly monitored by criminals or competitors for extended periods of time.

And they are not the only ones spying—look no further than the U.S. National Security Agency (NSA) scandal of 2013. With Edward Snowden's revelations, it is clear that governments are accessing, monitoring, and storing massive amounts of private data.

Where this stolen information is going and how it will be used is yet to be determined. But it is clear that possessing this competitive intelligence could give a government or company a huge advantage economically, competitively, diplomatically, and militarily.

The information assets of companies and government agencies are at risk globally. Some are invaded and eroded daily, without detection. The victims are losing economic advantage and national secrets to unscrupulous rivals, so it is imperative that IG policies are formed, followed, enforced, tested, and audited. It is also imperative to use the best available technology to counter or avoid such attacks.[5]

Insider Threat: Malicious or Not

Ibas, a global supplier of data recovery and computer forensics, conducted a survey of 400 business professionals about their attitudes toward intellectual property (IP) theft:

- Nearly 70 percent of employees have engaged in IP theft, taking corporate property upon (voluntary or involuntary) termination.
- Almost one-third have taken valuable customer contact information, databases, or other client data.
- Most employees send e-documents to their personal e-mail accounts when pilfering the information.
- Almost 60 percent of surveyed employees believe such actions are acceptable.
- Those who steal IP often feel that they are entitled to partial ownership rights, especially if they had a hand in creating the files.[6]

These survey statistics are alarming, and by all accounts the trend continuing to worsen today. Clearly, organizations have serious cultural challenges to combat prevailing attitudes toward IP theft. A strong and continuous program of IG aimed at securing confidential information assets can educate employees, raise their IP security

Attacks can continue in organizations for years before they are uncovered—if they are discovered at all.

Information assets are invaded and eroded daily, often without detection. This compromises competitive position and has real financial impact.

awareness, and train them on techniques to help secure valuable IP. And the change needs to be driven from the top: from the CEO and boardroom. However, the magnitude of the problem in any organization cannot be accurately known or measured. Without the necessary IG monitoring and enforcement tools, executives cannot know the extent of the erosion of information assets and the real cost in cash and intangible terms over the long term.

Countering the Insider Threat

Frequently ignored, the insider has increasingly become the main threat—more than the external threats outside of the perimeter. *Insider threat breaches can be more costly than outsider breaches.* Most of the insider incidents go unnoticed or unreported.[7]

Companies have been spending a lot of time and effort protecting their perimeters from outside attacks. In recent years, most companies have realized that the insider threat is something that needs to be taken more seriously.

Malicious Insider

Malicious insiders and saboteurs comprise a very small minority of employees. A disgruntled employee or sometimes an outright spy can cause a lot of damage. Malicious insiders have many methods at their disposal to harm the organization by destroying equipment, gaining unsanctioned access to IP, or removing sensitive information by USB drive, e-mail, or other methods.

Nonmalicious Insider

Fifty-eight percent of Wall Street workers say they would take data from their company if they were terminated, and believed they could get away with it, according to a recent survey by security firm CyberArk.[8] Frequently, they do this without malice. The majority of users indicated having sent out documents *accidentally* via e-mail. So, clearly it is easy to leak documents without meaning to do any harm, and that is the cause of most leaks.

Solution

Trust and regulation are not enough. In the case of a nonmalicious user, companies should invest in security, risk education, and IG training. A solid IG program can reduce IP leaks through education, training, monitoring, and enforcement.

Security professionals state that insider threat breaches are often more costly than outsider ones.

In the case of the malicious user, companies need to take a hard look and see whether they have any effective IG enforcement and **document life cycle security** (DLS) technology such as information rights management (IRM) in place. Most often, the answer is no.[9]

Privacy Laws

The protection of personally identifiable information (PII) is a core focus of IG efforts. PII is any information that can identify an individual, such as name, Social Security number, medical record number, credit card number, and so on. Various privacy laws have been enacted in an effort to protect privacy. You must consult your legal counsel to determine which laws and regulation apply to your organization and its data and documents.

In the United States, the Federal Wiretap Act "prohibits the unauthorized interception and disclosure of wire, oral, or electronic communications." The Electronic Communications Privacy Act (ECPA) of 1986 amended the Federal Wiretap Act significantly and included specific on e-mail privacy.[10] The Stored Communications and Transactional Records Act (SCTRA) was created as a part of ECPA and is "sometimes useful for protecting the privacy of e-mail and other Internet communications when discovery is sought." The Computer Fraud and Abuse Act makes it a crime to intentionally breach a "protected computer" (one used by a financial institution or for interstate commerce).

Also relevant for public entities is the Freedom of Information Act, which allows U.S. citizens to request government documents that have not previously been released, although sometime sensitive information is redacted (blacked out), and specifies the steps for disclosure as well as the exemptions. In the United Kingdom, the Freedom of Information Act 2000 provides for similar disclosure requirements and mandatory steps.

In the United Kingdom, privacy laws and regulations include these:

- Data Protection Act 1998
- Freedom of Information Act 2000
- Public Records Act 1958
- Common law duty of confidentiality
- Confidentiality National Health Service (NHS) Code of Practice
- NHS Care Record Guarantee for England
- Social Care Record Guarantee for England
- Information Security NHS Code of Practice
- Records Management NHS Code of Practice

Also, the international information security standard ISO/IEC 27002: 2005 comes into play when implementing security.

Redaction

Redaction is the process of blocking out sensitive fields of information. In a paper environment, this was done with a black marking pen; however, privacy software can redact certain fields in digital documents, making them unreadable. Redaction is used for confidential patient information in medical records as well as other confidential document types, such as birth certificates, financial documents, property deeds, and other unstructured information that is managed.

A complete audit trail should be enabled that shows when specific users accessed or printed specific confidential information.

Limitations of Perimeter Security

Traditionally, central computer system security has been primarily perimeter security—securing the firewalls and perimeters within which e-documents are stored and attempting to keep intruders out—rather than securing e-documents directly upon their creation. *The basic access security mechanisms implemented, such as passwords, two-factor authentication, and identity verification, are rendered totally ineffective once the confidential e-documents or records are legitimately accessed by an authorized employee.* The documents are usually bare and unsecured. This poses tremendous challenges if the employee is suddenly terminated, if the person is a rogue intent on doing harm, or if outside hackers are able to penetrate the secured perimeter. And, of course, it is common knowledge that they do it all the time. *The focus should be on securing the documents themselves, directly.*

Restricting access is the goal of conventional perimeter security, but it does not directly protect the information inside. Perimeter security protects information the same way a safe protects valuables; if safecrackers get in, the contents are theirs. There are no protections once the safe is opened. Similarly, if hackers penetrate the perimeter security, they have complete access to the information inside, which they can steal, alter, or misuse.[11] The perimeter security approach has four fundamental limitations:

1. *Limited effectiveness.* Perimeter protection stops dead at the firewall, even though sensitive information is sent past it and circulates around the Web, unsecured. Today's extended computing model and the trend toward global business means that business enterprises and government agencies frequently share sensitive information externally with other stakeholders, including business partners, customers, suppliers, and constituents.
2. *Haphazard protections.* In the normal course of business, knowledge workers send, work on, and store copies of the same information outside the organization's established perimeter. Even if the information's new digital environment is secured by other perimeters, each one utilizes different access controls or sometimes no access control at all (e.g., copying a price list from a sales folder to a marketing folder; an attorney copying a case brief or litigation strategy document from a paralegal's case folder).
3. *Too complex.* With this multi-perimeter scenario, there are simply too many perimeters to manage, and often they are out of the organization's direct control.
4. *No direct protections.* Attempts to create boundaries or portals protected by perimeter security within which stakeholders (partners, suppliers, shareholders, or customers) can share information causes more complexity and administrative overhead while it fails to protect the e-documents and data directly.[12]

Despite the current investment in e-document security, it is astounding that once information is shared today, it is largely unknown who will be accessing it tomorrow.

Defense in Depth

Defense in depth is an approach that uses multiple layers of security mechanisms to protect information assets and reduce the likelihood that rogue attacks can succeed.[13] The idea is based on military principles that an enemy is stymied by complex layers and approaches compared to a single line. That is, hackers may be able to penetrate one or two of the defense layers, but multiple security layers increase the chances of catching the attack before it gets too far. Defense in depth includes a firewall as a first line of defense and also antivirus and anti-spyware software, **identity and access management** (IAM), hierarchical passwords, intrusion detection, and biometric verification. Also, as a part of an overall IG program, physical security measures are deployed, such as smartcard or even biometric access to facilities and intensive IG training and auditing.

Controlling Access Using Identity Access Management

IAM software can provide an important piece of the security solution. It aims to prevent unauthorized people from accessing a system and to ensure that only authorized individuals engage with information, including confidential e-documents.

Today's business environment operates in a more extended and mobile model, often including stakeholders outside of the organization. With this more complex and fluctuating group of users accessing information management applications, the idea of identity management has gained increased importance.

The response to the growing number of software applications using inconsistent or incompatible security models is strong identity management enforcement software. These scattered applications offer opportunities not only for identity theft but also for *identity drag*, where the maintenance of identities does not keep up with changing identities, especially in organizations with a large workforce. This can result in theft of confidential information assets by unauthorized or out-of-date access and even failure to meet regulatory compliance, which can result in fines and imprisonment.[14]

IAM—along with sharp IG policies—"manages and governs user access to information through an automated, continuous process."[15] Implemented properly, good IAM does keep access limited to authorized users while increasing security, reducing IT complexity, and increasing operating efficiencies.

Critically, *"IAM addresses 'access creep' where employees move to a different department of business unit and their rights to access information fail to get updated"* (emphasis added).[16]

In France in 2007, a rogue stock trader at Société Générale had in-depth knowledge of the bank's access control procedures from his job at the home office.[17] He used that information to defraud the bank and its clients out of over €7 billion (over $10 billion). If the bank had implemented an IAM solution, the crime might not have been possible.

> "IAM addresses 'access creep' where employees move to a different department of business unit and their rights to access information fail to get updated."

A robust and effective IAM solution provides for:

- *Auditing.* Detailed audit trails of *who* attempted to access *which information*, and *when.* Stolen identities can be uncovered if, for instance, an authorized user attempts to log in from more than one computer at a time.
- *Constant updating.* Regular reviews of access rights assigned to individuals, including review and certification for user access, an automated recertification process (*attestation*), and enforcement of IG access policies that govern the way users access information in respect to segregation of duties.
- *Evolving roles.* Role life cycle management should be maintained on a continuous basis, to mine and manage roles and their associated access rights and policies.
- *Risk reduction.* Remediation regarding access to critical documents and information.

Enforcing IG: Protect Files with Rules and Permissions

One of the first tasks often needed when developing an IG program that secures confidential information assets is to define roles and responsibilities for those charged with implementing, maintaining, and enforcing IG policies. Corollaries that spring from that effort get down to the nitty-gritty of controlling information access by rules and permissions.

Rules and permissions specify *who* (by roles) is allowed access to *which* documents and information, and even contextually *from where* (office, home, travel) and *at what times* (work hours, or extended hours). Using the old policy of the *need-to-know* basis is a good rule of thumb to apply when setting up these access policies (i.e., only those who are at a certain level of the organization or are directly involved in certain projects are allowed access to confidential and sensitive information). The roles are relatively easy to define in a traditional hierarchical structure, but today's flatter and more collaborative enterprises present challenges.

To effectively wall off and secure information by management level, many companies and governments have put in place an information security framework—a model that delineates which levels of the organization have access to specific documents and databases as a part of implemented IG policy. This framework shows a hierarchy of the company's management distributed across a range of defined levels of information access. The U.S. Government Protection Profile for Authorization Server for Basic Robustness Environments is an example of such a framework.

Challenge of Securing Confidential E-Documents

Today's various document and content management systems were not initially designed to allow for secure document sharing and collaboration while also preventing document leakage. These software applications were mostly designed before the invention and adoption of newer business technologies that have extended the computing environment. The introduction of cloud computing, mobile PC devices, smartphones, social media, and online collaboration tools all came after most of today's document and content management systems were developed and brought to market.

> The glaring vulnerability in the security architecture of ECM systems is that few protections exist once the information is legitimately accessed.

Thus, vulnerabilities have arisen that need to be addressed with other, complementary technologies. We need to look no further than the WikiLeaks incident and the myriad of other major security breaches resulting in document and data leakage to see that there are serious information security issues in both the public and private sectors.

Technology is the tool, but without proper IG policies and a culture of compliance that supports the knowledge workers following IG policies, any effort to secure confidential information assets will fail. An old IT adage is that even *perfect technology will fail without user commitment.*

Protecting Confidential E-Documents: Limitations of Repository-Based Approaches

Organizations invest billions of dollars in IT solutions that manage e-documents and records in terms of security, auditing, search, records retention and disposition, version control, and so on. These information management solutions are predominantly repository-based, including enterprise content management (ECM) systems and collaborative workspaces (for unstructured information, such as e-documents). With content or document repositories, the focus has always been on perimeter security—keeping intruders out of the network. But that provides only partial protection. Once intruders are in, they are *in* and have full access to confidential e-documents. For those who are authorized to access the content, there are no protections, so they may freely copy, forward, print, or even edit and alter the information.[18]

The glaring vulnerability in the security architecture of ECM systems is that few protections exist once the information is legitimately accessed.

These confidential information assets, which may include military plans, price lists, patented designs, blueprints, drawings, and financial reports, often can be printed, e-mailed, or faxed to unauthorized parties without any security attached.[19]

Also, in the course of their normal work processes, knowledge workers tend to keep an extra copy of the electronic documents they are working on stored at their desktop, or they download and copy them to a tablet or laptop to work at home or while traveling. *This creates a situation where multiple copies of these e-documents are scattered about on various devices and media, which creates a security problem, since they are outside of the repository and no longer secured, managed, controlled, or audited.*

> Technologies like firewalls, access controls, and gateway filters can grant or deny access but cannot provide granular enforcement of acceptable use policies that define what users can and cannot do with confidential data and documents.

It also creates records management issues in terms of the various versions that might be out there and determining which one is the official business record.

Apply Better Technology for Better Enforcement in the Extended Enterprise

Protecting E-Documents in the Extended Enterprise

Sharing e-documents and collaborating are essential in today's increasingly mobile and global world. Businesses are operating in a more distributed model than ever before, and they are increasingly sharing and collaborating not only with coworkers but also with suppliers, customers, and even at times competitors (e.g., in pharmaceutical research). This reality presents a challenge to organizations dealing in sensitive and confidential information.[20]

Basic Security for the Microsoft Windows Office Desktop

The first level of protection for e-documents begins with basic protections at the desktop level. Microsoft Office provides ways to password-protect Microsoft Office files, such as those created in Word and Excel, quickly and easily. Many corporations and government agencies around the world use these basic protections. A key flaw or caveat is that *passwords used in protecting documents cannot be retrieved if they are forgotten or lost.*

Where Do Deleted Files Go?

When you delete a file it is gone, right? Actually, it is not (with the possible exception of solid state hard drives). For example, after a file is deleted in Windows, a simple undelete DOS command can bring back the file, if it has not been overwritten. That is because when files are deleted, they are not really deleted; rather, the space where they reside is marked for reuse and can be overwritten. If it is not yet overwritten, the file is still there. The same process occurs as drafts of documents are created and temp (for *temporary*) files are stored. The portions of a hard drive where deleted or temp files are stored can be overwritten. This is called unallocated space. *Most users are unaware that deleted files and fragments of documents and drafts are stored temporarily on their computer's unallocated space.* So it must be wiped clean and completely erased to ensure that any confidential documents or drafts are completely removed from the hard drive.

IG programs include the highest security measures, which means that an organization must have a policy that includes deleting sensitive materials from a computer's unallocated space and tests that verify such deletion actions are successful periodically.

Lock Down: Stop All External Access to Confidential E-Documents

Organizations are taking other approaches to stop document and data leakage: physically restricting access to a computer by disconnecting it from any network connections and forbidding or even blocking use of any ports. Although cumbersome, these methods are effective in highly classified or restricted areas where confidential e-documents are held. Access is controlled by utilizing multiple advanced identity verification methods, such as biometric means.

Secure Printing

Organizations normally expend a good amount of effort making sure that computers, documents, and private information are protected and secure. However, if your computer is hooked up to a network printer (shared by multiple knowledge workers), all of that effort might have been wasted.[21]

Some basic measures can be taken to protect confidential documents from being compromised as they are printed. You simply invoke some standard Microsoft Office protections, which allow you to print the documents once you arrive in the copy room or at the networked printer. This process varies slightly, depending on the printer's manufacturer. (Refer to the documentation for the printer for details.)

In Microsoft Office, there is an option in the Print Dialog Box for delayed printing of documents (when you physically arrive at the printer).

Serious Security Issues with Large Print Files of Confidential Data

According to Canadian output and print technology expert William Broddy, in a company's data center, a print file of, for instance, investment account statements or bank statements contains all the rich information that a hacker or malicious insider needs. *It is information distilled to the most important core data about customers, and has been referred to as data syrup since it has been boiled down and contains no mountains of extraneous data, only the culled, cleaned, essential data that gives criminals exactly what they need.*[22]

What most managers are not aware of is that entire print files and sometimes remnants of them stay on the hard drives of high-speed printers and are vulnerable to security breaches. Data center security personnel closely monitor calls to their database. To extract as much data as is contained in print files, a hacker requires hundreds or even thousands of calls to the database, which sets off alerts by system monitoring tools. But retrieving a print file takes only one intrusion, and it may go entirely unnoticed. The files are sitting there; a rogue service technician or field engineer can retrieve them on a routine service call.

To help secure print files, specialized hardware devices designed to sit between the print server and the network and cloak server print files are visible only to those who have a cloaking device on the other end.

Organizations must practice good IG and have specific procedures to erase sensitive print files once they have been utilized. For instance, in the example of preparing statements to mail to clients, files are exposed to possible intrusions in at least six points in the process (starting with print file preparation and ending with the actual mailing). These points must be tightly monitored and controlled. Typically, an

A print file contains all the distilled customer information a hacker might want. Retrieving a print file takes only one intrusion and may go entirely unnoticed.

Files are exposed to possible intrusions in at least six points between print file preparation and final hard-copy mailing.

organization retains a print file for about 14 days, though some keep files long enough for customers to receive statements in the mail and review them. *Organizations must make sure that print files or their remnants are secured and then completely erased when the printing job is finished.*

E-Mail Encryption

Encrypting (scrambling using advanced algorithms) sensitive e-mail messages is an effective step to securing confidential information assets while in transit. Encryption can also be applied to desktop folders and files and even entire disk drives (full disk encryption, or FDE). All confidential or sensitive data and e-documents that are exposed to third parties or transferred over public networks should be secured with file-level encryption, at a minimum.[23]

Secure Communications Using Record-Free E-Mail

What types of tools can you use to encourage the free flow of ideas in collaborative efforts without compromising your confidential information assets or risking litigation or compliance sanctions?

Stream messaging is an innovation that became commercially viable around 2006. It is similar in impact to IRM software, which limits the recipients' ability to forward, print, or alter data in an e-mail message (or reports, spreadsheets, etc.) *but goes further by leaving no record on any computer or server.*

Stream messaging is a simple, safe, secure electronic communications system ideal for ensuring that sensitive internal information is kept confidential and not publicly released. Stream messaging is not intended to be a replacement for enterprise e-mail but is a complement to it. If you need an electronic record, e-mail it; if not, use stream messaging.[24]

What makes stream messaging unique is its recordlessness. Streamed messages cannot be forwarded, edited, or saved. A copy cannot be printed as is possible with e-mail. That is because *stream messaging separates the sender's and receiver's names and the date from the body of the message, never allowing them to be seen together.* Even if the sender or receiver were to attempt to make a copy using the print-screen function, these elements are never captured together.[25]

With stream messaging, no record or trace of communication is left.

The instant a stream message is sent, it is placed in a temporary storage buffer space. When the recipient logs in to read the message, it is removed from the buffer space. By the time the recipient opens it, the complete stream message no longer exists on the server or any other computer.

This communications approach is Web based, meaning that no hardware or software purchases are required. It also works with existing e-mail systems and e-mail addresses and is completely immune to spam and viruses. Other solutions (both past and present) have been offered, but these have taken the approach of encrypting e-mail or generating e-mail that disappears after a preset time. Neither of these approaches is truly recordless.

Stream messaging is unique because its technology effectively eliminates the ability to print, cut, paste, forward, or save a message. It may be the only electronic communications system that separates the header information—date, name of sender, name of recipient—from the body of the message. This eliminates a traceable record of the communication. Soon many other renditions of secure messaging will be developed.

In addition, stream messaging offers the added protection of being an indiscriminate Web-based service, meaning that the messages and headers are never hosted on the subscribing companies' networks. This eliminates the risk that employers, competitors, or hackers could intercept stream messages, which is a great security benefit for end users.[26]

Digital Signatures

Digital signatures are more than just digitized autographs—they carry detailed audit information used to "detect unauthorized modifications" to e-documents and to "authenticate the identity of the signatory."[27]

Online transactions can be conducted with full trust that they are legal, proper, and binding. They prove that the person whose signature is on the e-document did, in fact, authorize it. A digital signature provides evidence in demonstrating to a third party that the signature was genuine, true, and authentic, which is known as *nonrepudiation*. To repudiate is to dispute, and with digital signatures, a signatory is unable to claim that the signature is forged.

Digital signatures can be implemented a variety of ways—not just through software but also through firmware (programmed microchips), computer hardware, or a combination of the three. Generally, hardware- and firmware-based implementations are more difficult to hack, since their instructions are hardwired.

Here is a key point: For those who are unfamiliar with the technology, *there is a big difference between electronic signatures and digital signatures.*[28]

An "electronic signature is likely to be a bit-map image, either from a scanned image, a fax copy or a picture of someone's signature, or may even be a typed acknowledgement or acceptance." *A digital signature contains "extra data appended to*

There is a big difference between digital and electronic signatures. Digital signatures contain additional authenticating information.

Requiring a physical signature can disrupt and slow business processes. Digital signatures speed that up and add a layer of security.

a message which identifies and authenticates the sender and message data using public-key encryption."[29]

So digital signatures are the only ones that offer any real security advantages.

Digital signatures are verified by the combination of applying a signatory's private signing key and the public key that comes from the signatory's personal ID certificate. After that, only the public key ID certificate is required for future verifications. *"In addition, a checksum mechanism confirms that there have been no modifications to the content."*[30]

A formal, trusted **certificate authority (CA)** issues the certificate associated with the public-private key. It is possible to generate self-certified public keys, but these do not verify and authenticate the recipient's identity and are therefore flawed from a security standpoint. The interchange of verified signatures is possible on a global scale, as "digital signature standards are mature and converging internationally."[31]

After more than 30 years of predictions, the paperless office is almost here. Business process cycles have been reduced, and great efficiencies have been gained since the majority of documents today are created digitally and spend most of their life cycle in digital form, and they can be routed through work steps using business process management (BPM) and work flow software. *However, the requirement for a physical signature frequently disrupts and holds up these business processes.* Documents have to be printed out, physically routed, and physically signed—and often they are scanned back into a document or records management (or contract management) system, which defeats the efficiencies sought.

Often *multiple* signatures are required in an approval process, and some organizations require each page to be initialed, which makes the process slow and cumbersome when it is executed without the benefit of digital signatures. Also, multiple copies are generated—as many as 20—so digital signature capability injected into a business process can account for significant time and cost savings.[32]

Document Encryption

There is some overlap and sometimes confusion between digital signatures and document encryption. Suffice it to say that they work differently, in that document encryption secures a document for those who share a secret key, and digital signatures prove that the document has not been altered and the signature is authentic.

There are e-records management implications of employing document encryption:

Unless it is absolutely essential, full document encryption is often advised against for use within electronic records management systems as it prevents full-text indexing, and requires that the decryption keys (and application) are available for any future access. Furthermore, if the decryption key is lost or an employee leaves without passing it on, encrypted documents and records will in effect be electronically shredded as no one will be able to read them.

Correctly certified digital signatures do not prevent unauthorized persons reading a document nor are they intended to. They do confirm that the person who signed it is who they say they are, and that the document has not been altered since they signed it. Within a records management system a digital signature is often considered to be an important part of the metadata of a document, confirming both its heritage and its integrity.[33]

Data Loss Prevention (DLP) Technology

The aforementioned document security challenges have given rise to an emerging but critical set of capabilities by a new breed of IT companies that provide **data loss prevention** (DLP) (also called data *leak* prevention). DLP providers create software and hardware appliances that thoroughly inspect all e-documents and e-mail messages before they leave the organization's perimeter and attempt to stop sensitive data from exiting the firewall.

This filtering is based on several factors, but mostly using specified critical content keywords that are flagged by the implementing organization. DLP can also stop the exit of information assets by document types, origin, time of day, and other factors.

DLP systems are designed to detect and prevent unauthorized use and transmission of confidential information.[34] In more detail, DLP is a computer security term referring to systems that identify, monitor, and protect data/documents in all three states: (1) *in use* (endpoint actions), (2) *in motion* (network actions), and (3) *at rest* (data/document storage). DLP accomplishes this by deep content inspection and contextual security analysis of transaction data (e.g., attributes of the originator, the data object, medium, timing, recipient/destination, etc.) with a centralized management framework.

Promise of DLP

Gartner reports that the DLP market reached an estimated $670 million in 2013, up from $425 million in 2011, and "with adoption of DLP technologies moving quickly down to the small to medium enterprise, DLP is no longer an unknown quantity." [35] Although the DLP market has matured, it suffers from confusion about how DLP best fits into the new mix of security approaches, how it is best utilized (endpoint or gateway), and even the definition of DLP itself.[36]

Data loss is very much on managers' and executives' minds today. The series of WikiLeaks incidents exposed hundreds of thousands of sensitive government and military documents. According to the Ponemon Institute (as reported by DLP Experts), data leaks continue to increase annually. Billions of dollars are lost every year as a result of data leaks, with the cost of each breach ranging from an average of $700,000 to $31 million. Some interesting statistics from the study include:

- Almost half of breaches happen while an enterprise's data was in the hands of a third party.
- Over one-third of breaches involved lost or stolen mobile devices.

- The cost per stolen record is approximately $200 to $225.
- One-quarter of breaches were conducted by criminals or with malicious intent.
- More than 80 percent of breaches compromised over 1,000 records.[37]

What DLP Does Well (and Not So Well)

DLP has been deployed successfully as a tool used to map the flow of data inside and exiting the organization to determine the paths that content takes, so that more sophisticated information mapping, monitoring, and content security can take place.

This use as a traffic monitor for analysis purposes has been much more successful than relying on DLP as the sole enforcement tool for compliance and to secure information assets. Today's technology is simply not fast enough to catch everything. It catches many e-mail messages and documents that users are authorized to send, which slows the network and the business down. This also adds unnecessary overhead, as someone has to go back and release each and every one of the e-mails or documents that were wrongly stopped.

Another downside: *Since DLP relies on content inspection, it cannot detect and monitor encrypted e-mail or documents.*

Basic DLP Methods

DLP solutions typically apply one of three methods:

1. Scanning traffic for keywords or regular expressions, such as customer credit card or Social Security numbers.
2. Classifying documents and content based on a predefined set to determine what is likely to be confidential and what is not.
3. Tainting (in the case of agent-based solutions), whereby documents are tagged and then monitored to determine how to classify derivative documents. For example, if someone copies a portion of a sensitive document into a different document, this document receives the same security clearance as the original document.[38]

All these methods involve the network administrator setting up a policy clearly defining what is allowed to be sent out and what should be kept in confidence. This policy creating effort is extremely difficult: Defining a policy that is *too broad* means accidentally letting sensitive information get out, and defining a policy that is *too narrow* means getting a significant amount of false positives and stopping the flow of normal business communications.

Although network security management is well established, defining these types of IG policies is extremely difficult for a network administrator. Leaving this job to network administrators means there will be no collaboration with business units, no standardization, and no real forethought. As a result, many installations are plagued with false positives that are flagged and stopped, which can stifle and frustrate knowledge workers. *The majority of DLP deployments simply use DLP for monitoring and auditing purposes.*

Examining the issue of the dissolving perimeter more closely, a deeper problem is revealed: DLP is binary; it is black or white. Either a certain e-document or e-mail can leave the organization's boundaries or it cannot. This process has been referred to as outbound content compliance.

But this is not how the real world works today. Now there is an increasing need for collaboration and for information to be shared or reside outside the organization on mobile devices or in the cloud.

Most of today's DLP technology cannot address these complex issues on its own. Often additional technology layers are needed.

Data Loss Prevention: Limitations

DLP has been hyped in the past few years, and major security players have made several large acquisitions—especially those in the IRM market. Much like firewalls, DLP started in the form of network gateways that searched e-mail, Web traffic, and other forms of information traveling out of the organization for data that was defined as internal. When it found such data, the DLP blocked transmission or monitored its use.

Soon agent-based solutions were introduced, performing the same actions locally on users' computers. The next step brought a consolidation of many agent- and network-based solutions to offer a comprehensive solution.

IG policy issues are key. What is the policy? All these methods depend on management setting up a policy that clearly defines what is acceptable to send out and what should be kept in confidence.

With DLP, a certain document can either leave the organization's boundaries or it can't. But this is not how the real world works. In today's world there is an increasing need for information to be shared or reside outside the organization on mobile devices or in the cloud. Simply put, *DLP is not capable of addressing this issue on its own, but it is a helpful piece of the overall technology solution.*

Missing Piece: Information Rights Management (IRM)

Another technology tool for securing information assets is information rights management (IRM) software (also referred to as enterprise rights management [ERM] and previously as enterprise digital rights management [e-DRM].) *For purposes of this book, we use the term "IRM" when referring to this technology set, so as not to be confused with electronic records management. Major software companies also use the term "IRM."*

IRM technology provides a sort of security wrapper around documents and protects sensitive information assets from unauthorized access.[39] We know that DLP can search for key terms and stop the exit of sensitive data from the organization by inspecting its content. But it can also prevent confidential data from being copied to external media or sent by e-mail if the person is not authorized to do so. If IRM is deployed, files and documents are protected wherever they may be, with persistent security. *The ability to apply security to an e-document in any state* (in use, in motion, and at rest), across media types, inside or outside of the organization, *is called persistent security.*

The ability to secure data at any time, in any state, is called persistent protection.

This is a key characteristic of IRM technology, and it is all done transparently without user intervention.[40]

IRM has the ability to protect e-documents and data wherever they may reside, however they may be used, and in all three data states (at rest, in use, and in transit).[41]

IRM allows for e-documents to be remote controlled, meaning that security protections can be enforced even if the document leaves the perimeter of the organization. This means that e-documents (and their control mechanisms) can be separately created, viewed, edited, and distributed.

IRM provides persistent, ever-present security and manages access to sensitive e-documents and data. IRM provides embedded file-level protections that travel with the document or data, regardless of media type.[42] These protections and prevent unauthorized viewing, editing, printing, copying, forwarding, or faxing. So, even if files are somehow copied to a thumb drive and taken out of the organization, e-document protections and usage are still controlled.

The major applications for IRM services include cross-protection of e-mails and attachments, dynamic content protection on Web portals, secure Web-based training, secure Web publishing, and secure content storage and e-mail repositories all while meeting compliance requirements of Sarbanes–Oxley, the Health Insurance Portability and Accountability Act, and others. Organizations can comply with regulations for securing and maintaining the integrity of digital records, and IRM will restrict and track access to spreadsheets and other financial data too.

In investment banking, research communications must be monitored, according to National Association of Securities Dealers rule (NASD) 2711, and IRM can help support compliance efforts. In consumer finance, personal financial information collected on paper forms and transmitted by fax (e.g., auto dealers faxing credit applications) or other low-security media can be secured using IRM, directly from a scanner or copier. Importers and exporters can use IRM to ensure data security and prevent the loss of cargo from theft or even terrorist activities, and they also can comply with U.S. Customs and trade regulations by deploying IRM software. Public sector data security needs are numerous, including intelligence gathering and distribution, espionage, and Homeland Security initiatives. Firms that generate intellectual property IP, such as research and consulting groups, can control and protect access to IP with it. In the highly collaborative pharmaceutical industry, IRM can secure research and testing data.

IRM protections can be added to nearly all e-document types including e-mail, word processing files, spreadsheets, graphic presentations, computer-aided design (CAD) plans, and blueprints. This security can be enforced globally on all documents or granularly down to the smallest level, protecting sensitive fields of information from prying eyes. This is true even if there are multiple copies of the e-documents scattered about on servers in varying geographic locations. Also, the protections can be applied permanently or within controlled time frames. For instance, a person may be granted access to a secure e-document for a day, a week, or a year.

Key IRM Characteristics

Three requirements are recommended to ensure effective IRM:

1. *Security* is foremost; documents, communications, and licenses should be encrypted, and documents should require authorization before being altered.

2. *The system can't be any harder to use* than working with unprotected documents.
3. *It must be easy to deploy and manage*, scale to enterprise proportions, and work with a variety of common desktop applications.[43]

IRM software enforces and manages document access policies and use rights (view, edit, print, copy, e-mail forward) of electronic documents and data. Controlled information can be text documents, spreadsheets, financial statements, e-mail messages, policy and procedure manuals, research, customer and project data, personnel files, medical records, intranet pages, and other sensitive information. IRM provides persistent enforcement of IG and access policies to allow an organization to control access to information that needs to be secured for privacy, competitive, or compliance reasons. *Persistent content security is a necessary part of an end-to-end enterprise security architecture.*

Well, it sounds like fabulous technology, but is IRM really so new? No, it has been has been around for a decade or more, and continues to mature and improve. It has essentially entered the mainstream around 2004/2005 (when this author began tracking its development and publishing researched articles on the topic).

IRM software currently is used for persistent file protection by thousands of organizations throughout the world. Its success depends on the quality and consistency of the deployment, which includes detailed policy-making efforts. *Difficulties in policy maintenance and lack of real support for external sharing and mobile devices have kept first-wave IRM deployments from becoming widespread, but this aspect is being addressed by a second wave of new IRM technology companies.*

Other Key Characteristics of IRM

Policy Creation and Management

IRM allows for the creation and enforcement of policies governing access and use of sensitive or confidential e-documents. The organization's IG team sets the policies for access based on role and organizational level, determining what employees can and cannot do with the secured e-documents.[44] The IG policy defined for a document type includes these following controls:

1. Viewing
2. Editing
3. Copy/Paste (including screen capture)
4. Printing
5. Forwarding e-mail containing secured e-documents

Access to sensitive e-documents may be revoked at any time, no matter where they are located or what media they are on, since each time a user tries to access a document, access rights are verified with a server or cloud IRM application. This can be done remotely—that is, when an attempt is made to open the document, an authorization must take place. In cloud-based implementations, it is a matter of simply denying access.

Decentralized Administration

One of the key challenges of e-document security traditionally is that a system administrator had access to documents and reports that were meant only for executives and senior managers. With IRM, the e-document owner administers the security of the data, which considerably reduces the risk of a document theft, alteration, or misuse.

Auditing

Auditing provides the smoking-gun evidence in the event of a true security breach. Good IRM software provides an audit trail of how all documents secured by it are used. Some go further, providing more detailed document analytics of usage.

Integration

To be viable, IRM must integrate with other enterprise-wide systems, such as ECM, customer relationship management, product life cycle management, enterprise resource planning, e-mail management, message archiving, e-discovery, and a myriad of cloud-based systems. This is a characteristic of today's newer wave of IRM software.

This ability to integrate with enterprise-based systems does not mean that IRM has to be deployed at an enterprise level. *The best approach is to target one critical department or area with a strong business need and to keep the scope of the project narrow to gain an early success before expanding the implementation into other departments.*

IRM embeds protection into the data (using encryption technology), allowing files to protect themselves. IRM may be the best available security technology for the new mobile computing world of the permeable perimeter.[45]

With IRM technology, a document owner can selectively prevent others from viewing, editing, copying, or printing it. Despite its promise, most enterprises do not use IRM, and if they do, they do not use it on an enterprisewide basis. This is due to the high complexity, rigidity, and cost of legacy IRM solutions.

It is clearly more difficult to use documents protected with IRM—especially when policy making and maintenance is not designed by role but rather by individual. Some early implementations of IRM by first-to-market software development firms had as many as 200,000 different policies to maintain (for 200,000 employees). These have since been replaced by newer, second-wave IRM vendors, who have reduced that number to a mere 200 policies, which is much more manageable. Older IRM installations require intrusive plug-in installation; they are limited in the platforms they support, and they largely prevent the use of newer platforms, such as smartphones, iPads, and other tablets. This is a real problem in a world where almost all executives carry a smartphone and use of tablets (especially the iPad) is growing.

Moreover, due to their basic design, first-wave or legacy IRM is not a good fit for organizations aiming to protect documents shared outside company boundaries. These outdated IRM solutions were designed and developed in a world where organizations were more concerned with keeping information inside the perimeter than protecting information beyond the perimeter.

IRM technology protects e-documents and data directly rather than relying on perimeter security.

Most initial providers of IRM focused on internal sharing and are heavily dependent on Microsoft Active Directory (AD) and lightweight directory access protocol (LDAP) for authentication. Also, the delivery model of older IRM solutions involves the deployment and management of multiple servers, SQL databases, AD/LDAP integration, and a great deal of configuration. This makes them expensive and cumbersome to implement and maintain. Furthermore, these older IRM solutions do not take advantage of or operate well in a cloud computing environment.

Although encryption and legacy IRM solutions have certain benefits, they are extremely unwieldy and complex and offer limited benefits in today's technical and business environment. Newer IRM solutions are needed to provide more complete DLS.

Embedded Protection

IRM embeds protection into the data (using encryption technology), allowing files to protect themselves. IRM may be the best available security technology for the new mobile computing world of the permeable perimeter.[46]

Is Encryption Enough?

Many of the early solutions for locking down data involved encryption in one form or another:

- E-mail encryption
- File encryption
- Full Disk Encryption (FDE)
- Enterprisewide encryption

These encryption solutions can be divided into two categories: encryption *in transit* (e.g., e-mail encryption) and encryption *at rest* (e.g., FDE).

The various encryption solutions mitigate some risks. In the case of data in transit, these risks could include an eavesdropper attempting to discern e-mail or network traffic. In the case of at-rest data, risks include loss of a laptop or unauthorized access to an employee's machine. The most advanced solutions are capable of applying a policy across the organization and encrypting files, e-mails, and even databases. However, encryption has its caveats.

Most simple encryption techniques necessarily involve the decryption of documents so they can be viewed or edited. At these points, the files are essentially exposed. Malware (e.g., Trojan horses, keystroke loggers) installed on a computer may use the opportunity to send out the plain-text file to unauthorized parties. Alternatively, an employee may copy the contents of these files and remove them from the enterprise.

Device Control Methods

Another method that is related to DLP is **device control**. Many vendors offer software or hardware that prevents users from copying data via the USB port to portable drives and removing them from the organization in this manner. These solutions are typically as simple as blocking the ports; however, some DLP solutions, when installed on the client side, can selectively prevent the copying of certain documents.[47]

Thin Clients

One last method worth mentioning is the use of thin clients to prevent data leaks. These provide a so-called walled garden containing only the applications users require to do their work, via a diskless terminal. This prevents users from copying any data onto portable media; however, if they have e-mail or Web access applications, they still can send information out via e-mail, blogs, or social networks.

Note about Database Security

Database security and monitoring is addressed in Chapter 10, "IG for IT."

Compliance Aspect

Compliance has been key in driving companies to invest in improving their security measures, such as firewalls, antivirus software, and DLP systems. More than 400 regulations exist worldwide mandating a plethora of information and data security requirements. One example is the Payment Card Industry Data Security Standard (PCI-DSS), which is one of the strictest regulations for credit card processors. Companies that fail to comply with these regulations are subject to penalties of up to $500,000 per month for lost financial data or credit card information. It is estimated that the per-record cost of a breach is $90 to $305."[48] But do compliance activities always result in adequate protection of your sensitive data? In many cases the answer is no. It is important to keep in mind that *being formally compliant does not mean the organization is actually secure.* In fact, compliance is sometimes used as a fig leaf, covering a lack of real document security. One needs to look no further than to the recent series of major document leakage incidents to understand this. Those all came from highly secure and regulated entities, such as banks, hospitals, and the military.

Hybrid Approach: Combining DLP and IRM Technologies

An idea being promoted recently is to make IRM an enforcement mechanism for platforms like DLP. Together, DLP and IRM accomplish what they independently cannot. Enterprises may be able to use their DLP tools to discover data flows, map them out, and detect transmissions of sensitive information. They can then apply their IRM or encryption protection to enforce their confidentiality and information integrity goals.[49]

Several vendors in the fields of DLP, encryption, and IRM have already announced integrated products. However, at this point in time, most IRM solutions are by no means ready for prime time when it comes to this use. Only a select few second-wave IRM software providers can offer comprehensive, streamlined, persistent security across many platforms.

As the enterprise perimeter dissolves, document and data security should become the focus of the Internet security field. However, most legacy solutions, such as encryption and legacy IRM, are complex and expensive and provide only a partial solution to the key problems. Combining several methods offers effective countermeasures, but an ultimate solution has not yet arrived.

Securing Trade Secrets after Layoffs and Terminations

In today's global economy—which has shifted labor demands—huge layoffs are not uncommon in the corporate and public sectors. The act of terminating an employee creates document security and IP challenges while raising the question: How does the organization retrieve and retain its IP and confidential data? An IG program to secure information assets must also deal with everyday resignations of employees who are in possession of sensitive documents and information.[50]

According to Peter Abatan, author of the Enterprise Digital Rights Management blog, "As a general rule *all organizations should classify all their documents with the aim of identifying the ones that need persistent protection*" (emphasis added). That is to say, documents should be protected at all times, regardless of where they travel and who is using them, while the organization still retains control of usage rights. There are two basic technological approaches to this protection:

1. The first, as discussed earlier in this chapter, is combining *IRM with DLP*; DLP is used to conduct deep content inspection and identify all documents that may contain sensitive information, then the DLP agent "notifies the enterprise [information] rights management engine that sensitive information is about to be copied to external media or outside the firewall and therefore needs to be encrypted."
2. The second is using a form of *context-sensitive IRM* "in which all documents that contain sensitive data defined in the [global] data dictionary [are] automatically encrypted."

These two technological approaches must be fostered by an IG program. They can have significant positive impact in protecting sensitive information, no matter where it is located, and can help document owners withdraw access to its sensitive documents at any time.

Organizations must educate their employees to increase awareness of the financial and competitive impact of breaches and to clarify that sensitive documents are the property of the organization. If those handling sensitive documents are informed of the benefits of IRM and related technologies, they will be more vigilant in their efforts to keep information assets secure.

Persistently Protecting Blueprints and CAD Documents

Certain IRM software providers have focused on securing large-format engineering and design documents, and they have made great strides in the protection of

As much as 95 percent of CAD files are proprietary designs and represent valuable IP.

computer-aided design files. As much as *95 percent of CAD files are proprietary designs and represent valuable, proprietary IP of businesses worldwide.* And CAD files are just as vulnerable as any other e-document in that, when unprotected, they "can be emailed or transferred to another party without the knowledge of the owner of the content."[51]

In today's global economy, it is common to conduct manufacturing operations in markets where labor is inexpensive and regulations are lax. Many designs are sent to China, Indonesia, and India for manufacturing. Although they usually are accompanied by binding confidential disclosure contracts, but these agreements are often difficult to enforce, especially given the disparity in cultures and laws. And what happens if a rogue employee in possession of designs and trade secrets absconds with them and sells them to a competitor? Or starts a competing business? There are a number of examples of this happening.

Owners of valuable proprietary IP must vigilantly protect it; the very survival of the business may depend on it. Monitoring and securing IP wherever it might travel is now a business imperative.

Theft of IP and confidential information represents a clear and present danger to all types of businesses, especially global brands dependent on proprietary designs for a competitive advantage. Immediate IG action by executive management is required to identify possible leaks and plug the holes. Not safeguarding IP and confidential or sensitive documents puts the organization's competitive position, strategic plans, revenue stream, and very future at risk.

Securing Internal Price Lists

In 2010, it was reported that confidential information about the advertising expenditures of some of Google's major accounts was leaked to the public.[52] This may not seem like a significant breach, but, in fact, with this information, Google's customers can determine if they are getting a preferred price schedule, and competitors can easily undercut Google's pricing for major customers. According to Peter Abatan, "[It is clear] why this information is so critical to Google that this information is tightly secured."

Is your company's price list secured at all times? Price lists are confidential information assets, and if they are revealed publicly, major customers could demand steeper discounts and business relationships could suffer irreparable damage, especially if customers find out they are paying more for a product or service than their competitors.

A company's price list is critical to an organization because it impacts all aspects of the business, from the ability to generate revenue to private dealings with customers and suppliers. IRM should be used to protect price lists, and printing of these valuable lists must be monitored and controlled using secure printing methods and document analytics.

Confidential information should be persistently protected throughout their document life cycle in all three states (at rest, in motion, and in use) *so that if they are compromised or stolen, they are still protected and controlled by the owning organization.*

Approaches for Securing Data Once It Leaves the Organization

It is obvious with today's trends that, as Andrew Jaquith of SilverSky (formerly with Forrester Research) states, "The enterprise security perimeter is quickly dissolving." A lot of valuable information is routed outside the owning organization through unsecured e-mail. A breach can compromise competitive position, especially in cases dealing with personnel files and marketing plans or merger details. Consider for a moment that even proprietary software and company financial statements are sent out. Exposure of this data can have real financial impact. Without additional protections, such as IRM and e-mail encryption, these valuable information assets are often out of the control of the IT department of the owning organization.[53]

Third-party possession or control of enterprise data is a critical point of vulnerability, and many organizations realize that securing data outside the organizational perimeter is a high priority. But a new concept has cropped up of late that bucks unconventional wisdom: *"Control does not require ownership."*

Instead of focusing on securing devices where confidential data is accessed, the new thinking focuses on securing the data and documents directly. With this new mind-set, security can be planned under the assumption that the enterprise owns its data but none of the devices that access it. As Forrester's report states, "Don't trust the endpoints. Treat them as hostile". This is referred to as the zero-trust model of information security. The report states: "...trust but verify applies here. Enterprises must put teeth into their contractual language and audit their partners."[54]

Forrester has developed a new network architecture that builds security into the DNA of a network, using a mixture of five data security design patterns:

1. *Thin client.* Access information online only, with no local operations, using a diskless terminal that cannot store data, documents, or programs so confidential information stays stored and secured centrally. For additional security, "IT can restrict host copy-and-paste operations, limit data transfers, and require strong or two-factor authentication using SecurID or other tokens."

2. *Thin device.* Devices such as smartphones, which have limited computing resources, Web surfing, e-mail, and basic Web apps that locally conduct no real information processing, are categorized as thin devices. In practice, these devices do not hold original documents but merely copies, so the official business record or master copy cannot be altered or deleted. A nice feature of many smartphones is the ability to erase or wipe data remotely, in the event the device is lost. According to the Forrester report, "For insurance, thin devices can be remotely wiped—making them truly 'disposable,' unlike PCs."[55]

3. *Protected process.* This approach allows local processing with a PC where confidential e-documents and data are stored and processed in a partition that is highly secure and controlled. This processing can occur even if the PC is not

owned and controlled by the organization. "The protected process pattern has many advantages: local execution, offline operation, central management, and a high degree of granular security control, including remote wipe [erase]." A mitigating factor to consider here is most business PCs today are Windows based, and the world is rapidly moving to other, more nimble platforms.

4. *Protected data.* Deploying IRM and embedding security into the documents (or data) provides complete DLS. The newer wave of more sophisticated, easier-to-use IRM vendors have role-based policy implementation and such features as "contextual" enforcement, where document rights are dependent on the *context*—that is, *where* and *when* a user attempts access. For instance, allow access to documents on workers' desktops but not on their laptops; or provide access to printing confidential documents at the facility during office hours but not after. "*Of all the patterns in the Zero Trust data security strategy, protected data is the most fine-grained and effective because it focuses on the information, not its containers.*"

5. *Eye in the sky.* This design pattern uses technologies such as DLP to scan network traffic content and halt confidential documents or sensitive data at the perimeter. Deployed properly, DLP is "ideal for understanding the velocity and direction of information flow and for detecting potential breaches, outliers, or anomalous transmissions." It should be noted that DLP does not provide complete protection. To do so would mean that many legitimate and sanctioned e-mails and documents would be held up for inspection, thus slowing the business process. As stated earlier, DLP is best for discovering information flows and monitoring network traffic. Another negative is that you cannot always require partner organizations and suppliers to install DLP on their computers. So this is a complementary technology, not a complete solution to securing confidential information assets.

By discarding the "age-old conflation of ownership and control, enterprises will be able to build data protection programs that encompass all possible ownership scenarios, including Tech Populism, offshoring, and outsourcing."

Document Labeling

Document labeling is "an easy way to *increase user awareness about the sensitivity of information* in a document"(emphasis added).[56] What is it? It is the process of attaching a label to classify a document. For instance, who would not know that a document labeled "confidential" is indeed confidential? If the label appears prominently at the top of a document, it is difficult for persons accessing it to claim they did not know it was sensitive.

The challenge is to *standardize and formalize the process* of *getting the label onto the document—enterprisewide.* This issue would be addressed in an IG effort focused on securing confidential e-documents, or may also be a part of a classification and taxonomy design effort. It cannot simply be left up to users to type in labels themselves, or it will not be sufficiently executed and will end up leaving a mishmash of labeled documents without any formal classification.

Another great challenge are legacy or archived documents, which are the lion's share of an organization's information assets. How do you go back and label those? One by one? Nope. Not practical.

Some content repositories or portals, such as Microsoft SharePoint®, provide some functionality toward addressing the document labeling challenge. SharePoint is the most popular platform for sharing documents today.

SharePoint has an information management policy tool called Labels, which can be used to add document labels, such as *Confidential*, to the top of documents:

There are several options available for administrators to customize the labels, including the ability to:

1. Prompt users to add the label when they save or print, rather than relying on the user to click the Label button in the ribbon;

2. Specify labels containing static text and/or variables such as Project Name;

3. Control the appearance of the labels, such as font, size, and justification.[57]

The labels are easily added from within Microsoft Office Word, PowerPoint, and Excel. One method that can be used is for the user to click the Label button on the Insert ribbon group; another method is to add the label through a prompt that appears when a user saves or prints a document (if the administrator has configured this option).

The labeling capabilities in document and content management systems such as Microsoft's SharePoint are a good start for increasing user awareness and improving the handling of sensitive documents. However, *the document labeling capabilities of Share-Point are basic and limited.* These basic capabilities may provide a partial or temporary solution, although organizations aiming for a high level of security and confidentiality for their documents will need to search for supplemental technologies from third-party software providers. For instance, finding the capabilities to label documents in bulk rather than one by one, add watermarks, or force users to save or print documents with a standard document label that cannot be altered may require looking at alternatives. Some are software vendors have enhanced the SharePoint document labeling capability and may provide the complete solution.

Document Analytics

Some software providers also provide document analytics capabilities that monitor the access, use, and printing of documents and create real-time graphical reports of document use activities. These capabilities are *very* valuable.

Document analytics allows a compliance officer or system administrator to view exactly how many documents a user accesses in a day and how many documents the user accesses *on average.* Using this information, analytics monitors can look for spikes or anomalies in use. It is also possible to establish baselines and compare usage with that of an employee's peers, as well as with his or her past document usage. If, for instance, a user normally accesses an average of 25 documents a day and that suddenly spikes to 200, the system sends an alert, and perhaps it is time to pay a visit to that person's office. Or, if an employee normally prints 50 pages per day, then one day prints 250 pages, a flag is raised. Document analytics capabilities can go so far as to calculate the average time a user spends reading a document; significant time fluctuations can be flagged as potentially suspicious activity.

Confidential Stream Messaging

E-mail is dangerous. It contains much of an organization's confidential information, and 99 percent of the time it is sent out unsecured. It has been estimated that as many as 20 percent of e-mail messages transmitted pose a legal, financial, or regulatory threat to the organization. Specifically, "34 of employers investigated a leak of confidential business information via email, and an additional 26% of organizations suffered the exposure of embarrassing or sensitive information during the course of a year," according to Nancy Flynn, Executive Director of the ePolicy Institute. These numbers are rising, giving managers and business owners cause to look for confidential messaging solutions.[58]

Since stream messaging separates the header and identifying information from the message, sends them separately, and leaves no record or trace, it is a good option for executives and managers, particularly when engaged in sensitive negotiations, litigation, or other highly confidential activities. Whereas e-mail leaves behind an indelible fingerprint that lives forever on multiple servers and systems, stream messaging does not.

Business records, IP and trade secrets, and confidential executive communications can be protected by implementing stream messaging. It can be implemented alongside and in concert with a regular e-mail system, but clear rules on the use of stream messaging must be established, and access to it must be tightly restricted to a small circle of key executives and managers.

The ePolicy Institute offers seven steps to controlling stream messaging:

1. Work with your legal counsel to define "business record" for your organization on a companywide basis. Establish written records retention policies, disposition and destruction schedules. And litigation hold rules. Support the email retention policy with a bona fide email archiving solution to facilitate the indexing, preservation and production of legally authentic records. Implement a formal electronic records management system to manage all records.

2. Work with your legal counsel to determine when, how, why, and with whom confidential stream messaging is the most appropriate, effective—and legally compliant—way to hold recordless, confidential business discussions *when permanent records are not required.*

3. In order to preserve attorney-client privilege, a phone call or confidential electronic messaging may be preferable to email. Have corporate counsel spell out the manner in which executives and employees should communicate with lawyers when discussing business, seeking legal advice, or asking questions related to specific litigation.

4. Define key terms for employees. Don't assume employees understand what management means when using terms like "confidential," "proprietary," or "private" or "intellectual property," etc. Employees must clearly understand definitions If they are to comply with confidentiality rules.

5. Implement written rules and policies governing the use of email and confidential stream messaging. E-policies should be written clearly and should

be easy for employees to access, and understand. Make them [as] "short and sweet" as possible. Do not leave anything up to interpretation.

6. Distribute a hard copy of the new confidential messaging policy, email policy and other electronic communications (e.g., social media, blogs). Insist that each and every employee signs and dates the policy, acknowledging that they understand and accept it and that disciplinary action including termination may result from violation of the organization's established policies.

7. Educate, educate, educate. Ensure that all employees who need to know the difference between email which leaves a potential business record and stream messaging which does not, and is confidential. [59]

Securing personal, classified, or confidential information effectively requires an eclectic, multifaceted approach. It takes clear and enforced IG policies, a collection of technologies, and regular testing and audits, both internally and by a trusted third party.

CHAPTER SUMMARY: **KEY POINTS**

- The average cost of a data breach in 2013 was over $5 million.

- Attacks on organizations' networks and theft of their IP continue to increase. There were an estimated 354 million privacy breaches between 2005 and 2010 in the United States alone.

- Attacks can continue in organizations for years before they are uncovered—if they are discovered at all.

- All organizations should classify all their documents with the aim of identifying the ones that need persistent security protection.

- Today's ECM and document management solutions rely mostly on perimeter security and were not designed to allow for secure document sharing and collaboration.

- Businesses are operating in a more distributed model than ever before, and they are increasingly sharing and collaborating—exposing confidential documents.

- Secure document printing reduces the chance that files can be compromised during or after printing. There are various methods to secure the print stream, depending on the print manufacturer. Copies or remnants of large print files often exist unsecured on the hard drives of high-speed printers. These files must be completely wiped to ensure security.

- Identity and access management (IAM) software governs user access to information through an automated, continuous process that addresses access creep, whereby employees move to a different business unit and their access rights are not updated.

CHAPTER SUMMARY: **KEY POINTS** (*Continued*)

- Data governance software is another tool that looks at who is accessing which documents and creates a matrix of roles and access along behavioral lines.

- Encrypting sensitive e-mail messages is an effective step to securing confidential information assets while in transit. Encryption can be applied to desktop folders and files.

- For e-mail communication with no trace or record, stream messaging is a solution.

- Digital signatures authenticate the identity of the signatory and prove that the signature was, in fact, generated by the claimed signatory. This is known as nonrepudiation.

- Data loss prevention technology performs a "deep content inspection" of all e-documents and e-mails before they leave the organization's perimeter to stop sensitive data from exiting the firewall.

- DLP can be used to discover the flow of information within an organization. Additional security tools can then be applied. This may be the best use for DLP.

- Information rights management software enforces and manages use rights of electronic documents. IRM provides a sort of security wrapper around documents and protects sensitive information assets from unauthorized use or copying. IRM is also known as enterprise rights management.

- Persistent security tools like IRM should be enforced on price lists, proprietary blueprints, and CAD designs. Printing these documents should be highly restricted.

- Most legacy or first-to-market providers of IRM focused on internal sharing and are heavily dependent on Microsoft Active Directory and lightweight directory access protocol (LDAP) for authentication. These early solutions were not built for cloud use or the distributed enterprises of today, where mobile devices are proliferating.

- DLP started in the form of network gateways (much like firewalls) that searched e-mails, Web traffic, and other forms of information for data that was defined as internal. When it detected such data, it blocked it from leaving the perimeter or monitored its use.

- Soon agent-based DLP technologies were introduced, performing the same action locally on users' computers. The next step brought a consolidation of many agent- and network-based technologies to offer a more comprehensive solution.

(*continued*)

CHAPTER SUMMARY: **KEY POINTS** (*Continued*)

- Combining IRM and DLP technologies is the best available approach to securing e-documents and data. Other encryption methods should also be utilized, such as e-mail encryption and FDE).

- The use of thin-client and thin-device architecture can reduce security threats to confidential information assets.

- Document analytics monitor the access, use, and printing of documents and create real-time graphical reports of document use activities.

- Document labeling is an easy way to increase user awareness about the sensitivity of information in a document.

- Stream messaging is a way to conduct sensitive business negotiations and activities without leaving a business record. Legal counsel must be consulted, and clear policies for regular e-mail versus stream messaging must be established and enforced.

Notes

1. Ponemon Institute Research Report, "2013 Cost of Data Breach Study: United States," May 2013, www.symantec.com/content/en/us/about/media/pdfs/b-cost-of-a-data-breach-us-report-2013.en-us.pdf
2. Jim Finkle, "'State Actor' behind Slew of Cyber Attacks," Reuters, August 3, 2011, www.reuters.com/article/2011/08/03/us-cyberattacks-idUSTRE7720HU20110803 (accessed August 18, 2011).
3. Ibid.
4. Ibid.
5. Ibid.
6. Peter Abatan, "Persistently Protecting Your Computer Aided Designs," Enterprise Digital Rights Management, http://enterprisedrm.tumblr.com/post/1423979379/persistently-protecting-your-computer-aided-designs (accessed August 18, 2011).
7. Ari Ruppin, March 20, 2011 via e-mail.
8. Sam Narisi, "IT's role in secure staff cuts," March 2, 2009. www.financetechnews.com/its-role-in-secure-staff-cuts/
9. Ibid.
10. Shira Scheindlin and Daniel Capra, The Sedona Conference, *Electronic Discovery and Digital Evidence*, Thomson Reuters, 2009, p. 204, www.amazon.com/Scheindlin-Conferences-Electronic-Discovery-Evidence-ebook/dp/B00AUE0LRI
11. Oracle White Paper, "Oracle Information Rights Management 11g—Managing Information Everywhere It Is Stored and Used," March 2010 p. 4, www.oracle.com/technetwork/middleware/webcenter/content/irm-technical-whitepaper-134345.pdf (accessed December 23, 2011).
12. Ibid.
13. Open Web Application Security Project, "Defense in Depth," https://www.owasp.org/index.php/Defense_in_depth (accessed June 24, 2013).
14. HCL, "Identity and Access Management Services," www.hclisd.com/identity-and-access-management.aspx (accessed September 2, 2011).
15. Ibid.
16. Ibid.
17. Nicola Clark and David Jolly, "Fraud Costs Bank 7.1 Billion," *New York Times*, January 25, 2008, www.nytimes.com/2008/01/25/business/worldbusiness/25bank-web.html?hp (accessed September 2, 2011).

INFORMATION GOVERNANCE AND PRIVACY AND SECURITY FUNCTIONS 237

18. Oracle White Paper, "Oracle Information Rights Management 11g."
19. Robert Smallwood, "E-DRM Plugs ECM Security Gap," *KM World*, April 1, 2008, www.kmworld.com/Articles/News/News-Analysis/E-DRM-plugs-ECM-security-gap-41333.aspx (accessed March 30, 2012).
20. Adi Ruppin, March 20, 2011, via e-mail to author.
21. Annik Stahl, "Secure Printing: No More Mad Dashes to the Copy Room," http://office.microsoft.com/en-us/help/secure-printing-no-more-mad-dashes-to-the-copy-room-HA001227631.aspx (accessed August 22, 2011).
22. Telephone interview of William Broddy by author, August 7, 2011.
23. Bill Blake, "WikiLeaks, the Pearl Harbor of the 21st Century," eDocument Sciences LLC, December 6, 2010, http://edocumentsciences.com/wikileaks-the-pearl-harbor-of-the-21st-century.
24. VaporStream, www.vaporstream.com (accessed December 9, 2013).
25. Ibid.
26. Ibid.
27. NIST, "Federal Information Processing Standards Publication," FIPS PUB 186-3, issued June 2009, http://csrc.nist.gov/publications/fips/fips186-3/fips_186-3.pdf (accessed August 15, 2011). FIPS Publication 186-3 (dated June 2009), was superseded on July 19, 2013 and is provided here only for historical purposes. For the most current revision of this publication, see: http://csrc.nist.gov/publications/PubsFIPS.html
28. Doug Miles, AIIM White Paper, "Digital Signatures – Making the Business Case," http://www.arx.com/files/DOCUMENTS/Digital-Signatures-for-Document-Workflow-and-SharePoint-Survey.pdf (accessed December 9, 2013).
29. Computer Desktop Encyclopedia, www.computerlanguage.com, retrieved March 30, 2012.
30. Doug Miles, AIIM White Paper, "Digital Signatures – Making the Business Case."
31. Ibid.
32. Ibid.
33. Ibid.
34. Ari Ruppin, March 20, 2011, via e-mail.
35. Fred Donovan, "Gartner: Enterprise Content-Aware Data Loss Prevention Market to Reach $670 Million This Year," February 7, 2013, www.fierceenterprisecommunications.com/story/gartner-enterprise-content-aware-data-loss-prevention-market-reach-670-mill/2013-02-07
36. Data Loss Prevention Experts, "DLP Product Guide for RSA Conference Expo 2011," January 17, 2011, www.dlpexperts.com/dlpxblog/2011/1/17/dlp-product-guide-for-rsa-conference-expo-2011.html (accessed August 22, 2011).
37. Ibid.
38. Ibid.
39. Ibid.
40. Peter Abatan, "Who Should Be Blamed for a Data Breach?" Enterprise Digital Rights Management, http://enterprisedrm.tumblr.com/post/1087100940/who-should-be-blamed-for-a-data-breach (accessed December 9, 2013).
41. Peter Abatan, "Understanding Enterprise Rights Management," Enterprise Digital Rights Management, www.enterprisedrm.info/page/2 (accessed August 3, 2011).
42. Robert Smallwood, "Securing Documents in the WikiLeaks Era," May 28, 2011, www.kmworld.com/Articles/Editorial/Feature/Securing-documents-in-the-WikiLeaks-era-75642.aspx (accessed August 1, 2011).
43. Oracle, *IRM Technical White Paper*, Oracle.com, February 2008 (accessed December 9, 2013).
44. Abatan, "Understanding Enterprise Rights Management," http://enterprisedrm.tumblr.com/page/3 (accessed December 9, 2013).
45. Ibid.
46. Ibid.
47. Ibid.
48. "http://www.bankersonline.com/bankrobbery/2007/04/if-you-remember-old-tv-commercials-for.html?"
49. Abatan, "Understanding Enterprise Rights Management," http://enterprisedrm.tumblr.com/page/3 (accessed December 9, 2013).
50. This discussion and quotes are from Peter Abatan, "Preparing for Staff Layoffs/Resignations where Confidential Information Is Concerned," Enterprise Digital Rights Management, http://enterprisedrm.tumblr.com /post/1230356519/preparing-for-staff-layoffs-resignations (accessed December 9, 2013).
51. Ibid.
52. This discussion and quotes are from Peter Abatan, "Is Your Price List under Lock and Key?" Enterprise Digital Rights Management, http://enterprisedrm.tumblr.com/post/1120104758/is-your-price-list-under-lock-and-key (accessed August 18, 2011).

53. This discussion and quotes are from "Own Nothing. Control Everything", Forrester Research, Inc., January 22, 2010.

54. "Own Nothing. Control Everything", Forrester Research, Inc., January 22, 2010.

55. "Own Nothing. Control Everything", Forrester Research, Inc., January 22, 2010.

56. This discussion and quotes are from Charlie Pulfer, "Document Labeling in SharePoint," September 13, 2009, www.contentmanagementconnection.com/Home/21196/ (accessed January 28, 2014.

57. Ibid.

58. Nancy Flynn, *The E-Policy Handbook: Rules and Best Practices to Safely Manage Your Company's E-Mail, Blogs, Social Networking, and Other Electronic Communication Tools*, 2nd ed. (New York: AMACOM, 2009), p. 57.

59. Ibid., pp. 68–70.

PART FOUR

Information Governance for Delivery Platforms

CHAPTER 12

Information Governance for E-Mail and Instant Messaging*

E-mail is a major area of focus for information governance (IG) efforts: It is the most common business software application and the backbone of business communications today, and e-mail is the leading piece of evidence requested during the discovery phase of civil trials, so it is critically important to implement IG measures for e-mail communications.

Employees utilize e-mail all day, including during their personal time, sometimes mixing business and personal use of e-mail. Social media use has skyrocketed in recent years and actually has surpassed e-mail for personal use, but the fact remains that in business, knowledge workers rely on e-mail for almost all communications, *including those of a sensitive nature.* A 2013 survey of 2,400 corporate e-mail users worldwide found that nearly two-thirds stated that e-mail was their favorite form of business communication, surpassing not only social media but also telephone and in-person contact.[1]

These e-mail communications may contain discoverable information in litigation, and a percentage of them will be declared formal business records. E-mail often contains records, such as financial spreadsheets and reports, product price lists, marketing plans, competitive analyses, safety data, recruitment and salary details, progressing contract negotiations, and other information that may be considered as constituting a business record.

E-mail systems can be hacked, monitored, and compromised and cause far-reaching damage to a victimized organization. The damage may occur slowly and go undetected while information assets—and business value—are eroded.

In mid-2011, the "hacktivist" group AntiSec claimed responsibility for hacking a U.S. government contractor, Booz Allen Hamilton, and publicly exposing 90,000 military e-mail addresses and passwords from the contractor by posting them online. It was the second attack on a government defense contractor in a single week.[2]

Booz Allen employees "maintain high government security clearances" while working with the defense sector (yet in 2013 another Booz Allen employee, Edward Snowden, gained access to secret communications monitoring programs that the U.S.

---

*Portions of this chapter are adapted from Chapter 11, Robert F. Smallwood, *Managing Electronic Records: Methods, Best Practices, and Technologies,* © John Wiley & Sons, Inc., 2013. Reproduced with permission of John Wiley & Sons, Inc.

National Security Agency operated to capture metadata and other information from the private e-mail and telephone conversations of American citizens on a broad scale). AntiSec penetrated the communications systems with relative ease and noted there were "basically had no security measures in place."[3] AntiSec was able to go even further, by running its own rogue application to steal software source code and to search and find access credentials to steal data from other servers, which the group said would help it to infiltrate other federal contractors and agencies. It even stated it might pass the security information on to other hackers.

The attack did not stop there. Later that week, another federal defense and FBI contractor, IRC Federal, was hacked, databases were invaded, the Web site was modified, and information from internal e-mail messages was posted online.[4]

Employees Regularly Expose Organizations to E-Mail Risk

A 2011 global e-mail survey, commissioned by a leading hosted e-mail services provider, found that nearly 80 percent of all employees send work e-mail to and from their personal accounts, and 20 percent do so regularly, which means that critical information assets are exposed to uncontrolled security risks.[5]

"Awareness of the security risks this behavior poses does not act as a deterrent" (emphasis added). Over 70 percent of people questioned recognize that there is an additional risk in sending work documents outside the corporate e-mail environment, but almost half of "these same respondents feel it is acceptable to send work emails and documents to personal email accounts anyway." According to the survey, the reasons for using personal e-mail accounts for work purposes range from working on documents remotely (71 percent), to sending files that are too big for the company mailbox (21 percent), to taking documents with them when they leave a company (18 percent), to simply not wanting to carry a laptop home (9 percent). The top two frustrations users had with work e-mail were restrictions on mailbox size, which has a negative impact on e-mail management, and the inability to send large attachments. This second issue often forces workers to use a personal account to send and receive necessary files. If size limits are imposed on mailboxes and attachments, companies must provide a secure alternative for file storage and transfer. Otherwise, employees are pushed into risking corporate information assets via personal e-mail. This scenario not only complicates things for e-mail administrators but has serious legal and regulatory implications. Clearly, as stated by Paul Mah in his "Email Admin" blog, "email retention and archival becomes an impossible task when emails are routed in a haphazard manner via personal accounts."[6]

This means that security, privacy, and records management issues must be addressed by first creating IG policies to control and manage the use of e-mail. These policies can utilize the e-mail system's included security features and also employ additional monitoring and security technologies where needed.

The e-mail survey also found an overall lack of clear e-mail policies and weak communication of existing guidelines. *This means a lack of IG.* Nearly half of the respondents stated either that their company had no e-mail policy or that they were unaware of one. Among those aware of a corporate e-mail policy, 4 in 10 think it could be communicated better. Among companies that have a policy, most (88 percent) deal with the appropriate use of e-mail as a business tool, but less than one-third (30 percent) address e-mail retention from a security standpoint.

Generally, employees are aware that sending work documents outside of their corporate network is unsafe, yet they continue to do so. It is abundantly clear that *e-mail policies have to be updated and upgraded to accommodate and manage the increasingly sophisticated and computer-savvy generation* of users who are able to find ways to work around corporate e-mail restrictions. (These users have been dubbed *Generation Gmail.*) In addition, new e-mail monitoring and security technologies need to be deployed to counter this risky practice, which exposes information assets to prying eyes or malicious attacks.

E-Mail Polices Should Be Realistic and Technology Agnostic

E-mail policies as part of your IG program must not be too restrictive. It may be tempting to include catchall policies that attempt to tamp down user behavior, but such efforts cannot succeed.[7] An important step is consulting with stakeholders to understand their usage patterns and needs and then going through a series of drafts of the policy, allowing for input. It may be determined that some exceptions and changes in technologies need to be factored in and that some additional technology is needed to accommodate users while keeping information assets safer and meeting compliance and legal demands. Specifics of these policies and tools should be progressively tightened on a regular basis as the process moves forward.

These new IG guidelines and policies need to refer to technology in a generic sense—a "technology-neutral" sense—rather than specifying proprietary software programs or features.[8] That is to say, they should be written so that they are *not* in need of revision as soon as new technologies are deployed.

Developing organization-wide IG policies is time consuming and expensive; they are a defensive measure that does not produce revenue, so managers, pressed for performance, often relegate policy making to the low-priority list. Certainly, it is a tedious, difficult task, so organizations should aim to develop policies that are flexible enough to stand the test of time. But it is also necessary to establish a review process to periodically revise policies to accommodate changes in the business environment, the law, and technology.

Here is an example of a technology-agnostic policy directive:

> All confidential information must be encrypted before being transmitted over the Internet.

This statement does not specify the technology to be used, or the mode of transmission. The policy is neutral enough to cover not only e-mail and instant messaging (IM) but also social media, cloud computing, mobile computing, and other means of communication. The policy also does not specify the method or brand of the encryption technology, so the organization can select the best method and technology available in the future without adapting the policy.[9]

E-Record Retention: Fundamentally a Legal Issue

Considering the massive volume of e-mail exchanged in business today, most e-mail messages do not rise to the level of being formal business records. But many of them do and are subject to IG, regulatory compliance, and legal requirements for maintaining and producing business records.

> Managing e-records is primarily a legal issue, especially for public and heavily regulated companies.

Although often lumped in with other information technology (IT) concerns, the retention of e-mail and other e-records is ultimately a legal issue. Other departments, including records management and business units, should certainly have input and should work to assist the legal team to record retention challenges and archiving solutions. But e-mail and e-record retention is "fundamentally a *legal* issue," particularly for public or highly regulated companies. According to Nancy Flynn of the ePolicy Institute, "It is essential for the organization's legal department to take the lead in determining *precisely* which types of email messages will be preserved, *exactly* how and where data will be stored, and *specifically when*—if ever—electronically stored information [ESI] will be deleted"[10] (emphasis added).

Since they are often shot out in the heat of battle, many times e-mail messages are evidence of a smoking gun in lawsuits and investigations. In fact, they are the most requested type of evidence in civil litigation today. The content and timing of e-mail messages can provide exonerating information too.

In January 2010, a U.S. House of Representatives committee probing bailout deals subpoenaed the Federal Reserve Bank of New York for e-mail and other correspondence from Treasury Secretary Timothy Geithner (former president of the New York Federal Reserve Bank) and other officials. The House Oversight and Government Reform Committee was in the process of examining New York Fed decisions that funneled billions of dollars to big banks, including Goldman Sachs Group and Morgan Stanley.[11]

This is just one example of how crucial e-mail messages can be in legal investigations and how they play an important role in reconstructing events and motives for legal purposes.

Preserve E-Mail Integrity and Admissibility with Automatic Archiving

Most users are not aware that e-mail contents and characteristics can be changed— "and rendered legally invalid"—by anyone with malicious motives, including those who are essentially "covering their tracks." Not only can the content be edited, but metadata that includes such information as the time, date, and total number of characters in the message can also be changed retroactively.[12]

To offset this risk and ensure that **spoliation** (i.e., the loss of proven authenticity of an e-mail) does not occur, *all messages, both inbound and outbound, should be captured and archived automatically and in real time.* This preserves legal validity and forensic compliance. Additionally, e-mail should be indexed to facilitate the searching process, and all messages should be secured in a single location. With these measures, e-mail records can be assured to be authentic and reliable.

E-Mail Archiving Rationale: Compliance, Legal, and Business Reasons

There are good reasons to archive e-mail and retain it according to a specific retention schedule that follows your organization's IG policies. Having a handle on managing voluminous e-mail archives translates to being able to effectively and rapidly search and retrieve exactly the right messages, which can provide a significant legal advantage. It gives your legal team more and better information and more time to figure out how to leverage it in legal strategy sessions. This means the odds are tipped in your organization's favor in the inevitable litigation arena. Your legal opponent may be driven to settle a weak claim when confronted with indisputable e-mail evidence, and, in fact, "email often produces supportive evidence that may help 'save the day' by providing valuable legal proof" of innocence.[13] This evidence may stop frivolous lawsuits in their tracks. Further, reliable e-mail evidence also can curtail lengthy and expensive lawsuits, and prevail. And if your company is public, Sarbanes–Oxley regulations require the archiving of e-mail.

Don't Confuse E-Mail Archiving with Backup

All backups are not created equal. *There is a big difference between traditional system backups and specialized e-mail archiving software.*

Backups are huge dumps to mass storage, where the data is stored sequentially and not compressed or indexed.[14] It is impossible to search backups except by date, and even doing that would mean combing through troves of raw, non-indexed data.

The chief executive may not be aware of it, but without true e-mail archiving, system administrators could spend long nights loading old tapes and churning out volumes of data, and legal teams will bill hourly for manual searches through troves of data. This compromises your enterprise's legal position and not only increases raw costs but also leads to less capable and informed legal representation. According to one study, fully one-third of IT managers state they would have difficulty producing an e-mail that is more than one year old. *"A backup system is no substitute for automatic archiving technology"*[15] (emphasis added).

No Personal Archiving in the Workplace

Employees are naturally going to want to back up their most important files, just as they probably do at home. But for an overall IG information-security program to be effective, personal archiving at work must be prohibited. This underground archiving results in hidden shadow files and is time consuming and risky. According to Flynn, *"Self-managed email can result in the deletion of electronic records, alteration of email evidence, time-consuming searches for back-up tapes, and failure to comply with legal discovery demands"* (emphasis added). Also, users may compromise formal electronic records, or they may work from unofficial records, which therefore by definition might be inaccurate or out-of-date, posing compliance and legal ramifications.[16]

Are All E-Mails Records?

Are e-mail messages records? This question has been debated for years. The short answer is no, not all e-mail messages constitute a record. But how do you determine whether certain messages are a business record or not? The general answer is that a record documents a transaction or business-related event that may have legal ramifications or historic value. Most important are business activities that may relate to compliance requirements or those that could possibly come into dispute in litigation. Particular consideration should be given to financial transactions of any type.

Certainly evidence that required governance oversight or compliance activities have been completed needs to be documented and becomes a business record. Also, business transactions, in which there is an exchange of money or the equivalent in goods or services, are also business records. Today, these transactions are often documented by a quick e-mail. And, of course, any contracts (and any progressively developed or edited versions) that are exchanged through e-mail become business records.

The form or format of a potential record is irrelevant in determining whether it should be classified as a business record. For instance, if a meeting of the board of directors is recorded by a digital video recorder and saved to DVD, it constitutes a record. If photographs are taken of a ground-breaking ceremony for a new manufacturing plant, the photos are records too. If the company's founders tape-recorded a message to future generations of management on reel-to-reel tape, it is a record also, since it has historical value. But most records are going to be in the form of paper, microfilm, or an electronic document.

Here are three guidelines for determining whether an e-mail message should be considered a business record:

1. The e-mail documents a transaction or the progress toward an ultimate transaction where anything of value is exchanged between two or more parties. All parts or characteristics of the transaction, including who (the parties to it), what, when, how much, and the composition of its components, are parts of the transaction. Often seemingly minor parts of a transaction are found buried within an e-mail message. One example would be a last-minute discount offered by a supplier based on an order being placed or delivery being made within a specified time frame.

2. The e-mail documents or provides support of a business activity occurring that pertains to internal corporate governance policies or compliance to externally mandated regulations.

3. The e-mail message documents other business activities that may possibly be disputed in the future, whether it ultimately involves litigation or not. (Most business disputes actually are resolved without litigation, provided that proof of your organization's position can be shown.) For instance, your supplier may dispute the discount you take that was offered in an e-mail message and, once you forward the e-mail thread to the supplier, it acquiesces.[17]

Destructive Retention of E-Mail

Destructive retention is an approach to e-mail archiving where e-mail messages are retained for a limited time (say, 90 days or six months), followed by their permanent manual or automatic deletion of messages from the company's network, so long as there is no litigation hold or the e-mail has not been declared a record in accordance with IG and records management policies. Implementing this as a policy may shield the enterprise from retaining potentially libelous or litigious e-mail that is not a formal business record (e.g., off-color jokes or other personnel violations).

For heavily regulated industries, such as health care, energy, and financial services, organizations may need to archive e-mail for longer periods of time.

Instant Messaging

Instant messaging (IM) use in enterprises has proliferated—despite the fact that frequently proper policies, controls, and security measures are not in place to prevent e-document and data loss. There are a variety of threats to IM use that enterprises must defend against to keep their information assets secure.

The first basic IM systems, which came into use in the mid-1960s, had real-time text capabilities for routing messages to users logged on to the same mainframe computer. Early chat systems, such as AOL Instant Messenger, have been in use since the late 1980s, but true IM systems that included buddy list features appeared on the scene in the mid-1990s, followed by the release of Yahoo! and Microsoft IM systems. The use of these personal IM products in the workplace has created new security risks.[18]

More secure enterprise instant messaging (EIM) products can be deployed. Leading EIM installed systems include IBM Lotus Sametime, Microsoft Office Communications Server, Cisco Unified Presence, and Jabber XCP. In the financial sector, Bloomberg Messaging and Reuters Messaging are leading platforms.

By the year 2000, it was estimated that nearly 250 million people worldwide were making use of IM, and today estimates are that more than 2 billion people use IM, with the addition of hundreds of millions of users in China.

As with many technologies, IM became popular first for personal use, then crept into the workplace—and exploded. IM is seen as a quicker and more efficient way to communicate short messages than engaging in a telephone conversation or going through rounds of sending and receiving endless e-mail messages. *The problem with IM is that many organizations are blind to the fact that their employees are going to use it one way or another*, sometimes for short personal conversations outside the organization. If unchecked, such messaging exposes the organization to a myriad of risks and gives hackers another way to compromise confidential information assets.

Best Practices for Business IM Use

Employing best practices for enterprise IM use can help mitigate its security risks while helping to capitalize on the business agility and velocity benefits IM can provide. Best practices must be built in to IG policies governing the use of IM, although "the specifics of these best practices must be tailored for each organization's unique needs."

A methodology for forming IM-specific IG policies and implementing more secure use of IM must begin with surveying and documenting the proliferation of IM use in the organization. It should also discover how and why users are relying on IM—perhaps there is a shortcoming with their available IT tools and IM is a work-around.

Typically, executives will deny there is much use of IM and that if it is being used, its impact is not worth worrying about. Also, getting users to come clean about

Documenting IM use in the organization is the first step in building IG policies to govern its use. Those policies must be tailored to the organization and its IM use.

their IM use may be difficult, since this may involve personal conversations and violations of corporate policy. A survey is a good place to start, but more sophisticated network monitoring tools need to be used to factually discover what IM systems are actually in use.

Once this discovery process has concluded and the use of IM is mapped out, the IG team or steering committee must create or update policies to: decide which IM systems it will allow to be used, how, when, and by whom; decide what restrictions or safeguards must be imposed; and create guidelines as to appropriate use and content. As a part of an overall IG effort, Quest Software determined that a successful IM policy will:

- *Clearly and explicitly explain the organization's instant messaging objectives.* Users should know why the organization permits IM and how it is expected to be used.
- *Define expectations of privacy.* Users should be made aware that the organization has the right to monitor and log all IM sessions for corporate compliance, safety, and security reasons.
- *Detail acceptable and unacceptable uses.* An exhaustive list of permitted and forbidden activities may not be necessary, but specific examples are helpful in establishing a framework of IM behaviors for users.
- *Detail content and contact restrictions (if any).* Most organizations will want to limit the amount of idle IM chat that may occur with family, friends, and other nonbusiness-related contacts. There may also be additional issues related to information confidentiality and privacy. Some businesses may choose to block the distribution of certain types of information via live IM chat session or file transfer.
- *Define consequences for violations of the policy.* Users should be advised of the consequences of policy violations. Generally these should be aligned with the company's personnel and acceptable use policies.

The use of a standard disclaimer, to be inserted into all users' IM sessions, can remind employees of appropriate IM use and that all chat sessions are being monitored and archived, and can be used in court or compliance hearings.

The next major step is to work with the IT staff to find the best and most appropriate security and network monitoring tools, given the computing environment. Alternatives must be researched, selected, and deployed. In this research and selection process, it is best to start with at least an informal survey of enterprises within the same industry to attempt to learn what has worked best for them.

The key to any compliance effort or legal action will be ensuring that IM records are true and authentic, so the exact, unaltered archiving of IM messages along with associated metadata should be implemented in real time. This is the only way to

Records of IM use must be captured in real time and preserved to ensure they are reliable and accurate.

preserve business records that may be needed in the future. But in addition, a policy for deleting IM messages after a period of time, so long as they are not declared business records, must be formulated.

IG requires that these policies and practices not be static; rather, they must be regularly revisited and updated to reflect changes in technology and legal requirements and to address any shortcoming or failure of the IG policies or technologies deployed.

Technology to Monitor IM

Today, it has been estimated that as much as 80 percent of all IM used by corporate employees comes from free IM providers like Yahoo!, MSN, or AOL. These programs are also the least secure. Messages using these IM platforms can fly around the Internet unprotected. Any monitoring technology implemented must have the capability to apply and enforce established IM use policies by constantly monitoring Internet traffic to discover IM conversations. Traffic containing certain keywords can be monitored or blocked, and chat sessions between forbidden users (e.g., those who are party to a lawsuit) can be stopped before they start. But this all necessarily starts with IG and policy formulation.

Tips for Safer IM

Organizations should assume that IM is being used, whether they have sanctioned it or not. And that may not be a bad thing—employees may have found a reasonable business use for which IM is expedient and effective. So management should not rush to ban its use in a knee-jerk reaction. Here are some tips for safer use of corporate IM:

- Just as e-mail attachments and embedded links are suspect and can contain malicious executable files, *beware of IM attachments* too. The same rules governing e-mail use apply to IM, in that employees should never open attachments from people they do not know. Even if they do know them, with phishing and social engineering scams, these attachments should first be scanned for malware using antivirus tools.
- *Do not divulge any more personal information than is necessary.* This comes into play even when creating screen names—so the naming convention for IM screen names must be standardized for the enterprise. Microsoft advises, "Your screen name should not provide or allude to personal information. For example, use a nickname such as SoccerFan instead of BaltimoreJenny."[19]
- *Keep IM screen names private;* treat them as another information asset that needs to be protected to reduce unwanted IM requests, phishing, or spam (actually *spim*, in IM parlance).

- *Prohibit transmission of confidential corporate information.* It is fine to set up a meeting with auditors, but do not attach and route the latest financial report through unsecured IM.
- *Restrict IM contacts to known business colleagues.* If personal contacts are allowed for emergencies, limit personal use for everyday communication. In other words, do not get into a long personal IM conversation with a spouse or teenager while at work. Remember, these conversations are going to be monitored and archived.
- *Use caution when displaying default messages when you are unavailable or away.* Details such as where an employee is going to have lunch or where their child is being picked up from school may expose the organization to liability if a hacker takes the information and uses it for criminal purposes. Employees may be unknowingly putting themselves in harm's way by giving out too much personal information.
- *Ensure that IM policies are being enforced by utilizing IM monitoring and filtering tools and by archiving messages in real time* for a future verifiable record, should it be needed.
- *Conduct an IM usage policy review at least annually*; more often in the early stages of policy development.

CHAPTER SUMMARY: **KEY POINTS**

- E-mail is a critical area for IG implementation, as it is a ubiquitous business communication tool and the leading piece of evidence requested at civil trials.

- Nearly 80 percent of all employees send work e-mail messages to and from their personal e-mail accounts, which exposes critical information assets to uncontrolled security risks.

- Meeting e-mail retention and archival requirements becomes an impossible task when e-mail messages are routed in a haphazard manner via personal accounts.

- In developing e-mail policies, an important step is consulting with stakeholders.

- E-mail policies must not be too restrictive or tied to a specific technology. They should be flexible enough to accommodate changes in technology and should be reviewed and updated regularly.

- Not all e-mail messages constitute a business record.

- Not all e-mail rises to the level of admissible legal evidence. Certain conditions must be met.

- Automatic archiving protects the integrity of e-mail for legal purposes.

CHAPTER SUMMARY: **KEY POINTS** (*Continued*)

- Instant messaging use in business and the public sector has become widespread, despite the fact that often few controls or security measures are in place.

- Typically as much as 80 percent of all IM use in corporations today is over free public networks, which heightens security concerns.

- IM monitoring and management technology provides the crucial components that enable the organization to fully implement best practices for business IM.

- Enterprise IM systems provide a greater level of security than IM from free services.

- Regular analysis and modification (if necessary) of business IM policies and practices will help organizations leverage the maximum benefit from the technology.

- Records of IM use must be captured in real time and preserved to ensure they are reliable and accurate.

Notes

1. "Research Finds that Restrictive Email Policies are Creating Hidden Security Risks for Businesses," *BusinessWire*, March 9, 2011, www.businesswire.com/news/home/20110309005960/en/Research-Finds-Restrictive-Email-Policies-Creating-Hidden.
2. Elizabeth Montalbano, "AntiSec Hacks Booz Allen, Posts Confidential Military Email," *InformationWeek*, July 12, 2011, www.informationweek.com/news/security/attacks/231001418?cid=nl_IW_daily_2011-07-12_html.
3. Ibid.
4. Mathew J. Schwartz, "AntiSec Hacks FBI Contractor," *InformationWeek*, July 11, 2011, www.informationweek.com/news/security/attacks/231001326.
5. Quotes from this survey are from "Research Finds That Restrictive Email Policies Are Creating Hidden Security Risks for Businesses."
6. Paul Mah, "How to Reduce the Email Security Risks to Your Business," *EmailAdmin*, March 10, 2011, www.theemailadmin.com/2011/03/how-to-reduce-the-email-security-risks-to-your-business/.
7. Blair Kahn, *Information Nation: Seven Keys to Information Management Compliance* (Silver Spring, MD: AIIM International, 2004), pp. 98–99.
8. Ibid, pp. 95–96.
9. Ibid.
10. Nancy Flynn, *The E-Policy Handbook: Rules and Best Practices to Safely Manage Your Company's E-Mail, Blogs, Social Networking, and Other Electronic Communication Tools*, 2nd ed. (New York: AMACOM, 2009), 20.
11. Hugh Son and Andrew Frye, "Geithner's E-mails, Phone Logs Subpoenaed by House (update3)," January 13, 2010, www.bloomberg.com/apps/news?pid=newsarchive&sid=aGzbhrSxFlXw,.
12. Flynn, *E-Policy Handbook*, p. 37.
13. Flynn, *E-Policy Handbook*, pp. 40–41.
14. Nancy Flynn and Randolph Kahn, *Email Rules, A Business Guide to Managing Policies, Security, and Legal Issues for E-Mail and Digital Communication* (New York: AMACOM, 2003), pp. 81–82.

15. Flynn, *The E-Policy Handbook*, p. 41.
16. Ibid., p. 43.
17. Robert F. Smallwood, *Taming the Email Tiger: Email Management for Compliance, Governance, & Litigation Readiness* (New Orleans, LA: Bacchus Business Books, 2008).
18. This discussion is based on Quest Software White Paper, "Best Practices in Instant Messaging Management" (October 2008), http://media.govtech.net/Digital_Communities/Quest%20Software/Best_Practices_in_Instant_Messaging_Management.pdf, p. 5.
19. M. Adeel Ansari, "10 Tips for Safer IM Instant Messaging," July 6, 2008, http://adeelansari.wordpress.com/tag/safer-im-instant-messaging/.

CHAPTER 13

Information Governance for Social Media*

By Dr. Patricia Franks and Robert Smallwood

nformation is the lifeblood of every organization, and an increasing volume of information today is created and exchanged through the use of social networks and Web 2.0 tools like blogs, microblogs, and wikis.

Corporations use public social media technology to create a visible brand, strengthen relations with current customers while attracting new connections and clients, highlight their products and services, and gather intelligence that can be used in decision making.

Governments use public social media technologies to consult with and engage citizens, provide services, and keep pace with fast-moving events (e.g., natural disasters).

Both types of enterprises also benefit from the use of internal social media solutions that facilitate communication and collaboration, improve employee engagement, and boost productivity and efficiency.

Content created through or posted to these new social media platforms must be managed, monitored, and, quite often, archived. Content that meets the organization's definition of a record (i.e., documents business activities) must be retained in accordance with the organization's records retention and disposition policy.

Too often, social media content is not managed by information governance (IG) policies or monitored with controls that ensure protection of the brand and critical information assets and preservation of business records.

Types of Social Media in Web 2.0

The term "Web 2.0" was coined to characterize the move from static Web sites that passively provided information to consumers to more participative, interactive, collaborative, and user-oriented Web sites and Web applications that allow for input, discussion, and sharing. Users can add content, increasing the value of the Web site or service. Examples include blogs and Web pages containing podcasts (digital media, usually audio) where readers can post comments or pose questions; wikis that

---

*Portions of this chapter are adapted from Chapter 13, Robert F. Smallwood, *Managing Electronic Records: Methods, Best Practices, and Technologies*, © John Wiley & Sons, Inc., 2013. Reproduced with permission of John Wiley & Sons, Inc.

hyperlink to related information to create a knowledge base that shows interrelationships and allow users to add content; and RSS (really simple syndication) feeds that provide a stream of fresh content to the user or consumer.

Web 2.0 is the term used to describe the second generation of the World Wide Web, which is comprised of a combination of technologies that allow consumers of Web content to participate, collaborate, and share information online. The improved functionality reflects consumer needs and preferences that surfaced as a result of increased use of the Web for daily information and communications.

Social media sites like LinkedIn, Twitter, and Facebook encourage social interactions by allowing users to create their own close network of business associates or friends—essentially a hand-picked audience—and to post their own content in the form of comments, links, photos, videos, and so forth. Others in their social network may view, forward, share, organize, and comment on this content.[1]

Web 2.0 and social media platforms began as outward-facing, public Web services that could link users from around the world. Subsequently, businesses discovered that social media technology could also be leveraged for internal use in various ways, such as by creating a directory and network of subject matter experts that users can search when working on special projects or by sending out microblog messages to keep their workforce informed. These internal social networks may be extended to include external stakeholders, such as suppliers and customers, in a controlled environment. A number of platform and software options exist for enterprise social media development and use.

According to the U.S. National Archives and Records Administration:

> Social media platforms can be grouped into the categories below. Some specific platforms may fit into more than one category depending on how the platform is used.
>
> - *Web Publishing.* Platforms used to create, publish, and reuse content.
>   - Microblogging (Twitter, Plurk)
>   - Blogs (WordPress, Blogger)
>   - Wikis (Wikispaces, PBWiki)
>   - Mashups (Google Maps, popurls)
> - *Social networking.* Platforms used to provide interactions and collaboration among users.
>   - Social networking tools (Facebook, LinkedIn)
>   - Social bookmarks (Delicious, Digg)
>   - Virtual worlds (Second Life, OpenSim)
>   - Crowdsourcing/Social voting (IdeaScale, Chaordix)
> - *File sharing/storage.* Platforms used to share files and host content storage.
>   - Photo libraries (Flickr, Picasa)
>   - Video sharing (YouTube, Vimeo)
>   - Storage (Google Drive, Dropbox)
>   - Content management (SharePoint, Drupal)
>
> Agencies [and businesses] use a variety of software tools and platforms. The examples given above are not meant to be an exhaustive list.[2]

Additional Social Media Categories

Breaking out the categories of social media further, we can see in Table 13.1 examples of the wide range of social media applications that exist in the marketplace today. These categories will increase and fluctuate as the market matures and the companies providing the social media technologies and services expand, merge, are acquired, or die off.

There are certainly additional categories, and the categories will continue to grow. In addition, social media companies do not always fit neatly into one category. Applications (apps) for smartphones and tablets offer instant gratification and combine several functions. For example, Snapchat allows the sender to share an experience by snapping an image or video, adding a caption, and sending it to a friend.[3] The image, unless saved by the recipient, is visible only for the number of seconds set by the sender. The goal is to share a moment in time by sending a fleeting message. Another app, Vine, introduced by Twitter in early 2013, allows anyone to capture and share short looping videos.[4] Popular for personal use, a number of firms (e.g., GE, Urban Outfitters, and

Table 13.1   Social Media by Application Type

Category	Examples
Content curation	Buzzfeed, Flipboard, Skygrid, Storify, Summify
Content sharing	Yelp, Scribd, Slideshare, Digg, Topix
Photo sharing	Flickr, Picasa, SmugMug, Photobucket
Social ad networks	Lifestreet, AdKnowledge, Media6degrees, BurstMedia
Social analytics	Awe.sm, Bluefin Labs, Mixpanel, Webtrends
Social bookmarking	BibSonomy, Delicious, Diigo, Folkd
Social business software	Lithium, Jive, Pluck, Mzinga, Telligent, Ingage, Leverage Software, Huddle, Cubetree, Yammer (Microsoft), Socialcast, Igloo, Socialtext, Watchtoo, Acquia*
Social brand engagement	Socialvibe, Mylikes, Adly, Sharethrough
Social commerce platforms	Ecwid, Moontoast, Shop Tab, Dotbox, Storenvy, VendorShop
Social community platforms	Ning, Mixxt, Grou.ps, Groupsite
Social data	GNIP, DataSift, Rapleaf, RavenPack
Social intelligence software	SDL, Netbase, Postrank, Google Analytics, Trendrr, Trackur, Visible
Social marketing management	Shoutlet, Syncapse, Objective Marketer, Immobi, MediaFunnel
Social promotion platforms	Offerpop, Seesmic, Strutta, Votigo, Fanzila, Zuberance, Extole, Social AppsHQ, Social Amp
Social publishing platforms	Hootsuite, Spredfast, Hearsaysocial, MutualMind, SproutSocial, Flowtown, Socialware
Social referral	500Friends, Curebit, Tip or Skip, Turnto
Social search and browsing	StumbleUpon, Topsy, Wink, Kurrently, SocialMention
Social scoring	Klout, EmpireAvenue, PeerIndex

Source: Luma Partners and Terry Kawaja, http://static5.businessinsider.com/image/4fb5077becad04 5f47000003-960/buddy-media-social-marketing.jpg (accessed May 21, 2012).

20th Century Fox) have begun to integrate Vine into their marketing/branding strategy, including major brands.

Social Media in the Enterprise

Public-facing social media integrates Internet-based applications, technology, social interaction, and content creation to enable communication, collaboration, and content sharing within and across subnetworks of millions of public users. Implementing tight security on these types of mass networks would likely slow response time and inhibit the user experience, and it may not provide a sufficient level of security to warrant the investment on the part of the social media provider.

While popular consumer-based technologies (Facebook, Twitter, and LinkedIn) top the list of social media technologies used in enterprises today,[5] *these services were not designed with the business in mind.* Enterprises that need tight security but wish to take advantage of the many benefits of social media use are increasingly implementing enterprisewide social media solutions in addition to or in place of public-facing social media.

In the business world, Facebook-like social networking software is offered for private, closed networks with a finite number of users. In this computing environment, implementing security is more manageable and practical. Some services are cloud based; others operate internally behind the enterprise firewall; and some operate either way or in conjunction as hybrid architecture. Usage statistics that reflect trends, adoption rates, and areas of content interest can be provided to help feed the metrics needed to chart the progress and effectiveness of the enterprise social network.[6]

Enterprise social networking is being adopted by business and public-sector entities at a rapid rate. With the entry of *Generation Gmail* into the workforce, many of these initiatives took on an experimental, "cool" image. However, it is crucial to establish social media business objectives, to define time-limited metrics, and to measure progress. There does need to be some leeway, as calculating return on investment (ROI) for enterprise social networks is very new, and all the benefits (and pitfalls) have not yet been discovered or defined. Certainly the network load and required bandwidth for e-mail and attachments will decrease; instead of sending a 25MB PowerPoint file back and forth among 10 coworkers, the file can sit in a common workspace for collaboration.

Another intangible benefit is the competitive value in being a market leader or industry innovator. But to keep that edge, companies need to continually scan the horizon for new technologies and services. Engaging in online conversations with customers and other stakeholders is the norm rather than the exception. One sign of a progressive-thinking organization is its ability to leverage social media technology to refine operations, improve customer services, and make employees' lives easier. An organization with a strong social media reputation likely will be better able to attract, recruit, and retain qualified, high-achieving employees.

> Implementing security is more manageable and practical with enterprise social networking software.

Key Ways Social Media Is Different from E-Mail and Instant Messaging

Social media offers some of the same functionality as other communication and collaboration systems like e-mail and instant messaging (IM), yet its architecture and underlying assumptions are quite different.

When implementing enterprise versions of social media applications, a company may exert more control over the computing and networking environment through in-house implementation rather than outsourcing. Consumer-oriented social media applications, such as Facebook and Twitter, reside on application servers outside the enterprise controlled by third-party providers. This creates IG and records management (RM) challenges and poses legal risks.[7]

Obviously, social media is an emerging technology, so standards, design, and architecture are in flux, whereas e-mail has been stable and established for 15 to 20 years. E-mail is a mature technology set, meaning it is unlikely to change much. There are standard e-mail communications protocols, and the technology's use is pervasive and constant. So when e-mail IG policies are formed, less updating and fine-tuning are required over time. With social media, new features are being added, standards are nonexistent, privacy settings change overnight, and the legalese in terms of service agreements is continually modified to include new features and settings, which means that your social media policy must be more closely monitored and frequently fine-tuned.

E-mail, IM, and social media are all communication tools used to share content and collaborate, but social media also offers user interaction features, such as "Like" on Facebook or "retweet" (copying and posting a 140-character tweet) on Twitter, that bring attention to the content in the user's network and can be construed as an endorsement or rejection of content based on user opinions expressed and associated with the content.[8]

Further confounding the organization's ability to control the social media environment is the fact that the social media sites are dynamic and ever changing, with comments and opinions being published in real time. This is not true with e-mail and IM systems, which are more structured, stable, and technologically mature.

Biggest Risks of Social Media

Social media is the Wild West of collaboration and communication. Vulnerabilities still are being exposed, and rules still are being established. Users often are unsure of exactly who can see what they have posted. They may believe that they have posted a comment only for the eyes of a friend or colleague, not realizing it may have been posted publicly. "One of the biggest risks that social networking poses to organizations

Social media differs greatly from e-mail use. E-mail is mature and stable. Social media is not. These distinctions have important ramifications for IG policy development.

is that *employees may be exposing information that's not meant for public consumption*, especially in highly regulated environments like banking and healthcare, in industries that rely heavily on proprietary research and development, or even in the military"[9] (emphasis added).

Organizations that believe they can ban social media in order to avoid risks are mistaken. Prohibition of social media can result in social media use being driven underground. Employees accustomed to the ease of communicating and collaborating through social networks may turn to the use of personal devices and accounts outside the control of the organization. Even strict adherence to a nonuse policy can harm the organization's reputation, finances, ability to gather information that can be used to improve operations, and ability to remain competitive.

Once an organization decides it will engage in social media initiatives, it must identify different types of risks to initiate its IG effort in this area. According to Chris Nerney of *Network World*, two of the greatest social media security threats are:

1. *Lack of a social media policy.* Many organizations are just now discovering the extent to which social media has popped up in various pockets of their organization. They may believe that their e-mail and communications policy will pretty much cover social media use and that it is not worth the time and expense to update IG policies to include social media.

   This invites complexities, vagaries, and potential disaster. A simple Twitter comment could invite litigation: "Our new project is almost ready, but I'm not sure about the widget assembly." It's out there. There is a record of it. *Instant potential liability in 140 characters or less.*

   Social media can add value to an organization's efforts to reach out to customers and other stakeholders, but this must be weighed carefully against the accompanying risks.

   The objectives of a social media initiative must be spelled out, and metrics must be in place to measure progress. But more than that, *who can utilize social media on behalf of the company and what they can state needs to be established with clarity in the IG policy.* If not, employees are essentially flying blindly without controls, and they are more likely to put the enterprise at risk.[10]

   More than policy development is needed. If your organization is going to embark on a social media program, it needs an executive sponsor to champion and drive the program, communicating policy to key leaders. You will also need to conduct training—on a consistent basis. *Training is key, since social media is a moving target.*

2. *Employees—the accidental and intentional insider threat.* This may be in part due to lack of social media policy or due to lack of monitoring and enforcement. Sometimes an employee harms an organization intentionally. Remember Private Bradley Manning's release of hundreds of thousands of classified government documents to WikiLeaks?[11] But *most times* employees do not realize the negative impact of their behavior in posting to social media sites. People might use social media to vent about a bad day at work, but the underlying message can damage the company's reputation and alienate coworkers and clients. Other times a post that is seemingly unrelated to work can backfire and take a toll on business. We're all human and sometimes emotion gets the better of us, before we have rationally thought out the consequences. And that

is especially true in the new world of social media, where it may be unclear exactly who can see a comment.

The dangers of social media are quite different from those posed by an isolated, off-color, or offensive verbal comment made in the workplace, or even one errant e-mail. With social media it is possible that the whole world will be able to see a comment meant only for a limited and controlled audience. For example, consider Ketchum public relations vice president James Andrews, who in 2009 "fired off an infamous tweet trashing the city of Memphis, hometown of a little Ketchum client called FedEx, the day before he was to make a presentation to more than 150 FedEx employees (on digital media, no less!)." FedEx employees complained to Ketchum and their own executives, pointing out that while they suffered salary reductions, money was being spent on Ketchum, which had been clearly disrespectful of FedEx. Andrews was forced to make a "very public and humiliating apology."[12]

This story shows that high-level executives must be just as careful as lower-level employees. Andrews was not only a corporate vice president, but also a public relations, communications, and social media expert, well versed in the firm's policies and mission. He also had no ill intent. Knowing this, consider what a rogue employee intent on damaging the company might do. Such impact could be much worse. For instance, what if a chief executive's assistant were to release details of strategic plans, litigation, or ethics investigations to the public? Or embarrassing details of the CEO's private life? The impact could be quite costly.

Legal Risks of Social Media Posts

With over 554 million active registered users and an estimated average of 58 million tweets per day in 2013 to the microblogging site Twitter,[13] a number that continues to increase, surely some employees in your organization are tweeting. As of the first quarter of 2013, more than 225 million professionals in over 200 countries and territories were members of the LinkedIn network, and the network continues to expand, with students and recent college graduates being the fastest-growing segment. Approximately 33 percent of members are in the United States.[14]

The casual use of public comments can easily create liability for a company. *With no IG policy, guidelines, monitoring, or governance, legal risks of using social media increase significantly. This is an avoidable risk.*

Many people are posting birthday wishes and pictures of what they had for dinner, but others may be venting about specific companies and individuals within those companies. There's a difference between "I can't stand Wall Street," and "Goldman is run by Satan, and his name is John Smith. We're going to sue his butt off." *Instant liability.*

Two of the biggest threats of social media use for organizations come from the lack of a social media policy and threats presented by employee use.

> With no IG policy, guidelines, monitoring, or governance, legal risks of using social media increase significantly. This is an avoidable risk.

The specifics of where and how an employee posted or tweeted a message may mean whether a lawsuit against your company is successful or not. If a personal LinkedIn or Twitter account is used, and it was posted after hours using a PC from home, the company *may* be off the hook. But if it was done using a company computer or network, or from a company-authorized account, a defense will be difficult. Opposing counsel likely will ask questions about the policy for posting first. One thing is true: "Much of this remains unsettled ground."[15]

Just when compliance and records managers thought they had nailed down IG for e-mail, IM, and electronic records, social media came on the scene creating new, dynamic challenges!

Even though not all social media content will rise to the level of a record, according to the definition in use, the organization still may be responsible for managing the nonrecord content. For example, an organization may consider a social networking profile a record but consider comments nonrecords. That decision will have an impact on what must be retained according to the records retentions schedule. It does not, however, absolve the organization from monitoring and evaluating the comments.[16]

"Tweets are no different from letters, e-mail, or text messages—they can be damaging and discoverable, which is especially problematic for companies that are required to preserve electronic records, such as the securities industry and federal contractors. Yet another compliance headache is born."

Blogs are simply Web logs, a sort of online journal that is focused on a particular topic. Blog readers can become followers and receive notices when new content is posted as well as add their own comments, which may be moderated or restricted. It seems confounding, but with the explosion in the use of blogs, there have been actual incidents where employees have "disclosed trade secrets and insider trading information on their blogs. Blogs have also led to wrongful termination and harassment suits."

So the liability and potential for leakage or erosion of information assets is not theoretical; it is *real*.

To safeguard the enterprise that sanctions and supports blog use, *IG policies must be clear, and real-time capture and management of blog posts should be implemented.* Remember, these can be business records that are subject to legal holds, and authenticity and accuracy are crucial in supporting a legal case. So a true and original copy must be retained. This may, in fact, be a legal or regulatory requirement, depending on the industry.

If content-posting guidelines are not clear, then the informal nature of social media posts potentially can be damaging to an organization. The usual fact checking and vetting that is done for traditional press releases and advertising may not be conducted, so social media posts can be unscreened and unfiltered, which poses problems when IG policies are not clear and fully enforced.[17] Beyond that, the consequences of violating policy should be severe and clearly stated in policies, as should the penalties imposed, a message that should be reinforced consistently over time.

Tools to Archive Social Media

New approaches to capture, manage, and archive social media are emerging. Some are free or inexpensive and appropriate for personal and small business use. Others require a more substantial investment of resources but better meet the needs of midsize and large organizations.

Public Social Media Solutions

Launched as a personal cloud organizing service in March 2012, Jolicloud took a file system approach to social media so Facebook, Flickr, Instagram, Picasa, and Twitter content that was previously interacted with or shared could be sorted and searched.[18] The service "slurps" (extracts) content from social media sites and makes it available for viewing through any mainstream Internet browser, tablet, or smartphone. As users perform social media functions like sharing, "liking," and "favoriting" content on their various social media services, the content is automatically saved to their Jolicloud account, which can later be sorted and searched.

Jolicloud has similarities with other "personal social Web memory" products, such as Facebook Timeline and TimeHop. In 2013, Jolicloud added the ability to view and edit files and rebranded its unified cloud platform Jolidrive.[19]

If you prefer to maintain copies of all files on your own computer, an alternative to Jolicloud is a product called SocialFolders. This app lives on your computer and connects directly to your favorite social media sites so you can manage, backup, and sync your photos, videos, and documents in a centralized location.[20]

Since Facebook and Twitter initially did not provide archiving tools, some third-party applications have popped up to perform the task.

TwInbox is a free MS Outlook plug-in that archives Twitter postings and allows users to install a (Twitter) menu option to send tweets directly from Outlook; these tweets are archived into a standard Outlook folder. The folder can be configured to capture tweets that a user sends outside of Outlook, so that everything is stored in one folder.

TweetTake is a free utility that archives followers and tweet posts. It does not require a software download, and the archive can be stored as a zip file and then imported into a spreadsheet (e.g., Excel) for further analysis. By the time this book goes to press, there will be even more options, and the existing ones will have changed and (it is hoped) improved.

If your organization uses Twitter and social media archiving is required by law, regulations, or internal IG policies, a good place to start your research is with software like TwInbox (if you operate in a Microsoft Office environment) and TweetTake as well as other new entrants to the market or other options your organization may have.[21]

For archiving Facebook posts, there are several options. Facebook users can download and archive their Facebook data from their account settings page. Also, there are free plug-ins for Mozilla's Firefox browser. One comes directly from Mozilla, which archives everything but fan pages into a zip file. Another is a Firefox add-on called ArchiveFacebook, which allows you to save Facebook content directly to your hard drive and view the content exactly as it looks on Facebook. Other tools, including SocialSafe, PageFreezer, and Wayback Machine, charge a small fee. All of these options and new ones need to be evaluated when selecting an archiving solution for Facebook that meets your organization's requirements.

For archiving LinkedIn posts and information, SocialSafe, PageFreezer, and Way-back Machine can be used, and other tools will surface.

To convert records to a standard format for use outside of the social media application, there are also options to create PDF documents out of social media posts using products like PDF995 and PrimoPDF.[22] Nuance Software also provides PDFCreate.

Additional archiving tools are being developed as the social media market matures. Bear in mind that tools developed by third parties always carry some risk that tools directly from the software or service provider do not.

These tools may not provide a legally defensible audit trail in court. Choosing among the tools requires a critical analysis and may require additional technology layers. Other alternatives, such as real-time content archiving tools and even in-house developed customizations, also have to be considered.

Government and Industry Solutions

Most of the products and methods that could be of use for personal or small business archiving of social media content involves manual intervention, which can be time consuming. All organizations must focus on their core business and would benefit from tools and services that streamline and automate the archiving process as much as possible—however, there is a cost. Midsize and large organizations, often using both public and enterprise social media technologies, may find the investment in commercial products and services worth the additional cost, especially those products that integrate and manage social media content with other enterprise content. Capture and management of social media content is an area that must be addressed as part of an overall IG strategy. Some of the solutions available at this time are described in Table 13.2; however, because of the recent increased focus on archiving solutions for public and enterprise social media content, the landscape will continue to become more efficient, effective, and possibly *unified*.

In addition to providing archiving functions, unified and integrated solutions provide business intelligence applications and tools to enable the enterprise to better achieve its organizational goals, processes, and performance requirements.

IG Considerations for Social Media

The report "How Federal Agencies Can Effectively Manage Records Created Using Social Media Tools" addresses building an IG framework for social media. An IG model provides the overarching policies, guidelines, and boundaries for social media initiatives.[23]

An IG framework for social media should incorporate social media policy, controls, and operational guidelines as well as spell out consequences for violations. Best practices for social media still are being established, and those that have been established are evolving. In addition to establishing policies to govern the use of social media across the organization, best practices should include industry-specific, vertical market considerations. A cross-section of functional groups within the enterprise should provide input into the policy-making process. At the very minimum, internal audit, marketing, finance, information technology (IT), legal, human resources, and RM must be consulted, and all

Table 13.2   Social Media Archiving and Management Software

Type of Solution	Description	Examples
Archiving solution	Services that capture, protect, and retain social media for compliance, e-discovery, digital preservation, and records management	Archives Social; Smarsh; RegEd by Arkovi
Unified solutions	Services and software that facilitate the management of various file types across the enterprise (e.g., social media, legacy data, word files, SharePoint files) for storage, optimization, e-discovery, compliance, and records management	Unified Archive® by ZL Technologies; Symantec Enterprise Vault; HP Autonomy
Integrated solutions	Services that integrate various types of systems (e.g., customer relationship management in the cloud with social media tools, enterprise content management [ECM], and/or records management) to manage records and information for business operations and compliance.	Microsoft SharePoint 2013 and Yammer (contains social and collaboration features as well as RM and compliance features); Salesforce and Chatter (integrates social collaboration technology and potential to integrate with ECM content repository and ECM Documentum Records Manager).

business units should be represented. Clear roles and responsibilities must be spelled out, and controls must be established to govern acceptable use—essentially what is allowed and what is not. Even writing style, logo format, branding, and other marketing considerations should be weighed. The enterprise's image and brand are at risk, and prudent steps must be taken to protect this valuable, intangible asset. And most important, all legal and regulatory considerations must be folded into the new IG policy governing the use of social media.

Key Social Media Policy Guidelines

Your social media policy development process can begin by examining the published policies of major organizations in your industry or closely related industries. It should also be based on changes in the workplace as well as established standards, such as guidance developed as the result of a January 2013 ruling by the National Labor Relations Board. *More important, social media policies must be hand-crafted and customized for each organization.*

An IG framework for social media should incorporate social media policy, controls, and operational guidelines, and spell out consequences for violations.

A prudent and properly crafted social media policy:

- Specifies who is authorized to create social media accounts for the organization.
- Authorizes specifically who can speak on the organization's behalf and who cannot (by role/responsibility).
- Outlines the types of negative impact on the company's brand and reputation that unscreened, poorly considered posts may have.[24]
- Draws clear distinctions between business and personal use of social media and specifies whether personal access is allowed during work hours.
- Underscores the fact that employees should not have any expectation of privacy when using social media for corporate purposes, just as in using other forms of communications such as e-mail, IM, and voicemail, which may be monitored.
- Clearly states what is proper and allowed on the organization's behalf and what is forbidden in social media posts or using organization resources.
- Instructs employees to always avoid engaging in company-confidential or even controversial discussions.
- Encourages/requires employees to include a standard disclaimer when publishing content that makes clear the views shared are representative of the employee and not the organization.
- Strictly forbids the use of profanity and uses a professional business tone, albeit more informal than in other corporate communications.
- Strictly forbids any statements that could be construed as defamatory, discriminative, or inflammatory.
- Outlines clear punishments and negative actions that will occur to enforce social media policy.
- Draws clear rules on the use of the company name and logo.[25]

The policy need not be long but should be clear. Best Buy's social media policy, for example, uses the slogan, "Be smart. Be respectful. Be human."[26] It then breaks the guidance into two major sections: what you should do and what you should never disclose. A word of caution contained in the Best Buy Social Media Policy explains the rationale for the employee to abide by the social media policy: *Protect the brand, protect yourself.*

To ensure compliance with the organization's IG strategy, it is also necessary to include a reference to the organization's related policies, including the records and information management policy.

Records Management and Litigation Considerations for Social Media

Legal requirements and demands trump all others when making decisions about capturing and preserving social media records. Social media is no different from other forms of **electronically stored information** (ESI) in that it is potentially discoverable during litigation.[27] Not all ESI residing in social media are records, but all are discoverable. If an organization employs social media and makes a conscious decision *not* to archive all or some portion of that data, it is taking risks. A legally defensible records retention schedule must be in place, and it must be based on specific laws that identify the records that must be retained and to a records retention policy that explains the process for identifying, categorizing, and managing information and records.

U.S. corporations that utilize social media are compelled to preserve those records, including metadata and associated linked content, according to Rule 34 of the **Federal Rules of Civil Procedure** (FRCP), which states that opposing parties in litigation may request "any designated documents or ESI—including writings, drawings, graphs, charts, photographs, sound recordings, images, and other data or data compilations—stored in any medium from which information can be obtained either directly or, if necessary, after translation by the responding party into a usable form."[28] This echoes a key principle of the Sedona *Conference®*, a leading RM and legal retention think tank. Also, Rule 26 of the FRCP requires that any and all information that might be discoverable or "potentially responsive" must be preserved and produced if requested by the opposing party. So it is clear that there is a legal duty to preserve social media records.

From an RM perspective, it is critical to consider that social media posts are more than the posts themselves; for legal or compliance purposes, they include metadata and hyperlinks to external content—*and that external content in its native format*—that must also be preserved, preferably in real time. That external content may be a PDF document, a PowerPoint presentation, Web site content, or even a video on YouTube, which would require that video archiving, along with associated metadata, is in place.

To truly capture the necessary content required by law, records and compliance managers must understand how software programs communicate with each other in order to recommend possible solutions to the IT department. One way to preserve the Web-based data of social media applications is to use the application programming interfaces (APIs) that social media providers offer. APIs offer standard "hooks" into an application. Another way, perhaps preferable, is to enlist a service that can capture and archive information from multiple social networks. Further innovations in tools and services that will make capturing these records easier are being developed.

Content found in social media networks can be static or dynamic. Profiles in Facebook and blog posts are examples of static content. They can be captured before being posted to the Web. Blog comments and endorsements through "liking" or "favoriting" a post are examples of dynamic content. The ideal method from a RM standpoint is to capture all dynamic social media content *in real time* in order to be able to prove authenticity and fight claims of records **spoliation** (corruption or adulteration of evidence) in the event of a discovery request.

Regardless of method of capture, social media content that meets record status criteria should be moved to a repository in an **electronic records management**

U.S. corporations must archive social media records under Rule 34 of the FRCP.

Social media policy must be unique to each particular organization.

(ERM) system application. Then business rules for retention should be applied to those records. Typical functions of an ERM system include these:

- Marking an electronic document as a read-only electronic record
- Protecting the record against modification or tampering
- Filing a record against an organizational file plan or taxonomy for categorization
- Marking records as vital records
- Assigning disposal (archival or destruction rules) to records
- Freezing and unfreezing disposal rules
- Applying access and security controls (Security rules may differ from the source electronic document in an electronic document management system or **enterprise content management [ECM] software.)**
- Executing disposal processing (usually an administrative function)
- Maintaining organizational/historical metadata that preserves the business context of the record in the case of organizational change
- Providing a history/audit trail[29]

Robust search capabilities are perhaps the most crucial component of a social media ERM or archiving solution. It is fine to preserve the records and their associated metadata perfectly, but if you cannot easily *find and produce* the information, compliance and e-discovery efforts will fall short and may cost the organization dearly.

Social media policy will be unique to each particular organization. It is fine to start with a social media policy example or template, but it must be tailored to the needs of the organization for it to be effective and legally defensible.[30]

Records Retention Guidelines

Here are some basic records retention guidelines:

- *Make records threshold determinations.* Examine the content to see if it in fact constitutes a record *by your own organization's definition of a record*, which should be contained in your IG policies. This records determination process likely also will require consultation with your legal counsel. If the social media site has not been kept operating, or it was used for a specific project that has been completed (and all pertinent records for that project have been retained), then its content may not require retention of records.[31]
- *Use existing retention schedules if they apply.* If your organization already has retention policies for, say, e-mail, then any e-mail sent by social media should adhere to that same scheduling guideline, unless there is some legal reason to change it.
- *Apply basic content management principles.* Focus on capturing all related content for social media posts, including conversation threads, and associated metadata that may be required in legal discovery to provide context and maintain the completeness, authenticity, and integrity of the records.

- *Risk avoidance in content creation.* Instruct and reinforce the message to employees participating in corporate social media that content on the Web stays there indefinitely and that it carries potential legal risks. In addition, once something is posted on the Web, completely erasing and destroying the content at the end of its retention period is nearly impossible.

Content Control Models

There are several basic ways to manage social media content, ranging from tightly controlling it through one single, accountable person, to delegating control to the business unit level, all the way to letting the social media participants post their thoughts, unmoderated and unfettered, to encourage spontaneity and enthusiastic use of the tool. The approach your organization takes will depend on the specified business objectives you have for utilizing social media and your organization's appetite for risk.

Emerging Best Practices for Managing Social Media Records

Best practices for managing social media business records are still evolving, and will continue to develop as records and information practitioners gain more experience with social media records. Here are some emerging best practices:

- *Identify records during the social media planning stage.* Both a social media policy and the records and information policy should refer to a form to be completed by the person or unit proposing a new social media initiative. The person completing the form should indicate if records will be created and, if so, how they will be managed.
- *Promote cross-functional communications.* A social media team of representatives from various departments, such as IT, social media, legal, compliance, records management, and other stakeholders, is formed, and communication and collaboration is encouraged and supported.
- *Require consultation in policy development.* Extending beyond the social media team, input and advice from multiple stakeholder groups is essential for creating IG policies that cover social media records management.
- *Establish clear roles and responsibilities.* The cross-functional social media team must lay out clear expectations and responsibilities and draw lines of accountability so that stakeholders understand what is expected of them.
- *Utilize content management principles.* Management of social media content should fall under an ECM software implementation, which can capture and track content, including associated metadata and external content, and manage that social media content through its life cycle.
- *Implement RM functionality.* Management by an ERM system that offers features that enable records retention and disposition, implementation of legal holds, and lifting of legal holds is essential.
- *Control the content.* Clear guidelines and monitoring mechanisms must be in place to control and manage content *before* it gets published on the Web, when possible (e.g., static content on blogs and profiles in social networks) if there is any potential legal risk at all.

- *Capture content in real time.* By implementing a real-time content capture solution for content posted directly to social media (e.g., comments on blogs and posting of someone else's content or retweets), organizations will begin their control and management of the content at soonest point and can more easily prove it is authentic and reliable from a legal perspective.
- *Champion search capabilities.* After capture and preservation of records and associated metadata, search capabilities are the single most important feature that the technology must provide.
- *Train, train, train.* Social media is a new and emerging technology that changes rapidly. Users must be trained, and that training must be updated and reinforced on a regular basis so that employees have clear guidelines, understand the technology, and understand the business objectives for its use.

CHAPTER SUMMARY: KEY POINTS

- Organizations are increasingly using social media and Web 2.0 platforms to connect people to companies and government.

- Social media use presents unique challenges because of key differences with other electronic communications systems, such as e-mail and IM.

- Two of the biggest risks that social networking poses to organizations are (1) not having a social media policy; and (2) employees may be—intentionally or not—exposing information that is not meant for public consumption.

- Enterprise social networking software has many of the features of consumer social applications such as Facebook, but with more oversight and control, and they come with analytics features to measure adoption and use.

- Various software tools have become available in recent years for archiving social media posts and followers for RM purposes.

- An IG framework provides the overarching policies, guidelines, and boundaries for social media initiatives, so that they may be controlled, monitored, and archived.

- Social media posts are more than the post itself; they include metadata and also include hyperlinks to external content—and that external content must be preserved in its native format to meet legal standards.

- Robust search capabilities are the most crucial component of a social media ERM or archiving solution.

- Social media policy will be unique to each particular organization.

- Best practices for managing social media business records are still evolving but include forming cross-functional social media teams with clear responsibilities, encouraging communication, and capturing complete content in real time.

Notes

1. U.S. National Archives and Records Administration, NARA Bulletin 2011-02, "Guidance on Managing Records in Web 2.0/Social Media Platforms," October 20, 2010, www.archives.gov/records-mgmt/bulletins/2011/2011-02.html.
2. Ibid.
3. See www.snapchat.com/ (accessed June 3, 2013).
4. See http://vine.com/ (accessed June 3, 2013).
5. Nancy Gohring, "Facebook and Twitter Rule the Enterprise, Too," May 20, 2013, www.citeworld.com/social/21893/facebook-twitter-rule-enterprise (accessed June 4, 2013).
6. Andrew Conry-Murray, "Can Enterprise Social Networking Pay Off?" Internet Evolution, March 21, 2009, www.internetevolution.com/document.asp?doc_id=173854.
7. Patricia C. Franks, "How Federal Agencies Can Effectively Manage Records Created Using New Social Media Tools," IBM Center for the Business of Government, San Jose State University, 2010, www.businessofgovernment.org/sites/default/files/How%20Federal%20Agencies%20Can%20Effectively%20Manage%20Records%20Created%20Using%20New%20Social%20Media%20Tools.pdf, pp. 20–21 (accessed March 30, 2012).
8. Ibid.
9. Paul McDougall, "Social Networking Here to Stay Despite Security Risks," Information Week, May 12, 2011, www.informationweek.com/news/security/privacy/229500138.
10. Chris Nerney, "5 Top Social Media Security Threats," Network World, May 31, 2011, www.networkworld.com/news/2011/053111-social-media-security.html.
11. C. Savage, "Soldier Admits Providing Files to WikiLeaks," New York Times, February 23, 2013, www.nytimes.com/2013/03/01/us/bradley-manning-admits-giving-trove-of-military-data-to-wikileaks.html?ref=bradleyemanning&_r=0 (accessed May 19, 2013).
12. Ibid.
13. Twitter Statistics, Statistic Brain, www.statisticbrain.com/twitter-statistics/ (accessed May 18, 2013).
14. LinkedIn, "About Us," www.linkedin.com/about-us (accessed May 18, 2013).
15. Sharon Nelson, John Simek, and Jason Foltin, "Capturing Quicksilver: Records Management for Blogs, Twittering and Social Networks," Sensei Enterprises, 2009, www.senseient.com/storage/articles/Capturing_Quicksilver.pdf (accessed December 10, 2013).
16. This discussion and the next quotes in this section are from Patricia C. Franks, Records and Information Management (Chicago: American Library Association Neal-Schuman, 2013), p. 179.
17. Sharon Nelson and John Simek, "Mitigating Legal Risks of Using Social Media," Information Management 45, no. 5 (September/October 2011), ARMA International.
18. Liz Gannes, "Saving the Social Web for Later Use: Jolicloud Organizes Everything You've Shared, Liked, and Favorited," March 19, 2012, http://allthingsd.com/20120319/saving-the-social-web-for-later-use-jolicloud-organizes-everything-youve-shared-liked-and-favorited/.
19. Nick Summers, "Jolicloud Rebrands Its Unified Cloud Platform as Jolidrive, Adds the Ability to View and Edit Files," TNW, March 6, 2013, http://thenextweb.com/insider/2013/03/06/jolicloud-rebrands-its-unified-cloud-service-as-jolidrive-adding-the-ability-to-edit-and-view-files/ (accessed May 18, 2013).
20. Social Folders, "About Us," http://socialfolders.me/about-us/ (accessed May 18, 2013).
21. Andy Opsahl, "Backing Up Twitter and Facebook Posts Challenges Governments," Government Technology, January 20, 2010, www.govtech.com/policy-management/Backing-Up-Twitter-and-Facebook-Posts.html?utm_source=related&utm_medium=direct&utm_campaign=Backing-Up-Twitter-and-Facebook-Posts.
22. Ibid.
23. The next discussion is based on Franks, "How Federal Agencies Can Effectively Manage Records."
24. Nelson and Simek, "Mitigating Legal Risks of Using Social Media."
25. Ibid.
26. Best Buy Social Media Policy, http://forums.bestbuy.com/t5/Welcome-News/Best-Buy-Social-Media-Policy/td-p/20492 (accessed December 10, 2013).
27. The next discussion is based on Rakesh Madhava, "10 Things to Know about Preserving Social Media," Information Management (September/October 2011): 34–35, 37. ARMA International.
28. Federal Rules of Civil Procedure, http://www.uscourts.gov/uscourts/rulesandpolicies/rules/cv2009.pdf (accessed 2/20/14).
29. Franks, Records and Information Management, p. 151.
30. Ibid., pp. 36–37.
31. Guidelines here and in the next section are from New York State Archives, "Records Advisory: Preliminary Guidance on Social Media," May 24, 2010, www.archives.nysed.gov/a/records/mr_social_media.shtml.

CHAPTER 14

Information Governance for Mobile Devices*

The use of mobile devices is ubiquitous in today's society. According to CTIA (the Wireless Association), over 326 million mobile devices were in use within the United States as of December 2012.[1] This is a more than 100 percent penetration rate, since many users have more than one mobile device, and usage continues to grow. Citizens of China, India, and the European Union (EU) have even greater mobile phone usage than those in the United States.

Mobile computing has vastly accelerated in popularity over the last decade. Several factors have contributed to this: Improved network coverage, physically smaller devices, improved processing power, better price points, a move to next-generation operating systems (OSs) such as Google's Android and Apple's iOS, and a more mobile workforce have fueled the proliferation of mobile devices.

Mobile devices include laptops, netbooks, tablet PCs, personal digital assistants (PDAs) such as BlackBerries, and smartphones such as Apple's iPhone and those based on Google's Android platform. What used to be simple cell phones are now small computers with nearly complete functionality and some unique communications capabilities. These devices all link to an entire spectrum of public and private networks.

Gartner has estimated that "by 2016, *40 percent of the global workforce will be mobile*, with 67 percent of workers using smartphones"[2] (emphasis added).

With these new types of devices and operating environments come new demands for information governance (IG) policies and unknown security risks.[3] The Digital Systems Knowledge Transfer Network, a UK think tank, found: "The plethora of mobile computing devices flooding into the market will be one of the biggest ongoing security challenges [moving forward]." "With mobile devices connecting to Wi-Fi and Bluetooth networks, there are suddenly many more opportunities [for hackers] to get in and steal personal information."[4]

Due to this rapid shift toward mobile computing, companies with mobile personnel, such as salespeople and service technicians, need to be aware of and vigilant toward these impending security threats, which can compromise confidential information.

Securing mobile devices is critical: A survey by Aberdeen Group, an IT research and analysis firm, estimates that that *data leakage or loss can cost an organization anywhere from $10,600 to over $400,000.*[5]

---

*Portions of this chapter are adapted from Chapter 7, Robert F. Smallwood, *Safeguarding Critical E-Documents: Implementing a Program for Securing Confidential Information Assets*, © John Wiley & Sons, Inc., 2012. Reproduced with permission of John Wiley & Sons, Inc.

The reality is that most mobile devices *are not designed with security in mind*; in fact, some compromises have been made to enable new smartphone operating systems to run on a variety of hardware, such as the Android OS from Google. This is analogous to the trade-offs Microsoft made when developing the Windows OS to run across a variety of hardware designs from many PC manufacturers.

Smartphone virus infections are particularly difficult to detect and thorny to remove. Users may be unaware that all their data is being monitored and captured and that a hacker is waiting for just the right time to use it. Businesses can suffer economic and other damage, such as erosion of information assets or even negative goodwill from a damaged image.

The smartphone market is rapidly expanding with new developments almost daily, each providing criminals with a new opportunity. An International Data Corporation report indicated that "*smartphone sales outpaced PC sales for the first time ever in the fourth quarter of 2010*, with 100.9 million smartphones shipped versus 92.1 million PCs" (emphasis added).[6] The growth in smartphone sales and new services from banks—such as making deposits remotely by snapping a picture of a check—means that there are new and growing opportunities for fraud and identity theft.

Awareness and education are key. *The first line of defense is for users to better understand cybercriminal techniques and to become savvier in their use of information and communications technologies.*

A large part of the battle will be won when biometric authentication technologies (those that use retina, voice, and fingerprint recognition) are mature enough to positively identify a user to ensure the correct person is accessing financial or confidential accounts. Application suppliers are first concerned about functionality and widespread adoption; security is not their top priority. Users must be aware and vigilant to protect themselves from theft and fraud. On a corporate level, organizations must step up their training efforts in addition to adding layers of security technology to safeguard critical electronic documents and data and to protect information assets.

Social engineering—using various ways of fooling the user into providing private data—*is the most common approach criminal hackers use*, and it is on the rise. Machines do their job, and software performs exactly as it is programmed to do, but human beings are the weakest link in the security chain. As usage trends in the direction of a more mobile and remote workforce, people need to be trained as to what threats exist and constantly updated on new criminal schemes and approaches. This training is all part of an overall IG effort, controlling *who* has access to *what* information, *when*, and from *where*.

With more and more sensitive business information being pushed out to mobile devices (e.g., financial spreadsheets, business contracts, strategic plans, etc.) and advancing and evolving threats to mobile the mobile realm, *IG becomes an imperative; and the most important part of IG is that it is done on an ongoing basis, consistently and regularly.* Policies must be reviewed when a new mobile device starts to be utilized, when new threats are uncovered, as employees use unsecured public Wi-Fi networks more and more, and as business operations change to include more and more mobile strategies. Information technology (IT) divisions must ensure their mobile devices are protected from the latest security risks, and users must regularly be apprised of changing security threats and new criminal approaches by hackers.

Mobile device management (MDM) is critical to secure confidential information assets and managing mobile devices. Some available technologies can wipe devices free of confidential documents and data remotely, even after they are lost or stolen. These types of utilities need to be deployed to protect an enterprise's information assets.

Current Trends in Mobile Computing

With the rapid pace of change in mobile computing, it is crucial to convey an understanding of trends, to better know what developments to anticipate and how to plan for them. When a new mobile device or operating system is released, the best thing may be to wait to see what security threats pop up. It is important to understand the direction mobile computing usage and deployment are taking in order to plan and develop IG policies to protect information assets.

From CIOZone.com, here are the top trends in mobile computing:

1. *Long Term Evolution (LTE).* The so-called fourth generation of mobile computing (4G) is expected to be rolled out across North America over the next several years [2013–2015], making it possible for corporate users to run business applications on their devices simultaneously with Voice over IP (VoIP) capabilities.

2. *WiMax* [Worldwide Interoperability for Microwave Access]. As LTE and WiMax networks are deployed in the U.S. through [2013 and beyond], expect to see more netbooks and laptops equipped with built-in radio frequency identification (RFID) and wireless support. [WiMax is protocol for communications that provides up to 40 megabits/second speeds (much faster than Wi-Fi) for fixed and mobile Internet access. The next IEEE 802.16m update will push the speed to up to 1 gigabyte bit/second fixed speeds.]

3. *3G and 4G interoperability.* Sprint has developed a dual mode card which will enable mobile device users to work on both 3G and 4G networks. Other carriers are expected to follow suit.

4. *Smartphone applications.* Third-party software vendors will increasingly make enterprise applications available for smartphones, including inventory management, electronic medical records management, warehousing, distribution and even architectural and building inspection data for the construction industry.

5. *GPS.* Global Positioning Systems (GPS) will increasingly be used to identify end users by their whereabouts and also to analyze route optimization for delivery workers and service technicians.

6. *Security.* As new and different types of mobile devices are introduced, corporate IT departments will find it increasingly challenging to identify and authenticate individual end users. As such, expect to see a combination of improvements in both Virtual Private Network (VPN) software and hardware-based VPNs to support multiple device types.

7. *Antivirus.* As more third-party business applications are made available on smartphones and other mobile devices, CIOs [chief information officers] will also have to be cognizant about the potential for viruses and worms.

8. *Push-button applications.* Let's say a waste disposal truck arrives at an industrial site and is unable to empty a Dumpster because a vehicle is blocking its path. Smartphones will increasingly have applications built into them that would make it possible for the disposal truck driver to photograph the impeding object and route the picture to a dispatcher to document and time-stamp the obstruction.

9. *Supplemental broadband.* As carriers implement LTE and WiMax networks, companies such as Sprint and Verizon are looking at potentially extending wireless broadband capabilities to small businesses which don't have fiber optic or copper connections on the ground. Under this scenario, a small packaging company in New Jersey could potentially be able to receive T-1 level (high-speed) broadband capabilities in regions of the U.S. where it has offices but doesn't have wireline broadband connections.

10. *Solid State Drives (SSDs).* Corporate customers should expect to see continued improvements in the controllers and firmware built into SSDs in order to improve the longevity of the write cycles in notebooks.[7]

Security Risks of Mobile Computing

Considering their small size, mobile computing devices store a tremendous amount of data, and storage capacities are increasing with the continued shrinking of circuits and advancement in SSD technologies. Add to that the fact that they are highly portable and often unsecured and you have a vulnerable mix that criminals can target. Considering how often people lose or misplace their mobile devices daily, and what valuable targets they are for physical theft (this author had a laptop stolen in the Barcelona airport, right from under his nose), and it is clear that the use of mobile devices represents an inherent security risk.

But they do not have to be lost or stolen to be compromised, according to Stanford University's guidelines, which are intended to help mobile computing device users protect the information the devices contain. "*Intruders can sometimes gain all the access they need if the device is left alone and unprotected, or if data is 'sniffed out of the air' during wireless communications*"[8] (emphasis added). The devices can be compromised with the use of keystroke loggers that capture every single entry a user makes. This can be done without the user having any knowledge of it. That means company passwords, confidential databases, and financial data (including personal and corporate credit card numbers) are all at risk.

Securing Mobile Data

The first and best way to protect confidential information assets is to remove confidential, unnecessary, or unneeded data from the mobile device. Confidential data should not be stored on the device unless explicit permission is given by the IT department, business unit head, or the IG board to do so. This includes price lists, strategic plans, competitive information, photo images of corporate buildings or coworkers, and financial data such as tax identification numbers, company credit card or banking details, and other confidential information.

If it is necessary for sensitive data to be stored on mobile devices, there are options to secure the data more tightly, using USB drives, flash drives, and hard drives that have integrated digital identity and cryptographic (encryption) capabilities.

Mobile Device Management

MDM software helps organizations to remotely monitor, secure, and manage devices such as smartphones and tablet PCs.[9] MDM improves security and streamlines enterprise management of mobile devices by providing ways to contact the remote devices individually or en masse to add, upgrade, or delete software, change configuration settings, and "wipe," or erase, data, and make other security-related changes and updates. More sophisticated MDM offerings can manage not only homogenous company-owned mobile devices but also those that employees use in the workplace in a **bring-your-own-device (BYOD)** environment.

The ability to control configuration settings and secure data remotely allows organizations to better manage and control mobile devices, which reduces the risk of data leakage and reduces support costs by providing more uniformity and the ability to monitor enforce company-dictated IG policy for mobile devices.

Key vendors in the MDM marketplace include AirWatch, Apple (Profile Manager) AppSense, BoxTone, Centrify, Citrix, Good Technology, IBM (Endpoint Manager for Mobile Devices), LANDesk, MobileIron, SAP (Afaria MDM), and Symantec (Mobile Management Suite).

Rapid growth is expected in the MDM marketplace, with Gartner projecting that nearly two-thirds of organizations will deploy MDM software by 2018.[10] And Frost & Sullivan projects that "the market for enterprise MDM will grow from $178.6 million in 2011 to $712.4 million by 2018."[11]

Trends in MDM

Six key trends in the MDM marketplace are discussed next.

1. *MDM software expansion and maturity.* Many experts believe that MDM will develop and reach beyond just mobile endpoints to include deep integration with mobile infrastructure and applications (apps).[12] What is important is securing and authenticating data. To ensure that, MDM must expand beyond remote device locking, tracking, and wiping. A more comprehensive life cycle management approach will emerge beginning with the acquisition or introduction of the device into the enterprise network until its retirement or destruction. In addition, monitoring and controlling costs through integrated expense management will likely occur.

2. *Consolidation of MDM major players.* Acquisitions by Citrix, Good Technology, and others signal that fewer but stronger market leaders are likely to emerge.

3. *Cloud-based MDM.* This will become the norm, not the exception, and it will happen quite rapidly.
4. *Emphasis on mobile device policy.* Technology can do only so much—an organization must have its IG policies, processes, and audit practices formalized, tested, and monitored. The IT department must have clear direction on which data and devices to monitor and secure, and employee rights and responsibilities must be clearly delineated and communicated.
5. *Diversifying and expanding mobile monitoring and security.* This means that MDM may go beyond today's mobile devices and include remote instruments and machines that are churning out data in applications, such as process management, transportation management, and enterprise resource management.
6. *Infrastructure consolidation.* The currently disparate pieces, including social computing, mobile computing, and cloud computing, may consolidate and become the new construct for the infrastructure paradigm. This means that tools will emerge to manage all these pieces in a centralized and holistic way.

IG for Mobile Computing

Stanford University's guidelines are a helpful foundation for IG of mobile devices. They are "relatively easy to implement and use and can protect your privacy" and safeguard data "in the event that the device becomes compromised, lost or stolen."[13]

Smartphones and Tablets

- *Encrypt communications.* For phones that support encrypted communication (secure sockets layer [SSL], virtual private network [VPN], hypertext transfer protocol secure [https]), *always configure defaults to use encryption.*
- *Encrypt storage.* Phones approved to access confidential information assets must encrypt their bulk storage with hardware encryption.
- *Password protect.* Configure a password to gain access and or use the device. Passwords for devices that access confidential information assets should be at least seven characters in length and use upper- and lowercase letters as well as some numerical characters. Passcodes should be changed every 30 days.
- *Timeout.* Set the device so that it is locked after a period of idleness or timeout, perhaps as short as a few minutes.
- *Update.* Keep all system and application patches up to date, including mobile OSs and installed applications. This allows for the latest security measures and patches to be installed to counter ongoing threats.
- *Protect from hacking.* Phones approved to access confidential and restricted data must not be jailbroken (hacked to gain privileged access on a smartphone using the Apple iOS) or rooted (typically refers to jailbreaking on a smartphone running the Android OS). The process of rooting varies widely by device. It usually includes exploiting a security weakness in the firmware shipped from the factory. "'Jailbreaking' and 'rooting' removes the manufacturer's protection against malware."
- *Manage.* Phones approved to gain access to confidential information assets must be operating in a managed environment to maintain the most current security and privacy settings, and monitor use for possible attacks.

Portable Storage Devices

These include thumb drives or memory sticks, removable hard drives, and even devices like iPods that are essentially mobile disc storage units with extra bells and whistles.

- *Create a user name and password* to protect the device from unauthorized access—especially if lost or stolen.
- *Utilize encryption* to protect data on devices used to store and/or transport confidential information assets.
- *Use additional levels of authentication and management* for accessing the device, where possible.
- *Use biometric identification* to authenticate users, where possible.

Laptops, Netbooks, Tablets, and Portable Computers

- *Password protect.* This is the most basic protection, yet it is often not used. Create a user name and password to protect the device from unauthorized access; require that they are entered each time the computer is used.
- *Timeout.* Require that the password is reentered after a timeout period for the screensaver.
- *Encrypt.* Laptops, notebooks, or tablets used to access confidential information assets should be required to be encrypted with whole disk encryption.
- *Secure physically.* Physical locks should be used *"whenever the system is in a stationary location for extended periods of times."*

Building Security into Mobile Applications

While it is a relatively new channel, mobile electronic commerce (e-commerce) is growing rapidly, and new software apps are emerging for consumers as well as business and public sector enterprises. These apps are reducing business process cycle times and making the organizations more agile, more efficient, and more productive. Some key strategies can be used to build secure apps.

As is the case with any new online delivery channel, security is at the forefront for organizations as they rush to deploy or enhance mobile business apps in the fast-growing smartphone market. Their priorities are different from those of the software developers churning out apps.

In the banking sector, initially many mobile apps limited customers to a walled-off set of basic functions—checking account balances and transaction histories, finding a branch or automated teller machine location, and initiating transfers—but "a new wave of apps is bringing person-to-person payments, remote deposit capture and bill pay to the mobile channel. Simply, the apps are getting smarter and more capable. *But with those capabilities comes the potential for greater threats"*[14] (emphasis added).

Security experts state that the majority of the challenges that could result from mobile fraud have not been seen before. Mobile e-commerce is relatively new and has not been heavily targeted—yet. But industrial espionage and the theft of trade secrets by targeting mobile devices is going to be on the rise and the focus of rogue competitive intelligence-gathering organizations. User organizations have to be even more proactive, systematic, and diligent in designing and deploying mobile apps than they did with Web-based apps.

Software developers of mobile apps necessarily seek the widest audience possible, so they often deploy them across multiple platforms, which forces some security trade-offs: Enterprises *have to build apps for the "strengths and weaknesses intrinsic to every device, which adds to the security challenges"*[15] (emphasis added).

A side effect of mobile app development efforts from the user perspective is that it can reshape the way users interact with core information management (IM) applications within the enterprise.

The back-office IM systems, such as accounting, customer relationship management, human resources, and other enterprise apps that are driving online and mobile, are the same as before, but the big difference comes in how stakeholders (employees, customers, and suppliers) are interacting with the enterprise. In the past, when deploying basic online applications for browser access, there was much more control over the operating environment; with newer mobile applications running on smartphones and tablets, that functionality has been pushed out to end user devices.

Real Threats Are Poorly Understood

The list of threats to mobile apps is growing, and existing threats are poorly understood, in general. They are just too new, because mobile commerce by downloadable app is a relatively new phenomenon—the Apple iTunes App Store and the Android Marketplace debuted in the second half of 2008. "But that doesn't mean the threat isn't real—even if the app itself is not the problem."[16] The problem could be the unsecure network users are on or a device infection of some sort.

For mobile apps, antivirus protection is not the focus as it is in the PC world; the security effort mostly focuses on keeping malware off the device itself by addressing software development methods and network vulnerabilities. Surely, new types of attacks on mobile devices will continue to be introduced. That is the one thing that can be counted on.

There already have been some high-profile examples of mobile devices being compromised. For example, in 2010:

> New York–based Citibank's iPhone app was found to be storing customers' [private] data on their phones, with obvious privacy implications [and exposing it to theft and fraud]. Meanwhile, Google (New York) has had to pull a number of apps from the Android Marketplace built by an anonymous [criminal] developer who was creating fake bank apps [with realistic and usable features] that attempted to exploit information on users' devices to commit banking and [credit] card fraud.

There are many more examples, but the cited incidents make it imperative to understand the mobile app marketplace itself in order that effective IG policies and controls may be developed, deployed, and enforced. Simply knowing how Google has approached soliciting app development is key to developing an IG strategy for Android devices. Google's relatively open-door approach initially meant that almost anyone could develop and deploy an app for Google Android. Although the policy has evolved somewhat to protect Android users, it is still quite easy for any app developer—well intentioned or malicious—to release an app to the Android Marketplace. This in itself can pose a risk to end users, who sometimes cannot tell the difference between a real app released by a bank and a banking app built by a third party, which may be fraudulent. Apple has taken a more prudent and measured approach by enforcing a quality-controlled approval process for all apps released to its iTunes App Store. Sure, it slows development, but it also means apps will be more thoroughly tested and secure.

Both approaches have their positives and negatives the companies and for the device users. But clearly, Apple's curated and quality-controlled approach is better from a security risk standpoint.

Understanding the inherent strengths and, perhaps more important, weaknesses of specific mobile hardware devices and OS—and their interaction with each other— is key when entering the software design phase for mobile apps.

The development environment is altogether different. Windows programmers will experience a learning curve. Mobile apps under Android or Apple OS operate in a more restricted and less transparent file management environment.

Bearing that in mind—regardless of the mobile OS—*first ensure that data is secured, and then check the security of the application itself.* That is, practice good IT governance to ensure that the software source code is also secure. Malicious code can be inserted into the program; once it is deployed, hackers will have an easy time stealing confidential data or documents.

Innovation versus Security: Choices and Trade-offs

As organizations deploy mobile apps, they must make choices, given the limited or confined software development environment and the need to make agile, intuitive apps that run fast so users will adopt them. To ensure that a mobile offering is secure, many businesses are limiting their apps' functionality. So stakeholder users get mobile access that they didn't have before and a new interface with new functionality, but it is not possible to offer as much functionality as in Web apps. And more security means some sacrifices and choices will need to be made versus speed and innovative new features.

Some of the lessons learned in the deployment of online Web apps still apply to mobile apps. Hackers are going to try social engineering like phishing (duping users into providing access or private information) and assuming the identity of an account holder, bank, or business. They will also attempt man-in-the-middle attacks. (More on that topic soon).

With mobile applications, typically the app is operated directly on a mobile device, such as a smartphone. *This is a key difference between apps and traditional PC-based interfaces that rely on browser access or using basic mobile phone text messaging.* Connecting to a business via app can be more secure than relying on a browser or texting platform, which require an additional layer of software (e.g., the browser, texting platform, or Wi-Fi connection) to execute sensitive tasks. These security vulnerabilities can compromise the safety of information transmitted to a secure site. Thankfully, *if the app is developed in a secure environment, it can be entirely self-contained, and the opportunity to keep mobile data secure is greatest when using the app as opposed to a browser-based platform.*

This is because a mobile app provides a direct connection between the user's device and the business, governmental agency, or e-commerce provider. Some security experts believe that mobile apps potentially could be more secure than browser-based access from the desktop because they can communicate on an app-to-app (or computer-to-computer) level.

In fact, "a customer using a bank app on a mobile network might just be safer than a customer accessing online banking on a PC using an open Wi-Fi connection" that anyone can monitor.

How do you combat this browser-based vulnerability if it is required to access an online interface? *The most effective and simplest way to counter security threats in the PC-based browser environment and to eliminate* man-in-the-browser *or* man-in-the-middle *attacks is to use two different devices* rather than communicate over a standard Internet connection. This approach can be built into IG guidelines.

Consider this: Mobile apps actually can *bring about greater security*. For example, do you receive alerts from your bank when hitting a low-balance threshold? Or a courtesy e-mail when a transaction is posted? Just by utilizing these types of alerts—and they can be applied to any type of software application beyond banking—tech-savvy users themselves can serve as an added layer of protection. If they receive an alert of account activity regularly, they may be able to identify fraudulent activity immediately and take action to counter it and stop it in its tracks, limiting the damage and potential exposure of additional private data or confidential information assets.

Best Practices to Secure Mobile Applications

Mobile computing is not going away; it is only going to increase in the future. Most businesses and governments are going to be forced to deploy mobile apps to compete and provide services customers will require. There is the potential for exposure of confidential data and e-documents, but this does not mean that organizations must shy away from deploying mobile apps.[17] Some proven best practice approaches can help to ensure that mobile apps are secure.

Some steps can be taken to improve security—although there can never be any guarantees— and some of these should be folded into IG guidelines in the policy development process. *BankTech* magazine identified six best practices that can shape an organization's app development process:

1. Make sure your organization or outside development firm uses seasoned application developers who have had secure-coding training and use a *secure software development life cycle* (SDLC).

2. [Developed for banking apps, this approach can be applied to other vertical apps too.] Follow the guidance suggested by the Federal Deposit Insurance Corp. (FDIC FIL-103-2005) regarding authentication in an Internet banking environment. The guidance describes *enhanced authentication methods*, such as multifactor authentication, that regulators expect banks to use when authenticating the identity of customers using the bank's online products and services.

3. Make sure that the customer (or employee) is *required to re-enter his or her credentials after a certain time period* to prevent someone other than the mobile device's owner from obtaining access to private account information.

4. *Hire an information security expert* to assess the security around your mobile application servers. Unfortunately, *an organization's servers are often over-looked* during a risk assessment, as they require a specialized skill set to test them.

5. *Encrypt sensitive data* that is stored on a mobile device and account data that travels from the handset across the Internet. Ensure that the encryption is implemented properly.

6. Hire a security expert *to test the security of a mobile application* before you implement it across your customer base.[18] (Emphasis added throughout.)

Developing Mobile Device Policies

Where do you start? Developing a comprehensive mobile strategy is key before you craft your mobile device policies. You will need input from a variety of stakeholders, and you will need to understand where mobile devices fit in your overall technology infrastructure and strategy. Here are some best practices for developing your mobile device policies.

1. *Form a cross-functional mobility strategy team.* You will need the input of primary stakeholder groups, including IT, field business units, and human resources (for policy creation and distribution). Your strategy development process should also tap into the expertise of your risk management, compliance, records management, and legal departments. The aim will be to balance risks and benefits to improve employee productivity and guard against risk while focusing on the goals and business objectives of the organization.[19]

2. *Clarify goals for your mobile strategy.* Start your discussion with the big picture, the "30,000 foot view" of the business drivers, challenges, threats, and opportunities that mobile computing provides in today's technology context and your business context. Draw a direct line from your mobile business needs to your planned mobile support strategy and infrastructure. Keep your business goals in mind and link them to the discussion.

3. *Drill down into policy requirement details.* You may want to survey other existing mobile device policies to inform your mobility strategy team. Those from peer organizations and competitors will be most relevant. Then start with the basics: which types of devices and OS make sense for your organization to support, what changes and trends are occurring in the technology market-place, which sensitive e-documents and data you must protect (or disallow) on mobile devices, and what available security technologies (e.g. MDM, mobile VPNs, encryption, information rights management) you might deploy. It may be helpful to segment your mobile users into broad categories, and break out a list of their specific business needs related to mobile computing. Your strategy and policies for executives will be somewhat different than those for users in field business units. And you will need BYOD policies if your organization opts to go this route.

4. *Budgeting and expense control.* Is the organization going buy devices and pay all mobile expenses through direct billing each month? What cost controls need

to be in place? Or will mobile device use expenses be reimbursed by a flat rate or by processing expense reports? What about BYOD? Roaming charge limits? Decisions on the financial and cost control aspects of mobile computing use must be made by your mobility policy team, under the guidance of an executive sponsor.

5. *Consider legal aspects and liability issues.* Consult your legal counsel on this. What key laws and regulations apply to mobile use? Where could users run afoul? What privacy and security issues are most prominent to consider? What about the private data that users may hold on their own (BYOD) devices? An overarching consideration is to maintain security for private information and to have a policy in place for data leaks and lost or stolen devices. That includes your policy on remote "wipes" of sensitive data or perhaps *all* data.

6. *Weigh device and data security issues.* Since most mobile devices—especially smartphones—were not designed with security as a foremost consideration, you must take steps to protect your sensitive data and to secure the devices themselves without impeding business or making operation too difficult for the end user. The world of mobile computing presents new challenges that were not present when IT had full control of endpoint devices and internal networks. Clear mobile security policies and controls must be in place.

7. *Develop your communications and training plan.* Users must be apprised and reminded of your mobile device policy if they are going to adhere to it. They also need to know the consequences of violating your policies. Your communications and training plan should be creative—from wall posters to text and e-mail messages, from corporate newsletters to group training sessions. You may want to first pilot your new policy with a small group of users. But communication and training are key: A perfect mobile device policy will not work if it is not communicated properly and users are not trained properly.

8. *Update and fine-tune.* There will be some misses, some places where after your deploy your mobile policy you find room for improvement. You will receive user feedback, which should be considered too. And there will be changes in the technology marketplace and user trends. A program must be in place to periodically (every six months, perhaps) review your mobile device policy and any audit information to make improvements in the policy.

If your organization sanctions the use of mobile devices, you must have a clear, updated IG policy for their use, and you must be able to monitor, test, and audit compliance with the policy. Bear in mind that mobile devices are inherently unsecured and have many vulnerabilities, and you will have to consider possible security threats. If your organization plans to utilize a BYOD approach, your support for mobile devices will be more challenging and complex. Critical to success in leveraging mobile devices is training employees on your IG policy and policy updates and consistently reinforcing the message of cautiousness with confidential company data. If you are using mobile devices to conduct business, there will be business records that are created that must be captured and archived with their integrity and authenticity intact. All information on an employee's smartphone or tablet is potentially discoverable in legal proceedings, so you must include your legal team in policy development and periodic updates. Mobile device use can allow for great productivity gains, but the gains come with associated risks.

CHAPTER SUMMARY: **KEY POINTS**

- The plethora of mobile computing devices flooding into the market will be one of the biggest ongoing security challenges moving forward.

- An IDC report indicated that smartphone sales outpaced PC sales for the first time ever in the fourth quarter of 2010.

- As businesses work to deploy mobile apps, they walk a fine line between innovation and risk. To ensure that a mobile offering is secure, many businesses are limiting their apps' functionality.

- Human beings remain the weakest link in security, particularly with the increasing use of mobile devices. IG policies must be established and employees must be trained to be aware of security and privacy risks.

- Connecting to a business directly via an app can be more secure than relying on a browser or texting platform, which require an additional layer of software.

- Over the next several years North America will be upgrading to 4G networks, faster WiMax will be deployed, and there will be 3G and 4G interoperability.

- MDM software helps organizations to remotely monitor, secure, and manage devices such as smartphones and tablet PCs.

- There will be new enhanced security and antivirus products developed to combat the increasing threat of cyberattacks.

- Mobile computing security challenges require that organizations follow best practices when developing and deploying apps. Some keys are: encrypting sensitive data, using the secure software development life cycle (SDLC) methodology and enhanced authentication methods, and hiring a security expert to test new apps.

- Develop a comprehensive mobile strategy before you craft your mobile device policies. You will need input from a variety of stakeholders, and you will need to understand where mobile devices fit in your overall technology infrastructure and strategy.

Notes

1. CTIA, "Wireless Quick Facts," www.ctia.org/advocacy/research/index.cfm/aid/10323 (accessed May 13, 2013).
2. Alan Joch, "How to Create an Effective Mobile Device Policy," *Biztech*, www.biztechmagazine.com/article/2013/03/how-create-effective-mobile-device-policy, March 26, 2013.
3. "Current Mobile Computing Calls for Security as Powerful as Titanium," http://techreview.blogpool.co.uk/2011/02/10/modern-day-mobile-computing-calls-for-security-as-powerful-as-titanium (accessed March 30, 2012).

4. Warwick Ashford, "Mobility among the Top IT Security Threats in 2011, Says UK Think Tank," *Computer Weekly*, January 7, 2011, www.computerweekly.com/Articles/2011/01/07/244797/Mobility-among-the-top-IT-security-threats-in-2011-says-UK-think.htm (accessed March 30, 2012).

5. Ann All, "Mobile Device Management: 6 Trends to Watch," *eSecurity Planet*, www.esecurityplanet.com/mobile-security/mobile-device-management-6-trends-to-watch.html (accessed February 8, 2013).

6. Matt Gunn, "How to Build a Secure Mobile App," *Bank Systems and Technology*, July 6, 2011, www.banktech.com/risk-management/231001058?itc=edit_stub (accessed December 19, 2011).

7. "Top Ten Trends in Mobile Computing," *CIO Zone*, www.ciozone.com/index.php/Editorial-Research/Top-Ten-Trends-in-Mobile-Computing/2.html (accessed December 19, 2011).

8. Stanford University, "Guidelines for Securing Mobile Computing Devices," www.stanford.edu/group/security/securecomputing/mobile_devices.html (accessed December 19, 2011).

9. Symantec, "Business Challenge: Mobile Device Management," www.symantec.com/mobile-device-management (accessed May 14, 2013).

10. All, "Mobile Device Management: 6 Trends to Watch."

11. Vikrant Gandhi, "U.S. Mobile Device Management (MDM) Market," October 4, 2012, www.frost.com/sublib/display-report.do?ctxixpLink=FcmCtx1&searchQuery=mdm&bdata=aHR0cDovL3d3d y5mcm9zdC5jb20vc3JjaC9jYXRhbG9nLXNlYXJjaC5kbz9xdWVyeVRleHQ9bWRtQH5AU2Vhc-mNoIFJlc3VsdHNAfkAxMzYwMzI5NTg4NTc5&ctxixpLabel=FcmCtx2&id=NB29-01-00-00-00

12. All, "Mobile Device Management: 6 Trends to Watch."

13. Quotes in this section are from Stanford University, "Guidelines for Securing Mobile Computing Devices." www.stanford.edu/group/security/securecomputing/mobile_devices.html

14. Quotations in this section are from Matt Gunn, "How to Build a Secure Mobile App," *Bank Systems and Technology*, July 6, 2011, www.banktech.com/risk-management/231001058?itc=edit_stub (accessed March 30, 2012).

15. Ibid.

16. Ibid.

17. Beau Woods, "6 Ways to Secure Mobile Apps," *Bank Systems and Technology*, May 26, 2011, www.banktech.com/architecture-infrastructure/229700033 (accessed March 30, 2012).

18. Ibid.

19. Joch, "How to Create an Effective Mobile Device Policy."

CHAPTER 15

Information Governance for Cloud Computing*

By Monica Crocker CRM, PMP, CIP, and Robert Smallwood

C loud computing represents one of the most significant paradigm shifts in information technology (IT) history. It may have evolved as an extension of sharing an application-hosting provider, which has been around for a half century and was common in highly regulated vertical industries, such as banks and health care institutions. But cloud computing is a very different computing resource, utilizing advances in IT architecture, system software, improved hardware speeds, and lower storage costs.

The impetus behind cloud computing is that it provides economies of scale by spreading costs across many client organizations and pooling computing resources while matching client computing needs to consumption in a flexible, (nearly) real-time way. Cloud computing can be treated as a utility that is vastly scalable and can be readily modulated, just as the temperature control on your furnace regulates your energy consumption. This approach has great potential, promising on-demand computing power, off-site backups, strong security, and "innovations we cannot yet imagine."[1]

When executives hear of the potential cost savings and elimination of capital outlays associated with cloud computing, their ears perk up. Cloud deployments can give users some autonomy and independence from their IT department, and IT departments are enthused to have instant resources at their disposal and to shed some of the responsibilities for infrastructure so they can focus on business applications. Most of all, they are excited by the agility offered by the on-demand provisioning of computing and the ability to align IT with business strategies more nimbly and readily.

But for all the hoopla and excitement, *there are also grave concerns about security risks and loss of direct IT control*, which call for strict information governance (IG) policies and processes. Managers and IT leaders who are customers of cloud computing services are ultimately responsible for IT performance. A number of critical IG challenges associated with cloud computing must be addressed. These include privacy and security issues, records management (RM) issues, and compliance issues, such as the ability to

---

*Portions of this chapter are adapted from Chapter 12, Robert F. Smallwood, *Managing Electronic Records: Methods, Best Practices, and Technologies*, © John Wiley & Sons, Inc., 2013. Reproduced with permission of John Wiley & Sons, Inc.

respond to legal discovery orders. In addition, there are metadata management and custody challenges to consider. An investigation and analysis of how the cloud services provider(s) will deliver RM capability is crucial to supporting IG functions, such as archiving and e-discovery, and meeting IG policy requirements.

Organizations need to understand the security risks of cloud computing, and they must have IG policies and controls in place for leveraging cloud technology to manage electronic information before moving forward with a cloud computing strategy.

Defining Cloud Computing

The definition of **cloud computing** is, rather, well, *cloudy*, if you will. The flurry of developments in cloud computing makes it difficult for managers and policy makers to define it clearly and succinctly, and to evaluate available options. Many misconceptions and vagaries surround cloud computing. Some misconceptions and questions include:

- "That hosting thing is like SaaS"
- "Cloud, SaaS, all the same, we don't own anything"
- "OnDemand is Cloud Computing"
- "ASP, Hosting, SaaS seems all the same"
- "It all costs the same so what does it matter to me?"
- "Why should I care if it's multi-tenant or not?"
- "What's this private cloud versus public cloud?"[2]

Cloud computing is a shared resource that provides dynamic access to computing services that may range from raw computing power, to basic infrastructure, to fully operational and supported applications.

It is a set of newer information technologies that provides for on-demand, modulated, shared use of computing services remotely. This is accomplished by telecommunications via the Internet or a virtual private network (which may provide more security). It eliminates the need to purchase server hardware and deploy IT infrastructure to support computing resources and gives users access to applications, data, and storage within their own business unit environments or networks.[3] Perhaps the best feature of all is that services can be turned on or off, increased or decreased, depending on user needs.

There are a range of interpretations and definitions of cloud computing, some of which are not completely accurate. Some merely define it as renting storage space or applications on a host organization's servers; others center definitions around Web-based applications like social media and hosted application services.

Someone has to be the official referee, especially in the public sector. The National Institute of Standards and Technology (NIST) is the official federal arbiter of

"Cloud computing encompasses any subscription-based or pay-per-use service that, in (near) real time over the Internet, extends IT's existing capabilities."

definitions, standards, and guidelines for cloud computing. NIST defines cloud computing as:

> a model for enabling convenient, on-demand network access to a shared pool of configurable computing resources (e.g., networks, servers, storage, applications, and services) that can be rapidly provisioned and released with minimal management effort or service provider interaction.[4]

NIST has offered its official definition, but "the problem is that (as with Web 2.0) everyone seems to have a different definition."[5] The phrase "the cloud" has entered the mainstream—it is promoted on prime-time TV—but its meaning and description are in flux: that is, if you ask 10 different people to define it, you will likely get 10 different answers. According to Eric Knorr and Galen Gruman in *InfoWorld*, it's really just "a metaphor for the Internet," but when you throw in "computing" alongside it, "the meaning gets bigger and fuzzier." Cloud computing provides "a way to increase capacity [e.g., computing power, network connections, storage] or add capabilities dynamically on the fly without investing in new infrastructure, training new personnel, or licensing new software. Cloud computing encompasses any subscription-based or pay-per-use service that, in (near) real time over the Internet, extends IT's existing capabilities."[6]

Given the changing nature of IT, especially for newer developments, NIST has stated that the definition of cloud computing "is evolving." People looking for the latest official definition should consult the most current definition available from NIST's Web site at www.nist.gov (and other resources).

Key Characteristics of Cloud Computing

NIST also identifies five essential characteristics of cloud computing:

1. *On-demand self-service.* A [computing] consumer can unilaterally provision computing capabilities, such as server time and network storage, as needed automatically without requiring human interaction with each service's provider.
2. *Broad network access.* Capabilities are available over the network and accessed through standard mechanisms that promote use by heterogeneous thin or thick client platforms (e.g., mobile phones, laptops, and PDAs [personal digital assistants]).
3. *Resource pooling.* The [hosting] provider's computing resources are pooled to serve multiple consumers using a multi-tenant model, with different physical and virtual resources dynamically assigned and reassigned according to

Cloud computing enables convenient, on-demand network access to a shared pool of configurable computing resources that can be rapidly provisioned.

consumer demand. There is a sense of location independence in that the customer generally has no control or knowledge over the exact location of the provided resources but may be able to specify location at a higher level of abstraction (e.g., country, state, or datacenter). Examples of resources include storage, processing, memory, network bandwidth, and virtual machines.

4. *Rapid elasticity.* Capabilities can be rapidly and elastically provisioned, in some cases automatically, to quickly scale out, and rapidly released to quickly scale in. To the consumer, the capabilities available for provisioning often appear to be unlimited and can be purchased in any quantity at any time.

5. *Measured service.* Cloud systems automatically control and optimize resource use by leveraging a metering capability at some level of abstraction appropriate to the type of service (e.g., storage, processing, bandwidth, and active user accounts). Resource usage can be monitored, controlled, and reported, providing transparency for both the provider and consumer of the utilized service.[7]

What Cloud Computing Really Means

Cloud computing growth is expected to continue to climb dramatically. A recent Gartner study shows that the United States is the leader in adopting cloud computing, and the market is expanding rapidly.[8] The cloud computing market is expected to grow 21 percent annually from 2012 to 2016, exceeding $16 billion in 2014 and growing to over $22 billion in 2016.[9]

The use of **service-oriented architecture**—which separates infrastructure, applications, and data into layers—permeates enterprise applications, and the idea of loosely coupled services running on an agile, scalable infrastructure may eventually "make every enterprise a node in the cloud." That is the direction the trend is headed.

A common misconception is that an organization "moves to the cloud." In reality, the organization may decide to transition some specific business applications to the cloud. Those specific business applications are selected because a cloud architecture may offer crucial functions that the internally hosted solution does not or because the internal solution is burdensome to maintain. Some examples of business applications that frequently are moved to the cloud include advertising, collaboration, e-mail, office productivity applications, sales support solutions, customer response systems, file storage, and system backups.

Another common misconception is that if your organization does not decide to migrate to a cloud solution, you are protected from all the dangers of cloud computing. The hard facts are that, for the vast majority of organizations, users are already putting information in the cloud. They are simply using cloud solutions to compensate for

Among metatrends, "Cloud computing is the hardest one to argue with in the long term."

> The idea of loosely coupled services running on an agile, scalable infrastructure should eventually "make every enterprise a node in the cloud."

limitations of the current environment. They may be using Box.com to get at information when working remotely or Dropbox.com to share information with an outside business partner. Or they are using SkyDrive get to documents from their iPad. They may not even realize they have posted company information to a cloud environment, so they do not realize they violated any policy against doing that. To complicate matters, they probably also left a copy of the information within your organization's firewall. Internal users might not realize they are not using the current version, and your records manager does not know another copy is floating around out there. *This is completely ungoverned information in the cloud.* The best defense against it is to deliver solutions for those business needs so that users do not have to find their own.

Cloud Deployment Models

Depending on user needs and other considerations, cloud computing services typically are deployed using one of four models, as defined by NIST:

1. *Private cloud.* This is dedicated to and operated by a single enterprise. This is a particularly prudent approach when privacy and security are key issues, such as in the health care and financial services industries and also for sensitive government or military applications and data. A private cloud may be managed by the organization or a third party and may exist on or off premises.
2. *Community cloud.* Think co-ops, nonprofit organizations, and nongovernmental organizations. In this deployment, the cloud infrastructure is *shared by several organizations* and supports a specific community that has shared concerns (e.g., mission, security requirements, policy, and compliance considerations). It may be managed by the organizations or a third party and may exist on or off premises.
3. *Public cloud.* Open to the public, this cloud can be maintained by a user group or even a fan club. In this case, "the cloud infrastructure is made available to the general public or a large industry group and is owned by an organization selling cloud services."
4. *Hybrid cloud.* This utilizes a combined approach, using parts of the aforementioned deployment models: private, community, and/or public. The cloud infrastructure is a "*composition of two or more clouds*, (private, community, or public) that remain unique entities but are bound together by standardized

> There are four basic cloud computing models: private, public, community, and hybrid (which is a combined approach).

or proprietary technology that enables data and application portability (e.g., cloud bursting for load-balancing between clouds)" (emphasis added).[11]

Security Threats with Cloud Computing

Cloud computing comes with serious security risks—some of which have not yet been uncovered. In planning your cloud deployment, these risks must be borne in mind and dealt with through controls and countermeasures. Controls must be tested and audited, and the actual enforcement must be carried out by management. Key cloud computing security threats are discussed next, along with specific examples and remedial measures that can be taken (fixes). The majority of this information and quotations are from the Cloud Security Alliance.[12]

Information Loss

When information is deleted or altered without a backup, it may be lost forever. Information also can be lost by unlinking it from its indices, deleting its identifying metadata, or losing its encoding key, which may render it unrecoverable. Another way data/document loss can occur is by storing it on unreliable media. And as with any architecture—not just cloud computing—unauthorized parties must be prevented from hacking into the system and gaining access to sensitive data. In general, providers of cloud services have more resources at their disposal than their individual clients typically have.

Examples

- Basic operational failures, such as server or disk drive crashes.
- Data center reliability, backup, and disaster recovery/business continuity issues.
- Implementation of information purging without your approval (e.g., purging all data over three years old without regard to your retention schedule or existing legal holds).

The Fixes

- Agreement by cloud provider to follow standard operating procedures for data backup, archiving, and retention.
- Standard procedures for information purges that require your signoff before they are completed.
- Check your insurance coverage. Are you covered for the costs or liability associated with a breach or loss of information that is stored in the cloud?
- Clear delineation of the process for notifying the client of a security breach or data loss.

Cloud computing carries serious security risks—some of which have not yet been uncovered.

Lack of training on cloud use can lead to users compromising sensitive data.

Information Breaches

Many times damage to information is malicious, while other times damage is unintentional. *Lack of training and awareness, for example, can cause an information user to accidentally compromise sensitive data.* Organizations must have proactive IG policies that combat either type of breach. The loss of data, documents, and records is always a threat and can occur whether cloud computing is utilized or not.

But the threat of data compromise inherently increases when using cloud computing, due to "the number of and interactions between risks and challenges which are either unique to cloud, or more dangerous because of the architectural or operational characteristics of the cloud environment."

Examples

- Lack of **document life cycle security** (DLS) technologies, such as data loss prevention (DLP) and information rights management (IRM) technologies.
- Insufficient **authentication, authorization, and audit** controls to govern log-in access.
- Ineffective encryption and software keys, including lost keys or inconsistent encryption.
- Security challenges related to persistent data or ineffective disposal methods.
- Inability to verify disposal at the end of information lifecycle.

The Fixes

- DLS implementation where needed to protect information from creation to their final disposition.
- Strong **encryption** to protect sensitive data at rest, in use, and in transit.
- IG policies for data and document security during the software application design phase as well as testing and auditing the controls for those policies during live operation.
- Secure storage, management, and document destruction practices.
- Contractual agreement by cloud service providers to completely delete data before storage media are reused by other clients.
- Check your insurance coverage. Are you covered for the costs or liability associated with a breach or loss of information that is stored in the cloud?
- Clear delineation of the process for notifying the client of a security breach or data loss.

The Enemy Within: Insider Threats

Since the advent of the National Security Agency controversy and the slew of examples in the corporate world, the threat of the malicious insider is well known. "*This threat is amplified for consumers of cloud services by the convergence of IT services and customers under*

> It is prudent to investigate the security and personnel screening processes of a potential cloud provider.

a single management domain, combined with a general lack of transparency into provider process and procedure" (emphasis added). It is important to understand your cloud provider's security procedures for its employees: How are they screened? Are background checks performed? How is physical access to the building and data center granted and monitored? What are its remedial procedures for noncompliance?

When these security, privacy, and support issues are not fully investigated, it creates an opportunity for identity thieves, industrial spies, and even "nation-state sponsored intrusion. The level of access granted could enable such an adversary to harvest confidential data or gain complete control over the cloud services with little or no risk of detection."

Examples

- A cloud provider's employee steals information to give or sell to one of your company's competitors.
- Inadequate screening processes (by your company or a cloud provider) can result in the hiring of people with criminal records, granting them access to sensitive information.
- A cloud provider's subcontractor steals information to give or sell to one of your company's competitors.
- A cloud provider's employee allows unauthorized access to data that your company believes is secure in the cloud.
- The physical cloud storage facility lacks security, so anyone can enter the building and access information.

The Fixes

- Implementation of DLP and IRM technologies and related technology sets at all stages of DLS.
- Assessment of suppliers' practices and complete supply chain, especially those services that are subcontracted.
- Screening and hiring requirements (e.g., background checks) for employees as part of contract with cloud provider.
- Transparent policies regarding information security, data management, compliance, and reporting, as approved by the client.
- Clear delineation of the process for notifying the client of a security breach or data loss.

Hacking and Rogue Intrusions

Although cloud computing providers, as a rule, invest heavily in security, they also can be the target of attacks, and those attacks can affect many client enterprises. Providers of cloud infrastructure service (e.g., network management, computing power,

Easy sign-up procedures for cloud services mean that hackers can easily assume multiple identities and carry out malicious attacks.

databases, storage) offer their customers the illusion of unlimited infrastructure expansion in the form of computing, network resources, and storage capacity. Often this is coupled with a very easy sign-up process, free trials (even for anonymous users), and simple activation with a credit card. This is a boon to hackers who can assume multiple identities. Using these anonymous accounts to their advantage, hackers and spammers can engage in criminal operations while remaining elusive.

Examples

- Cloud services providers have often unknowingly hosted malicious code, including Trojan horses, keystroke loggers, bot applications, and other programs that facilitate data theft. Recent examples include the Zeus botnet and InfoStealer.
- Malware can masquerade as downloads for Microsoft Office, Adobe PDFs, or other innocuous files.
- Botnets can infect a cloud provider to gain access to a wide range of data, while leveraging the cloud provider's control capabilities.
- Spam is a perennial problem—each new countermeasure is met with new ways to sneak spam through filters to phish for sensitive data.

The Fixes

- IG policies and monitoring controls must require tighter initial registration and thorough user verification processes.
- IG policies and technologies to combat credit card fraud.
- Total network monitoring, including deep content inspection.
- Requirement that the cloud provider regularly monitor public blacklists to check for exploitation.

Insecure Points of Cloud Connection

By their very nature, cloud computing solutions involve the movement of information. Information moves from a workstation in your network to the cloud, from the cloud to a mobile device user, from an external partner to the cloud and then to one of your workstations, and so on. Further, information may be moved automatically from an application in the cloud to an application you host internally and vice versa. The movement of information complicates the process of securing it, as it now must be protected at the point of origin, the point of receipt, on the device that transmits it, on the device that receives it and at all times when it is in transit.

An **application programming interface** (API) is a way of standardizing the connection between two software applications. APIs are essentially standard hooks that an application uses to connect to another software application—in this case, a system in

> APIs must be thoroughly tested to ensure they are secure and abide by policy.

the cloud. System actions like provisioning, management, orchestration, and monitoring can be performed using these API interfaces.

It comes down to this: A chain is only as strong as its weakest link, so *APIs must be thoroughly tested to ensure that all connections abide by established policy.* Doing this will thwart hackers seeking work-arounds for ill intent as well as valid users who have made a mistake. It is possible for third parties to piggyback value-added services on APIs, resulting in a layered interface that is more vulnerable to security breaches.

Examples

- Anonymous logins and reusable passwords can undermine the security of an entire cloud community.
- Unencrypted transmission or storage and unencrypted verification allow successful man-in-the-middle data theft.
- Rigid basic access controls or false authorizations pose a threat.
- Poor management, monitoring, and recording of cloud logins and activity make it difficult to detect malicious behavior.
- Weak APIs provide opportunities for data compromise.
- Dependency on unregulated API interfaces, especially third-party add-ons, can allow critical information to be stolen as necessary connections are made.

The Fixes

- Utilization of multiple logon authentication steps and strong access controls.
- Encryption of sensitive data during transmission.
- More robust and secure API access control.
- An understanding of the security model of cloud provider APIs and interfaces, including any third-party or organization-created dependencies.
- Understanding how the API impacts associated cloud usage.

Issues with Multitenancy and Technology Sharing

Basic cloud infrastructure is designed to leverage scale through the sharing of components. Despite this, many component manufacturers have not designed their products to function in a multitenant system. Newer architectures will evolve to address this issue.

In the meantime, virtual computing is often used, allowing for multiple instances of an operating system (OS) (and applications) to be walled off from others that are running on the same computer. Essentially, each instance of the OS runs independently, as if it were the only one on the computer. A "virtualization hypervisor mediates access between guest operating systems and the physical compute resources" (like central processing unit processing power). Yet flaws have been found in these hypervisors "that have enabled guest operating systems to gain inappropriate levels of control or influence on the underlying platform"—and therefore indirectly impact

Cloud providers use virtualization heavily and hypervisors may allow intrusions.

the other guest OSs running on the machine. To combat this, "security enforcement and monitoring" of all shared computing resources must be employed. Solid partitions between the guest OSs—known as compartmentalization—should be employed to ensure that one client's activities do not interfere with others running on the same cloud provider. Customers should *never* have access to any other tenant's "actual or residual data, network traffic" or other proprietary data.

Examples

- Joanna Rutkowska's Blue Pill root technique, which describes how an unauthorized user could intercept data by using virtual hardware called a hypervisor. The Blue Pill would be undetectable as long as the host system was functioning properly. Rutkowska also developed a Red Pill, which could detect a Blue Pill hypervisor, allowing the owner to eliminate it.
- Kostya Kortchinksy's CloudBurst is another example of hypervisor exploitation.

The Fixes

- Security IG that leverages best practices for installation, configuration, monitoring, testing, and auditing of cloud computing resources.
- Requirements for monitoring the computing environment for any rogue intrusions or misuse of cloud resources.
- Control and verification of access. Promote a more secure two-factor authentication procedure.
- Enforceable service-level agreements (SLAs) for patching software bugs, addressing data breaches, and fixing vulnerabilities.
- An IG policy that requires regular audits and evaluations to detect weaknesses in cloud security and configuration.

Hacking, Hijacking, and Unauthorized Access

Hacking into accounts to assume the identity of an authorized user has been happening almost since personal e-mail existed. It can be as simple as stealing passwords with a keystroke logger. Attack methods such as social engineering (e.g., phishing), fraud by identity theft, and exploitation of software vulnerabilities are still effective at compromising systems. Most people recycle a few passwords and reuse them for multiple accounts, so once one is breached, criminals can gain access to additional accounts. If login credentials are compromised, a hacker can monitor nearly everything your organization is doing: A less passive hacker might alter or destroy sensitive documents, create false information, or replace your links with fraudulent ones that direct users to sites harboring malware or phishing scams. Once they have control, it can look like *your organization* is the origin of the malicious downloads or information capture. From here, the attackers can assume the good name and reputation of an organization to further their attacks.

Examples

- Examples are widespread in the general population; however, no clear instances of this occurring with cloud services providers are known (as this book goes to press).

The Fixes

- IG policies should clearly state that users and providers should never reveal their account information to anyone.
- An IG policy should require more secure two-factor authentication techniques to verify login identity, where possible.
- Require your cloud services provider to actively monitor and log all activity in order to quickly identify users engaging in fraudulent actions or those that otherwise fail to comply with the client's IG policy.
- Understand, analyze, and evaluate the cloud provider's contract, especially regarding security protocols. Negotiate improved terms in SLAs to improve or enhance security and privacy.

Who Are Your Neighbors?

Knowing your neighbors—those who are sharing the same infrastructure with you—is also important, and, as we all know, good fences make good neighbors. If the cloud services provider will not or cannot be forthcoming about who else is sharing its infrastructure services with your organization and this becomes a significant issue, you may want to insert contract language that forbids any direct competitor from sharing your servers. These types of terms are always difficult to verify and enforce, so moving to a private cloud architecture may be the best option.

Examples

- The Internal Revenue Service (IRS) utilized Amazon's Elastic Compute Cloud service. When the IRS asked Amazon for a certification and accreditation (C&A) report, Amazon declined. (Note: The C&A process was developed to help ensure compliance with NIST standards and mandated by the Office of Management and Budget, which oversees Federal Information Security Management Act of 2002 compliance.)
- Heartland, a payment processing corporation, suffered a data breach in 2008. Hackers stole account details for over 100 million credit and debit cards. This data was stored on Heartland's network, which the hackers broke into using information (pertaining to employees, corporate structure, company networks, and related systems) it had stolen in the weeks leading up to the major breach.

It is important to know what other clients are being hosted with your cloud services provider, as they may represent a threat. Moving to a private cloud architecture is a solution.

The Fixes

- An IG policy that requires full disclosure of activity and usage logs, and related information. Audit the policy for compliance.
- Investigate the architecture of your cloud services provider (e.g., version levels, network OSs, firewalls, etc.).
- Robust and vigilant supervision, logs, and reporting of all system activity, particularly requesting expansive and detailed reports on the handling of sensitive information.

Additional IG Threats and Concerns

A primary selling point of cloud computing is that enterprises are freed up to focus on their core business rather than being focused on providing IT services. Modulating computer hardware and software resources without making capital expenditures is another key advantage. Both of these business benefits allow companies to invest more heavily in line-of-business activities and focus on their core products, services, and operations. However, the security risks must be weighed against the financial and operational advantages. Further complicating things is the fact that cloud deployments often are enthusiastically driven by advocates who focus inordinately on potential benefits and do not factor in risk and security issues. Additional examples of IG concerns are listed next.

- Lack of clarity about who owns the information (and if that changes at any point).
- Risk of association with any larger failures of the cloud provider.
- Inability of the cloud services provider to manage records *at the file level.*
- Inability to closely *follow the user's retention schedule* and produce certificates of destruction at the end of the information life cycle. This may result in information that is held for too long and ends up costing the client unnecessary expense if it is deemed to be responsive to litigation or other legal action.
- Lack of RM functionality in many cloud-based applications. This problem is not unique to cloud platforms, but the key difference is that internal storage resource systems may have functionality that supports integration with a RM solution. It is unlikely that a cloud provider will provide the option of integrating your in-house RM system with its system. Too many potential security, access control, and performance issues may result.
- Inability to *implement legal holds* when litigation is pending or anticipated.
- *Poor response time*—inability to deliver files quickly and in line with user expectations.
- *Limited ability to ensure your cloud provider meets your duties to follow regulations related to the governance of your information.*
- Jurisdiction and political issues that may arise due to the fact that the cloud provider resides outside of the client's geographic region.
- Storage of personally identifiable information (PII) on servers in Europe or other locales that *prohibit or restrict the release of PII back to the United States* (or home country of the cloud services client organization).[13]

An analysis of an organization's exposure to risk *must* include checking on software versions and revision levels, overall security design, and general IG practices. This includes updating software, tools, and policy, as needed.

Finally, for each of these challenges, "IG policies and controls to secure information assets" and "IG policies and controls to protect the most sensitive documents and data" are a key part of the solution.

Benefits of the Cloud

The risks and security vulnerabilities of cloud computing have been reviewed in this chapter—so much so that perhaps some readers wondering whether cloud computing really is worth it. The answer is a *qualified* yes—it can be, based on your organization's business needs and computing resource capabilities. Besides the obvious benefit of getting your company out of the IT infrastructure business and back to focusing on its real business goals, there are many benefits to be gained from cloud computing solutions.

Some of the specific benefits offered by cloud computing solution are listed next.

- Cloud computing solutions provide a means to support bring-your-own-device (BYOD) initiatives. As long as users have an Internet browser and Internet connectivity, they can use any device to access an application deployed in the cloud.
- Your workers need to be able to access corporate information via a mobile device. Some cloud solutions allow them to access information stored in a secure location that only requires a smart phone and a login. Some of these solutions can even ensure that the information is not actually stored on the device itself. Entire applications, such as expense reporting, can be deployed this way and incorporate mobile capture technology as well.
- Cloud computing solutions provide a mechanism to support collaboration with external business partners. You need to exchange information with an outside business partner in a manner that e-mail just will not support. For instance, you want to create one copy of the information that anyone on your team or on a business partner's team can access and that reflects any updates or changes on an ongoing basis. Or you need to exchange files that are large or in a format that is prohibited by your e-mail servers. And you do not want to grant partners access to information within your firewall and they do not want to grant you access to information within theirs. A third-party cloud-based file-sharing solution may provide the answer. You can post files there, partners can access them, you can update them as necessary, and everyone always has access to the most current version of the information without compromising security to your network.
- A cloud file storage solution provides a better alternative to remote information access than having users copy information to unsecured removable media or send an e-mail to their personal e-mail account. Again, it prevents duplication of information, provides access to the most current version of information, and stores information in an environment that only authenticated users can access.
- Cloud computing solutions also can form a key part of your organization's disaster recovery/business continuity strategy. If your data center is rendered inoperable, users still can access applications and information hosted by cloud

providers. Most cloud providers have redundant data centers so that even if one of their data centers was affected by the same incident that rendered your data center inaccessible, all your information is available. Many organizations deploy solutions to back up their in-house applications to a cloud-based storage provider for just this reason. It is a way to provide geographic diversification.

The business benefits of cloud computing may largely outweigh the security threats for the vast majority of enterprises, so long as they are anticipated and the preventive actions described are taken.

Managing Documents and Records in the Cloud

The National Archives and Records Administration has established guidelines for creating standards and policies for managing an organization's e-documents records that are created, used, or stored in cloud computing environments.

1. Include the Chief Records Management Officer and/or lead RM staff in the planning, development, deployment, and use of cloud computing solutions.

2. Define which copy of records will be declared as the organization's record copy and manage these in accordance with information governance policies and regulations. . . . Remember, the value of records in the cloud may be greater than the value of any other set because of indexing or other reasons. In such instances, this added value may require designation of the copies as records.

3. Include instructions for determining if records in a cloud environment are covered under an existing records retention schedule.

4. Include instructions on how all records will be captured, managed, retained, made available to authorized users, and retention periods applied.

5. Include instructions on conducting a records analysis, developing and submitting records retention schedules to an organization's central records department for unscheduled records in a cloud environment. These instructions should include scheduling system documentation, metadata, and related records.

6. Include instructions to periodically test transfers of records to other environments, including departmental servers, to ensure the records remain portable.

7. Include instructions on how data will be migrated to new formats, operating systems, etc., so that records are readable throughout their entire life cycles. Include in your migration planning provisions for transferring permanent records in the cloud to central records.

8. Resolve portability and accessibility issues through good records management policies and other data governance practices. Data governance typically addresses interoperability of computing systems, portability of data (able to move from one system to another), and information security

and access. However, such policies by themselves will not address an organization's compliance and information governance demands and requirements.[14]

IG Guidelines for Cloud Computing Solutions

A set of guidelines aimed at helping you leverage cloud computing in a way that meets your business objectives without compromising your IG profile is presented next.

1. As with any technology implementation, it is critical that you define your business objectives first, then select the provider that best meets your business objectives—provided, of course, it can meet your IG requirements. This is consistent with applying a proven IT project management methodology to the initiative. Even though the solution may reside outside your environment, the same basic phases for your project approach still apply, especially for those tasks related to documentation.

2. As part of the project documentation, make sure to identify roles and responsibilities related to the system in at *least* the same level of detail you do for internally supported systems (preferably in more detail).

3. The biggest deviation from your standard approach is the need to incorporate the investigation and application of the appropriate fixes described in the "Security Threats with Cloud Computing" section into your project plan. Again, as with any service contract, it is helpful to involve a good contract negotiator. The contract negotiation phase is when you have the most influence with your provider. Therefore, you have the greatest chance of mitigating potential risks and optimizing the benefits if you can incorporate specific requirements into the contract language.

4. If the cloud computing paradigm is relatively new to your organization, try to figure out approaches to issues and high-level processes that can be reused in subsequent cloud computing projects. For instance, during the course of your project, you need to figure out:
   - How to migrate information, including metadata, to the cloud solution.
   - How to get your information, including metadata, back if you quit using that solution.
   - How to implement a legal hold.

Utilizing cloud computing resources provides an economic way to scale IT resources which allows more focus on core business operations. It can render significant business benefits, but its risks must be carefully weighed, and specific threats must be countered, in the context of a long-range cloud deployment plan.

Most cloud services providers do not have mass content migration or RM capabilities.

CHAPTER SUMMARY: **KEY POINTS**

- Cloud computing represents a paradigm shift in computing capabilities. It can streamline operations and cut costs but because it also has inherent risks, a well-researched and documented IG policy is needed.

- Organizations need to understand cloud computing's security risks and formulate IG policies and controls before deploying it.

- Organizations are rapidly moving applications and storage to the cloud. Cloud computing allows users to access and use shared data and computing services via the Internet or a VPN.

- Five key characteristics of cloud computing are: (1) on-demand self-service, (2) broad network access, (3) resource pooling, (4) rapid elasticity, and (5) measured service.

- Cloud computing services typically are deployed using one of four models: (1) private cloud, (2) public cloud, (3) community cloud, and (4) hybrid cloud.

- Utilizing cloud computing carries significant security risks, which can be offset by establishing IG policies and preventive measures so that the business benefits of agility and reduced cost may be exploited.

- Cloud application services may have weaknesses related to supporting RM functions, such as: the inability to manage records at the file level; the inability to closely follow the user's RM retention schedule, the inability to migrate data and documents to other platforms for preservation, and the inability to enforce legal holds when litigation is pending or anticipated.

Notes

1. Cloud Security Alliance, "Top Threats to Cloud Computing V1.0," March 2010, https://cloudsecurity-alliance.org/topthreats/csathreats.v1.0.pdf, p. 6.
2. R. "Ray" Wang, "Tuesday's Tip: Understanding the Many Flavors of Cloud Computing and SaaS," March 22, 2010, http://blog.softwareinsider.org/2010/03/22/tuesdays-tip-understanding-the-many-flavors-of-cloud-computing-and-saas/.
3. NARA Bulletin 2010-05, "Guidance on Managing Records in Cloud Computing Environments," September 8, 2010, www.archives.gov/records-mgmt/bulletins/2010/2010-05.html.
4. Peter Mell and Tim Grance, "NIST Definition of Cloud Computing," Version 15, 10-07-09, www.nist.gov/itl/cloud/upload/cloud-def-v15.pdf (accessed December 12, 2013).
5. Knorr and Gruman, "What Cloud Computing Really Means."
6. Ibid.
7. Mell and Grance, "NIST Definition of Cloud Computing."
8. Gartner Press Release, "Gartner Says Worldwide Public Cloud Services Market to Total $131 Billion," February 28, 2013, www.gartner.com/newsroom/id/2352816 (accessed October 11, 2013).
9. This and the next quotes in this section are from Louis Columbus, "451 Research: Cloud-Enabling

Technologies Revenue Will Reach $22.6B by 2016," September 26, 2013, http://softwarestrategies-blog.com/2013/09/26/451-research-cloud-enabling-technologies-revenue-will-reach-22-6b-by-2016/ (accessed October 11, 2013).

10. It's a long-running trend with a far-out horizon. But among big metatrends, cloud computing is the hardest one to argue with in the long term. (emphasis added).

11. All definitions are from Mell and Grance, "NIST Definition of Cloud Computing."

12. Cloud Security Alliance, "Top Threats to Cloud Computing V1.0."

13. Gordon E. J. Hoke, CRM, e-mail to author, June 10, 2012.

14. NARA Bulletin 2010-05, "Guidance on Managing Records in Cloud Computing Environments."

CHAPTER 16

SharePoint®
Information
Governance*

By Monica Crocker, CRM, PMP, CIP,
edited by Robert Smallwood

Microsoft's SharePoint® server product dramatically altered the content and records management (RM) markets. Previous to SharePoint, solutions were somewhat cumbersome, managed large quantities of documents, and required extensive implementation effort for each business application. SharePoint provided an enterprise level platform for the remaining small-volume, ad hoc solutions.

At a basic level, it is a collaboration platform, but it is often leveraged to be a content repository as well. If properly implemented, SharePoint can reduce duplication of information, automate business processes, serve up a common lexicon for categorizing information, provide a social media platform, give users access to current and historical e-documents, dramatically reduce network traffic loads (by cutting the number of e-mails with attachments), and stop the growth of shared drives. It can also provide a secure platform to support bring-your-own-device (BYOD) mobile programs and other mobile solutions.

Given all its stated capabilities, SharePoint can be used to help organizations govern their information. But, in order to achieve those benefits, the implementing organization must take a structured approach to the deployment of its SharePoint environment. The 2006 amendment to the U.S. Federal Rules of Civil Procedure require American organizations to produce any and all "electronically stored information that is relevant, not privileged, and reasonably accessible." Similar legal requirements exist in Canada, the United Kingdom and Europe, Australia, and other developed countries. Information stored in SharePoint often is included in the "relevant" information that must be produced. *So SharePoint should be deployed in a manner that makes all information contained within it findable, accessible, securable by a legal hold notification (LHN) and available for production in a timely manner.*

For SharePoint deployments, an ounce of prevention truly is worth a pound of cure. Since every SharePoint environment includes corporate information, organizations can avoid a lot of headaches and future **information governance** (IG) risks if they invest time and deliberation in *planning* how they will deploy SharePoint. These plans should be based on the business objectives for SharePoint that are tied to the

---

*Portions of this chapter are adapted from Chapter 14, Robert F. Smallwood, *Managing Electronic Records: Methods, Best Practices, and Technologies,* © John Wiley & Sons, Inc., 2013. Reproduced with permission of John Wiley & Sons, Inc.

organization's overall business objectives and include making all the necessary IG policy decisions *before* rolling out the solution to users.

SharePoint itself is a tool; it is not a panacea for poor IG, and simply deploying it will not resolve business issues or compliance problems. When it comes to managing business records, "Like any RM solution, SharePoint alone will not solve your needs unless it is used to support clearly defined [business] processes."[1] Therefore, IG policy development and business process analysis are critical in the planning process.

SharePoint often is expected to perform content management and records management, and also support e-discovery requests and legal holds. But sometimes, instead of solving records and IG problems, they become worse in an ungoverned SharePoint environment, since users often:

- Do not understand which SharePoint content (documents, discussions, announcements, lists) should be managed as a record.
- Are not clear on when or how to declare content a business record (and as a result make either everything a record or nothing a record).
- Simply replicate their existing file share folder structure, creating a new (often redundant) set of disorganized documents on SharePoint.
- Do not know how to attach well-defined metadata to information to make it findable in the long term.
- Do not understand how to apply appropriate security restrictions to information.

The unacceptable result of this lack of governance is that, instead of being a platform that can positively transform business processes, SharePoint actually can make it *more difficult* for people to do their jobs. And if users decide that SharePoint is actually making their work harder, they will begin to revert back to old, familiar (disorganized) ways of managing their information. In other words, they may continue to keep duplicate documents on their local C drives, go back to their existing shared drives, and keep sharing information by attaching documents to e-mails.

The **SharePoint governance model** should make it clear *where and how users should both store and find information.* A well-governed SharePoint environment provides enough consistency in how information is categorized to support sorting and filtering of search results so that users can quickly narrow results to the specific information or documents they need.

But keep in mind that a SharePoint governance model *needs to be tailored to your organization.* It will not work if it does not fit with your culture, technology standards, and staffing resources.

There is no such thing as one set of SharePoint governance best practices that every organization can adopt. Rather, developing a SharePoint governance model involves determining the appropriate answer to a series of questions regarding your organization's business goals, resource limitations and policy constraints. Once the initial plan is developed, it should be validated against a broad sample of use cases for the system.

Process Change, People Change

As with any initiative that requires behavior change or additional effort, *you will encounter resistance.* The nature of the resistance will depend on the culture of your organization and the personalities of the individuals involved. Some of the

As with any initiative that requires behavior change or additional effort, you will encounter resistance when implementing a new SharePoint system.

SharePoint-specific objections you should be prepared to counter include the premise that nothing in SharePoint is a record or that the very nature of SharePoint dictates that it should just be turned on and allowed to spread virally. Others are that "Users won't follow those procedures" and "Governance is too much of a burden to the user." And then, of course, there is all the standard user resistance to any system change implementation.

Too many organizations deploy SharePoint *without* putting the necessary effort into planning how this technology tool will be governed. *The result is similar to what is often found with e-mail or network shared drives*—scattered information and documents with no organization or governing policies. Only the situation is *worse*, because SharePoint has more types of content and quickly collects an even greater volume of information. At the highest level, all these types of content are part of SharePoint: sites, pages, libraries, and lists. And there are many subtypes within each of these content types. For instance, the list content type includes announcements, calendars, contacts, tasks, discussions, issues, surveys, and custom lists. And the site content type includes "MySites," which allows users to store a vast array of content, including their own documents (which could be personal and/or work related) and social content, such as tags and ratings of content on other sites.

Another contributing risk factor for SharePoint is that, to a large degree, it is self-provisioned. This means that, while the environment typically is deployed by central information technology (IT) staff, business users usually are given the authority to create new repositories for information within that environment without IT intervention. This allows SharePoint to function as a dynamic collaboration platform.

Because of its nature, in an ungoverned SharePoint environment, you may have:

- *Information chaos* because there is no way to identify who owns specific information, no context for information, and no consistent organization or hierarchy to information.
- *Orphaned information*, which results when the individual who understood the context of the information leaves the organization or when the site, page, list, or library is no longer in use.
- *Redundant information.* If no one knows *who* should put *what* on SharePoint, multiple users may upload the same new document to a dozen different locations, and users have no way to identify the "authentic" version of a piece of information when multiples are found.
- *Unfindable information*, which results when everyone decides for themselves how to secure a given piece of information and if and how to tag it with metadata. Then no one can find anything outside the sphere of the information they control or know if they have found everything in a search.
- *Noncompliant retention.* The organization cannot apply any records retention periods to information if there is no means to determine which records series applies to specific information.

Lack of governance can significantly diminish the business value and increase the risk of your SharePoint deployment.

- *E-discovery risk.* Ungoverned information limits the means to narrow the list of potentially responsive information, requiring the organization to find and review *a lot* of information in response to an e-discovery request.
- *Inappropriate use.* Lack of governance means the organization is at risk from individuals or teams deciding to use SharePoint in a way that may not be appropriate or legally defensible.

In sum, *lack of governance can significantly diminish the business value and increase the risk of your SharePoint deployment.*

This is more than a mess. It is a *costly* mess, because the organization is not achieving the maximum business benefit from SharePoint. Further, retrieving information during e-discovery for legal proceedings will be fraught with search and retrieval challenges and will be more costly and less efficient.

However, even if you have already started your SharePoint project or need to deploy before you feel your governance model is complete, you still can implement some IG strategies. That is, late is better than never, and gradual implementation of governance is better than none at all.

Where to Begin the Planning Process

As with any well-managed project, *the first step in a SharePoint deployment is to draft a **project charter** that defines the scope, budget, timeline, and business objectives* for your SharePoint environment.

The next step is to draft a **project schedule** that includes *copious* amounts of time for the up-front planning effort necessary to create the SharePoint Governance Model. Have the project **executive sponsor** sign off on this timeline so that he or she understands that the project will include time to think through key issues prior to deployment and why that is critical for your organization.

Then assemble your governance team. Include someone who understands the organization's culture and the business objectives for SharePoint (such as a business analyst), someone who understands the technical aspects of SharePoint (like a system administrator), someone who understands the compliance aspects of SharePoint (such as a compliance officer, records manager, or legal counsel), and someone who can help

Critical to success in SharePoint deployments is consulting with users about their processes and needs.

Governance decisions can be very controversial and require documentation.

implement the training and communications plan (perhaps from the human resources department). And, most important, make sure your governance team has the necessary authority level to determine the governance approach.

The SharePoint governance model planning process necessarily involves consulting with users about their collaboration, business process, document usage, and information storage needs. If the governance structure interferes with their ability to do their jobs, users will start creating and storing documents without knowing what rules to follow, or why the rules exist, and they will find their own work-arounds to satisfy their business requirements. For instance, if you restrict file size requirements too much, users still will store large files somewhere—perhaps unsecured in the cloud. If you do not allow certain file types and users need them, they will find another place to store them where they might be difficult for other users to find. And soon you will have all sorts of variations of folder and file systems and scattered documents and information, which results in the aforementioned information chaos scenario.

Regulatory and compliance factors also must be incorporated into SharePoint governance decisions for most organizations. Therefore, the process must include RM staff for guidance on crucial RM issues and legal staff for legal and compliance requirements.

Finally, create a formal SharePoint governance model "document." Do not rely on meeting notes or design documents to reflect the decisions made during governance discussions, though it may be valuable to keep those as a way to retain the reasoning and decision paths that led to the final model. *Governance decisions can be controversial, so the governance model selected should be explicitly stated in a dedicated document and officially "approved" by the appropriate stakeholders.*

Begin at a High Level

Start from a high level, with strategy and corporate governance issues. *Develop a problem statement in your project charter so that you know what you are trying to accomplish,* and then develop measureable, time-constrained business objectives so progress and success toward milestones can be measured. Next, be sure to align these objectives with your organization's overall vision statement or strategic plan. Aligning the technology with business considerations is key to a successful SharePoint deployment.

First, develop a problem statement and formulate business objectives for the SharePoint deployment. Then align those objectives with your overall Strategic Plan.

In order to identify specific business objectives for SharePoint, you may find it useful to conduct some focus group sessions with thought leaders from across the organization. Some examples of questions you might ask are listed next:

- How do you find information owned by your unit?
- How do you share information within your team?
- How do you find information owned by other units?
- How do you share information with other teams?
- How do you find expertise to assemble a project team?
- How do you find expertise to perform a single task?
- How do you exchange information with external business partners?
- What processes are particularly painful?
- How comfortable would you be sharing information with others in your unit? With others outside your unit?
- How would you like to connect with others in your organization?

Look for these themes in survey responses that might apply to your organization:

- It is difficult to find information without prior knowledge of its existence and location.
- It is difficult to find personnel resources with specific expertise (a **subject matter expert**).
- It is difficult to determine whether a given piece of information is the current version.
- The organization relies heavily on e-mail to create, share, and manage information. Therefore, the effort spent managing e-mail is burdensome.
- Most document creation processes included review and approval steps among multiple users, which slow down critical business processes.
- Users are struggling to find a way to communicate outside their immediate work group, but they have strong motivation to do so.
- It takes too long to onboard a new employee.
- Users want solutions that provide seamless access for remote workers.

Understanding the organization's current information management challenges allows the SharePoint governance team to identify business objectives for SharePoint and ensure that each individual governance decision supports accomplishment of the business objectives while at the same time supporting compliance with IG policy.

Once business objectives are formed, use them to define the **guiding principles** for the SharePoint governance model. It is prudent to lay out the guiding principles early in the governance document, since they provide a framework for everything that follows. Decision categories that can help shape the guiding principles are:

- *Required or optional.* Is this governance model a "mandated" approach or just "recommendations"? The answer must be clear to users, and enforcement actions against violations must be taken if governance is mandated.
- *Appropriate use.* What are the rules for SharePoint usage? For instance, you could declare that SharePoint is for business information only so that users know it is not OK to run their fantasy football league on a SharePoint site.

- *Information access policy.* Clarify your organization's philosophy about access to information; is it open to every authenticated user by default, or is it strictly secured and available on a need-to-know basis only? As a compromise, sites could be open to all by default, with secured information as an exception.
- *Accountability.* Who is accountable for information and managing governance at a site level?
- *Level of control.* Clarify how tightly SharePoint will be managed. This might range from rigid control, where a typical user can publish only information that has gone through a review process; to "semicontrolled," which permits superusers to create libraries and lists; to very loosely controlled, where site owners in the business are given complete site collections to manage according to their needs.
- *Information ownership.* Since users come and go and site administrators are very often administrative staff with little authority, information ownership must be clearly defined (e.g., the responsibility of the manager or director of a business unit).

Each of these guiding principles should be linked to any appropriate organizational policy or applicable law. In addition, they all should be linked to the business objectives for SharePoint. For instance, this could be a guiding principle:

Every site and page in SharePoint must have a clearly identified owner and a backup owner.

This sets a standard for the project team to follow, which helps end users identify the authoritative copy of information and addresses the governance issue regarding orphaned content.

Establish Scope

After business objectives are formed and sharpened and guiding principles are established, determine the *scope* of the SharePoint deployment: Just where are the boundaries of information you are going to govern? Any governance model likely will cover sites and pages and documents. But will it also include specific types of content, such as calendar items, announcements, discussions, and lists? Which specific documents will be governed in SharePoint (all/only those declared "records"/ only those that are flagged as "final")? How will documents be managed in the different stages of their life cycle (delete anything that has not been modified for a year/move anything declared final to an archive)? How will your organization address e-discovery requirements? Which document and content types are *not* governed in SharePoint? For instance, some organizations govern down to the

> Once business objectives are formed, use them to define the guiding principles for the SharePoint governance model.

> Be sure to clearly state the selection criteria for storing information in SharePoint.

"X" level (e.g., three levels deep in the site structure) but not below. Some choose to manage content on MySites while others simply impose a storage size limit on MySites.

These are the types of questions you should be asking, not only from an IG perspective but also to optimize future system performance of SharePoint. Better processes and fewer documents means faster performance when you are in the heat of the business battle.

Your governance model needs to address the two issues related to scope:

1. *Describe the scope of SharePoint as a technology solution.* In terms of the scope of SharePoint itself, document whether it is purely for internal use or whether it also includes external access, whether MySites are deployed, and which existing systems it was designed to replace, if applicable. Add any other information you can about what is included when you refer to "the SharePoint solution" in your organization, such as interfaces with other systems

2. *Define the scope of the governance model.* In your description of the scope of the governance model, you should enumerate whether governance applies to all types of sites, all types of content, all users, or some subset of those; and who has the authority to change the scope of SharePoint governance.

Exactly *what* information will be stored and managed in SharePoint? And, of that, which information or documents rise to the level of being records?

The selection criteria for storing information in SharePoint must be clear to all system users and administrators. They need to know not only what file sizes are allowed but also what file formats are permitted—or prohibited—as well as size limits for lists, libraries, and the entire site itself.

Policy Considerations

You must determine how your organization's IG policies relate to SharePoint. Microsoft has structured SharePoint so that every piece of information is a "content type." In addition, the tool allows you to configure RM policies/actions at various levels in the system; you can set them at a site collection level, a site level, a library or list level, or all the way down to the specific item level. Every particular instance of every content type could have a retention schedule and resulting actions associated with it, but that might be a lot of overhead for very little payback. *What do you manage and what do you not manage?* Examples of things you might *not* manage are work flow configurations, views, searches, and page templates. Examples of things you probably want to manage are documents and lists.

Your IG policy section should answer these questions:

- How is each type of content in SharePoint governed?
- Who decides what gets governed?
- At what point in the information's SharePoint existence is a governance action taken?

Any existing retention schedules must be translated into defensible disposition policies within your SharePoint environment. Finally, *specific processes for managing business records* must be established.

For instance, if your SharePoint charter identified "sharing administrative information such as meeting agendas and minutes" as a primary objective of your deployment, you could create standard libraries for "administrative" documents on each division's site, create an "administrative record" content type to categorize any document in that library, and associate the retention policy for that content to all those documents. This method would automate the purging of all administrative documents after the retention period has expired.

At some point in the SharePoint governance model document, you also need to address if and how you going to use document IDs and how major and minor versions of information are used and retained. For example, you could decide not to keep any previous versions of meeting agendas but to keep previous versions of policies for a number of years after they are superseded with new versions. The IG policy section is a good place for those items.

Roles and Responsibilities

Clear roles and their associated responsibilities for contributing to, maintaining, and utilizing the information in SharePoint must be established during the governance planning process. Only by spelling out who is responsible for what are you able to expect that your SharePoint environment will continue to follow the governance model.

Questions to ask with regard to definition of roles and responsibilities include these:

- Who is the executive sponsor for the solution?
- Who "owns" the system (and what does "ownership" entail)?
- Who is the sponsor/steward for a specific site or site collection?
- Who owns the information in the site?
- Who is responsible for completing the initial deployment of a site or collection?
- Who is responsible for day-to-day administration of the site?
- Who defines and sets up various information architecture components, such as content types, columns (metadata), and the term store (enterprise taxonomy)?
- Who is responsible for controlling access to a site? For making changes to security access as users' roles change or as users are terminated?
- Who will train super users and users initially? On an ongoing basis?
- Who will contribute information?
- Who will be allowed to view and/or edit information?

Some examples of possible SharePoint roles within a given organization are listed next.

- Executive sponsor
- Information owner or "steward" for a site or site collection
- Site owner
- Site member
- Site contributor
- Site visitor
- System administrator
- Site collection administrator
- Business analyst
- Training, education, and user support
- Information architect/taxonomist
- IG representative

The roles and responsibilities section of the SharePoint governance model will need to describe how users can request a site and how they get support for their sites, including the support escalation process. For this purpose, a **service-level agreement** (SLA) that outlines the basic support levels, time frames, problem escalation processes, cost allocations, and other issues related to service is useful. Wherever possible, create an SLA and refer to it so that users have clear expectations regarding how long it will take them to get a new site or get support for an existing site.

Establish Processes

Guiding principles provide the "what" of SharePoint governance. Roles and responsibilities define the "who." The governance model, or a separate set of procedures referenced by the model, also needs to describe the "how" of governance. Most important, it should detail the process of requesting and creating SharePoint sites. Also critical, the model must include a process for decommissioning sites. Further, as the ownership of the site may change in the future, the process of transferring site ownership must be established and standardized. In addition, more specific processes, such as those for migrating information into SharePoint, must be created. If a business record is created, you need a process to manage it accordingly, whether that is by sending it to a central records repository to complete its life cycle or by managing it in the library where it originated. When legal holds are required, standard processes must be established to produce information requested during e-discovery. A demonstrated ability to produce trustworthy information—information that can be proven to be authentic and unaltered—is an absolute requirement. All these processes must be designed to be as efficient and low cost as possible.

> While guiding principles provide the "what" of SharePoint Governance, roles and responsibilities provide the "who"—that is, who can store information, access it, and make changes to the system.

Your training plan needs to recognize that a given individual may fill more than one role on different SharePoint sites.

Training Plan

A well-defined training model as part of your SharePoint governance plan shows that your organization gave users the rules about SharePoint usage and the necessary tools to comply with those rules.

The training section of your SharePoint governance model should break down the overall training strategy: train everyone, just train site owners, or simply refer users to training resources. This section should explain the process for requesting training. It also should describe or include a reference to a detailed training plan. The training plan describes the ways training will be delivered and how training content will be created. It should include a level of detail sufficient to identify the different types of training (site owner training, information custodian training, user training, basic training, advanced training, etc.). As you define the training plan, remember that any given individual may fill more than one role; one person might be an owner on one site, a contributor on another, and a reader on many. So the training plan should allow people to get all the training they need, without having to endure the same training modules (such as "Introduction to Our SharePoint environment") multiple times.

An important training consideration is that SharePoint is a popular technology right now, and individuals with SharePoint skills are hot commodities in the marketplace. Therefore, in order to eliminate any single points of failure in your SharePoint roles, make sure to cross-train key roles to ensure that more than one person can perform critical functions.

Communication Plan

Your communication plan for SharePoint governance needs to take into account that you are asking people to change the fundamental way in which they manage much of the core information they use to do their work. So your communication plan needs to clearly state that the proposed SharePoint governance model:

- Is *good* for the organization as a whole, not just for IT or the compliance office.
- Makes it easier for team members to manage and find the information they need to do their jobs.

Your communication plan needs to recognize that you are asking people to change the fundamental way they access and manage documents.

An understanding of the SharePoint governance model should make it clear to users what the organization intends to do with SharePoint: the business drivers behind the deployment. It also should be very clear what users are expected to do and the training they will receive so that they can work well in the SharePoint environment. Every person assigned a SharePoint role should be able to review the communications regarding governance and understand how, exactly, it will impact them.

CHAPTER SUMMARY: **KEY POINTS**

- As with any initiative that requires behavior or attitude change, you will encounter resistance when implementing IG within SharePoint.

- Lack of governance can significantly diminish the business value and increase the risk of your SharePoint deployment.

- Critical to success in most SharePoint deployments is an understanding of the business objectives for the solution and how those map to the organization's strategic plan.

- Your SharePoint governance model needs to be tailored to your organization.

- Governance decisions can be very controversial and require documentation.

- First, develop a problem statement and formulate business objectives for the SharePoint deployment. Then align those objectives with your overall strategic plan.

- Once business objectives are formed, use them to define the guiding principles for the SharePoint governance model.

- While guiding principles provide the "what" of SharePoint governance, roles and responsibilities provide the "who"—that is, who can store information, access it, and make changes to the system.

- Be sure to clearly state the selection criteria for storing information in SharePoint.

- Your communication plan needs to consider that you are asking people to change the fundamental way they access, share and manage documents.

- A well-designed SharePoint governance model can help your organization achieve its IG objectives and can contribute to the achievement of business objectives.

Note

1. Don Lueders, "It's All About the Processes," June 18, 2009, http://sharepointrecordsmanagement.com/2009/06/18/its-all-about-the-processes/.

PART FIVE

Long-Term Program Issues

CHAPTER 17

Long-Term Digital Preservation*

By Charles M. Dollar and Lori J. Ashley

Every organization—public, private, or not for profit—now has electronic records and digital content that it wants to access and retain for periods in excess of 10 years. This may be due to regulatory or legal reasons, a desire to preserve organizational memory and history, or entirely by operational reasons. But *long-term continuity of digital information does not happen by accident*—it takes information governance (IG), planning, sustainable resources, and a keen awareness of the information technology (IT) and file formats in use by the organization, as well as evolving standards and computing trends.

Defining Long-Term Digital Preservation

Information is universally recognized as a key asset that is essential to organizational success. Digital information, which relies on complex computing platforms and networks, is created, received, and used daily to deliver services to citizens, consumers and customers, businesses, and government agencies. Organizations face tremendous challenges in the 21st century to manage, preserve, and provide access to electronic records for as long as they are needed.

Digital preservation is defined as long-term, error-free storage of digital information, with means for retrieval and interpretation, for the entire time span the information is required to be retained. *Digital preservation applies to content that is born digital as well as content that is converted to digital form.*

Some digital information assets must be preserved permanently as part of an organization's documentary heritage. Dedicated repositories for historical and cultural memory, such as libraries, archives, and museums, need to move forward to put in place trustworthy digital repositories that can match the security, environmental controls, and wealth of descriptive metadata that these institutions have created for analog assets (such as books and paper records). Digital challenges associated with records management affect all sectors of society—academic, government, private and not-for-profit enterprises—and ultimately all citizens of all developed nations.

---

*Portions of this chapter are adapted from Chapter 17, Robert F. Smallwood, *Managing Electronic Records: Methods, Best Practices, and Technologies*, © John Wiley & Sons, Inc., 2013. Reproduced with permission of John Wiley & Sons, Inc.

Digital preservation is defined as long-term, error-free storage of digital information, with means for retrieval and interpretation, for the entire time span that the information is required to be retained.

The term "preservation" implies permanence, but it has been found that electronic records, data, and information that is retained for only 5 to 10 years is likely to face challenges related to storage media failure and computer hardware/software obsolescence. A useful point of reference for the definition of "long term" comes from the International Organization for Standardization (ISO) standard 14721, which defines long-term as "long enough to be concerned with the impacts of changing technologies, including support for new media and data formats, or with a changing user community. Long Term may extend indefinitely."[1]

Long-term records are common in many different sectors, including government, health care, energy, utilities, engineering and architecture, construction, and manufacturing. During the course of routine business, thousands or millions of electronic records are generated in a wide variety of information systems. Most records are useful for only a short period of time (up to seven years), *but some may need to be retained for long periods or permanently.* For those records, organizations must plan for and allocate resources for preservation efforts to ensure that the data remains accessible, usable, understandable, and trustworthy over time.

In addition, *there may be the requirement to retain the metadata associated with records even longer than the records themselves.*[2] A record may have been destroyed according to its scheduled disposition at the end of its life cycle, but the organization still may need its metadata to identify the record, its life cycle dates, and the authority or person who authorized its destruction.

Key Factors in Long-Term Digital Preservation

Some electronic records must be preserved, protected, and monitored over long periods of time to ensure they remain authentic, complete, and unaltered and available into the future. Planning for the proper care of these records is a component of an overall records management program and should be integrated into the organization's **information governance** (IG) policies and technology portfolio as well as its privacy and security protocols.

Total capability for properly ensuring access to authentic electronic records over time, (in addition to the challenges of technological obsolescence), is a sophisticated combination of policies, strategies, processes, specialized resources, and adoption of standards.

Most records are useful for only a short period of time, but some may need to be retained for long periods or permanently.

Enterprise strategies for sustainable and trustworthy digital preservation repositories have to take into account several prevailing and compound conditions: the complexity of electronic records, decentralization of the computing environment, obsolescence and aging of storage media, massive volumes of electronic records, and software and hardware dependencies.

The challenges of managing electronic records significantly increased with the trend of decentralization of the computing environment. In the centralized environment of a mainframe computer, prevalent from the 1960s to 1980s but also in use today, it is relatively easy to identify, assess, and manage electronic records. This is not the case in the decentralized environment of specialized business applications and office automation systems, where each user creates electronic objects that may constitute a formal record and thus will have to be preserved under IG polices that address record retention and disposition rules, processes, and accountability.

Electronic records have evolved from simple text-based word processing files or reports to include complex mixed media digital objects that may contain embedded images (still and animated), drawings, sounds, hyperlinks, or spreadsheets with computational formulas. Some portions of electronic records, such as the content of dynamic Web pages, are created on demand from databases and exist only for the duration of the viewing session. Other digital objects, such as electronic mail, may contain multiple attachments, and they may be threaded (i.e., related e-mail messages linked in send-reply chains). These records cannot be converted to paper or text formats for preservation without the loss of context, functionality, and metadata.

Electronic records are being created at rates that pose significant threats to our ability to organize, control, and make them accessible for as long as they are needed. This continued volume increase includes documents that are digitally scanned or imaged from a variety of formats to be stored as electronic records.

Electronic records are stored as representations of bits—1s and 0s—and therefore depend on software applications and hardware networks for the entire period of retention, whether it is 3 days, 3 years, or 30 years or longer. As information technologies become obsolete and are replaced by new generations, the capability of a specific software application to read the representations of 1s and 0s and render them into human-understandable form will degrade to the point that the records are neither readable nor understandable. As a practical matter, this means that the readability and understandability of the records can never be recovered, and there can be serious legal consequences.

Electronic records are being created at rates that pose significant threats to our ability to organize, control, and make them accessible for as long as they are needed.

Storage media are affected by the dual problems of obsolescence and decay. They are fragile, have limited shelf life, and become obsolete in a matter of a few years. *Mitigating media obsolescence is critical to long-term digital preservation* (LTDP) because the bitstreams of 1s and 0s that comprise electronic records must be kept "alive" through periodic transfer to new storage media.

In addition to these current conditions associated with technology and records management, organizations face tremendous internal **change management** challenges with regard to reallocation of resources, business process improvements, collaboration and coordination between business areas, accountability, and the dynamic integration of evolving recordkeeping requirements. Building and sustaining the capability to manage digital information over long periods of time is a shared responsibility of all stakeholders.

Threats to Preserving Records

A number of known threats may degrade or destroy electronic records and data:

- *Failure of storage media.* Storage media is inherently vulnerable to errors and malfunction, including disk crashes. Solid-state drives (SSD) largely address these concerns, as there are no moving parts and data can be stored without needing electrical power.
- *Failure of computer systems.* Computer hardware has moving parts and circuits that deteriorate and fail over time, at an average rate called mean time between failure. Some failures are complete and irrecoverable, and some are minor and can be fixed with no loss of data. Computer software is prone to bugs and malware that can compromise the safekeeping of data.
- *Systems and network communications failures.* A small number of network communications is likely to contain errors or misreads, especially undetected checksum errors, which may impact the authenticity of a record. Network errors can occur from changes or redirection of URLs, and any communication over a network is subject to intrusions, errors, and hackers.
- *Component obsolescence.* As hardware, software, and media age, they become obsolete over time, due to the continued innovation and advances by the computer industry. Sometimes obsolescence is due to outdated component parts, changes in software routines, or changes in the hardware to read removable media.
- *Human error.* People make mistakes, and they can make mistakes in selecting, classifying, storing, or handling archived records. Some of these errors may be detected and can be remedied; some go unnoticed or cannot be fixed.
- *Natural disaster.* Hurricane Katrina is the clearest U.S. example of how a natural disaster can interrupt business operations and destroy business records, although in some instances, damaged records were able to be recovered. Floods, fires, earthquakes, and other natural disasters can completely destroy or cause media or computer hardware/software failures.
- *Attacks.* Archived electronic records are subject to external attacks from malware, such as viruses and worms, so preserved records must be scanned for malware and kept separate from external threats. Preserved records also can be subject to theft or damage from insiders, such as the theft of historical ra-

Threats to LTDP of records can be internal or external, from natural disasters, computer or storage failures, and even from the financial viability of an organization.

dio recordings by a National Archives And Records Administration employee, which was reported in 2012. Proper monitoring and auditing procedures must be in place to detect and avoid these types of attacks.

- *Financial shortfall.* It is expensive to preserve and maintain digital records. Power, cooling and heating systems, personnel costs, and other preservation-associated costs must be budgeted and funded.
- *Business viability.* If an organization has financial or legal difficulties or suffers a catastrophic disaster, it may not survive, placing the preserved records at risk. Part of the planning process is to include consideration of successor organization alternatives, should the originating organization go out of business. [3]

The impact on the preserved records can be gauged by determining what percentage of the data has been lost and cannot be recovered or, for the data that can be recovered, what the impact or delay to users may be.

It should be noted that threats can be interrelated and more than one type of threat may impact records at a time. For instance, in the event of a natural disaster, operators are more likely to make mistakes, and computer hardware failures can create new software failures.

Digital Preservation Standards

The digital preservation community recognizes that open standard technology-neutral standards play a key role in ensuring that digital records are usable, understandable, and reliable for as far into the future as may be required.

There are two broad categories of digital preservation standards. The first category involves systems infrastructure capabilities and services that support a trustworthy repository. The second category relates to open standard technology-neutral file formats.

Digital preservation infrastructure capabilities and services that support trustworthy digital repositories include the international standard **ISO 14721:2003**, 2012 **Space Data and Information Transfer Systems—Open Archival Information System (OAIS)—Reference Model**, which is a key standard applicable to LTDP.[4]

The fragility of digital storage media in concert with ongoing and sometimes rapid changes in computer software and hardware poses a fundamental challenge to ensuring access to trustworthy and reliable digital content over time. Eventually, every digital repository committed to LTDP must have a strategy to mitigate computer technology obsolescence. Toward this end, the Consultative Committee for Space Data Systems developed an **Open Archival Information System** (OAIS) reference model to support formal standards for the long-term preservation of space science data and information assets. OAIS was not designed as an implementation model.

The OAIS Reference Model defines an archival information system as an archive, consisting of an organization of people and systems that has accepted the responsibility to preserve information and make it available and understandable for a designated community (i.e., potential users or consumers), who should be able to understand the information. Thus, the context of an OAIS-compliant digital repository includes producers who originate the information to be preserved in the repository, consumers who retrieve the information, and a management/organization that hosts and administers the digital assets being preserved.

OAIS encapsulates digital objects into information packages. Each information package includes the digital object content (a sequence of bits) and representation information that enables rendering of an object into human usable information along with **preservation description information** (PDI) such as provenance, context, and fixity.

The OAIS Information Model employs three types of information packages: a **submission information package** (SIP), an **archival information package** (AIP), and a **dissemination information package** (DIP). An OAIS-compliant digital repository preserves AIPs and any PDI associated with them. A SIP encompasses digital content that a producer has organized for submission to the OAIS. After the completion of quality assurance and transformation procedures, an AIP is created, which is the focus of preservation activity. Subsequently, a DIP is created that consists of an AIP or information extracted from an AIP customized to the requirements of the designated community of users and consumers.

The core of OAIS is a functional model that consists of six entities:

1. *Ingest* processes the formal incorporation (in archival terms, *accession*) of submitted information (i.e., a SIP) into the digital repository. It acknowledges the transfer, conducts quality assurance, extracts metadata from the SIP, generates the appropriate AIP, and populates PDI and extracted metadata into the AIP.

2. *Archival storage* encompasses all of the activities associated with storage of AIPs. They include receipt of AIPs, transferring AIPs to the appropriate storage location, replacing media as necessary, transforming AIPs to new file formats as necessary, conducting quality assurance tests, supporting backups and business continuity procedures, and providing copies of AIPs to the access entity.

3. *Data management* manages the storage of description and system information, generates reports, and tracks use of storage media.

4. *Administration* encompasses a host of technical and human processes that include audit, policy making, strategy, and provider and customer service, among other management and business functions. OAIS administration connects with all of the other OAIS functions.

5. *Preservation planning* does not execute any preservation activities. Rather, it supports a technology watch program for sustainable standards, file formats, and software for digital preservation, monitoring changes in the access needs of the designated community, and recommending updated digital preservation strategies and activities.

6. *Access* receives queries from the designated community, passes them to archival storage, and makes them available as DIPs to the designated community.

Figure 17.1 displays the relationships between these six functional entities.[5]

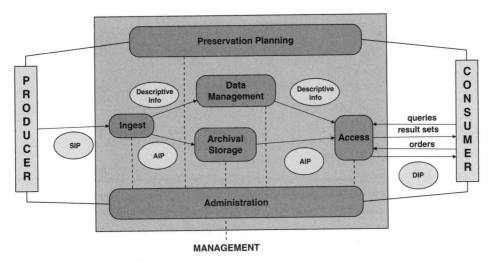

Figure 17.1   Open Archival Information System Reference Model

In archival storage, the OAIS reference model articulates a migration strategy based on four primary types of AIP migration that are ordered by an increasing risk of potential information loss: refreshment, replication, repackage, and transformation.[6]

1. *Migration refreshment* occurs when one or more AIPs are copied exactly to the same type of storage media with no alterations occurring in the packaging information, the content information, the PDI, or the AIP location and access archival storage mapping infrastructure.
2. *Migration replication* occurs when one or more AIPs are copied exactly to the same or new storage media with no alterations occurring in the packaging information, the content information, and the PDI. However, there is a change in the AIP location and access archival storage mapping infrastructure.
3. *Migration repackage* occurs when one or more AIPs are copied exactly to new storage media with no alterations in the content information and the PDI. However, there are changes in the packaging information and the AIP location and to the access to the archival storage mapping infrastructure.
4. *Migration transformation* occurs when changes in bitstreams result when a new content encoding procedure replaces the current encoding procedure (e.g., Unicode representation of A through Z replaces the ASCII representation of A through Z), a new file format replaces an existing one, or a new software application is required to access and render the AIP content.

OAIS is the lingua franca of digital preservation. The international digital preservation community has embraced it as the framework for viable and technologically sustainable digital preservation repositories. *An LTDP strategy that is OAIS-conforming offers the best means available today for preserving the digital heritage of all organizations, private and public.*

An OAIS-conforming LTDP strategy is the best way to preserve an organization's digital heritage.

ISO TR 18492 (2005), Long-Term Preservation of Electronic Document-Based Information

ISO 18492 provides practical methodological guidance for the long-term preservation and retrieval of authentic electronic document-based information, when the retention period exceeds the expected life of the technology (hardware and software) used to create and maintain the information assets. It emphasizes both the role of open standard technology-neutral formats in supporting long-term access and the engagement of IT specialists, document managers, records managers, and archivists in a collaborative environment to promote and sustain a viable digital preservation program.

ISO 18492 takes note of the role of ISO 15489 but does not cover processes for the capture, classification, and disposition of authentic electronic document-based information. Ensuring the usability and trustworthiness of electronic document-based information for as long as necessary in the face of limited media durability and technology obsolescence requires a robust and comprehensive digital preservation strategy. ISO 18492 describes such a strategy, which includes media renewal, software dependence, migration, open standard technology-neutral formats, authenticity protection, and security:

- *Media renewal.* ISO 18492 defines media renewal as a baseline requirement for digital preservation because it is the only known way to keep bitstreams of information based on electronic documents alive. It specifies the conditions under which copying and reformatting of storage media and storage devices should occur.
- *Open standard technology-neutral formats.* The fundamental premise of ISO 18492 is that open standard technology-neutral formats are at the core of a viable and technologically sustainable digital preservation strategy because they help mitigate software obsolescence. ISO 18492 recommends the use of several standard formats, including: eXtensible Markup Language (XML), Portable Document Format/Archival (PDF/A), tagged image file format (TIFF), and Joint Photographic Experts Group (JPEG).
- *Migrating electronic content.* ISO 18492 recommends two ways of migrating electronic content to new technologies. The first relies on backwardly compatible new open standard technology-neutral formats that are displacing existing ones. Generally, this is a straightforward process that typically can be executed with minimal human intervention. The second involves writing computer code that exports the electronic content to a new target application or open standard technology-neutral format. This can be a very labor-intensive activity and requires rigorous quality control.
- *Authenticity.* ISO 18492 recommends the use of hash digest algorithms to validate the integrity of electronic content after execution of media renewal activities that do not alter underlying bit streams of electronic content. In

ISO 18492 provides practical methodological guidance for the long-term preservation of e-documents when the retention period exceeds the expected life of the technology that created it.

instances where bitstreams are a result of format conversion, comprehensive preservation metadata should be captured that documents the process.

- *Security.* ISO 18492 recommends protecting the security of electronic records by creating a firewall between electronic content in a repository and external users. In addition, procedures should be in place to maintain backup/disaster recovery capability, including at least one off-site storage location.

ISO 16363 (2012)—Space Data and Information Transfer Systems—Audit and Certification of Trustworthy Digital Repositories

ISO 14721 (OAIS) acknowledged that an audit and certification standard was needed that incorporated the functional specifications for records producers, records users, ingest of digital content into a trusted repository, archival storage of this content, and digital preserving planning and administration. *ISO 16363 is this audit and certification standard.* Its use enables independent audits and certification of trustworthy digital repositories and thereby promotes public trust in digital repositories that claim they are trustworthy. To date only a handful of ISO 16363 test audits have been undertaken; additional time is required to determine how widely adopted the standard becomes.

ISO 16363 is organized into three broad categories: organization infrastructure, digital object management, and technical infrastructure and security risk management. Each category is decomposed into a series of primary elements or components, some of which may be more appropriate for digital libraries than for public records digital repositories. In some instances there are secondary elements or components. An explanatory discussion of each element accompanies "empirical metrics" relevant to that element. The "empirical metrics" typically include high-level examples of how conformance can be demonstrated. Hence, they are subjective high-level conformance metrics rather than explicit performance metrics.

Organizational infrastructure[7] consists of these primary elements:

- *Mission statement* that reflects a commitment to the preservation of, long-term retention of, management of, and access to digital information
- *Preservation strategic plan* that defines the approach the repository will take in the long-term support of its mission

ISO 16363 is an audit and certification standard organized into three broad categories: organization infrastructure, digital object management, and technical infrastructure and security risk management.

- *Collection policy* or other document that specifies the types of information it will preserve, retain, manage, and provide access to
- *Identification and establishment of the duties identified* and establishment of the duties and roles that are required to perform along with a staff with adequate skills and experience to fulfill these duties
- *Dissemination of the definitions* of its designated community and associated knowledge base(s)
- *Preservation policies* that ensure that the preservation strategic plan will be met
- *Documentation* of the history of changes to operations, procedures, software, and hardware
- *Commitment to transparency and accountability* in all actions supporting the operation and management of the repository that affect the preservation of digital content over time
- *Dissemination* as appropriate of the definition, collection, and tracking of information integrity measurements
- *Commitment to a regular schedule of self-assessment* and external certification
- *Short- and long-term business planning* processes in place to sustain the repository over time
- *Deposit agreements* for digital materials transferred to the custody of the organization
- *Written policies* that specify when the preservation responsibility for contents of each set of submitted data objects occurs
- *Intellectual property ownership rights* policies and procedures

Digital object management,[8] *which is the core of the standard*, comprises these primary elements:

- Methods and factors used to determine the different types of information for which an organization accepts preservation responsibility
- An understanding of digital collections sufficient to carry out the preservation necessary for as long as required
- Specifications that enable recognition and parsing of SIPs
- An ingest procedure that verifies each SIP for completion and correctness
- An ingest procedure that validates successful ingest of each SIP
- Definitions for each AIP or class of AIPs used that are adequate for parsing and suitable for long-term preservation requirements
- Descriptions of how AIPs are constructed from SIPs, including extraction of metadata
- Documentation of the final disposition of SIPs, including those not ingested
- A convention that generates unique, persistent identifiers of all AIPs
- Reliable linking services that support the location of each uniquely identified object, regardless of its physical location
- Tools and resources that support authoritative representation information for all of the digital objects in the repository, including file type
- Documented processes for acquiring and creating PDI
- Understandable content information for the designated community at the time of creation of the AIPs

- Verification of the completeness and correctness of AIPs at the point of their creation
- Contemporaneous capture of documentation of actions and administration processes that are relevant to AIP creation
- Documented digital preservation strategies
- Mechanisms for monitoring the digital preservation environment
- Documented evidence of the effectiveness of digital preservation activities
- Specifications for storage of AIPs down to the bit level
- Preservation of the content information of AIPs
- Monitoring the integrity of AIPs
- Documentation that preservation actions associated with AIPs complied with the specifications for those actions
- Specification of minimum information requirements that enable the designated community to discover and identify material of interest
- Bidirectional linkage between each AIP and its associated descriptive information
- Compliance with access policies
- Policies and procedures that enable the dissemination of digital objects that are traceable to the "originals," with evidence supporting their authenticity
- Procedures that require documentation of actions taken in response to reports about errors in data or responses from users

Technical infrastructure and security risk management primary elements[9] include these:

- Technology watches or other monitoring systems that track when hardware and software is expected to become obsolete
- Procedures, commitment, and funding when it is necessary to replace hardware
- Procedures, commitment, and funding when it is necessary to replace software
- Adequate hardware and software support for backup functionality sufficient for preserving the repository content and tracking repository functions
- Effective mechanisms that identify bit corruption or loss
- Documentation captures of all incidents of data corruption or loss, and steps taken to repair/replace corrupt or lost data
- Defined processes for storage media and/or hardware change (e.g., refreshing, migration)
- Management of the number and location of copies of all digital objects
- Systematic analysis of security risk factors associated with data, systems, personnel, and physical plant
- Suitable written disaster preparedness and recovery plan(s), including at least one off-site backup of all preserved information together with an offsite copy of the recovery plan(s)

ISO 16363 represents the gold standard of audit and certification for trustworthy digital repositories. In some instances the resources available to a trusted repository may not support full implementation of the audit and certification specifications. Decisions about where full and partial implementation is appropriate should be based on a risk assessment analysis.

ISO 16363 represents the gold standard of audit and certification for trustworthy digital repositories.

PREMIS Preservation Metadata Standard

ISO 14721 specifies that preservation metadata associated with all archival storage activities (e.g., generation of hash digests, transformation, and media renewal) should be captured and stored in PDI. *This high-level guidance requirement demands greater specificity in an operational environment.*

Toward this end, the U.S. Library of Congress and the Research Library Group supported a new international working group called PREservation Metadata Information Strategies (PREMIS)[10] to define a core set of preservation metadata elements with a supporting data dictionary that would be applicable to a broad range of digital preservation activities and to identify and evaluate alternative strategies for encoding, managing, and exchanging preservation metadata. Version 2.2 was released in June 2012.[11]

PREMIS enables designers and managers of digital repositories to have a clear understanding of the information required to support the "functions of viability, renderability, understandability, authenticity, and identity in a preservation context." PREMIS accomplishes this through a data model that consists of five "semantic units" (think of them as high-level metadata elements, each of which is decomposed into subelements) and a data dictionary that decomposes these "semantic units" into a structure hierarchy. The five semantic units and their relationships are displayed in Figure 17.2.

Note the arrows that define relationships between these entities:

- *Intellectual entities* are considered a single intellectual unit such as a book, map, photograph, database, or records (e.g., an AIP).

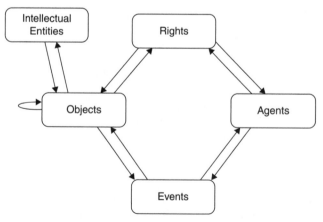

Figure 17.2   PREMIS Data Model
Source: Library of Congress, *P REMIS Data Dictionary for Preservation Metadata* , Version 2.1 (January 2011).

The PREMIS standard defines a core set of preservation metadata elements with a supporting data dictionary applicable to a broad range of digital preservation activities.

- *Objects* are discrete units of information in digital form that may exist as a bitstream, a file or a representation.
- *Events* denote actions that involve at least one digital object and/or agent known to the repository. Events may include the type of event (e.g., media renewal), a description of the event, and the agents involved in the event. Events support the chain of custody of digital objects.
- *Agents* are actors in digital preservation that have roles. An agent can be an individual, organization, or a software application.
- *Rights* involve the assertion of access rights and access privileges that relate to intellectual property, privacy, or other related rights

The PREMIS Data Dictionary decomposes objects, events, agents, and rights into a structured hierarchical schema. In addition, it contains semantic units that support documentation of relationships between Objects. An important feature of the PREMIS is an XML schema for the PREMIS Data Dictionary. The primary rationale for the XML schema is to support the exchange of metadata information, which is crucial in ingest and archival storage. The XML schema enables automated extraction of preservation related metadata in SIPs and population of this preservation metadata into AIPs. In addition, the XML schema can enable automatic capture of preservation events that are foundational for maintaining a chain of custody in archival storage.

Recommended Open Standard Technology-Neutral Formats

A digital file format specifies the internal logical structure of digital objects (i.e., binary bits of 1s and 0s) and signal encoding (e.g., text, image, sound, etc.). File formats are crucial to long-term preservation because a computer can open, process, and render file formats that it recognizes. *Many file formats are proprietary* (also known as native), *meaning that digital content can be opened and rendered only by the software application used to create, use, and store it.* However, as IT changed, some software vendors introduced new products that no longer support earlier versions of a file format. In such instances these formats become "legacy" format, and digital content embedded in them can be opened only with computer code written expressly for this purpose. Other vendors, such as Microsoft, support backward compatibility across multiple generations of technology so Microsoft Word 2010 can open and render documents in Microsoft Word 95. Nonetheless, it is unrealistic to expect any software vendor to support backward compatibility for its proprietary file formats for digital content that will be preserved for multiple decades.

Many digital file formats are proprietary, meaning that content can be viewed and controlled only by the software application used to create, use, and store it.

In the late 1980s, an alternative to vendor-supported backward compatibility emerged to mitigate dependence on proprietary file formats through open system interoperable file formats. Essentially, this meant that digital content could be exported from one proprietary file format and imported to one or more other proprietary file formats. Over time, interoperable file formats evolved into open standard technology-neutral formats that today have these characteristics:

- *Open* means that the process is transparent and that participants in the process reach a consensus on the properties of the standard.
- *Standard* means that a recognized regional or international organization (e.g., the ISO) published the standard.
- *Technology neutral* means that the standard is interoperable on almost any technology platform that asserts conformance to the standard.

Because even open standard technology-neutral formats are not immune to technology obsolescence, their selection must take into account their technical sustainability and implementation in digital repositories. The PRONON program of the National Archives of the United Kingdom and long-term sustainability of file formats of the U.S. Library of Congress assess the sustainability of open standard technology-neutral formats.

The recommended open standard technology-neutral formats for nine content types listed in Table 17.1 are based on this ongoing work, along with preferred file formats supported by Library and Archives Canada and other national archives. Unlike PDF/A, several of these file formats (e.g., XML, JPEG 2000, and Scalable Vector

Table 17.1 Recommended Open Standard Technology-Neutral Formats

	PDF/A	XML	TIFF	PNG	JPEG 2000	SVG	MPEG-2	BWF	WARC
Text	√	√							
Spreadsheets	√								
Images (raster)	√		√	√					
Photographs (digital)					√				
Vector graphics						√			
Moving images							√		
Audio								√	
Web									√
Databases		√							

> The PDF/A file format was designed specifically for digital preservation.

Graphics [SVG]) were not explicitly designed for digital preservation. *It cannot be emphasized too strongly that this list of recommended open standard technology-neutral formats (or any other comparable list) is not static and will change over time as technology changes.*

ISO 19005 (PDF/A)—Document Management—Electronic Document File Format for Long-Term Preservation (2005, 2011, and 2012)

PDF/A is an open standard technology-neutral format that enables the accurate representation of the visual appearance of digital content without regard for the proprietary format or application in which it was created or used. PDF/A is widely used in digital repositories as a preservation format for static textual and image content. Note that PDF/A is agnostic with regard to digital imaging processes or storage media. PDFA/A supports conversion of TIFF and PNG images to PDF/A. There are two levels of conformance to PDF/A specifications. PDF/A-1a references the use of a "well-formed" hierarchical structure with XML tags that enable searching for a specific tag in a very large digital document. PDF/A-1b does not require this conformance, and as a practical matter, it does not affect the accurate representation of visual appearance.

Since its publication in 2005, there have been two revisions of PDF/A. The first revision, PDF/A-2, was aligned with the Adobe Portable Document Format 1.7 published specifications, which Adobe released to the public domain in 2011. The second revision, PDF/A-3, supports embedding documents in other formats, such as the original source document, in a PDF document.

Extensible Markup Language (XML)—World Wide Web Consortium (W3C) Internet Engineering Group (1998)

XML is a markup language that is a derivative of **Standard General Markup Language** (SGML) that logically separates the rendering of a digital document from its content to enable interoperability across multiple technology platforms. Essentially XML defines rules for marking up the structure of content and its content in American Standard Code for Information Interchange (ASCII) text. Any conforming interoperable XML parser can render the original structure and content. XML-encoded text is human-readable because any text editor can display the marked-up text and content. XML is ubiquitous in IT environments because many communities of users have developed document type definitions unique to their purposes, including genealogy, math, and relational databases. Structure data elements work with relational databases, so this enables relational database portability.

Tagged Image File Format (1992)

Tagged image file format (TIFF) was initially developed by the Aldus Corporation in 1982 for storing black-and-white images created by scanners and desktop publishing application. Over the next six years, several new features were added, including a wide range of color images and compression techniques, including lossless compression. The most recent version of TIFF 6.0 was released by Aldus in 1992. Subsequently, Adobe purchased Aldus and chose not to support any further significant revisions and updates. Nonetheless, TIFF is widely used in desktop scanners for creating digital images for preservation. With such a large base of users, it is likely to persist for some time, but Adobe's decision to discontinue further development of TIFF means that it will lack features of other current and future image file formats. Fortunately, there are tools available to convert TIFF images to PDF and PNG images.

ISO/IEC 15498:2003—Information Technology—Computer Graphics and Image Processing-Portable Network Graphics (PNG)—Functional Specifications

The W3C Internet Engineering Task Force supported the development of PNG as a replacement for graphics image format (GIF) because the GIF compression algorithm was protected by patent rights rather than being in the public domain, as many believed. In 2003, PNG became an international standard that supports lossless compression, grayscale, and true-color images with bit depths that range from 1 to 16 bits per pixel, file integrity checking, and streaming capability.

Scalable Vector Graphics (SVG)—W3C Internet Engineering Task Force (2003)

Vector graphics images consist of two-dimensional lines, colors, curves, or other geometrical shapes and attributes that are stored as mathematical expressions, such as where a line begins, its shape, where it ends, and its color. Changes in these mathematical expressions will result in changes in the image. Unlike raster images, there is no loss of clarity of a vector graphics image when it is made larger. SVG images and their behavior properties are defined in XML text files, which means any named element in a SVG image can be indexed and searched. SVG images also can be accessed by any text editor, which minimizes on a specific software application to render and edit the images.

ISO/IEC 15444-1:2004—Joint Photographic Engineers Group (JPEG 2000)

JPEG 2000 *is an international standard for compressing full-color and grayscale digital images* and rendering them as full-size images and thumbnail images. Unlike JPEG, its predecessor, which supported only lossy compression, JPEG 2000 supports both lossy and lossless compression. Lossy compression means that during compression, bits that are considered technically redundant are permanently deleted. Lossless compression means no bits are lost or deleted. *The latter is very important for LTDP because lossy*

PNG replaced GIF as an international standard for grayscale and color images in 2004.

JPEG 2000 is an international standard for compressing and rendering full-color and grayscale digital images in full size or as thumbnails.

compression is irreversible. JPEG 2000 is widely used in producing digital images in digital cameras and is an optional format in many digital scanners.

ISO/IEC 13818-3:2000—Motion Picture Expert Group (MPEG-2)

MPEG-2 is an international broadcast standard for lossy compression of moving images and associated audio. The major competitor for MPEG-2 appears to be Motion JPEG 2000, which is used in small devices, such as cell phones.

European Broadcasting Tech 3285—Broadcast Wave Format (BWF) (2011)

First issued by the European Broadcasting Union in 1997 and revised in 2001 (v1) and 2011 (v2), BWF is a file format for audio data that is an extension of the Microsoft Wave audio format. Its support of metadata ensures that it can be used for the seamless exchange of audio material between different broadcast environments and between equipment based on different computer platforms.

ISO 28500:2009—WebARChive (WARC)

WebARChive (WARC) is an extension of the Internet Archive's ARC format to store digital content harvested through "Web crawls." WARC was developed to support the storage, management, and exchange of large volumes of "constituent data objects" in a single file. Currently, WARC is used to store and manage digital content collected through Web crawls and data collected by environmental sensing equipment, among others.

Digital Preservation Requirements

Implementing a sustainable LTDP program is not an effort that should be undertaken lightly. Digital preservation is complex and costly and requires collaboration with all of the stakeholders who are accountable for or have an interest in ensuring access to usable, understandable, and trustworthy electronic records for as far into the future as may be required.

As noted earlier, ISO 14721 and ISO 16363 establish the baseline functions and specifications for ensuring access to usable, understandable, and trustworthy electronic records, whether this involves regulatory and legal compliance for a business entity, vital records, accountability for a government unit, or cultural memory for a public or private institution. Most first-time readers who review the functions and specifications of ISO 14721 and ISO 16363 are likely to be overwhelmed by the detail and complexity of almost 150 specifications.

Long-Term Digital Preservation Capability Maturity Model®

A useful approach that both simplifies these specifications and provides explicit criteria regarding conformance to ISO 14721 and ISO 16363 is the Long-Term Digital Preservation Capability Maturity Model® (DPCMM).[12] The DPCMM, which is described in some detail in this section, draws on functions and preservation services identified in ISO 14721 (OAIS) as well as attributes specified in ISO 16363, Audit and Certification of Trustworthy Repositories. It is important to note that the DPCMM is not a one-size-fits-all approach to ensuring long-term access to authentic electronic records. Rather, it is a flexible approach that can be adapted to an organization's specific requirements and resources.

DPCMM can be used to identify the *current state* capabilities of digital preservation that form the basis for debate and dialogue regarding the *desired future state* of digital preservation capabilities, and the level of risk that the organization is willing to assume. In many instances, this is likely to come down to the question of what constitutes digital preservation that is good enough to fulfill the organization's mission and meet the expectations of its stakeholders. The DPCMM has five incremental stages, which are depicted in Figure 17.3. In Stage 1, a systematic digital preservation

> The Long-Term Digital Preservation Capability Maturity Model (DPCMM) systematically organizes high-level conformance to ISO 14721 and ISO 16363.

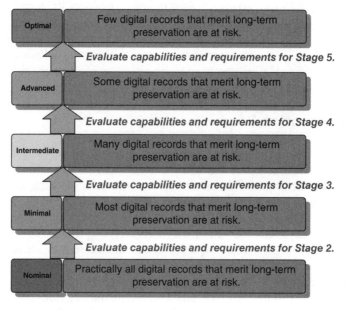

Figure 17.3 Five Levels of Digital Preservation Capabilities

program has not been undertaken or the digital preservation program exists only on paper, whereas Stage 5 represents the highest level of sustainable digital preservation capability and repository trustworthiness that an organization can achieve.

The DPCMM is based on the functional specifications of ISO 14721 and ISO 16363 and accepted best practices in operational digital repositories. It is a systems-based tool for charting an evolutionary path from disorganized and undisciplined management of electronic records, or the lack of a systematic electronic records management program, into increasingly mature stages of digital preservation capability.

The goal of the DPCMM is to identify at a high level where an electronic records management program is in relation to optimal digital preservation capabilities, report gaps, capability levels, and preservation performance metrics to resource allocators and other stakeholders to establish priorities for achieving enhanced capabilities to preserve and ensure access to long-term electronic records.

Stage 5: Optimal Digital Preservation Capability

Stage 5 is the highest level of digital preservation readiness capability that an organization can achieve. It includes a strategic focus on digital preservation outcomes by continuously improving the manner in which electronic records life cycle management is executed. Stage 5 digital preservation capability also involves benchmarking the digital preservation infrastructure and processes relative to other best-in-class digital preservation programs and conducting proactive monitoring for breakthrough technologies that can enable the program to significantly change and improve its digital preservation performance. *In Stage 5, few if any electronic records that merit long-term preservation are at risk.*

Stage 4: Advanced Digital Preservation Capability

Stage 4 capability is characterized by an organization with a robust infrastructure and digital preservation processes that are based on ISO 14721 specifications and ISO 16363 audit and certification criteria. At this stage, the preservation of electronic records is framed entirely within a collaborative environment in which there are multiple participating stakeholders. Lessons learned from this collaborative framework serve as the basis for adapting and improving capabilities to identify and proactively bring long-term electronic records under lifecycle control and management. *Some electronic records that merit long-term preservation still may be at risk.*

Stage 3: Intermediate Digital Preservation Capability

Stage 3 describes an environment that embraces the ISO 14721 specifications and other best practice standards and schemas and thereby establishes the foundation for sustaining an enhanced digital preservation capability over time. This foundation includes successfully completing repeatable projects and outcomes that support the enterprise digital preservation capability and enables collaboration, including shared resources, between record-producing units and entities responsible for managing and maintaining trustworthy digital repositories. *In this environment, many electronic records that merit long-term preservation are likely to remain at risk.*

Stage 2: Minimal Digital Preservation Capability

Stage 2 describes an environment where an ISO 14721–based digital repository is not yet in place. Instead, a surrogate repository for electronic records is available to some records producers that satisfies some but not all of the ISO 14721 specifications. Typically, the digital preservation infrastructure and processes of the surrogate repository are not systematically integrated into business processes or universally available, so the state of digital preservation is somewhat rudimentary and life cycle management of the organization's electronic records is incomplete. There is some understanding of digital preservation issues, but it is limited to a relatively few individuals. There may be virtually no relationship between the success or failure of one digital preservation initiative and the success or failure of another one. Success is largely the result of exceptional (perhaps even heroic) actions of an individual or a project team. Knowledge about such success is not widely shared or institutionalized. *Most electronic records that merit long-term preservation are at risk.*

Stage 1: Nominal Digital Preservation Capability

Stage 1 describes an environment in which the specifications of ISO 14721 and other standards may be known, accepted in principle, or under consideration, but they have not been formally adopted or implemented by the record-producing organization. Generally, there may be some understanding of digital preservation issues and concerns, but this understanding is likely to consist of ad hoc electronic records management and digital preservation infrastructure, processes, and initiatives. Although there may be some isolated instances of individuals attempting to preserve electronic records on a workstation or removable storage media (e.g., DVD or hard drive), *practically all electronic records that merit long-term preservation are at risk.*

Scope of the Capability Maturity Model

This capability maturity model consists of 15 components, or key process areas, that are necessary and required for the long-term preservation of usable, understandable, accessible, and trustworthy electronic records. Each component is identified and is accompanied by explicit performance metrics for each of the five levels of digital preservation capability.

The objective of the model is to provide a process and performance framework (or benchmark) against best practice standards and foundational principles of digital preservation, records management, information governance, and archival science. Figure 17.4 displays the components of the DPCMM.

Scope notes for each of the graphic elements in Figure 17.4 diagram are provided next for additional clarity. Numbered components in the model are associated with performance metrics and capability levels described in the next section.

- **Producers and Users**
  - *Records creators and owners* are stakeholders who have either the obligation or the option to transfer permanent and long-term (10+-year retention) electronic records to one or more specified digital repositories for safekeeping and access.

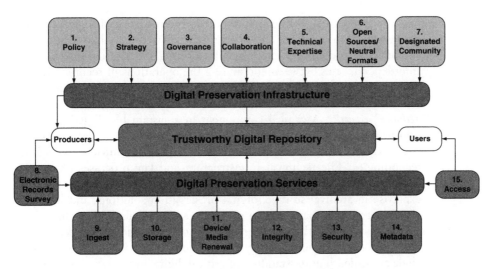

Figure 17.4   Digital Preservation Capability Maturity Model

■ *Users.* Individuals or groups that have an interest in and/or right to access records held in the digital repository. These stakeholders represent a variety of interests and access requirements that may change over time.

■ *Digital preservation infrastructure.* Seven key organizational process areas required to ensure sustained commitment and adequate resources for the long-term preservation of electronic records are:

1. *Digital preservation policy.* The organization charged with ensuring preservation and access to long-term and permanent legal, fiscal, operational, and historical records should issue its digital preservation policy in writing, including the purpose, scope, accountability, and approach to the operational management and sustainability of trustworthy repositories.

2. *Digital preservation strategy.* The organization charged with the preservation of long-term and permanent business, government, or historical electronic records must proactively address the risks associated with technology obsolescence, including plans related to periodic renewal of storage devices, storage media, and adoption of preferred preservation file formats.

3. *Governance.* The organization has a formal decision-making framework that assigns accountability and authority for the preservation of electronic records with long-term and permanent historical, fiscal, operational, or legal value, and articulates approaches and practices for trustworthy digital repositories sufficient to meet stakeholder needs. Governance is exercised in conjunction with information management and technology functions and with other custodians and digital preservation stakeholders, such as records-producing units and records consumers, and enables compliance with applicable laws, regulations, record retention schedules, and disposition authorities.

4. *Collaboration.* Digital preservation is a shared responsibility. The organization with a mandate to preserve long-term and permanent electronic

business, government, or historical records in accordance with accepted digital preservation standards and best practices is well served by maintaining and promoting collaboration among its internal and external stakeholders. Interdependencies between and among the operations of records producing units, legal and statutory requirements, IT policies and governance, and historical accountability should be addressed systematically.

5. *Technical expertise.* A critical component in a sustainable digital preservation program is access to professional technical expertise that can proactively address business requirements and respond to impacts of evolving technologies. The technical infrastructure and key processes of an ISO 14721/ISO 16363–conforming archival repository requires professional expertise in archival storage, digital preservation solutions, and life cycle electronic records management processes and controls. This technical expertise may exist within the organization or be provided by a centralized function or service bureau or by external service providers, and should include an in-depth understanding of critical digital preservation actions and their associated recommended practices.

6. *Open standard technology-neutral formats.* A fundamental requisite for a sustainable digital preservation program that ensures long-term access to usable and understandable electronic records is mitigation of obsolescence of file formats. Open standard platform-neutral file formats are developed in an open public setting, issued by a certified standards organization, and have few or no technology dependencies. Current preferred open standard technology file format examples include:
   - XML and PDF/A for text
   - PDF/A for spreadsheets
   - JPEG 2000 for photographs
   - PDF/A, PNG, and TIFF for scanned images
   - SVG for vector graphics
   - BWF for audio
   - MPEG-4 for video
   - WARC for Web pages

   Over time, new digital preservation tools and solutions will emerge that will require new open standard technology-neutral standard file formats. Open standard technology-neutral formats are backwardly compatible so they can support interoperability across technology platforms over an extended period of time.

7. *Designated community.* The organization that has responsibility for preservation and access to long-term and permanent legal, operational, fiscal, or historical government records is well served through proactive outreach and engagement with its designated community. There are written procedures and formal agreements with records-producing units that document the content, rights, and conditions under which the digital repository will ingest, preserve, and provide access to electronic records. Written procedures are in place regarding the ingest of electronic records and access to its digital collections. Records producers will submit fully conforming ISO 14721/ISO 16363 SIPs while DIPs are developed and updated in conjunction with its user communities.

■ *Trustworthy digital repository.* This includes the integrated people, processes, and technologies committed to ensuring the continuous and reliable design, operation, and management of digital repositories entrusted with long-term and permanent electronic records. A trustworthy digital repository may range from a simple system that involves a low-cost file server and software that provide nonintegrated preservation services, to complex systems comprising data centers and server farms, computer hardware and software, and communication networks that interoperate.

The most complete trustworthy digital repository is based on models and standards that include ISO 14721, ISO 16363, and generally accepted best digital preservation practices. The repository may be managed by the organization that owns the electronic records or may be provided as a service by an external third party. It is likely that many organizations initially will rely on surrogate digital preservation capabilities and services that approximate some but not all of the capabilities and services of a conforming ISO14721/ISO 16363 trustworthy digital repository.

■ *Digital preservation processes and services.* Eight key business process areas needed for continuous monitoring of the external and internal environments in order to plan and take actions to sustain the integrity, security, usability and accessibility of electronic records stored in trustworthy digital repositories.

1. *Electronic records survey.* A trustworthy repository cannot fully execute its mission or engage in realistic digital preservation planning without a projected volume and scope of electronic records that will come into its custody. It is likely that some information already exists in approved retention schedules, but it may require further elaboration as well as periodic updates, especially with regard to preservation ready, near preservation ready, and legacy electronic records held by records-producing units.

2. *Ingest.* A digital repository that conforms to ISO 14721/ISO 16363 has the capability to systematically ingest (receive and accept) electronic records from records-producing units in the form of SIPs, move them to a staging area where virus checks and content and format validations are performed, transform electronic records into designated preservation formats as appropriate, extract metadata from SIPs and write it to PDI, create AIPs, and transfer the AIPs to the repository's storage function. This process is considered the minimal work flow for transferring records into a digital repository for long-term preservation and access.

3. *Archival storage.* ISO 14721 delineates systematic automated storage services that support receipt and validation of successful transfer of AIPs from ingest, creation of PDI for each AIP that confirms its "fixity"[13] during any preservation actions through the generation of hash digests, capture and maintenance of error logs, updates to PDI including transformation of electronic records to new formats, production of DIPs from access, and collection of operational statistics.

4. *Device and media renewal.* No known digital device or storage medium is invulnerable to decay and obsolescence. A foundational digital preservation capability is ensuring the readability of the bitstreams underlying the

electronic records. ISO 14721/ ISO 16363 specify that a trustworthy digital repository's storage devices and storage media should be monitored and renewed ("refreshed") periodically to ensure that the bitstreams remain readable over time. A projected life expectancy of removable storage media does not necessarily apply in a specific instance of storage media. Hence, it is important that a trustworthy digital repository have a protocol for continuously monitoring removable storage media (e.g., magnetic tape, external tape drive, or other media) to identify any that face imminent catastrophic loss. Ideally, this renewal protocol would execute renewal automatically after review by the repository.

5. *Integrity.* A key capability in conforming ISO 14721/ISO 16363 digital repositories is ensuring the integrity of the records in its custody, which involves two related preservation actions. The first action generates a hash digest algorithm (also known as a cyclical redundancy code) to address a vulnerability to accidental or intentional alterations to electronic records that can occur during device/media renewal and internal data transfers. The second action involves integrity documentation that supports an unbroken electronic chain of custody captured in the PDI in AIPs.

6. *Security.* Contemporary enterprise information systems typically execute a number of shared or common services that may include communication, name services, temporary storage allocation, exception handling, role-based access rights, security, backup and business continuity, and directory services, among others. A conforming ISO 14721/ISO 16363 digital repository is likely to be part of an information system that may routinely provide some or perhaps all of the core security, backup, and business continuity services, including firewalls, role-based access rights, data-transfer-integrity validations, and logs for all preservation activities, including failures and anomalies, to demonstrate an unbroken chain of custody.

7. *Preservation metadata.* A digital repository collects and maintains metadata that describes actions associated with custody of long-term and permanent records, including an audit trail that documents preservation actions carried out, why and when they were performed, how they were carried out, and with what results. *A current best practice is the use of a PREMIS-based data dictionary to support an electronic chain of custody that documents authenticity over time as preservation actions are executed.* Capture of all related metadata, transfer of the metadata to any new formats/systems, and secure storage of metadata are critical. All metadata is stored in the PDI component of conforming AIPs.

8. *Access.* Organizations with a mandate to support access to permanent business, government, or historical records are subject to authorized restrictions. A conforming ISO 14721/ISO 16363 digital repository will provide consumers with trustworthy records in "disclosure-free" DIPs redacted to protect, privacy, confidentiality, and other rights, where appropriate, and searchable metadata that users can query to identify and retrieve records of interest to them. Production of DIPs is tracked, especially when they involve extractions, to verify their trustworthiness and to

identify query trends that are used to update electronic accessibility tools to support these trends.

Digital Preservation Capability Performance Metrics

Digital preservation performance metrics for each level of the five levels of the model have been mapped to each of the 15 numbered components described in the previous section. The performance metrics are explicit empirical indicators that reflect an incremental level of digital preservation capability. The digital preservation capability performance metrics for digital preservation strategy listed in Table 17.2 illustrate the results of this mapping exercise.[14]

Conducting a gap analysis of its digital preservation capabilities using these performance metrics enables the organization to identify both its current state and desired future state of digital preservation capabilities. In all likelihood, this desired future state will depend on available resources, the organization's mission, and stakeholder expectations. "Good-enough" digital preservation capabilities will vary by organization; what is good enough for one organization is unlikely to coincide with what is good enough for another.

Digital Preservation Strategies and Techniques

Any organization with long-term or permanent electronic records in its custody must ensure that the electronic records can be read and correctly interpreted by a computer application, rendered in an understandable form to humans, and trusted as

Table 17.2   Digital Preservation Performance Metrics

Level	Capability Description
0	A formal strategy to address technology obsolescence does not exist.
1	A strategy to mitigate technology obsolescence consists of accepting electronic records in their native format with the expectation that new software will become available to support these formats. During this interim period, viewer technologies will be relied on to render usable and understandable electronic records.
2	Electronic records in interoperable "preservation-ready"* file formats and transformation of one native file format to an open standard technology-neutral file format are supported. Changes in information technologies that may impact electronic records collections and the digital repository are monitored proactively and systematically.
3	The organization supports transformation of selected native file formats to preferred/supported preservation file formats in the trustworthy digital repository. Records-producing units are advised to use preservation-ready file formats for permanent or indefinite long-term (e.g., case files, infrastructure files) electronic records in their custody.
4	Electronic records in all native formats are transformed to available open standard technology-neutral file formats.

* The term "preservation-ready file formats" refers to open standard technology-neutral formats that the organization has identified as preferred for long-term digital preservation.

accurate representations of their logical and physical structure, substantive content, and context. To achieve these goals, a digital repository should operate under the mandate of a digital preservation strategy that addresses 10 digital preservation processes and activities:

1. *Adopt preferred open standard technology-neutral formats.* Earlier, nine open standard technology-neutral file formats that covered text, images, photographs, vector graphics, moving images, audio, and Web pages were discussed. Adoption of these file formats means that the digital repository will support their use in its internal digital preservation activities and notify the producers of records of the preferred formats for preservation-ready electronic records to be transferred to the repository's custody.

2. *Acquire electronic records in preservation-ready formats.* Likely many born-digital electronic records along with scanned images will be created or captured in a preservation-ready format. Acquisition or ingest of electronic records already in preservation-ready formats can significantly reduce the workload of the repository because it will not be necessary to transform records to open standard technology-neutral formats.

3. *Acquire and transform electronic records in near-preservation-ready formats.* Near-preservation-ready formats are native proprietary file formats that can be easily transformed to preservation-ready file formats through widely available software plug-ins. Ideally, over time, the volume of near-preservation-ready records will diminish as records producers increasingly convert records scheduled for long-term retention into preservation-ready formats before they are transferred to the repository.

4. *Acquire legacy electronic records.* Legacy electronic records initially were created in a proprietary file format that is obsolete and no longer supported by a vendor. In most instances, electronic records embedded in legacy file formats can be recovered and saved in a preservation-ready format only if special computer code is written to extract the records from their legacy format. Once extracted from the legacy format, they can be written to a contemporary format. Niche vendors provide this kind of service, but it is relatively expensive and perhaps beyond the resources of many repositories.

   An alternative is to forgo this costly process in the hope that a future technology, such as **emulation**, will be widely available and relatively inexpensive. Meanwhile, the repository would rely on a file viewer technology, such as Inside Out, to render legacy electronic records into format understandable to humans with the exact logical and physical structure and representation at the time they were created and used.

5. *Maintain bitstream readability through device/media removal.* No known digital storage device or media is exempt from degradation and technology obsolescence. Consequently, the bitstreams of 1s and 0s that underlie electronic records are stored on media that are vulnerable to degradation and technology obsolescence. Technology obsolescence may occur when a vendor introduces a new form factor for storage device/media, such as the transition from 5.25-inch disk drives and disks to 3.5-inch disk drives and media to thumb drives. With today's technology, periodic device/medial renewal is the only known way to keep bitstreams available. *A rule of thumb is to renew storage*

device/media at least every 10 years. Failure to maintain the readability of bit-streams over time is an absolute guarantee the electronic records cannot be recovered and that the records will be permanently lost for all practical purposes.

6. *Migrate to new open standard technology-neutral formats.* These formats are not immune to technology obsolescence. The inevitable changes in IT mean that new open standard technology formats will be created that displace current ones. The solution to this issue is migration from an older or current open standard technology-neutral format to newer ones. Seamless migration from old to new open standard technology-neutral formats is made possible through backward compatibility. "Backward compatibility" means that a new standard can interpret digital content in an old standard and then save it in the new format standard. Migration is the most widely used tool to mitigate file format obsolescence.

7. *Protect the integrity and security of electronic records.* Imperfect information technologies inevitably have glitches that, along with accidental human error and intentional human actions, can corrupt or otherwise compromise the trust-worthiness of electronic records though some alteration in the underlying bitstream. Accidental alteration occurs when preservation actions are initiated for electronic records. These actions may occur during transformation, migration, media renewal, accessions to digital records, and relocation of electronic records from one part of the repository to another. The most effective tool for validating that no unauthorized changes to electronic records occur is to compute a hash digest before a preservation action occurs and after the action is completed. If there is change of only one bit, a comparison of the two will identify it. Capturing these pre- and posthash digests and saving them as preservation description information can contribute to an electronic chain of custody.

   A robust firewall that blocks unauthorized access with tightly controlled role-based permission rights will help protect the security of records in the custody of the repository.

   A further enhancement to protect against a cataclysmic natural or man-made disaster is maintaining a backup copy of the repository's holdings at an off-site facility.

8. *Capture and save preservation metadata.* Preservation metadata, which consists of tracking, capturing, and maintaining documentation of all preservation actions associated with electronic records, involves identifying these events, the agents that executed the actions, and the results of the actions, including any corrective action taken. Saving this metadata along with the hash digest integrity validations just discussed enables a robust electronic chain of custody and establishes a strong basis for the trustworthiness of electronic records in the custody of the digital repository

9. *Provide access. Access to usable and trustworthy records is the ultimate justification for digital preservation.* In some respects, this may be the most challenging aspect of digital preservation because user expectations for customized retrieval tools, access speed, and delivery formats of electronic records may exceed the current resources of a trusted digital repository. Nonetheless, some form of user access through replication of records in a single open standard technology format, such as PDF/A for text and scanned images and JPEG 2000 for digital photographs, would be a major accomplishment and form the basis for a more aggressive access program over time.

10. *Engage proactively with records producers and other stakeholders.* The traditional notion of an archive being in a reactive mode with regard records producers and other stakeholders in LTDP simply will not work in today's world. Proactive engagement with records producers about how capturing electronic records in open standard technology-neutral formats can support both current business operation requirements and long-term requirements for usable, understandable, and trustworthy archives can be a win-win for the digital repository and the records producers. Equally important is the notion of proactive engagement with all of the stakeholders in ensuring long-term access to usable, understandable, and trustworthy electronic records. Support of other stakeholders can be leveraged to gain broad organizational support for the digital repository.

Evolving Marketplace

The design and implementation of a digital repository that operates under this digital preservation strategy can be carried out in several different ways. One way is to use internal expertise to build a stand-alone repository that conforms to these digital preservation strategy requirements. Typically, an internally built repository is costly, takes considerable time to implement, and may not meet all expectations because of technical inexperience. An alternative is to use the services and/or solutions offered by an external institution or supplier. A third-party solution is offered by Archivematica, a Vancouver, British Columbia, company that specializes in the use of open-source software and conformance to the specifications of ISO 14721. "Archivematica is a free and open-source digital preservation system that is designed to maintain standards-based, long-term access to collections of digital objects."[15] Another company, Tessella Technology & Consulting,[16] has an ISO 14721–conforming digital preservation solution called Safety Deposit Box that has been implemented in a number of national archives. In June 2012, Tessella introduced Preservica,[17] a cloud-based implementation of the Safety Deposit Box that runs on Amazon Web Services. *It is likely that other repository solutions, preservation services, and cloud-based digital preservation services will emerge over the next few years.* The digital preservation strategy discussed earlier can be used to assess the capabilities of these solutions.

Looking Forward

Organizations face significant challenges in meeting their LTDP needs, especially organizations whose primary mission is to preserve and provide access to permanent records. They must collaborate with internal and external stakeholders, develop governance policies and strategies to govern and control information assets over long periods of time, inventory records in the custody of records producers, monitor technology changes and evolving standards, and sustain trustworthy digital repositories. The most important consideration is to determine what level of LTDP maturity is appropriate, achievable, and affordable for the organization and to begin working methodically toward that goal for the good of the organization and its stakeholders over the long term. In addition, organizations should focus on what is doable over the next 10 to 20 years rather than the next 50 or 100 years.

CHAPTER SUMMARY: **KEY POINTS**

- Digital preservation is defined as long-term, error-free storage of digital information, with means for retrieval and interpretation, for the entire time span the information is required to be retained.

- Digital preservation applies to content that is born digital as well as content that is converted to digital form.

- Capability for properly ensuring access to authentic electronic records over time, (regardless of the challenges of technological obsolescence), is a sophisticated combination of policies, strategies, processes, specialized resources, and adoption of standards.

- Most records are useful for only a short period of time, but some may need to be retained for long periods or permanently. For those records, organizations will need to plan for their preservation to ensure that they remain accessible, trustworthy, and useful.

- Electronic records are being created at rates that pose significant threats to our ability to organize, control, and make them accessible for as long as they are needed.

- Threats to LTDP of records can be internal or external, from natural disasters, computer or storage failures, and even from the financial viability of an organization, which can limit needed funding.

- Building and sustaining the capability to manage digital information over long periods of time is a shared responsibility among all stakeholders.

- ISO 14721 is the lingua franca of digital preservation. The international digital preservation community has embraced it as the framework for viable and technologically sustainable digital preservation repositories.

- An ISO 14721 (OAIS)–compliant repository is the best way to preserve an organization's long-term digital assets.

- ISO/TR 18492 provides practical methodological guidance for the long-term preservation of e-documents, when the retention period exceeds the expected life of the technology that created it.

- ISO 16363 is an audit and certification standard organized into three broad categories: organization infrastructure, digital object management, and technical infrastructure and security risk management.

- ISO 16363 represents the gold standard of audit and certification for trustworthy digital repositories.

- The PREMIS standard defines a core set of preservation metadata elements with a supporting data dictionary applicable to a broad range of digital preservation activities.

(Continued)

CHAPTER SUMMARY: **KEY POINTS** (*Continued*)

- Many digital file formats are proprietary, meaning that content can be viewed and controlled only by the software application used to create, use, and store it.

- The digital preservation community recognizes that open standard technology-neutral standards play a key role in ensuring that digital records are usable, understandable, and reliable for as far into the future as may be required.

- The PDF/A file format was specifically designed for digital preservation.

- PNG replaced GIF as an international standard for grayscale and color images in 2004.

- JPEG 2000 is an international standard for compressing and rendering full-color and grayscale digital images in full size or as thumbnails.

- The Long-Term Digital Preservation Capability Maturity Model simplifies conformance to ISO 14721 and ISO 16363.

- Migration, refreshment, and replication are examples of specific preservation techniques.

- It is likely that new third-party repository solutions and preservation services, including cloud-based offerings, will emerge over the next few years.

Notes

1. Consultative Committee for Space Data Systems, *Reference Model for an Open Archival Information System (OAIS)* (Washington, DC: CCSDS Secretariat, 2002), pp. 1-1.
2. Kate Cumming, "Metadata Matters," in Julie McLeod and Catherine Hare, eds., *Managing Electronic Records*, p. 48 (London: Facet, 2005).
3. David Rosenthal et al., "Requirements for Digital Preservation Systems," *D-Lib Magazine* 11, no. 11 (November 2005), www.dlib.org/dlib/november05/rosenthal/11rosenthal.html.
4. "ISO 14721:2003, 2012 Space Data and Information Transfer Systems—Open Archival Information System—Reference Model," www.iso.org/iso/catalogue_detail.htm?csnumber=24683 (accessed May 21, 2012).
5. Ibid., section 4.1.
6. Ibid., section 5.4.
7. See ISO 16363:2012 (E), sections 3.1–3.5.2.
8. See ibid., sections 4.1–4/6/2/1.
9. See ibid., sections 5.1–5.2.3.
10. For a useful overview of PREMIS, see Priscilla Caplan, "Understanding PREMIS," Library of Congress, February 1, 2009, www.loc.gov/standards/premis/understanding-premis.pdf.
11. Library of Congress, "PREMIS Data Dictionary Version 2.2: Hierarchical Listing of Semantic Units," September 13, 2012, www.loc.gov/standards/premis/v2/premis-dd-Hierarchical-Listing-2-2.html.
12. Charles Dollar and Lori Ashley are codevelopers of this model. Since 2007 they have used it successfully in both the public and private sectors. The most recent instance is a digital preservation capability assessment for the U.S. Council of State Archivists (CoSA). For more information about the model, see "Digital Preservation Capability Maturity Model" at www.savingthedigitalworld.com (accessed December 12, 2013).
13. ISO 14721 uses "fixity" to express the notion that there have been no unauthorized changes to electronic records and associated Preservation Description Information in the custody of the repository. See ISO 14721:2003 (E): 1.6.

14. For information about digital preservation capability performance metrics, visit "Digital Preservation Capability Maturity Model."

15. Archivematica, "What Is Archivematica?" October 15, 2012, www.archivematica.org/wiki/Main_Page.

16. Tessella, "Tessella SDB" www.tessella.com/tag/safety-deposit-box/ (accessed June 28, 2012).

17. Tessella, "Preservica: Digital Preservation as a Service" January 2011, www.digital-preservation.com/wp-content/uploads/Paas-Description-V3-Alternate-Web.pdf.

CHAPTER 18

Maintaining an Information Governance Program and Culture of Compliance*

Maintaining your information governance (IG) program beyond an initial project effort is key to realizing continued and long-term benefits of IG. This means that the IG program must become an everyday part of an organization's operations and communications. It requires vigilant and consistent monitoring and auditing to ensure that IG policies and processes are effective and consistently followed and enforced. If proper controls are in place, IG-infused processes should become a regular part of the enterprise's operations. It also requires an ongoing training and communications program to keep employees apprised of approved processes and behaviors that support IG.

Monitoring and Accountability

Monitoring and accountability require a continuous tightening and expansion of protections and the implementation of newer, strategic technologies. Information technology (IT) developments and innovations that can foster the effort must be steadily monitored and evaluated, and those technology subsets that can assist in providing security need to be incorporated into the mix.

The IG policies themselves must be reviewed and updated periodically to accommodate changes in the business environment, laws, regulations, and technology. Program gaps and failures must be addressed, and the effort should continue to improve and adapt to new types of security threats.

That means accountability: Some individual must remain responsible for an IG policy's administration and results.[1] Perhaps the executive sponsor for the initial project becomes the chief information governance officer or IG czar of sorts; or the chief executive officer continues ownership of the program and drives its active

---

*Portions of this chapter are adapted from Chapter 17, Robert F. Smallwood, *Safeguarding Critical E-Documents: Implementing a Program for Securing Confidential Information Assets,* © John Wiley & Sons, Inc., 2012. Reproduced with permission of John Wiley & Sons, Inc.

> Maintaining an IG program for requires that someone is accountable for continual monitoring and refinement of policies and tools.

improvement. The organization also may decide to form a standing IG board, steering committee, or team with specific responsibilities for monitoring, maintaining, and advancing the program.

However it takes shape, an IG program must be ongoing, dynamic, and aggressive in its execution in order to remain effective.

Staffing Continuity Plan

In today's work environment, employees are more mobile in their careers: people take new career opportunities outside of the organization and also change jobs and move to other positions within an organization, so it is critical to have a continuity plan for your IG program. Backup and supporting designates must be named and kept current on the administration of the program. So you must have a supporting sponsor or senior sponsor to fill the role of executive sponsor, should the need arise; likewise, there needs to be other human resource/staffing redundancies built in to ensure the smooth and continued operation of the IG program, in the event of an unplanned incident that threatens it.

The approach to an IG program is similar to that of a a **vital records** (those critical business records that an organization must have to continue operations) program. Backups of backups must be built in. In vital records, there must be backups of backup copies of vital records, and they must be safely stored and also there needs to be backup IT systems and processes in place to ensure that an organization can continue its operations. These redundancies must be considered, tested, and implemented. This may mean that when the formal program manager is unable to execute his or her duties, an assistant or designated backup can carry out those duties.

It is also a good idea to cross-train employees. With this approach, the legal team, for instance, will better understand the needs and requirements of the records management function, and vice versa. Cross-training improves overall organization acceptance and understanding of the IG program while building in safeguards to ensure that it keeps running.

> IG programs need built-in staffing redundancies to ensure their continued operation in the event of employee turnover or transfer.

Continuous Process Improvement

Maintaining IG program effectives requires implementing principles of continuous process improvement (CPI). CPI is a "never-ending effort to discover and eliminate the main causes of problems. It accomplishes this by using small-steps improvements, rather than implementing one huge improvement." In Japan, the word *kaizen* reflects this gradual and constant process, as it is enacted throughout the organization, regardless of department, position, or level.[2] To remain effective, the program must continue using CPI methods and techniques.

Maintaining and improving the program will require monitoring tools, periodic audits, and regular meetings for discussion and approval of changes to improve the program. It will require a cross section of team leaders from IT, legal, records management, compliance, internal audit, and risk management as well as functional business units participating actively and discussing possible threats and sources of information leakage.

Why Continuous Improvement Is Needed

Although the specific drivers of change are always evolving, the reasons that organizations need to continuously improve their program for securing information assets are relatively constant. These reasons include:

- *Changing technology.* New technology capabilities need to be monitored and considered with an eye to improving, streamlining, or reducing the cost of IG. The IG program needs to anticipate new types of threats and also evaluate adding or replacing technologies to continue to improve it.
- *Changing laws and regulations.* Compliance with new or updated laws and regulations must be maintained.
- *Internal IG requirements.* As an organization updates and improves its overall IG, the program elements that concern critical information assets must be kept aligned and synchronized.
- *Changing business plans.* As the enterprise develops new business strategies and enters new markets, it must reconsider and update its IG program. If, for instance, a firm moves from being a domestic entity to a regional or global one, new laws and regulations will apply, and perhaps new threats will exist and new security strategies must be formed.
- *Evolving industry best practices.* Best practices change, and new best practices arise with the introduction of each successive wave of technology and with changes in the business environment. The program should consider and leverage new best practices.
- *Fixing program shortcomings.* Addressing flaws in the IG program that are discovered through testing, monitoring, and auditing; or addressing an actual breach of confidential information; or a legal sanction imposed due to noncompliance are all reasons why a program must be revisited periodically and kept updated.[3]

> Maintaining the IG program requires that a senior-level officer of the enterprise continues to push for enforcement, improvement, and expansion of the program to secure and control information.

Maintaining the IG program requires that a senior-level officer of the enterprise continues to sponsor it and pushes for enforcement, improvement, and expansion. This requires leadership and consistent and clear messages to employees. IG and the security of information assets must be on the minds of all members of the enterprise; it must be something they are aware of and think about daily. They must be on the lookout for ways to improve it, and they should be rewarded for those contributions.

Gaining this level of mindshare in employees' heads will require follow-up messages in the form of personal speeches and presentations, newsletters, corporate announcements, e-mail messages, and even posters placed at strategic points (e.g., near the shared printing station advising about secure procedures). Employees must be reminded that information governance is everyone's job and meeting compliance and legal demands help contribute to achieving business objectives, and also that losing, misusing, or leaking confidential information harms the organization over the long term and erodes its value.

CHAPTER SUMMARY: **KEY POINTS**

- Keeping an enterprise's IG program effective requires vigilant and consistent monitoring and auditing to ensure that IG are followed and enforced.

- Information technologies that can assist in advancing the program must be steadily monitored, evaluated, and implemented.

- To maintain and improve the IG program requires monitoring tools, regular audits, and regular meetings for discussion and approval of changes to the program to continually improve it.

- IG programs need built-in staffing redundancies to ensure their continued operation in the event of employee turnover or transfer.

- Organizations need to continuously improve their program for securing information assets due to:
  - Changing technology
  - Changing laws and regulations

CHAPTER SUMMARY: **KEY POINTS** (*Continued*)

- ■ Internal information governance requirements

- ■ Changing business plans

- ■ Evolving industry best practices

- ■ Program shortcomings

- ■ Maintaining an IG program requires that a senior-level officer of the enterprise continues to push for enforcement, improvement, and expansion of the program to secure and control information.

Notes

1. Mark Woeppel, "Is Your Continuous Improvement Organization a Profit Center?" June 15, 2009, www.processexcellencenetwork.com/process-management/articles/is-your-continuous-improvement-organization-a-prof/ (accessed September 12, 2011).
2. Donald Clark, "Continuous Process Improvement," Big Dog and Little Dog's Performance Juxtaposition (blog), March 11, 2010, www.nwlink.com/~donclark/perform/process.html (accessed September 12, 2011).
3. Randolph Kahn and Barclay T. Blair, *Information Nation: Seven Keys to Information Management Compliance* (New York: AIIM International, 2004), pp. 242–243.

APPENDIX A

Information Organization and Classification: Taxonomies and Metadata*

By Barb Blackburn, CRM, with Robert Smallwood; edited by Seth Earley

Information governance (IG) necessarily involves organizing and classifying information. IG is critical to enabling improved search results to base business decisions on, executing records retention schedule (RRS) tasks, and sifting through and finding responsive (relevant) information in the e-discovery process. Well-organized information constructs provide downstream benefits across the organization in not only compliance and legal efforts but also day-to-day decision-making and knowledge worker productivity. It is even more crucial in the era of Big Data.

The creation of electronic documents and records is exploding exponentially and multiplying at an increasing rate. Sifting through all this information results in a lot of wasted, unproductive (and expensive) knowledge worker time. This has real costs to the enterprise. According to the study "The High Cost of Not Finding Information," "knowledge workers spend at least 15 to 25 percent of the workday searching for information. Only half the searches are successful."[1] *Experts point to poor* **taxonomy** *design as being at the root of these failed searches and lost productivity.*

Taxonomies are at the heart of the solution to harnessing and governing information. *Taxonomies are hierarchical classification structures* used to standardize the naming and organization of information, and their role and use in managing electronic records cannot be overestimated.

Although the topic of taxonomies can get complex, in **electronic records management** (ERM) they are a sort of online card catalog that is cross-referenced with hyperlinks that is used to organize and manage records and documents.[2]

According to Forrester Research, taxonomies "represent agreed-upon terms and relationships between ideas or things and serve as a glossary or knowledge map helping to define how the business thinks about itself and represents itself, its products and services to the outside world."[3]

---

*Portions of this appendix are adapted from Chapter 6 and 16, Robert F. Smallwood, *Managing Electronic Records: Methods, Best Practices, and Technologies*, © John Wiley & Sons, Inc., 2013. Reproduced with permission of John Wiley & Sons, Inc.

Knowledge workers spend at least 15 to 25 percent of the workday searching for information with only half the searches being successful.

Gartner Group researchers warn that "to get value from the vast quantities of information and knowledge, enterprises must establish discipline and a system of governance over the creation, capture, organization, access, and utilization of information."[4]

Over time, organizations have implemented taxonomies to attempt to gain control over their mounting masses of information, creating an orderly structure to harness unstructured information (such as e-documents, e-mail messages, scanned records, and other digital assets), and to improve searchability and access.[5]

Taxonomies for ERM standardize the vocabulary used to describe records, making it easier and faster for searches and retrievals to be made.

Search engines are able to deliver faster and more accurate results from good taxonomy design by limiting and standardizing terms. A robust and efficient taxonomy design is the underpinning that indexes collections of documents uniformly and helps knowledge workers find the proper files to complete their work. The way a taxonomy is organized and implemented is critical to the long-term success of any enterprise, as it directly impacts the quality and productivity of knowledge workers who need organized, trusted information to make business decisions.

It does not sound so complicated, simply categorizing and cataloging information, yet most enterprises have had disappointing or inconsistent results from the taxonomies they use to organize information. *Designing taxonomies is hard work.* Developing an efficient and consistent taxonomy is a detailed, tedious, labor-intensive team effort on the front end, and its maintenance must be consistent and regular and follow established IG guidelines in order to maintain its effectiveness.

Once a taxonomy is in place, it requires systematic updates and reviews to ensure that guidelines are being followed and new document and record types are included in the taxonomy structure. Technology tools like **text mining, social tagging,** and **auto-classification** can help uncover trends and suggest candidate terms. (More on these technologies later in this chapter.)

When done correctly, the business benefits of good taxonomy design go much further than speeding search and retrieval; an efficient, operational taxonomy also is a part of IG efforts that help the organization to manage and control information so that it may efficiently respond to litigation requests, comply with governmental regulations, and meet customer needs (both external and internal).

Taxonomies are crucial to finding information and optimizing knowledge worker productivity, yet some surveys estimate that nearly half of organizations do not have a standardized taxonomy in place.[6]

To maximize efficient and effective retrieval of records for legal, business, and regulatory purposes, organizations must develop and implement taxonomies.

Taxonomies speed up the process of retrieving records because end users can select from subject categories or topics.

According to the Montague Institute:

The way your company organizes information (i.e., its taxonomy) is critical to its future. A taxonomy not only frames the way people make decisions, but also helps them find the information to weigh all the alternatives. *A good taxonomy helps decision makers see all the perspectives, and "drill down" to get details from each, and explore lateral relationships among them.*[7] (Emphasis added.)

Without a taxonomy, your company will find it difficult to leverage intellectual capital, engage in electronic commerce, keep up with employee training, and get the most out of strategic partnerships.

With the explosion in growth of electronic documents and records, a standardized classification structure that a taxonomy imposes optimizes records retrievals for daily business operations and also for legal and regulatory demands.[8]

Since end users can choose from topic areas, subject categories, or groups of documents rather than blindly typing word searches, *taxonomies narrow searches and speed search time and retrieval.*[9]

"The link between taxonomies and usability is a strong one. The best taxonomies efficiently guide users to exactly the content they need. Usability is judged in part by how easily content can be found," according to the Montague Institute.[10]

Importance of Navigation and Classification

Taxonomies need to be considered from two main perspectives: navigation and classification. *Most people consider the former, but not the latter.* The navigational construct that is represented by a taxonomy is evident in most file structures and file shares—the nesting of folders within folders—and in many Web applications where users are navigating hierarchical arrangements of pages or links. However, classification is frequently behind the scenes. A document can "live" in a folder that the user can navigate to. *But within that folder, the document can be classified in different ways through the application of metadata.* Metadata are descriptive fields that delineate a (document or) record's characteristics, such as author, title, department of origin, date created, length, number of pages or file size, and so forth. The metadata is also part of the taxonomy or related to the taxonomy. In this way, usability can be impacted by giving the user *multiple ways* to retrieve their information.[11]

Taxonomies need to be considered from two main perspectives: navigation and classification.

Poor search results, inconsistent or conflicting file plans, and the inability to locate information on a timely basis are indications taxonomy work is needed.

When Is a New Taxonomy Needed?

In some cases, organizations have existing taxonomy structures, but they have gone out of date or have not been maintained. They may not have been developed with best practices in mind or with correct representation of user groups, tasks, or applications. There are many reasons why taxonomies no longer provide the full value that they can offer. Certain situations clearly indicate that the organization needs a refactored or new taxonomy.[12]

If knowledge workers in your organization regularly conduct searches and receive hundreds of pages of results, then you need a new taxonomy. If you have developed a vast knowledge base of documents and records and designated **subject matter experts** (SMEs), yet employees struggle to find answers, you need a new taxonomy. If there is no standardization of the way content is classified and cataloged, or there is conflict between how different groups or business units classify content, you need a new taxonomy. And if your organization has experienced delays, fines, or undue costs in producing documentation to meet compliance requests or legal demands, your organization needs to work on a new taxonomy.[13]

Taxonomies Improve Search Results

Taxonomies can improve a search engine's ability to deliver results to user queries in finding documents and records in an enterprise. The way the digital content is indexed (e.g., spidering, crawling, rule sets, algorithms) is a separate issue, and a good taxonomy improves search results regardless of the indexing method.[14]

Search engines struggle to deliver accurate and refined results since the wording in queries may vary and since words can have multiple meanings. A taxonomy addresses these problems since the terms are set and defined in a **controlled vocabulary**.

Metadata (data fields that describe content, such as document type, creator, date of creation, etc.) *must be leveraged in the taxonomy design effort.*

A formal definition of metadata is "standardized administrative or descriptive data about a document [or record] that is common for all documents [or records] in a given repository." Standardized metadata elements of e-documents should be utilized and supported by including them in controlled vocabularies when possible.[15]

The goal of a taxonomy development effort is to help users find the information they need, in a logical and familiar way, even if they are not sure what the correct search terminology is. *Good taxonomy design makes it easier and more comfortable for users*

Taxonomies improve search results by increasing accuracy and also improving the user experience.

> Metadata, which are the characteristics of a document expressed in data fields, must be leveraged in taxonomy design.

to browse topics and drill down into more narrow searches to find the documents and records they need. Where it really becomes useful and helps contribute to productivity is when complex or compound searches are conducted.

Metadata and Taxonomy

One potential limitation of a purely hierarchical taxonomy is the lack of association between tiers (or nodes). There are often one-to-many or many-to-many associations between records. For example, an employee travels to a certification course. The resultant "expense report" is classified in the Finance/Accounts Payable/Travel Expense node of the taxonomy. The "course completion certificate" that is generated from the same travel (and is included as backup documentation for the expense report) is appropriately classified in the Human Resources/Training and Certification/Continuing Education node. *For ERM systems that do not provide the functionality for a multifaceted taxonomy, metadata is used to provide the link between the nodes in the taxonomy* (see Figure A.1).

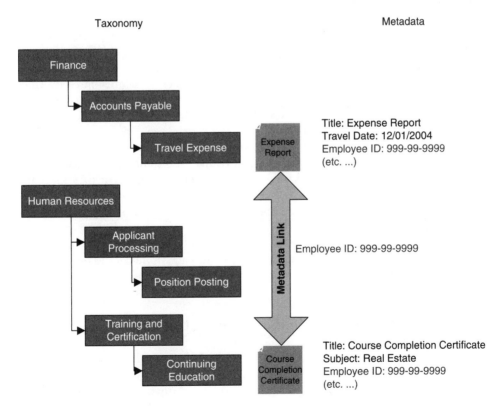

Figure A.1   Metadata Link to Taxonomy Example
Source: Blackburn Consulting

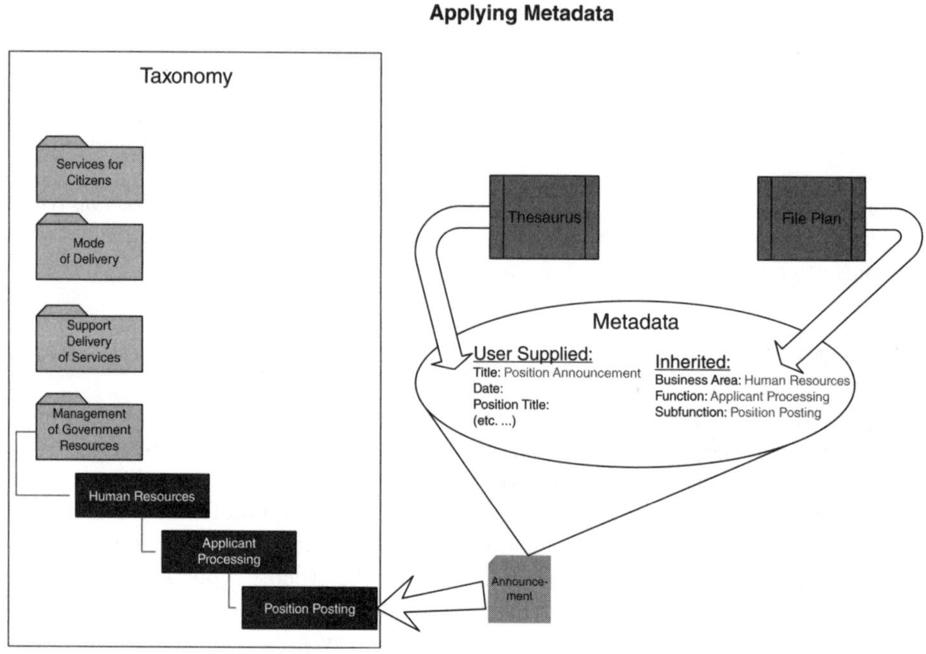

Applying Metadata

Figure A.2   Application of Metadata to Taxonomy Structure
Source: Blackburn Consulting

Metadata schema must be structured to provide the appropriate associations as well as meet the users' keyword search needs. *It is important to limit the number of metadata fields that a user must manually apply to records.* Most recordkeeping systems provide the functionality to automatically assign certain metadata to records based on rules that are established in advance and set up by a system administrator (referred in this book as **inherited metadata**). The record's classification or location in the taxonomy is appropriate for inherited metadata.

Metadata can also be applied by auto-categorization software. This can reduce the burden placed on the user and increase the quality and consistency of metadata. These approaches need to be tested and fine-tuned in order to ensure that they meet the needs of the organization.[16]

The file plan will provide the necessary data to link the taxonomy to the document via inherited metadata. In most systems, this metadata is applied by the system and is transparent to the users. Additional metadata will need to be applied by the user. To maintain consistency, a **thesaurus**, which contains all synonyms and definitions, is used to enforce naming conventions (see Figure A.2).

Metadata Governance, Standards, and Strategies

Metadata can be a scary term to a lot of people. It just *sounds* complicated. And it can get complicated. It is often defined as "data about data," which is true but somewhat confusing, and this does not provide enough information for most people to understand.

"Meta" derives from a Greek word that means "alongside, with, after, next." Metadata can be defined as "structured data about other data."[17]

In ERM, metadata identifies a record and its contents. *ERM metadata describes a record's characteristics so that it may be classified more easily and completely.* Metadata fields, or *terms,* for e-records can be as basic as identifying the name of the document, the creator or originating department, the subject, the date it was created, the document type, the length of the document, its security classification, and its file type.

Creating standardized metadata terms is part of an IG effort that enables faster, more complete, and more accurate searches and retrieval of records. This is important not only in everyday business operations but also, for example, when searching through potentially millions of records during the discovery phase of litigation.

Good metadata management also assists in the maintenance of corporate memory and in improving accountability in business operations.[18]

Using a standardized format and controlled vocabulary provides a "precise and comprehensible description of content, location, and value."[19] *Using a controlled vocabulary means your organization has standardized a set of terms used for metadata elements describing records.* This "ensures consistency across a collection" and helps with optimizing search and retrieval functions and records research as well as meeting e-discovery requests, compliance demands, and other legal and regulatory requirements. Your organization may, for instance, decide to use the standardized Library of Congress Subject Headings as standard terms for the "subject" metadata field.[20]

Metadata also describes a record's relationships with other documents and records and what actions may have been taken on the record over time. This helps to track its history and development.

The role of metadata in managing records is multifaceted; it helps to:

- Identify the records, record creators and users, and the areas within which they are utilized.
- Determine the relationships between records and the knowledge workers who use them, and the relationships between the records and the business processes they are supporting.
- Assist in managing and preserving the content and structure of the record.
- Support IG efforts that outline who has access to records and the context (when and where) in which access to the records is granted.
- Provide an audit trail to document changes to or actions on the record and its metadata.
- Support the finding and understanding of records and their relationships.[21]

In addition, good metadata management provides additional business benefits including increased management control over records, improved records authenticity and security, and reusability of metadata.[22]

Metadata terms or fields describe a record's characteristics so that it may be classified, managed, and found more easily.

> Metadata terms can be as basic as the name of the document, the creator, the subject, the date it was created, the document type, the length of the document, its security classification, and its file type.

Often, organizations will establish mandatory metadata terms that must accompany a record and some optional ones that may help in identifying and finding it. *A record is more complete with more metadata terms included, which also facilitates search and retrieval of records.*[23] This additional metadata is particularly helpful when knowledge workers are not quite sure which records they are searching for and therefore enter some vague or conceptual search terms. The more detail that is in the metadata fields, the more likely—and faster—that end users can find the records they need to complete their work. Populating metadata fields provides a measurable productivity benefit to the organization, although it is difficult to quantify. Certainly, search times will decrease upon implementation of a standardized metadata program, and improved work output and decisions will also follow.

Standardizing the metadata terms, definitions, and classifications for documents and records is done by developing and enforcing IG policy. This standardization effort gives users confidence that the records they are looking for are, in fact, the complete and current set they need to work with. And it provides the basis for a *legally defensible* records management (RM) program that will hold up in court.

A metadata governance program must be an ongoing effort that keeps metadata up to date and accurate. Often, once a metadata project is complete, attention to it wanes, maintenance tasks are not executed, and soon the accuracy and completeness of searches for documents and records deteriorates. So metadata maintenance is an ongoing process, and it must be formalized into a program that is periodically checked, tested, and audited.

Types of Metadata

Several types or categories of metadata are described next.

> *Administrative metadata.* Metadata that includes management information about the digital resource, such as ownership and rights management.
>
> *Descriptive metadata.* Metadata that describes the intellectual content of a resource and is used for the indexing, discovery, and identification of a digital resource.
>
> *Preservation metadata.* Metadata that specifically captures information that helps facilitate management and access to digital files over time. This inherently

> A metadata governance and management program must be ongoing.

The main types of metadata are: administrative, descriptive, preservation, structural, and technical metadata.

includes descriptive, administrative, structural, and technical metadata elements that focus on the provenance, authenticity, preservation activity, technical environment, and rights management of an object.

Structural metadata. Metadata that is used to display and navigate digital resources and describes relationships between multiple digital files, such as page order in a digitized book.

Technical metadata. Metadata that describes the features of the digital file, such as resolution, pixel dimension, and hardware. The information is critical for migration and long-term sustainability of the digital resource.[24]

Core Metadata Issues

Some key considerations and questions that need to be answered for effective implementation of a metadata governance program are listed next.

- *Who is the audience?* Which users will be using the metadata in their daily operations? What is their skill level? Which metadata terms/fields are most important to them? What has been their approach to working with documents and records in the past, and how can it be streamlined or improved? What terms are important to management? How can the metadata schema be designed to accommodate the primary audience and other secondary audiences? Answers to these questions will come only with close consultation with these key stakeholders.

- *Who else can help?* That is, which other stakeholders can help build a consensus on the best metadata strategy and approach? What other records creators, users, custodians, auditors, and legal counsel personnel can be added to the team to design a metadata approach that maximizes its value to the organization? Are there subject matter experts (SMEs)? What standards and best practices can be applied across functional boundaries to improve the ability of various groups to collaborate and leverage the metadata?

- *How can metadata governance be implemented and maintained?* Creating IG guidelines and rules for metadata assignment, input, and upkeep are a critical step—but how will the program continue to be updated to maintain its value to the organization? What business processes and audit checks should be in place? How will the quality of the metadata be monitored and controlled? Who is accountable?

- *What will the user training program look like?* How will users be trained initially, and how will continued education and reinforcement be communicated? Will there be periodic meetings of the IG or metadata team to discuss issues and concerns? What is the process for adding or amending metadata terms as the business progresses and changes? These questions must be answered, and a documented plan must be in place.

■ *What will the communications plan be?* Management time and resources are also needed to continue the practice of informing and updating users, and encouraging compliance with internal metadata standards and policies. Users need to know on a consistent basis why metadata is important and the value that good metadata management can bring to the organization.

International Metadata Standards and Guidance

Metadata is what gives an e-record its record status; in other words, electronic records metadata is what makes an electronic file a record. There are a number of established international standards for metadata structure, and additional guidance on strategy and implementation has been provided by standards groups, such as the International Organization for Standardization (ISO) and American National Standards Institute/ National Information Standards Organization (ANSI/NISO), and other bodies, such as the Dublin Core Metadata Initiative (DCMI).

ISO 15489 Records Management Definitions and Relevance

The international RM standard ISO 15489 states that "a record should correctly reflect what was communicated or decided or what action was taken. It should be able to support the needs of the business to which it relates and be used for accountability purposes." Its metadata definition is "data describing context, content, and structure of records and their management through time."[25]

A key difference between a document and a record is that a record is fixed, whereas a document can continue to be edited. Preventing records from being edited can be accomplished in part by indicating their formal record status in a metadata field, among other controls.

Proving that a record is, in fact, authentic and reliable necessarily includes proving that its metadata has remained intact and unaltered through the entire chain of custody of the record.

ISO Technical Specification 23081–1:2006 Information and Documentation—Records Management Processes—Metadata for Records—Part 1: Principles

[ISO 23081–1] covers the principles that underpin and govern records management metadata. These principles apply through time to:

■ Records and their metadata;
■ all processes that affect them;

Proving that a record is authentic and reliable includes proving that its metadata has remained intact and unaltered through the record's entire chain of custody.

ISO 23081 defines needed metadata for records and provides guidance for metadata management within the "framework" of ISO 15489.

- any system in which they reside;
- any organization that is responsible for their management.[26]

This standard provides guidance for metadata management within the "framework" of ISO 15489 and addresses the relevance and roles that metadata plays in RM intensive business processes. There are *no mandatory* metadata terms set, as these will differ by organization and by location and governing national and state/provincial laws.[27] The standard lists 10 purposes or benefits of using metadata in records management, which can help build the argument for convincing users and managers of the importance of good metadata governance and its resultant benefits.

Dublin Core Metadata Initiative

The DCMI produced a basic or core set of metadata terms that have served as the basis for many public and private sector metadata governance initiatives. Initial work in workshops filled with experts from around the world took place in 1995 in Dublin, Ohio (*not* Ireland). From these working groups arose the idea of a set of "core metadata" or essential metadata elements with generic descriptions. "The fifteen-element 'Dublin Core' achieved wide dissemination as part of the Open Archives Initiative Protocol for Metadata Harvesting (OAI-PMH) and has been ratified as IETF RFC 5013, ANSI/NISO Standard Z39.85–2007, and ISO Standard 15836:2009." [28]

Dublin Core has as its goals:

Simplicity of creation and maintenance

The Dublin Core element set has been kept as small and simple as possible to allow a nonspecialist to create simple descriptive records for information resources easily and inexpensively, while providing for effective retrieval of those resources in the networked environment.

Commonly understood semantics

Discovery of information across the vast commons of the Internet is hindered by differences in terminology and descriptive practices from one field of knowledge to the next. The Dublin Core can help the "digital tourist"—a nonspecialist searcher—find his or her way by supporting a common set of elements, the semantics of which are universally understood and supported. For example, scientists concerned with locating articles by a particular

Goals of the Dublin Core Metadata Initiative are simplicity, commonly understood semantics, international scope, and extensibility.

author, and art scholars interested in works by a particular artist, can agree on the importance of a "creator" element. Such convergence on a common, if slightly more generic, element set increases the visibility and accessibility of all resources, both within a given discipline and beyond.

International scope

The Dublin Core Element Set was originally developed in English, but versions are being created in many other languages, including Finnish, Norwegian, Thai, Japanese, French, Portuguese, German, Greek, Indonesian, and Spanish. The DCMI Localization and Internationalization Special Interest Group is coordinating efforts to link these versions in a distributed registry.

Although the technical challenges of internationalization on the World Wide Web have not been directly addressed by the Dublin Core development community, the involvement of representatives from virtually every continent has ensured that the development of the standard considers the multilingual and multicultural nature of the electronic information universe.

Extensibility

While balancing the needs for simplicity in describing digital resources with the need for precise retrieval, Dublin Core developers have recognized the importance of providing a mechanism for extending the DC [Dublin Core] element set for additional resource discovery needs. It is expected that other communities of metadata experts will create and administer additional metadata sets, specialized to the needs of their communities. Metadata elements from these sets could be used in conjunction with Dublin Core metadata to meet the need for interoperability. The DCMI Usage Board is presently working on a model for accomplishing this in the context of "application profiles." [29]

The fifteen element "Dublin Core" described in this standard is part of a larger set of metadata vocabularies and technical specifications maintained by the Dublin Core Metadata Initiative. . . . The full set of vocabularies, DCMI Metadata Terms . . . , also includes sets of resource classes (including the DCMI Type Vocabulary . . .), vocabulary encoding schemes, and syntax encoding schemes. The terms in DCMI vocabularies are intended to be used in combination with terms from other, compatible vocabularies in the context of application profiles and on the basis of the DCMI Abstract Model. [30]

Global Information Locator Service

Global Information Locator Service (GILS) is ISO 23950, the international standard for information searching over networked (client/server) computers, which is a simplified version of structured query language (SQL). ISO 23950 is a federated search protocol that equates to the U.S. standard ANSI/NISO Z39.50. The U.S. Library of Congress is the official maintenance agency for both standards, "which are technically identical (though with minor editorial differences)."[31]

ISO 23950 grew out of the library science community, although it is widely used, particularly in the public sector.[32] The use of GILS has tapered off as other metadata standards at the international, national, industry level, and agency level have been established.[33]

ISO 23950 (GILS) is the international standard for information searching over networked computers.

"It [GILS] specifies procedures and formats for a client to search a database provided by a server, retrieve database records, and perform related information retrieval functions." It does not specify a format, but information retrieval can be accomplished through full-text search, although it "also supports large, complex information collections."[34] The standard specifies how searches are made and how results are returned.

GILS helps people find information, especially in large, complex environments, such as across multiple government agencies. It is used in more than 40 U.S. states and a number of countries, including Argentina, Australia, Brazil, Canada, France, Germany, Hong Kong, India, Spain, Sweden, Switzerland, United Kingdom, and many others.

Text Mining

On a continuing basis, text mining can be conducted on documents to learn of emerging potential taxonomy terms. Text mining is simply performing detailed full-text searches on the content of document. And with more sophisticated tools like neural computing and artificial intelligence, *concepts*, not just keywords, can be discovered and leveraged for improving search quality for users.

Another tool is the **faceted search** (sometimes referred to as faceted navigation or faceted browsing), where, for instance, document collections are classified in multiple ways rather than in a single, rigid taxonomy. Knowledge workers may apply multiple filters to search across documents and records and find better and more complete results. And when they are not quite sure what they are looking for, or if it exists, a good taxonomy can help suggest terms, related terms, and associated content, truly contributing to enterprise **knowledge management** (KM) efforts, adding to corporate memory and increasing the organizational knowledge base.[35] Good KM helps to provide valuable training content for new employees and helps to reduce the impact of turnover and retiring employees.

Search is ultimately about metadata—whether your content has explicit metadata or not. The search engine creates a forward index and determines what words are contained in the documents being searched. It then inverts that index to provide the documents that words are contained in. This is effectively metadata about the content. A taxonomy can be used to enrich that search index in various ways. Index enrichment does require configuration and integration with search engines, but the result is the ability to increase both precision and recall of search results. Search results can also be grouped and clustered using a taxonomy. Doing this allows large numbers of results

Text mining is simply performing detailed full-text searches on the content of document.

to be scanned and understood by the user more easily. Many of these functions are determined by the capabilities of search tools and document and RM systems. As search functionality is developed, do not miss this opportunity to leverage the taxonomy.

Records Grouping Rationale

Records are grouped together for five primary reasons:

1. They tie together documents with like content, purpose, or theme.
2. To improve search and retrieval capabilities.
3. To identify content creators, owners, and managers.
4. To provide an understandable context.
5. For retention and disposition scheduling purposes.[36]

Taxonomies group records with common attributes. The groupings are constructed not only for RM classification and functions but also to support end users in their search and retrieval activities. Associating documents of a similar theme enables users to find documents when they do not know the exact document name. Choosing the theme or topic enables the users to narrow their search to find the relevant information.

The theme or grouping also places the document name into context. Words have many meanings and adding a theme to them further defines them. For example, the word "article" could pertain to a newspaper article, an item or object, or a section of a legal document. If it were grouped with publications, periodicals, and so on, the meaning would be clear. The challenge here is when to choose to have a separate category for "article" or to group "article" with other similar publications. Some people tend to develop finer levels of granularity in classification structures. These people can be called "splitters." Those who group things together are "lumpers." *But there can be clear rules for when to lump versus split.* Experts recommend splitting into another category when business needs demand that we treat the content differently or users need to segment the content for some purpose. This rule can be applied to many situations when trying to determine whether a new category is needed.[37]

Management, security, and access requirements are usually based on a user's role in a process. Grouping documents based on processes makes the job of assigning the responsibilities and access easier. For example, documents used in financial processes can be sensitive, and there is a need to restrict access to only those users that have the role in the business with a need to know.

Records retention periods are developed to be applied to a series (or group) of documents. When similar documents are grouped, it is easier to apply retention rules. However, when the grouping for retention is not the same as the grouping for other user views, a cross-mapping (**file plan**) scheme must be developed and incorporated into the taxonomy effort.

Business Classification Scheme, File Plans, and Taxonomy

In its simplest definition, a **business classification scheme** (BCS) is a hierarchical conceptual representation of the business activity performed by an organization.[38] The highest level of a BCS is called an *information series*, which signifies "high-level business functions" of a business or governmental agency. The next level is *themes*, which represent the specific activities that feed into the high-level functions at the information series level. These two top levels are rarely changed in an organization.[39]

A BCS is often viewed as synonymous with the term "file plan," which is the shared file structure in an ERM system, but it is *not a direct file plan*.

Yet a file plan can be developed and mapped back to the BCS and automated through an electronic document and records management system (EDRMS) or ERM system.[40]

A BCS is required by ISO 15489, the international RM standard. Together with the folders and records it contains, the BCS comprises what in the paper environment was called simply a "file plan." A BCS is therefore a full representation of the business of an organization.

Classification and Taxonomy

Classification of records extends beyond the categorization of records in the taxonomy. It also must include the application of retention requirements. These are legal and business requirements that specify the length of time a record must be maintained. A **records retention schedule** is a document that specifies the periods for which an organization's records should be retained to meet its operational needs and to comply with legal and other requirements. *The RRS groups documents into records series that relate to specific business activities.* This grouping is performed because laws and regulations are mainly based on the business activity that creates the documents. These business activities are not necessarily the same as the activities described in the hierarchy of the taxonomy. Therefore, there must be a method to map the RRS to the Taxonomy. This is accomplished with a File Plan. The File Plan facilitates the application of retention rules during document categorization without requiring a user to know or understand the RRS (see Figure A.3).

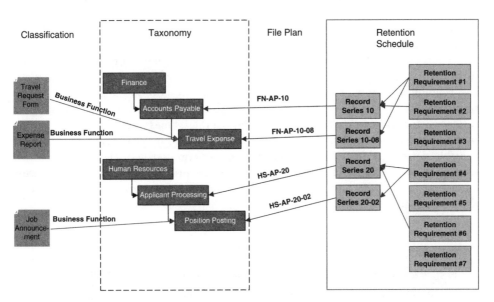

Figure A.3   Mapping the Records Retention Schedule to the Taxonomy
Source: Blackburn Consulting

Prebuilt versus Custom Taxonomies

Taxonomy templates for specific vertical industries (e.g., law, pharmaceuticals, aerospace) are provided by ECM, ERM/EDRMS, KM, enterprise search vendors, and trade associations. These prebuilt taxonomies use consistent terminology, have been tried and tested, and incorporate industry best practices, where possible. They can provide a jump-start and faster implementation at a lower cost than developing a custom taxonomy in-house or with external consulting assistance.

There are advantages and disadvantages to each approach. A prebuilt taxonomy typically will have some parameters that can be configured to better meet the business needs of an organization, yet compromises and trade-offs will have to be made. It also may introduce unfamiliar terminology that knowledge workers will be forced to adapt to, increasing training time and costs, and reducing overall effectiveness. These considerations must be factored into the build-or-buy decision. Using the custom-developed approach, a taxonomy can be tailored to meet the precise business needs of an organization or business unit and can include nuances such as company-specific nomenclature and terminology.[41]

Frequently, the longer and more costly customized approach must be used, since no prebuilt taxonomies fit well. This is especially the case with niche enterprises or those operating in developing or esoteric markets. For mature industries, more prebuilt taxonomies and template choices exist. *Attempting to tailor a prebuilt taxonomy actually can end up taking longer than building one from scratch if it is not a good fit in the first place*, so best practices dictate that organizations use prebuilt taxonomies where practical and custom-design taxonomies where needed.

There really is no one size fits all when it comes to taxonomy. And even when two organizations do the exact same thing in the exact same industry, differences in their culture, process, and content will require customization and tuning of the taxonomy. Standards are useful for improving efficiency of a process, and taxonomy projects really are internal standards projects. However, competitive advantage is attained through differentiation. A taxonomy specifically tuned to meet the needs of a particular enterprise is actually a competitive advantage.[42]

There is one other alternative, which is to "auto-generate" a taxonomy from the metadata in a collection of e-documents and records by using sophisticated statistical techniques, such as term frequency and entity extraction, to attempt to create a taxonomy.[43] This method seems to be perhaps the best of both worlds in that it offers instant customization at a low cost, but, although these types of tools can help provide useful insights into the data on the front end of a taxonomy project and help provide valuable statistical renderings, the only way to focus on user needs is to interview and work with users to gain insights into their business process needs and requirements while considering the business objectives of the taxonomy project. This cannot be done with mathematical computations—the human factor is key.

> Best practices dictate that taxonomy development includes designing the taxonomy structure and heuristic principles to align with user needs.

In essence, these auto-generated taxonomy tools can determine which terms and documents are used frequently, but they cannot assess the *real value* of information being used by knowledge workers and *how* they use the information. That takes consultation with stakeholders, studied observation, and business analysis.[44] *Machine-generated taxonomies look like they were generated by machines*—which is to say, they are not very usable by humans.[45]

Thesaurus Use in Taxonomies

In the use of taxonomies, a thesaurus contains the agreed-on synonyms and similar names for terms used in a controlled vocabulary. So, "invoice" may be listed as the equivalent term for "bill" when categorizing records. The thesaurus goes further and lists "information about each term and their relationships to other terms within the same thesaurus."

A thesaurus is similar to a hierarchical taxonomy but also includes "associative relationships."[46] An associative relationship is a conceptual relationship. *It is the "see also" that we may come across in the back of the book index.* But the question is, why do we want to see it? Associative relationships can provide a linkage to specific classes of information of interest to users and for particular processes. Use of associative relationships can provide a great deal of functionality in content and document management systems and needs to be considered in RM applications.[47]

There are international standards for thesauri creation from International ISO, ANSI, and the British Standards Institution (BSI).[48]

ISO 25964, "Information and Documentation—Thesauri and Interoperability with Other Vocabularies," "will draw on [the British standard, BS 8723] but reorganize the content to fit into two parts." Part 1, "Thesauri for Information Retrieval," of the standard ISO 25964 was published in August 2011. Part 2, "Interoperability with Other Vocabularies," was approved in 2013.[49]

Taxonomy Types

Taxonomies used in ERM systems are usually hierarchical where categories (nodes) in the hierarchy progress from general to specific. Each subsequent node is a subset of the higher level node. There are three basic types of hierarchical taxonomies: subject, business-unit, and functional.[50]

A *subject* taxonomy uses controlled terms for subjects. The subject headings are arranged in alphabetical order by the broadest subjects, with more precise subjects listed under them. An example is the Library of Congress subject headings used to categorize holdings in a library collection (see Figure A.4). Even the Yellow Pages could be considered a subject taxonomy.

There are three basic types of hierarchical taxonomies: subject, business unit, and functional.

```
...
H — SOCIAL SCIENCES
J — POLITICAL SCIENCE
K — LAW
L — EDUCATION
M — MUSIC AND BOOKS ON MUSIC
N — FINE ARTS
P — LANGUAGE AND LITERATURE
Q — SCIENCE
R — MEDICINE
 –   Subclass RA Public aspects of medicine
 –   Subclass RB Pathology
 –   Subclass RC Internal medicine
      –  RC31-1245 Internal medicine
      –  RC49-52 Psychosomatic medicine
      –  RC251 Constitutional diseases (General)
      –  RC254-282 Neoplasm. Tumors. Oncology
...
```

Figure A.4   Library of Congress Subject Headings

It is difficult to establish a universally recognized set of terms in a subject taxonomy. If users are unfamiliar with the topic, they may not know the appropriate term heading with which to begin their search. For example, say people are searching through the Yellow Pages for a place to purchase eyeglasses. They begin their search alphabetically by turning to the E's and scanning for the term "eyeglasses." Since there are no topics titled "eyeglasses," they consult the index, find the term "eyeglasses," and this provides a list of preferred terms or "see alsos" that direct them to "Optical—Retail" for a list of eyeglass businesses. (See Figure A.5.)

In both examples, the subject taxonomy is supported by a thesaurus. Again, a thesaurus is a controlled vocabulary that includes synonyms, related terms, and preferred terms. In the case of the Yellow Pages, the index functions as a basic thesaurus.

In a *business unit*–based taxonomy, the hierarchy reflects the organizational charts (e.g., department/division/unit). Records are categorized based on the business unit that manages them. Figure A.6 shows the partial detail of one node of a business unit–based taxonomy that was developed for a county government.

One advantage of a business unit–based taxonomy is that it mimics most existing paper-filing system schemas. Therefore, users are not required to learn a "new" system. However, conflicts arise when documents are managed or shared among multiple business units. As an example, for the county government referenced earlier, a property transfer document called the "TD1000" is submitted to the recording office for recording and then forwarded to the assessor for property tax evaluation processing. This poses a dilemma as to where to categorize the TD1000 in the taxonomy.

Another issue arises with organizational changes. When the organizational structure changes, so must the taxonomy based on business units.

In a *functional* taxonomy, records are categorized based on the functions and activities that produce them (function/activity/transaction). The organization's business processes are used to establish the taxonomy. The highest or broadest level represents the business functions. The next level down the hierarchy constitutes the

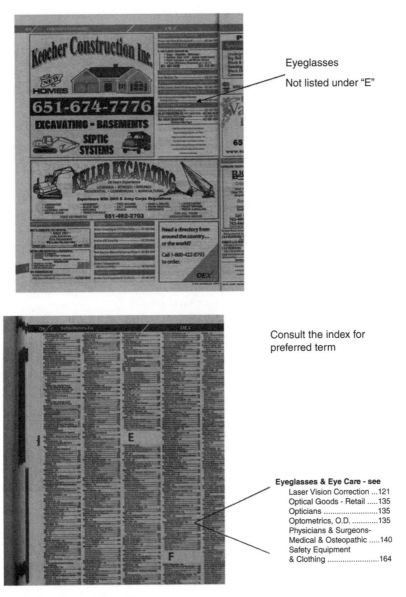

Eyeglasses
Not listed under "E"

Consult the index for
preferred term

Eyeglasses & Eye Care - see
Laser Vision Correction ...121
Optical Goods - Retail 135
Opticians 135
Optometrics, O.D. 135
Physicians & Surgeons-
Medical & Osteopathic 140
Safety Equipment
& Clothing 164

Figure A.5   Yellow Pages Example

activities performed for the function. The lowest level in the hierarchy consists of the records that are created as a result of the activity (the *transactions*).

Figure A.7 shows partial detail of one node of a functional taxonomy developed for a state government regulatory agency. The agency organizational structure is based on regulatory programs. Within the program areas are similar (repeated) functions and activities (e.g., permitting, compliance, and enforcement, etc.). When the repeated functions and activities are universalized, the results are a "flatter" taxonomy. *This type of taxonomy is better suited to endure organizational shifts and changes.* In addition, the process of universalizing the functions and activities inherently results in broader and

```
Assessor
Building
Commissioners
Coroner
District Attorney
Finance
Health and Environment
Human Resources
Human Services
Motor Vehicle
Clerk and Recorder  <-------- Department
•  Election          <-------- Divisions
•  Motor Vehicle
•  Recording
        - TD1000         <------- Records
        - Warranty Deed
...     - Quitclaim Deed
        - Subdivision Plat
Sheriff
Treasury
```

Figure A.6   County Government Business Unit Taxonomy

```
Accounting
Procurement
Contracts and Agreements
Licensing and Certification
Technical Assistance
Permitting
Compliance and Enforcement  <-- Function
•  Inspections              <-- Activities
•  Complaints
•  Emergency Response
•  Enforcement
        - Notice of Violation  <-- Transactions
        - Consent Decree
        - Request for Response Actions
        - Stipulation Agreement
```

Function	Activity
4. Permitting	4.1 Registration
	4.2 Application
	4.3 Public Notice
	4.4 Permit Development & Issuance
	4.5 Termination
5. Compliance and Enforcement	5.1 Inspections
	5.2 Complaints
	5.3 Emergency Response & Preparedness
	5.4 Monitoring Reporting
	5.5 Enforcement Actions

Figure A.7   State Government Regulatory Agency Functional Taxonomy

A functional taxonomy is better suited to endure organizational changes.

more generic naming conventions. A functional taxonomy provides flexibility when adding new record types (transactions) because there will be fewer changes to the hierarchy structure.

One disadvantage of a functional taxonomy is its inability to address case files (or project files). A case file is a collection of records that relate to a particular entity, person, or project. The records in the case file can be generated by multiple activities. For example, at the regulatory agency, enforcement files are maintained that contain records generated by enforcement activities (notice of violation, consent decree, etc.) and other ancillary but related activities, such as contracting, inspections, and permitting.

To address the case file issue at the regulatory agency, metadata cross-referencing was used to provide a virtual case file view of the records collection. (See Figure A.8.)

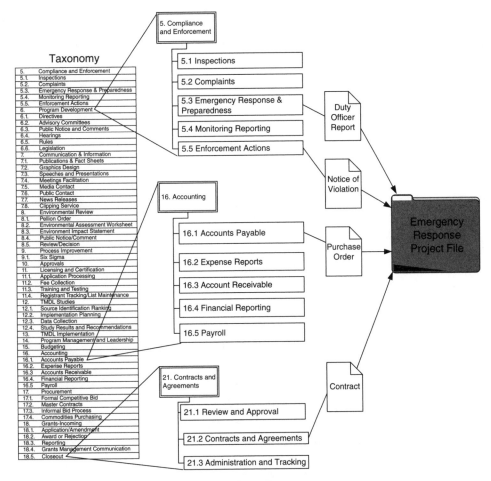

Figure A.8   Metadata Cross-Referencing within a Taxonomy
Source: Blackburn Consulting

One disadvantage of a functional taxonomy is its inability to address case files (or project files).

A *hybrid* taxonomy is usually the best approach. Certain business units usually do not change over time. For example, accounting and human resources activities are fairly constant. Those portions of the taxonomy could be constructed in a business unit manner even when other areas within the organization use a functional structure. (See Figure A.9.)

Faceted taxonomies allow for multiple organizing principles to be applied to information along various dimensions. Facets can contain subjects, departments, business units, processes, tasks, interests, security levels, and other attributes used to describe information. With faceted taxonomies, there is never really one single taxonomy but rather collections of taxonomies that describe different aspects of information. In the e-commerce world, facets are used to describe brand, size, color, price, and other context-specific attributes. RM systems can also be developed with knowledge and process attributes related to the enterprise.[51]

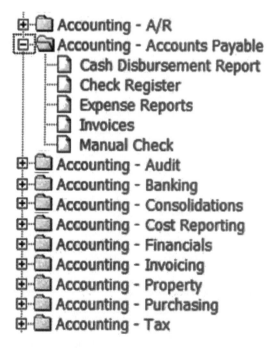

Figure A.9   Basic Accounting Business Unit Taxonomy
Source: Blackburn Consulting

A hybrid approach to taxonomy design is usually the best.

Business Process Analysis

To establish the taxonomy, business processes must be documented and analyzed. There are two basic process analysis methods: top down and bottom up. In the top-down method, a high-level analysis of business functions is performed to establish the higher tiers. Detailed analyses are performed on each business process to fill in the lower tiers. The detailed analyses usually are conducted in a phased approach, and the taxonomy is updated incrementally.

In order to use the bottom-up method, detailed analyses must be performed for all processes in one effort. Using this method ensures that there will be fewer modifications to the taxonomy. However, sometimes conducting a comprehensive analysis is not feasible for organizations with limited resources. A phased or incremental approach is usually more budget friendly and places fewer burdens on the organization's resources.

Many diagramming formats and tools will provide the details needed for the analysis. The most basic diagramming can be accomplished with a standard tool such as Visio® from Microsoft. More advanced modeling tools can be used to produce the diagrams that provide the functionality to statistically analyze process changes through simulation and provide information for architecture planning and other process initiatives within the organization.

Any diagramming format will suffice as long as it depicts the flow of data through the processes showing process steps, inputs, and outputs (documents), decision steps, organizational boundaries, and interaction with information systems. The diagrams should depict document movement within as well as between the subject department and other departments or outside entities.

Figure A.10 uses a swim-lane type diagram. Each horizontal "lane" represents a participant or role. The flow of data and sequence of process steps is shown with lines (the arrows note the direction). Process steps are shown as boxes.

Business processes must be documented and analyzed to develop a taxonomy.

Decision steps are shown as diamonds.

Documents are depicted as a rectangle with a curved bottom line.

The first step is to review any existing business process documentation (e.g., business plans, procedures manuals, employee training manuals, etc.) in order to gain a better understanding of the functions and processes. This is done in advance of interviews in order to provide a base-level understanding to reduce the amount of time required of the interviewees.

Two different types of interviews (high level and detailed business process) are conducted with key personnel from each department. The initial (high-level) interviews are conducted with a representative who will provide an overall high-level view of the department, including its mission, responsibilities, and identification of the functional areas. This person will identify those staff members who will provide details of the specific processes in each of the functional areas identified. For instance, if the department is human resources, functional areas of the department might include: applicant processing, classification, training, and personnel file management. It is expected that this first interview/meeting will last approximately one hour.

The second interviews are detailed interviews that focus on daily processes performed in each functional area. For example, if the function is human resources

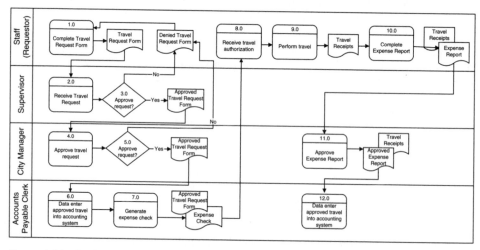

Figure A.10   Business Process Example—Travel Expense Process
Source: Blackburn Consulting

classification, the process may be the creation/management of position descriptions. It is only necessary to interview one person who represents a particular process—there is no need to interview multiple staff members performing the same function. These second interviews likely will last one to two hours each, depending on the complexity of the process.

When there are processes that "connect" (e.g., the output from one process is the input to another), it is useful to conduct group interviews with representatives for each process. This often results in a-ha moments when employees from one process finally understand why they are sending certain records to another process. It also brings to light **business process improvement** opportunities. When employees understand the big-picture process, they can identify unnecessary process steps and redundant or obsolete documents that can be eliminated.

One purpose of process analysis is to develop taxonomy facets that can be used to bring to the surface information for particular steps in the process. In some cases, process steps can directly inform the types of artifacts that are needed at a particular part of the process and therefore be used to develop content types in KM use cases. This is related to RM in that KM applications are simply another lens under which content can be viewed. Process analysis also can help determine the scope of metadata for content. For example, if developing an application to view invoices, if the process includes understanding line item detail, this will dictate a different metadata model than if the process sought only to determine whether invoices over a certain threshold were unpaid. Different processes, different use cases, different metadata.

Taxonomy Testing: A Necessary Step

Once a new taxonomy is developed, it must be tested and piloted to see if it meets user needs and expectations. To attempt the rollout of a new taxonomy without testing it first is imprudent, and will end up costing more time and resources in the long run. So budget the time and money for it.[52] Taxonomy testing is where the rubber meets the road; it provides real data to see if the taxonomy design has met user expectations and actually helps them in their work.

User testing provides valuable feedback and allows the taxonomist or taxonomy team to fine-tune the work they have done to more closely align the taxonomy with user needs and business objectives. What may have seemed an obvious term or category may, in fact, be way off. This may result from the sheer focus and myopia of the taxonomy team. So getting user feedback is essential.

Many taxonomy testing tools can assist in the design effort. Once an initial design is drafted, a low-tech approach is to hand-write classification categories and document types on Post-it notes or index cards. Then bring in a sampling of users and ask them to place the notes or cards in the proper category. Track and calculate the results.

Software is available to conduct this card sorting in a more high-tech way, and more sophisticated software can assist in the development and testing effort and to help to update and maintain the taxonomy.

Regardless of the method used, the taxonomy team or even IG team or task force needs to be the designated arbiter when conflicting opinions arise.

> There is nothing better than getting quantitative feedback to see if you are hitting the mark with users.

Taxonomy testing is not a one-shot task; with feedback and changes, you progress in iterations closer and closer to meeting user requirements, which may take several rounds of testing and changes.

Taxonomies can be tested in multiple ways. User acceptance throughout the derivation process can be simple conference room pilots or validation, formal usability testing based on use cases, card sorting (open and closed), and tagging processes. Autotagging of content with target taxonomies is also an area that requires testing.[53]

Taxonomy Maintenance

After a taxonomy has been implemented, it will need to be updated over time to reflect changes in document management processes as well to increase usability. Therefore, users should have the opportunity to suggest changes, addition, and deletions. *There should be a formal process in place to manage requests for changes.* A person or committee should be assigned the responsibility to determine how and if each requests will be facilitated.

There must be guidelines to follow in making changes to the taxonomy. A U.S. state agency organization uses these guidelines in determining taxonomy changes:

- The new term must have a definition, preferably provided by the proposer of the new term.
- It should be a term someone would recognize even if they have no background within our agency's workings; use of industry standard terminology is preferred.
- Terms should be mutually exclusive from other terms.
- Terms that can be derived using a combination of other terms or facilitated with metadata will not be added.
- The value should not be a "temporary" term—it should have some expectation to have a long life span.
- We should expect that there would be a significant volume of content that could be assigned the value—otherwise, use of a more general document type and clarification through the metadata on items is preferred: if enough

> There should be a formal process in place to manage requests for taxonomy changes.

> A folksonomy uses free-form words to classify documents. A folksonomy approach is useful for updating your taxonomy structure and improves the user search experience.

items are titled with the new term over time to warrant reconsideration, it will be reconsidered.

- For higher-level values in the hierarchy, the relationship between parents and children (functions and activities) is always "is a kind of . . ." Other relationships are not supported.
- Document type values should not reflect the underlying technology used to capture the content and should not reflect the format of the content directly.

Social Tagging and Folksonomies

Social tagging is a method that allows users to manage content with metadata they apply themselves using keywords or metadata tags. Unlike traditional classification, which uses a controlled vocabulary, *social tagging keywords are freely chosen by each individual.*

Folksonomy is the term used for this free-form, social approach to metadata assignment.

Folksonomies are not an ordered classification system; rather, they are a list of keywords input by users that are ranked by popularity.[54]

Taxonomies and folksonomies both have their place. *Folksonomies can be used in concert with taxonomies to nominate key terms for use in the taxonomy,* which contributes toward the updating and maintenance of the taxonomy while making the user experience better by utilizing users' own preferred terms.

A combined taxonomy and folksonomy approach may provide for an optional free-text metadata field for social tags that might be titled "Subject" or "Comment." Then users could search that free-form, uncontrolled field to narrow document searches. The folksonomy fields will be of most use to a user or departmental area, but if the terms are used frequently enough, they may need to be added to the formal taxonomy's controlled vocabulary to benefit the entire organization.

In sum, taxonomy development, testing, and maintenance is hard work—but it can yield significant and sustained benefits to the organization over the long haul by providing more complete and accurate information when knowledge workers make searches; better IG and control over the organization's documents, records, and information; and a more agile compliance and litigation readiness posture.

APPENDIX SUMMARY: **KEY POINTS**

- Knowledge workers spend 15 to 25 percent of an average workday searching for information, often due to poor taxonomy design.

- Taxonomies are hierarchical classification structures used to standardize the naming and organization of information using controlled vocabularies for terms.

- Taxonomies speed up the process of retrieving records because end users can select from subject categories or topics.

- Taxonomies need to be considered from two main perspectives: navigation and classification.

- Poor search results, inconsistent or conflicting file plans, and the inability to locate information on a timely basis are indications that taxonomy work is needed.

- Metadata, which are the characteristics of a document expressed in data fields, must be leveraged in taxonomy design.

- Best practices dictate that taxonomy development includes designing the taxonomy structure and heuristic principles to align with user needs.

- There are three basic types of hierarchical taxonomies: subject, business unit, and functional.

- A *hybrid* approach to taxonomy design is usually the best.

- An SME can be a valuable resource in taxonomy development. SMEs should not be relied on too heavily, though, or the taxonomy may end up filled with esoteric jargon.

- A document inventory is conducted to gather detailed information regarding the documents managed.

- Business processes must be documented and analyzed to develop a taxonomy.

- User testing is essential, provides valuable feedback, and allows the taxonomist or taxonomy team to fine-tune the work.

- Begin by using low-cost, simple tools for taxonomy development, and migrate to more capable ones as your organization's needs grow and maintenance is required.

- A folksonomy uses free-form words to classify documents. A folksonomy approach is useful for updating your taxonomy structure and improves the user search experience.

Notes

1. ARMA Metro Maryland Newsletter, Cadence Group, "Taxonomies: The Backbone of Enterprise Content Management," December 2008—January 2009, www.arma-metromd.org/wp-content/uploads/2012/11/2009-01NewImages.pdf.
2. Delphi Group White Paper, "Taxonomy and Content Classification: Market Milestone Report," 2002, www.delphigroup.com/whitepapers/pdf/WP_2002_TAXONOMY.PDF (accessed April 25, 2012).
3. Ibid.
4. Cadence Group, "Taxonomies."
5. Daniela Barbosa, "The Taxonomy Folksonomy Cookbook," www.slideshare.net/HeuvelMarketing/taxonomy-folksonomy-cookbook (accessed October 12, 2012).
6. Ibid.
7. Montague Institute Review, "Your Taxonomy Is Your Future" (February 2000), www.montague.com/abstracts/future.html.
8. Free Library, "Creating Order Out of Chaos with Taxonomies," 2005, www.thefreelibrary.com/Creating+order+out+of+chaos+with+taxonomies%3A+the+increasing+volume+of...-a0132679071 (accessed April 25, 2012).
9. Susan Cisco and Wanda Jackson, "Creating Order Out of Chaos with Taxonomies," *Information Management Journal* (May/June 2005), www.arma.org/bookstore/files/Cisco.pdf.
10. Marcia Morante, "Usability Guidelines for Taxonomy Development," April 2003, www.montague.com/abstracts/usability.html.
11. Seth Earley, e-mail to author, September 10, 2012.
12. Ibid.
13. Cadence Group, "Taxonomies," p. 3.
14. DAM News Staff, "8 Things You Need to Know about How Taxonomy Can Improve Search," May 17, 2010, http://damcoalition.com/index.php/metadata/story/8_things_you_need_to_know_about_how_taxonomy_can_improve_search/.
15. Ibid.
16. Earley e-mail.
17. National Archives of Australia, "AGLS Metadata Standard, Part 2—Usage Guide," Version 2.0, July 2010, www.naa.gov.au/Images/AGLS%20Metadata%20Standard%20Part%202%20%20Usage%20Guide_tcm16-47011.pdf.
18. Kate Cumming, "Metadata Matters," in Julie McLeod and Catherine Hare, eds., *Managing Electronic Records*, p. 34 (London: Facet, 2005).
19. Minnesota State Archives, "Electronic Records Management Guidelines: Metadata," March 12, 2012, www.mnhs.org/preserve/records/electronicrecords/ermetadata.html.
20. Ibid.
21. Cumming, "Metadata Matters," p. 35.
22. Ibid.
23. NISO, "Understanding Metadata," 2004, www.niso.org/publications/press/UnderstandingMetadata.pdf (accessed October 15, 2012).
24. This and the next section are based on Minnesota State Archives, "Electronic Records Management Guidelines."
25. National Archives, "Requirements for Electronic Records Management Systems: 2: Metadata Standard," 2002, www.nationalarchives.gov.uk/documents/metadatafinal.pdf (accessed June 21, 2012).
26. International Organization for Standardization, "ISO 23081-1:2006, Information and Documentation—Records Management Processes—Metadata for Records—Part 1: Principles," www.iso.org/iso/iso_catalogue/catalogue_tc/catalogue_detail.htm?csnumber=40832 (accessed June 26, 2012).
27. Carl Weise, "ISO 23081-1: 2006, Metadata for Records, Part 1: Principles," January 27, 2012, www.aiim.org/community/blogs/expert/ISO-23081-1-2006-Metadata-for-records-Part-1-principles.
28. Dublin Core Metadata Initiative, http://dublincore.org/metadata-basics/ (accessed June 26, 2012).
29. Diane Hillman, Dublin Core Metadata Initiative, "User Guide," November 7, 2005, http://dublincore.org/documents/usageguide/.
30. Dublin Core Metadata Initiative, "Dublin Core Metadata Element Set," Version 1.1, June 14, 2012, http://dublincore.org/documents/dces/.
31. International Standard Maintenance Agency, Z39.50, Library of Congress www.loc.gov/z3950/agency/ (accessed July 7, 2012).

32. National Information Standards Organization, "ANSI/NISO Z39.50-2003 (R2009) Information Retrieval: Application Service Definition & Protocol Specification," www.niso.org/apps/group_public/project/details.php?project_id=49 (accessed July 7, 2012).

33. Jenn Riley, "Glossary of Metadata Standards," 2009–2010, www.dlib.indiana.edu/~jenlrile/metadata-map/seeingstandards_glossary_pamphlet.pdf (accessed July 9, 2012).

34. Global Information Locator Service, "Initiatives—Includes Spatial Data Initiatives," www.gils.net/initiatives.html (accessed July 7, 2012).

35. Ibid.

36. Adventures in Records Management, "The Business Classification Scheme," October 15, 2006, http://adventuresinrecordsmanagement.blogspot.com/2006/10/business-classification-scheme.html.

37. Earley e-mail.

38. National Archives of Australia, www.naa.gov.au/Images/classifcation%20tools_tcm16-49550.pdf (accessed December 13, 2013).

39. Adventures in Records Management, "Business Classification Scheme."

40. Ibid.

41. Cisco and Jackson, "Creating Order Out of Chaos."

42. Earley e-mail.

43. www.earley.com/blog/the-popularity-contest-taxonomy-development-in-the-petabyte-era (accessed April 25, 2012).

44. Ibid.

45. Earley e-mail.

46. Hedden, "The Accidental Taxonomist," 10.

47. Earley e-mail.

48. Hedden, "The Accidental Taxonomist," 8.

49. NISO, "Project ISO 25964: Thesauri and Interoperability with Other Vocabularies," www.niso.org/workrooms/iso25964 (accessed April 25, 2012).

50. This section is adapted with permission from Barb Blackburn, "Taxonomy Design Types," *e-Doc Magazine* (May/June 2006): 14, 16, www.imergeconsult.com/img/114BB.pdf (accessed October 12, 2012).

51. Earley e-mail.

52. Details in this section are from Stephanie Lemieux, "The Pain and Gain of Taxonomy User Testing," July 8, 2008, www.earley.com/blog/the-pain-and-gain-of-taxonomy-user-testing.

53. Earley e-mail.

54. Tom Reamy, "Folksonomy Folktales," *KM World* 18, no. 9 (October 2009), www.kmworld.com/Articles/Editorial/Feature/Folksonomy-folktales-56210.aspx.

Laws and Major Regulations Related to Records Management

United States

Records management practices and standards are delineated in many federal regulations. Also, a number of state statutes have passed. In some cases they actually supersede federal regulations; therefore, it is crucial to understand compliance within the state or states where an organization operates.

On the federal level, public companies must be vigilant in verifying, protecting, and reporting financial information to comply with requirements under Sarbanes—Oxley (SOX) and the Gramm—Leach—Bliley Acts. Health care concerns must meet the requirements of the Health Insurance Portability and Accountability Act (HIPAA), and investment firms must comply with a myriad of regulations by the Securities and Exchange Commission (SEC) and National Association of Securities Dealers (NASD).

This appendix presents a brief description of current rules, laws, regulators, and their records retention and corporate policy requirements. *(Note: This is an overview, and firms should consult their own legal counsel for interpretation and applicability.)*

Gramm—Leach—Bliley Act

The Financial Institution Privacy Protection Act of 2001 and Financial Institution Privacy Protection Act of 2003 (Gramm—Leach—Bliley Act) was amended in 2003 to improve and increase protection of nonpublic personal information. Through this act, financial records must be properly secured, safeguarded, and eventually completely destroyed so that the information cannot be further accessed.

Health Insurance Portability and Accountability Act of 1996

HIPAA requires that security standards be adopted for:

- Controlling who may access health information.
- Providing audit trails for electronic record systems.
- Isolating health data, making it inaccessible to unauthorized access.
- Ensuring the confidentiality and safeguarding of health information when it is electronically transmitted to ensure it is physically, electronically, and administratively secure.
- Meeting the needs and capabilities of small and rural health care providers.

385

USA-PATRIOT Act (Uniting and Strengthening America by Providing Appropriate Tools Required to Intercept and Obstruct Terrorism Act of 2001)

The USA-PATRIOT Act does two things: It (1) requires that the identity of a person opening an account with any financial institution is verified by the financial institution, which must implement reasonable procedures to maintain identity information; and (2) provides law enforcement organizations broad investigatory rights, including warrantless searches.

Sarbanes–Oxley Act

The key provisions of SOX require that:

- Public corporations implement extensive policies, procedures, and tools to prevent fraudulent activities.
- Financial control and risk mitigation processes be documented and verified by independent auditors.
- Executives of publicly traded companies certify the validity of the company's financial statements.
- Business records must be kept for not less than five years.

SEC Rule 17A-4

SEC Rule 17A-4 requires that: (1) records that must be maintained and preserved must be available to be produced or reproduced using either micrographic media (such as microfilm or microfiche) or electronic storage media (any digital storage medium or system); and (2) original copies of all communications, such as interoffice memoranda, be preserved for no less than *three* years, the first two in an easily accessible location.

Code of Federal Regulations Title 21, Part 11—Pharmaceuticals

CFR Title 21, Part 11, requires that companies: (1) have controls in place to protect content stored on both open and closed systems to ensure the authenticity and integrity of electronic records; and (2) generate accurate and complete electronic copies of records so that the Food and Drug Administration may inspect them.

Code of Federal Regulations Title 47, Part 42—Telecommunications

CFR Title 47, Part 42, requires that telecommunications carriers keep original records or reproductions of original records, including memoranda, documents, papers, and correspondence that the carrier prepared or that were prepared on behalf of the carrier.

U.S. Federal Authority on Archives and Records: National Archives and Records Administration

The National Archives and Records Administration (NARA: go to nara.gov):

- Oversees physical and electronic recordkeeping policies and procedures of government agencies, requiring adequate and proper documentation on the conducting of U.S. government business.

- Defines "formal e-records" as machine-readable materials created or received by an agency of the U.S. federal government under federal law or in the course of the transaction of public business.
- Requires that organized records series be established for electronic records (e-records) on a particular subject or function to facilitate the management of these e-records.

NARA regulations affecting federal agencies and their records management programs are found in Subchapter B of 36 CFR Chapter XII.[1]

- Part 1220—Federal Records; General
- Part 1222—Creation and Maintenance of Records
- Part 1223—Managing Vital Records
- Part 1224—Records Disposition Program
- Part 1225—Scheduling Records
- Part 1226—Implementing Disposition
- Part 1227—General Records Schedule
- Part 1228—Loan of Permanent and Unscheduled Records
- Part 1229—Emergency Authorization to Destroy Records
- Part 1230—Unlawful or Accidental Removal, Defacing, Alteration, or Destruction of Records
- Part 1231—Transfer of Records from the Custody of One Executive Agency to Another
- Part 1232—Transfer of Records to Records Storage Facilities
- Part 1233—Transfer, Use, and Disposition of Records in a NARA Federal Records Center
- Part 1234—Facility Standards for Records Storage Facilities
- Part 1235—Transfer of Records to the National Archives of the United States
- Part 1236—Electronic Records Management
- Part 1237—Audiovisual, Cartographic, and Related Records Management
- Part 1238—Microform Records Management
- Part 1239—Program Assistance and Inspections
- Part 1240–1249 [Reserved]

U.S. Code of Federal Regulations

In the CFR, there are more than 5,000 references to retaining records. It can be found online at www.ecfr.gov/cgi-bin/ECFR?page=browse

Canada

By Ken Chasse, J.D., LL.M.

The National Standards of Canada for electronic records management are: (1) Electronic Records as Documentary Evidence, CAN/CGSB-72.34–2005 (72.34), published in December 2005; and (2) Microfilm and Electronic Images as Documentary Evidence, CAN/CGSB-72.11–93, first published in 1979 and updated to 2000 (72.11).[2] 72.34 incorporates all that 72.11 deals with and is therefore the more important of the two. Because of its age, 72.11 should not be relied on for its "legal" content. However,

72.11 has remained the industry standard for "imaging" procedures—converting original paper records to electronic storage. The Canada Revenue Agency has adopted these standards as applicable to records concerning taxation.[3]

72.34 deals with nine topics:

1. Management authorization and accountability
2. Documentation of procedures used to manage records
3. "Reliability testing" of electronic records according to existing legal rules
4. The procedures manual and the chief records officer
5. Readiness to produce (the "prime directive")
6. Records recorded and stored in accordance with "the usual and ordinary course of business" and "system integrity," key phrases from the Evidence Acts in Canada
7. Retention and disposal of electronic records
8. Backup and records system recovery
9. Security and protection

From these standards practitioners have derived many specific tests for auditing, establishing, and revising electronic records management systems (ERMS).[4]

The "prime directive" of these standards states: "An organization shall always be prepared to produce its records as evidence."[5] *The duty to establish the "prime directive" falls on senior management.*[6]

Senior management, the organization's own internal law-making authority, proclaims throughout the organization the integrity of the organization's records system (and, therefore, the integrity of its electronic records) by establishing and declaring:

1. The system's role in the usual and ordinary course of business.
2. The circumstances under which its records are made.
3. Its prime directive for all records management system purposes, i.e., an organization shall always be prepared to produce its records as evidence. This dominant principle applies to all of the organization's business records, including electronic, optical, original paper source records, microfilm, and other records of equivalent form and content.

Being prepared to produce records (the "dominant principle" of an organization's ERMS) means the duty to maintain compliance with the prime directive should fall on its senior management.

Because an electronic record is completely dependent on its ERM system for everything, compliance with these National Standards and their prime directive should be part of the determination of the "admissibility" (acceptability) of evidence and of electronic discovery in court proceedings (litigation) and in regulatory tribunal proceedings.[7]

There are 14 legal jurisdictions in Canada: 10 provinces; 3 territories; and the federal jurisdiction of the Government of Canada. Each has an Evidence Act (the Civil Code in the province of Quebec[8]), which applies to legal proceedings within its legislative jurisdiction. For example, criminal law and patents and copyrights are within federal legislative jurisdiction, and most civil litigation comes within provincial legislative jurisdiction.[9]

The admissibility of records as evidence is determined under the "business record" provisions of the Evidence Acts.[10] These acts require proof that a record was made "in the usual and ordinary course of business" and of "the circumstances of the making of the record." In addition, to obtain admissibility for electronic records, most of the Evidence Acts contain electronic record provisions, which state that an electronic record is admissible as evidence on proof of the "integrity of the electronic record system in which the data was recorded or stored."[11] This is the "system integrity" test for the admissibility of electronic records. The word "integrity" has yet to be defined by the courts.[12]

However, by way of sections such as the next one, the electronic record provisions of the Evidence Acts make reference to the use of standards such as the National Standards of Canada:

> For the purpose of determining under any rule of law whether an electronic record is admissible, evidence may be presented in respect of any standard, procedure, usage or practice on how electronic records are to be recorded or stored, having regard to the type of business or endeavor that used, recorded, or stored the electronic record and the nature and purpose of the electronic record.[13]

Six areas of law and records and information management (RIM) are applicable to paper and electronic records:

1. The laws of evidence applicable to electronic and paper records[14]
2. The National Standards of Canada concerning electronic records[15]
3. The records requirements of government agencies, such as the Canada Revenue Agency[16]
4. The electronic commerce legislation[17]
5. The privacy laws[18]
6. The guidelines for electronic discovery in legal proceedings[19]

These six areas are closely interrelated and are based on very similar concepts. They all make demands of records systems and of the chief records officer or others responsible for records. *Therefore, a failure to satisfy the records management needs of any one of them will likely mean a failure to satisfy all of them.* Agencies that manage these areas of law look to the decisions of the courts to determine the requirements for acceptable records.

Each of these areas of law affects RIM, just as these areas are affected by the laws governing the use of records as evidence in legal proceedings—the laws of evidence. These relationships make mandatory compliance with the prime directive provided by the National Standards, which states: "an organization shall always be prepared to produce its records as evidence."[20]

United Kingdom

Regulations and Legislation Impacting Records Retention

The following Acts and Statutory Instruments of the U.K. and Scottish Parliaments contain provisions that are relevant to records retention and disposal:

Acts of the U.K. Parliament

- 1957 c31 Occupiers Liability Act 1957
- 1969 c57 Employers' Liability (Compulsory Insurance) Act 1969
- 1970 c41 Equal Pay Act 1970
- 1970 c9 Taxes Management Act 1970
- 1973 c52 Prescription and Limitations (Scotland) Act 1973
- 1974 c37 Health and Safety at Work (etc.) Act 1974
- 1975 c65 Sex Discrimination Act 1975
- 1976 c74 Race Relations Act 1976
- 1980 c58 Limitation Act 1980
- 1992 c4 Social Security Contributions and Benefits Act 1992
- 1994 c30 Education Act 1994
- 1994 c23 Value Added Tax Act 1994
- 1995 c50 Disability Discrimination Act 1995
- 1998 c29 Data Protection Act 1998

Acts of the Scottish Parliament

- 2002 asp13 Freedom of Information (Scotland) Act 2002

Statutory Instruments of the U.K. Parliament

- SI 1977/500 The Safety Representatives and Safety Committees Regulations 1977
- SI 1981/917 The Health and Safety (First Aid) Regulations 1981
- SI 1982/894 The Statutory Sick Pay (General) Regulations 1982
- SI 1986/1960 The Statutory Maternity Pay (General) Regulations 1986
- SI 1989/1790 The Noise at Work Regulations 1989
- SI 1989/635 The Electricity at Work Regulations 1989
- SI 1989/682 The Health and Safety Information for Employees Regulations 1989
- SI 1991/2680 The Public Works Contracts Regulations 1991
- SI 1992/2792 The Health and Safety (Display Screen Equipment) Regulations 1992
- SI 1992/2793 The Manual Handling Operations Regulations 1992
- SI 1992/2932 The Provision and Use of Work Equipment Regulations 1992
- SI 1992/2966 The Personal Protective Equipment at Work Regulations 1992
- SI 1993/3228 The Public Services Contracts Regulations 1993
- SI 1993/744 The Income Tax (Employments) Regulations 1993
- SI 1995/201 The Public Supply Contracts Regulations 1995
- SI 1995/3163 The Reporting of Injuries, Diseases and Dangerous Occurrences Regulations 1995
- SI 1996/1513 The Health and Safety (Consultation with Employees) Regulations 1996
- SI 1996/341 The Health and Safety (Safety Signs and Signals) Regulations 1996

- SI 1996/972 The Special Waste Regulations 1996
- SI 1997/1840 The Fire Precautions (Workplace) Regulations 1997
- SI 1998/1833 The Working Time Regulations 1998
- SI 1998/2306 The Provision and Use of Work Equipment Regulations 1998
- SI 1998/2307 The Lifting Operations and Lifting Equipment Regulations 1998
- SI 1998/2573 The Employers' Liability (Compulsory Insurance) Regulations 1998
- SI 1999/3242 The Management of Health and Safety at Work Regulations 1999
- SI 1999/3312 The Maternity and Parental Leave (etc.) Regulations 1999
- SI 1999/584 The National Minimum Wage Regulations 1998
- SI 2002/2675 The Control of Asbestos at Work Regulations 2002
- SI 2002/2676 The Control of Lead at Work Regulations 2002
- SI 2002/2677 The Control of Substances Hazardous to Health Regulations 2002

Other Provisions

- HMCE 700/21 HM Customs and Excise Notice 700/21: Keeping [VAT] records and accounts
- IR CA30 Statutory Sick Pay Manual for Employers CA30[21]

Australia*

Archives Act

The Archives Act 1983 empowers the Archives to preserve the archival resources of the Australian Government—those records designated "national archives." Under the act, it is illegal to destroy Australian government records without permission from the Archives unless destruction is specified in another piece of legislation or allowed under a normal administrative practice.

The act also establishes a right of public access to nonexempt commonwealth records in the "open access period" (transitioning from 30 years to 20 years over the period 2011 to 2021 under amendments to the act passed in 2010). Different open access periods exist for cabinet notebooks (transitioning from 50 years to 30 years over the period 2011 to 2021) and records containing census information (99 years).

Freedom of Information Act

The Freedom of Information (FOI) Act 1982 gives individuals the legal right to access documents held by Australian government ministers, departments, and most agencies, including Norfolk Island government agencies. From November 1, 2010, the FOI Act also applies to documents created or held by contractors or subcontractors who provided services to the public or third parties on behalf of agencies.

*The information in this section is taken from www.naa.gov.au © Commonwealth of Australia (National Archives of Australia) 2013

The FOI Act applies to records that are not yet in the open access period under the Archives Act unless the document contains personal information (including personal information about a deceased person). The Archives Act regulates access to records in the open access period.

When a member of the public requests information, your agency must identify and preserve all relevant sources, including records, until a final decision on the request is made. The FOI Act also sets out how agencies may correct, annotate, or update records if a member of the public shows that any personal information relating to them is incomplete, incorrect, out of date, or misleading.

The FOI Act also establishes the Information Publication Scheme (IPS), which requires agencies subject to the FOI Act to take a proactive approach to publishing a broad range of information on their Web site. The IPS does not apply to a small number of security and intelligence agencies that are exempt from the FOI Act.

Australian Information Commissioner Act

The Australian Information Commissioner Act 2010 established the Office of the Australian Information Commissioner (OAIC). The OAIC has three sets of functions. These are:

1. *Freedom of information functions*—protecting the public's right of access to documents under the amended FOI Act and reviewing decisions made by agencies and ministers under that act.
2. *Privacy functions*—ensuring proper handling of personal information in accordance with the Privacy Act 1988.
3. *Government and information policy functions*, conferred on it by the Australian Information Commissioner Act 2010—these include strategic functions relating to information management and ensuring maximum coordination, efficiency, and transparency in government information policy and practice.

As part of its government and information policy function, the OAIC is committed to leading the development and implementation of a national information policy framework to promote secure and open government. It aims to achieve this by driving public access to government information and encouraging agencies to proactively publish information.

Privacy Act

The Privacy Act 1988 regulates the handling of personal information by Australian government agencies, Australian Capital Territory (ACT) government agencies, ACT government agencies, Norfolk Island government agencies, and a range of private and not-for-profit organizations. The Privacy Act regulates the way in which personal information can be collected, its accuracy, how it is kept secure, and how it is used and disclosed. It also provides rights to individuals to access and correct the information that organizations and government agencies hold about them. Records in the open access period as defined in the Archives Act 1983 *are* not covered by the Privacy Act. The Privacy Act also sets out requirements that may apply when an agency enters into a contract under which services are provided to the agency.

Evidence Act

The Evidence Act 1995 defines what documents, including records, can be used as evidence in a commonwealth court.[22]

All agencies need to take account of evidence legislation. A court may need to examine records as evidence of an organization's decisions and actions.[23]

Electronic Transactions Act

The Electronic Transactions Act 1999 encourages online business by ensuring that electronic evidence of transactions is not invalidated because of its format. This act does not authorize the destruction of any Australian government records, whether originals or copies. The obligations placed on agencies under the Archives Act 1983 for the preservation and disposal of commonwealth records continue to apply.

Financial Management and Accountability Act

The Financial Management and Accountability Act 1997 states that an Australian Public Service (APS) employee who misapplies, improperly disposes of, or improperly uses commonwealth records may be in breach of the Financial Management and Accountability Act (s. 41). Regulation 12 of the act requires that the terms of approval for a proposal to spend money be recorded in writing as soon as practicable.

Australian government records fall within the meaning of "public property" as defined in this act.

Crimes Act

The Crimes Act 1914 outlines crimes against the commonwealth. Several parts of the act relate to records. For example, section 70 prohibits public servants (or anyone working for the Australian government, including contractors, and consultants) from publishing or communicating facts, documents, or information that they gain access to through their work unless they have permission to do so. This includes taking or selling records that should be destroyed.

This act also makes it an offense for people to intentionally destroy documents that they know may be required as evidence in a judicial proceeding.

Identifying Records Management Requirements in Other Legislation

Your agency [or business] needs to be aware of the legislation governing its own records practices.

Some legislative requirements apply to many agencies [and businesses]. For example, occupational health and safety legislation requires an organization to keep certain types of records for prescribed periods of time. Requirements that apply to all agencies are included in the National Archives' Administrative Functions Disposal Authority.

Other legislative requirements may apply only to the particular business of one or a number of agencies.

Record-keeping requirements may be stipulated in your agency's enabling legislation (legislation that established the agency) or in specific legislation that your agency is responsible for administering.[24]

Notes

1. NARA Records Management Guidance and Regulations, www.archives.gov/records-mgmt/policy/guidance-regulations.html (accessed October 17, 2012).

2. These standards were developed by the Canadian General Standards Board, which is a standards-writing agency within Public Works and Government Services Canada (a department of the federal government). It is accredited by the Standards Council of Canada as a standards development agency. The council must certify that standards have been developed by the required procedures before it will designate them as being National Standards of Canada. 72.34 incorporates by reference as "normative references": (1) many of the standards of the International Organization for Standardization (ISO) in Geneva, Switzerland; and (2) several of the standards of the Canadian Standards Association. The "Normative references" section of 72.34 (p. 2) states that these "referenced documents are indispensable for the application of this document." 72.11 cites (p. 2, "Applicable Publications") several standards of the American National Standards Institute/Association for Information and Image Management (ANSI/AIIM) as publications "applicable to this standard." The process by which the National Standards of Canada are created and maintained is described within the standards themselves (reverse side of the front cover), and on the CGSB's Web site (see "Standards Development"), from which Web site these standards may be obtained; online: www.ongc-cgsb.gc.ca.

3. The Canada Revenue Agency informs the public of its policies and procedures by means, among others, of its Information Circulars and GST/HST Memoranda (GST: goods and services tax; HST: harmonized sales tax, i.e., the harmonization of federal and provincial sales taxes into one retail sales tax.) In particular, see: IC05-1, dated June 2010, entitled *Electronic Record Keeping*, paragraphs 24, 26, and 28. Note that use of the National Standard cited in paragraph 26, *Microfilm and Electronic Images as Documentary Evidence*, CAN/CGSB-72.11-93, is mandatory for "Imaging and microfilm (including microfiche) reproductions of books of original entry and source documents." Paragraph 24 recommends the use of the newer national standard, *Electronic Records as Documentary Evidence*, CAN/CGSB-72.34-2005, "To ensure the reliability, integrity and authenticity of electronic records." However, if this newer standard is given the same treatment by CRA as the older standard, it will be made mandatory as well. And similar statements appear in the GST Memoranda *Computerized Records* 500-1-2, *Books and Records* 500-1. IC05-1. *Electronic Record Keeping*, concludes with the note: "Most Canada Revenue Agency publications are available on the CRA website, www.cra.gc.ca, under the heading 'Forms and Publications.'"

4. More than 200 specific compliance tests can be applied to determine if the principles of 72.34 are being complied with. The analysts—a combined team of records management and legal expertise—analyze: (1) the nature of the business involved; (2) the uses and value of its records for its various functions; (3) the likelihood and risk of the various types of its records being the subject of legal proceedings, or of their being challenged by some regulating authority; and (4) the consequences of the unavailability of acceptable records—for example, the consequences of its records not being accepted in legal proceedings. Similarly, in regard to National Standard of Canada 72.11, a comparable series of more than 50 tests can be applied to determine the state of compliance with its principles.

5. *Electronic Records as Documentary Evidence*, CAN/CGSB-72.34-2005 (72.34), clause 5.4.3 c at p. 17; and *Microfilm and Electronic Images as Documentary Evidence*, CAN/CGSB-72.11-93 (72.11).

6. 72.34, Clause 5.4.3, ibid.

7. "Admissibility" refers to the procedure by which a presiding judge determines if a record or other proffered evidence is acceptable as evidence according the rules of evidence. "Electronic discovery" is the compulsory exchange of relevant records by the parties to legal proceedings prior to trial. As to the admissibility of records as evidence, see: Ken Chasse, "The Admissibility of Electronic Business Records," *Canadian Journal of Law and Technology* 8 (2010): 105; and Ken Chasse, "Electronic Records for Evidence and Disclosure and Discovery," *Criminal Law Quarterly* 57 (2011): 284. For the electronic discovery of records, see: Ken Chasse, "Electronic Discovery—*Sedona Canada* Is Inadequate on Records Management—Here's *Sedona Canada* in Amended Form," *Canadian Journal of Law and Technology* 9 (2011): 135; and Ken Chasse, "Electronic Discovery in the Criminal Court System" *Canadian Criminal Law Review* 14 (2010): 111.

8. For the province of Quebec, comparable provisions are contained in Articles 2831–2842, 2859–2862, 2869–2874 of Book 7 "Evidence" of the Civil Code of Quebec, S.Q. 1991, c. C-64, to be read in conjunction with "An Act to Establish a Legal Framework for Information Technology," R.S.Q. 2001, c. C-1.1, sections. 2, 5–8, and 68.

9. For the legislative jurisdiction of the federal and provincial governments in Canada, see the Constitution Act, 1867 (U.K.) 30 and 31 Victoria, c. 3, section 91 (federal) and section 92 (provincial); at online: www.canlii.org/en/ca/laws/stat/30—31-vict-c-3/latest/30—31-vict-c-3.html.

10. The two provinces of Alberta, and Newfoundland and Labrador do not have business record provisions in their Evidence Acts. Therefore "admissibility" in those jurisdictions would be determined by way of the court decisions that define the applicable common law rules; such decisions as *Ares v. Venner*, [1970] S.C.R. 608, 14 D.L.R. (3d) 4 (S.C.C.) and decisions that have applied it.

11. See, for example, the Canada Evidence Act, R.S.C. 1985, c. C-5, sections 31.1–31.8; Alberta Evidence Act, R.S.A. 2000, c. A-18, sections 41.1–41.8; (Ontario) Evidence Act, R.S.O. 1990, c. E.23, s. 34.1; and the (Nova Scotia) Evidence Act, R.S.N.S. 1989, c. 154, sections 23A–23G. The Evidence Acts of the two provinces of British Columbia and Newfoundland and Labrador do not contain electronic record provisions. However, because an electronic record is no better than the quality of the record system in which it is recorded or stored, its "integrity" (reliability, credibility) will have to be determined under the other provincial laws that determine the admissibility of records as evidence.

12. The electronic record provisions have been in the Evidence Acts in Canada since 2000. They have been applied to admit electronic records into evidence, but they have not yet received any detailed analysis by the courts.

13. This is the wording used in, for example, section 41.6 of the Alberta Evidence Act, section 34.1(8) of the (Ontario) Evidence Act; and section 23F of the (Nova Scotia) Evidence Act, *supra* note 10. Section 31.5 of the Canada Evidence Act, *supra* note 58, uses the same wording; the only significant difference is that the word "document" is used instead of "record." For the province of Quebec, see sections 12 and 68 of *An Act to Establish a Legal Framework for Information Technology*, R.S.Q., chapter C-1.1.

14. *Supra* notes 54 to 59 and accompanying texts.

15. *Supra* notes 49 and 52 and accompanying texts.

16. *Supra* note 50 and accompanying text.

17. All 14 jurisdictions of Canada have electronic commerce legislation except for the Northwest Territories. See, for example, the Personal Information Protection and Electronic Documents Act, S.C. 2000, c. 5, Parts 2 and 3; Ontario's Electronic Commerce Act, 2000, S.O. 2000, c. 17; and, British Columbia's Electronic Transactions Act, R.B.C. 20001, c. 10. The concept of "system integrity" in the Evidence Acts (*supra* note 58 and accompanying text), is also found in the electronic commerce legislation. See, for example, section 8 of the Ontario Electronic Commerce Act, 2000, under the heading "Legal Requirement re Original Documents."

18. For example, Part 1, "Personal Information Protection," of the federal Personal Information Protection and Electronic Documents Act (PIPEDA), S.C. 2000, c. 5, which applies within provincial legislative jurisdiction as well as federal, until a province enacts its own personal information protection act (a PIPA), which displaces it in the provincial sphere. British Columbia, Alberta, and Quebec are the only provinces that have done so.

19. The dominant guideline for electronic discovery in Canada is *The Sedona Canada Principles—Addressing Electronic Discovery*; online: The Sedona Conference, Canada, January 2008: www.thesedonaconference.com/content/miscFiles/canada_pincpls_FINAL_108.pdf or www.thesedonaconference.org/dltForm?did=canada_pincpls_FINAL_108.pdf; and E-Discovery Canada Web site, hosted by LexUM (at the University of Montreal), online: www. lexum.umontreal.ca/e-discovery. And see also the law journal articles concerning electronic discovery cited in note 54 *supra*.

20. *Supra* notes 52 and 53 and accompanying texts.

21. "Information Governance Record Retention Guidance," www.rec-man.stir.ac.uk/rec-ret/legislation.php (accessed October 17, 2012).

22. www.comlaw.gov.au/Details/C2012C00518, accessed Nov. 30, 2012.

23. General advice on the impact of the Evidence Act is given in the publication Commonwealth Records in Evidence (pdf). www.comlaw.gov.au/Details/C2012C00518 (accessed Nov. 30, 2012).

24. National Archives of Australia, www.naa.gov.au/records-management/strategic-information/standards/recordslegislation.aspx (accessed October 17, 2012).

Laws and Major Regulations Related to Privacy

United States

Note: This list is representative and not to be considered an exhaustive listing.[1] State laws and industry regulations may apply to your organization. Consult your legal counsel for definitive research.

Americans with Disabilities Act (ADA)

Cable Communications Policy Act of 1984 (Cable Act)

California Senate Bill 1386 (SB 1386)

Children's Internet Protection Act of 2001 (CIPA)

Children's Online Privacy Protection Act of 1998 (COPPA)

Communications Assistance for Law Enforcement Act of 1994

Computer Fraud and Abuse Act of 1986 (CFAA)

Computer Security Act of 1987: superseded by the Federal Information Security Management Act (FISMA)

Consumer Credit Reporting Reform Act of 1996 (CCRRA): modifies the Fair Credit Reporting Act (FCRA)

Controlling the Assault of Non-Solicited Pornography and Marketing (CAN-SPAM) Act of 2003

Driver's Privacy Protection Act of 1994

Electronic Communications Privacy Act of 1986 (ECPA)

Electronic Freedom of Information Act of 1996 (E-FOIA)

Electronic Funds Transfer Act (EFTA)

Fair and Accurate Credit Transactions Act (FACTA) of 2003

Fair Credit Reporting Act of 1999 (FCRA)

Family Education Rights and Privacy Act of 1974 (FERPA; aka the Buckley Amendment)

Federal Information Security Management Act (FISMA)

Federal Trade Commission Act (FTCA)

Gramm–Leach–Bliley Financial Services Modernization Act of 1999 (GLBA)

Privacy Act of 1974: including U.S. Department of Justice Overview

Privacy Protection Act of 1980 (PPA)

Right to Financial Privacy Act of 1978 (RFPA)

Telecommunications Act of 1996

Telephone Consumer Protection Act of 1991 (TCPA)

Uniting and Strengthening America by Providing Appropriate Tools Required to Intercept and Obstruct Terrorism Act of 2001 (USA-PATRIOT Act)

Video Privacy Protection Act of 1988

Major Privacy Laws Worldwide, by Country

Note: This list is representative and not to be considered an exhaustive listing.[2] State or provincial laws and industry regulations may apply to your organization. Consult your legal counsel for definitive research.

Argentina. Personal Data Protection Act of 2000 (aka Habeas Data)

Australia. Privacy Act of 1988

Austria. Data Protection Act 2000, Austrian Federal Law Gazette part I No. 165/1999 (Datenschutzgesetz 2000 or DSG 2000)

Belgium. Belgium Data Protection Law

Brazil. Privacy currently governed by Article 5 of the 1988 Constitution

Bulgaria. Bulgarian Personal Data Protection Act

Canada. Privacy Act—July 1983 Personal Information Protection and Electronic Data Act (PIPEDA) of 2000 (Bill C-6)

Chile. Act on the Protection of Personal Data, August 1998

Colombia. Law 1266 of 2008: (in Spanish) and Law 1273 of 2009 (in Spanish)

Czech Republic. Act on Protection of Personal Data (April 2000) No. 101

Denmark. Act on Processing of Personal Data, Act No. 429, May 2000

Estonia. Personal Data Protection Act of 2003. (June 1996, Consolidated July 2002)

European Union. European Union Data Protection Directive of 1998; EU Internet Privacy Law of 2002 (Directive 2002/58/EC)

Finland. Act on the Amendment of the Personal Data Act (986) 2000

France. Data Protection Act of 1978 (revised in 2004)

Germany. Federal Data Protection Act of 2001

Greece. Law No. 2472 on the Protection of Individuals with Regard to the Processing of Personal Data, April 1997

Guernsey. Data Protection (Bailiwick of Guernsey) Law of 2001

Hong Kong. Personal Data Ordinance (the Ordinance)

Hungary. Act LXIII of 1992 on the Protection of Personal Data and the Publicity of Data of Public Interests

Iceland. Act of Protection of Individual; Processing Personal Data, January 2000

Ireland. Data Protection (Amendment) Act, Number 6, of 2003

India. Information Technology Act of 2000

Italy. Processing of Personal Data Act, January 1997; Data Protection Code of 2003

Japan. Personal Information Protection Law (Act) Law for the Protection of Computer Processed Data Held by Administrative Organs, December 1988

Korea. Act on Personal Information Protection of Public Agencies Act on Information and Communication Network Usage

Latvia. Personal Data Protection Law, March 2000

Lithuania. Law on Legal Protection of Personal Data, June 1996

Luxembourg. Law of August 2002 on the Protection of Persons with Regard to the Processing of Personal Data

Malaysia. Common Law Principle of Confidentiality Personal Data Protection Bill Banking and Financial Institutions Act of 1989 Privacy Provisions

Malta. Data Protection Act (Act XXVI of 2001), amended March 22, 2002, November 15, 2002 and July 15, 2003

Mexico. Federal Law for the Protection of Personal Data Possessed by Private Persons (Spanish)

Morocco. Data Protection Act

Netherlands. Dutch Personal Data Protection Act 2000 as amended by Acts dated April 5, 2001, Bulletin of Acts, Orders and Decrees 180, December 6, 2001

New Zealand. Privacy Act, May 1993; Privacy Amendment Act, 1993; Privacy Amendment Act, 1994

Norway. Personal Data Act (April 2000)–Act of April 14, 2000 No. 31 Relating to the Processing of Personal Data (Personal Data Act)

Philippines. Data Privacy Act of 2011 (There is also a recognized right of privacy in civil law and a model data protection code.)

Romania. Law No. 677/2001 for the Protection of Persons Concerning the Processing of Personal Data and the Free Circulation of Such Data

Poland. Act of the Protection of Personal Data (August 1997)

Portugal. Act on the Protection of Personal Data (Law 67/98 of 26 October)

Singapore. E-commerce Code for the Protection of Personal Information and Communications of Consumers of Internet Commerce

Slovak Republic. Act No. 428 of July 3, 2002, on Personal Data Protection

Slovenia. Personal Data Protection Act, RS No. 55/99

South Africa. Electronic Communications and Transactions Act, 2002

South Korea. Act on Promotion of Information and Communications Network Utilization and Data Protection of 2000

Spain. Organic Law 15/1999 of December 13 on the Protection of Personal Data

Switzerland. Federal Law on Data Protection of 1992

Sweden. Personal Data Protection Act (1998: 204), October 24, 1998

Taiwan. Computer Processed Personal Data Protection Law (public institution applicability only)

Thailand. Official Information Act, B.E. 2540 (1997) (for state agencies)

United Kingdom. UK Data Protection Act 1998; Privacy and Electronic Communications (EC Directive) Regulations 2003

Vietnam. Law on Electronic Transactions 2008

Notes

1. Information Shield, "United States Privacy Laws," www.informationshield.com/usprivacylaws.html (accessed October 18, 2013).
2. Information Shield, "International Privacy Laws," www.informationshield.com/intprivacylaws.html (accessed February 1, 2014).

GLOSSARY

access control list In systems such as electronic records management, electronic document and records management systems, or document management systems, a list of individuals authorized to access, view, amend, transfer, or delete documents, records, or files. Access rights are enforced through software controls.

application programming interface (API) A way of standardizing the connection between two software applications. It is essentially a standard hook that an application uses to connect to another software application.

archival information package (AIP) One of three types of information packages that can be submitted in the Open Archival Information System (OAIS) preservation model.

archive Storing information and records for long-term or permanent preservation. With respect to e-mail, it is stored in a compressed and indexed format to reduce storage requirements and allow for rapid, complex searches. (This also can done for blogs, social media, or other applications.) Archiving of real-time applications like e-mail can be deemed reliable with record integrity only if it is performed immediately, in real time.

ARMA Association for Records Managers and Administrators, the United States-based nonprofit organization for records managers with a network of international chapters.

authentication, authorization, and audit (or accounting) (AAA) A network management and security framework that controls computer system logons and access to applications that enforces IG policies and audits usage.

authenticity of records Verified content and author information as original for the purposes of electronic records management; in a legal context, proof that the e-document is what it purports to be when electronically stored information is submitted during the e-discovery process.

auto-classification Setting predefined indices to classify documents and records and having the process performed automatically by using software rather than human intervention. A strong trend toward auto-classification is emerging due to the impact of Big Data and rapidly increasing volumes of documents and records.

backup A complete spare copy of data for purposes of disaster recovery. Backups are nonindexed mass storage and cannot substitute for indexed, archived information that can be quickly searched and retrieved (as in archiving).

best practices Those methods, processes, or procedures that have been proven to be the most effective, based on real-world experience and measured results.

Big Data More data than can be processed by today's database systems, or acutely high volume, velocity, and variety of information assets that demand IG to manage and leverage for decision-making insights and cost management.

bidders' conference A formal meeting where vendors bidding on a request for proposal (RFP) can ask questions and raise issues about the RFP, proposal requirements, and procurement process.

business activities The tasks performed to accomplish a particular business function. Several activities may be associated with each business function.

business case A written analysis of the financial, productivity, auditability, and other factors to justify the investment in software and hardware systems, implementation, and training.

business classification scheme (BCS) The overall structure an organization uses for organizing, searching, retrieving, storing, and managing documents and records in electronic records management. The BCS must be developed based on the business functions and activities. A file plan is a graphic representation of the BCS, usually a hierarchical structure consisting of headings and folders to indicate where and when records should be created during the conducting of the business of an office. In other words, *the file plan links the records to their business context.*

business driver A compelling business reason that motivates an organization to implement a solution to a problem. Business drivers can be based on financial, legal, or operational gaps or needs.

business functions Basic business units, such as accounting, legal, human resources, and purchasing.

business process A coordinated set of collaborative and transactional work activities carried out to complete work steps.

business process improvement (BPI) Analyzing and redesigning business processes to streamline them and gain efficiencies, reduce cycle times, and improve auditability and worker productivity.

business process outsourcing (BPO) Contracting with a third party to perform specific business processes. One example could be using a customer service center taking inbound telephone calls from U.S. customers and handling customer requests and complaints from a service center located offshore, in locations such as India, where labor costs are lower.

business process management (BPM) Managing the work steps and business activities of an organization's workers in an automated way.

business process management system (BPMS) A superset of workflow software, and more. BPMS software offers five main capabilities:

1. Puts existing and new application software under the direct control of business managers
2. Makes it easier to improve existing business processes and create new ones
3. Enables the automation of processes across the entire organization and beyond it
4. Gives managers real-time information on the performance of processes
5. Allows organizations to take full advantage of new computing services

capture Components that also often are called input components. There are several levels and technologies, from simple document scanning and capture to complex information preparation using automatic classification.

case records Records that are characterized as having a beginning and an end but are added to over time. Case records generally have titles that include names, dates, numbers, or places.

change management Methods and best practices to assist an organization and its employees in implementing changes to business processes, culture, and systems.

classification Systematic identification and arrangement of business activities and/ or records into categories according to logically structured conventions, methods, and procedural rules represented in a classification system. A coding of content items as members of a group for the purposes of cataloging them or associating them with a taxonomy.

cloud computing The provision of computational resources on demand via a network. Cloud computing can be compared to the supply of electricity and gas or the provision of telephone, television, and postal services. All of these services are presented to users in a simple way that is easy to understand without users' needing to know how the services are provided. This simplified view is called an abstraction. Similarly, cloud computing offers computer application developers and users an abstract view of services, which simplifies and ignores much of the details and inner workings. A provider's offering of abstracted Internet services is often called the cloud.

CobiT (Control Objectives for Information and related Technology) A process-based information technology governance framework that represents a consensus of experts worldwide. It was codeveloped by the IT Governance Institute and ISACA.

Code of Federal Regulations (CFR) The annual edition of the CFR contains all the rules published in the Federal Register by the departments and agencies of the federal government. It is divided into 50 broad subject areas and contain at least one individual volumes, and is update annually, on a staggered basis.

cold site An empty computer facility or data center that is ready for operation with air-conditioning, raised floors, telecommunication lines, and electric power. Backup hardware and software will have to be purchased and shipped in quickly to resume operations. Arrangements can be made with suppliers for rapid delivery in the event of a disaster.

compliance monitoring Being regularly apprised and updated on pertinent regulations and laws and examining processes in the organization to ensure compliance with them. In a records management sense, this involves reviewing and inspecting the various facets of a records management program to ensure it is in compliance. Compliance monitoring can be carried out by an internal audit, external organization, or records management and must be done on a regular basis.

computer memory Solid state volatile (erasable) storage capability built into central processing units of computers. At times memory size can be increased by expanding it to the computer's hard drive or external magnetic disks.

content In records, the actual information contained in the record; more broadly, content is information. For example, content is managed by enterprise content management systems and may be e-mail, e-documents, Web content, report content, and so on.

controlled vocabulary Set, defined terms used in a taxonomy.

corporate compliance The set of activities and processes that result in meeting and adhering to all regulations and laws that apply to an organization.

data cleansing (or data scrubbing) The process of removing corrupt, redundant, and inaccurate data in the data governance process.

data governance Processes and controls at the data level; a newer, hybrid quality control discipline that includes elements of data quality, data management, information governance policy development, business process improvement, and compliance and risk management.

data loss prevention (DLP; or data *leak* prevention) A computer security term referring to systems that identify, monitor, and protect data in use (e.g., endpoint actions), data in motion (e.g., network actions), and data at rest (e.g., data storage) through deep content inspection, contextual security analysis of transaction (attributes of originator, data object, medium, timing, recipient/ destination, etc.) and with a centralized management framework. Systems are designed to detect and prevent unauthorized use and transmission of confidential information.

declaration Assignment of metadata elements to associate the attributes of one or more record folder(s) to a record; for categories to be managed at the record level, providing the capability to associate a record category to a specific record.

de-duplication The process of identifying and eliminating redundant occurrences of data.

defensible deletion Disposing of unneeded data, e-documents, and reports based on set policy that can be defended in court. It reduces an organization's information footprint.

Designing and Implementing Recordkeeping Systems (DIRKS) An Australian methodology consisting of eight steps developed by the Archives Authority of New South Wales, included in ISO 15489, the international standard for records management. Roughly analogous to the Generally Accepted Recordkeeping Principles® developed by the Association for Records Managers and Administrators in the United States.

destruction The process of eliminating or deleting records, beyond any possible reconstruction.

destruction certificate A certificate issued once destruction of a record is complete. It verifies that destruction has taken place, who authorized the destruction, and who carried it out. It also may include some metadata about the record.

destructive retention policy Permanently destroying documents or e-documents (such as e-mail) after retaining them for a specified period of time.

disaster recovery (DR)/business continuity (BC)   The planning, preparation, and testing set of activities used to help a business plan for and recover from any major business interruption and to resume normal business operations.

discovery   The process of gathering and exchanging evidence in civil trials; or discovering information flows inside an organization using data loss prevention tools.

disposition   The range of processes associated with implementing records retention, destruction, or transfer decisions, which are documented in disposition authorities or other instruments.

dissemination information package (DIP)   One of three types of information packages that can be submitted in the Open Archival Information System (OAIS) preservation model.

document   Recorded information or object that can be treated as a unit.

document analytics   Detailed usage statistics on e-documents, such as time spent viewing, which pages were viewed and for how long, number of documents printed, where printed, number of copies printed, and other granular information about how and where a document is accessed, viewed, edited, or printed.

document imaging   Scanning and digitally capturing images of paper documents.

document life cycle   The span of a document's use, from creation, through active use, storage, and final disposition, which may be destruction or preservation.

document life cycle security (DLS)   Providing a secure and controlled environment for e-documents. This can be accomplished by properly implementing technologies including information rights management and data loss prevention, along with complementary technologies like digital signatures.

document management   Managing documents throughout their life cycle from creation to final disposition, including managing revisions. Also called document life cycle management.

document type   A term used by many software systems to refer to a grouping of related records.

e-document   An electronic document (i.e., a document in digital form).

electronic Code of Federal Regulations (e-CFR)   An unofficial, editorial compilation of CFR material and Federal Register amendments produced by the National Archives and Records Administration's Office of the Federal Register and the Government Printing Office.

electronic document and records management system (EDRMS)   Software that has the ability to manage documents and records.

electronic records management (ERM)   The management of electronic and nonelectronic records by software, including maintaining disposition schedules for keeping records for specified retention periods, archiving, or destruction. (For *enterprise rights management*, see *information rights management [IRM]*.)

electronic record Information recorded in a form that requires a computer or other machine to process and view it and that satisfies the legal or business definition of a record.

electronic records repository A direct access device on which the electronic records and associated metadata are stored.

electronically stored information (ESI) Any information stored by electronic means; this can include not just e-mail and e-documents but also audio and video recordings and any other type of information stored on electronic media. The term was created in 2006 when the U.S. Federal Rules of Civil Procedure were revised to include the governance of ESI in litigation.

e-mail and e-document encryption Encryption or scrambling (and often authentication) of e-mail messages, which can be done in order to protect the content from being read by unintended recipients.

enterprise content management (ECM) Software that manages unstructured information such as e-documents, document images, e-mail, word processing documents, spreadsheets, Web content, and other documents; most systems also include some records management capability.

enterprise process analytics Detailed statistics and analysis of business process cycle times and other data occurring throughout an enterprise. This business intelligence can help spot bottlenecks, optimize work flow, and improve worker productivity while improving input for decision making.

enterprise risk profile An assessment of the threats and risks an enterprise faces and the likelihood of those risks occurring.

event-based disposition A disposition instruction in which a record is eligible for the specified disposition (transfer or destroy) when or immediately after the specified event occurs. No retention period is applied, and there is no fixed waiting period, as with timed or combination timed-event dispositions. Example: *Destroy when no longer needed for current operations.*

faceted search Where document collections are classified in multiple ways rather than in a single, rigid taxonomy.

faceted taxonomy Allow for multiple organizing principles to be applied to information along various dimensions. Facets can contain subjects, departments, business units, processes, tasks, interests, security levels, and other attributes used to describe information. There is never really one single taxonomy but rather collections of taxonomies that describe different aspects of information.

Federal Rules of Civil Procedure (FRCP)—Amended 2006 In U.S. civil litigation, the FRCP governs the discovery and exchange of electronically stored information, which includes not only e-mail but all forms of information that can be stored electronically.

file plan A graphic representation of the business classification scheme, usually a hierarchical structure consisting of headings and folders to indicate where and when records should be created during the conduct of business of an office. In other words, the file plan links the records to their business context.

file transfer protocol (FTP) A standard network protocol used to copy a file from one host to another over a TCP-based network, such as the Internet. FTP is built on a client-server architecture and utilizes separate control and data connections between the client and server. FTP users may authenticate themselves using a clear-text sign-in protocol but can connect anonymously if the server is configured to allow it.

folksonomy The term used for a free-form, social approach to metadata assignment. Folksonomies are not an ordered classification system but are lists of keywords input by users that are ranked by popularity.

functional retention schedule A schedule that groups records series based on business functions, such as financial, legal, product management, or sales. Each function or grouping is also used for classification. Rather than detail every sequence of records, these larger functional groups are less numerous and are easier for users to understand.

Generally Accepted Recordkeeping Principles® (the Principles) A set of eight principles published in 2009 by U.S.-based ARMA International to foster awareness of good recordkeeping practices and to provide guidance for records management maturity in organizations. These principles and associated metrics provide an information governance framework that can support continuous improvement.

governance model A framework or model that can assist in guiding governance efforts. Examples include using a SharePoint governance model, the information governance reference model (IGRM), MIKE2.0, and others.

guiding principles The basic principles used to guide the development of a governance model (e.g., for a SharePoint deployment). They may include principles such accountability (who is accountable for managing the site, who is accountable for certain content), who has authorized access to which documents, and whether the governance model is required for use or is to be used optionally as a reference.

heat map A color-coded matrix generated by stakeholders voting on risk level by color (e.g., red being highest).

HIPAA The Healthcare Insurance Portability and Accountability Act enacted by the U.S. Congress in 1996. Title II of HIPAA, known as the administrative simplification (AS) provision, requires the establishment of national standards for electronic health care transactions and national identifiers for providers, health insurance plans, and employers.

hot site One that has identical or nearly identical hardware and operating system configurations and copies of application software, and receives live, real-time backup data from business operations. In the event of a business interruption, the information technology and electronic vital records operations can be switched over automatically, providing uninterrupted service.

information footprint The total size of the amount of information an organization manages.

information governance (IG) A subset of corporate governance. It is an all-encompassing term for how an organization manages the totality of its information. IG "encompasses the policies and leveraged technologies meant to dictate and manage what corporate information is retained, where and for how long, and also how it is retained (e.g., protected, replicated, and secured). Information governance spans retention, security, and life cycle management issues."[1] IG is an ongoing program that helps organizations meet external compliance and legal demands and internal governance rules.

information governance reference model (IGRM)   A graphically depicted practical framework that includes risk and profit considerations for the business, legal, informational technology, records and information management (RIM), and privacy and security functions of an organization. IGRM enables organizations to establish IG programs that more effectively deal with the rising volume and diversity of information and the risks, costs, and complications this presents. IGRM is most frequently used to facilitate dialogue and combine disparate information stakeholders and perspectives across legal, records, information technology, and business organizations.

information life cycle   The span of the use of information, from creation, through active use, storage, and final disposition, which may be destruction or preservation.

information map   A graphic diagram that shows where information is created, where it resides, and the path it takes.

information rights management (IRM)   Often referred to as enterprise rights management (ERM) or enterprise digital rights management (E-DRM). IRM applies to a technology set that protects sensitive information, usually documents or e-mail messages, from unauthorized access. IRM is technology that allows for information (mostly in the form of documents) to be remote controlled. Information and its control can be separately created, viewed, edited, and distributed.

information technology (IT)   Technology used to manage digital information.

IT governance   Controls and process to improve the effectiveness of information technology; also, the primary way that stakeholders can ensure that investments in IT create business value and contribute toward meeting business objectives.

IT governance framework   Constructs or frameworks that guide informational technology governance efforts, including CobiT® and ITIL.

ITIL (Information Technology Infrastructure Library)   A set of process-oriented best practices and guidance originally developed in the United Kingdom to standardize delivery of informational technology service management. ITIL is applicable to both the private and public sectors and, according to its Web site, is the "most widely accepted approach to IT service management in the world."

inherited metadata   Automatically assigning certain metadata to records based on rules that are established in advance and set up by a system administrator.

inventorying records   A descriptive listing of each record series or system, together with an indication of location and other pertinent data. It is not a list of each document or each folder but rather of each series or system.

ISO   International Organization for Standardization, a highly regarded and widely accepted global standards body.

jukebox (optical disk jukebox)   Optical disc autochanger units for mass storage that use robotics to pick and mount optical disks and remove and replace them after use; dubbed a "jukebox" for its similarity in mechanics to jukebox units for playing vinyl records and later CDs.

knowledge management (KM)   The accumulation, organization, and use of experience and lessons learned, which can be leveraged to improve future decision-making efforts. KM often involves listing and indexing subject matter experts, project categories, reports, studies, proposals, and other intellectual property sources or outputs that are retained to build corporate memory. Good KM systems help train new employees and reduce the impact of turnover and retirement of key employees.

legal hold or litigation hold   Also known as a preservation order or hold order. A temporary suspension of the company's document retention destruction policies for the documents that may be relevant to a lawsuit or that are reasonably anticipated to be relevant. It is a stipulation requiring the company to preserve all data that may relate to a legal action involving the company. A litigation hold ensures that the documents relating to the litigation are not destroyed and are available for the discovery process prior to litigation. The legal hold process is a foundational element of information governance.

legal hold notification (LHN)   The process of identifying information that may be requested in legal proceeding and locking that (data or documents) down to prevent editing or deletion while notifying all parties within an organization who may be involved in processing that information that it is subject to a legal hold. LHN management is arguably the absolute minimum an organization should be doing in order to meet the guidelines provided by court rules, common law, and case law precedent.

limitation period   The length of time after which a legal action cannot be brought before the courts. Limitation periods determine the length of time records must be kept to support court actions, including subsequent appeal periods.

long-term digital preservation (LTDP)   The managed activities, methods, standards, and technologies used to provide long-term, error-free storage of digital information, with means for retrieval and interpretation, for the entire time span the information is required to be retained.

magnetic disk drives   A common data storage device using erasable magnetic media. Magnetic disk drives are common peripherals and built-in storage devices in desktop PCs, minicomputers, and mainframe computers.

master retention schedule   A retention schedule that includes the retention and disposition requirements for records series that cross business unit boundaries. The master retention schedule contains all records series in the entire enterprise.

metadata   Data about data, or detailed information describing context, content, and structure of records and their management through time. Examples include the author, department, document type, date created, and length, among others.

migration   The act of moving records from one system to another while maintaining their authenticity, integrity, reliability, and usability.

negotiated procurement   A way to acquire a new system or components when the buying organization wants to make a rapid decision and requirements are known (e.g., making a bulk purchase of additional workstations or tablet computers that will be added to an existing network). Often a trusted consulting firm is engaged to solicit bids, negotiate with vendors, and make a recommendation for procurement. This approach can be a better fit than issuing a request for proposal when cost and time are leading issues.

NENR   Nonerasable, nonrewritable media (e.g., optical, magnetic) that, once written, do not allow for erasure or overwriting of the original data.

OAIS (Open Archival Information System)   Describes how to prepare and submit digital objects for long-term digital preservation and retrieval but does not specify technologies, techniques, or content types. The OAIS Reference Model defines an archival information system as an archive, consisting of an organization of people and systems that has accepted the responsibility to preserve information and make it available and understandable for a designated community (i.e., potential users or consumers), who should be able to understand the information. Thus, the context of an OAIS-compliant digital repository includes producers who originate the information to be preserved in the repository, consumers who retrieve the information, and a management/organization that hosts and administers the digital assets being preserved. The OAIS Information Model employs three types of information packages: a Submission Information Package (SIP), an Archival Information Package (AIP), and a Dissemination Information Package (DIP). An OAIS-compliant digital repository preserves AIPs and any preservation description information (PDI) associated with them. A SIP encompasses digital content that a producer has organized for submission to the OAIS. After the completion of quality assurance and normalization procedures, an AIP is created, which is the focus of preservation activity. Subsequently, a DIP is created that consists of an AIP or information extracted from an AIP that is customized to the requirements of the designated community of users and consumers.

optical character recognition (OCR)   A visual recognition process that involves photo-scanning text character by character.

optical disk   Round, platter-shape storage media written to using laser technologies. Optical disk drives use lasers to record and retrieve information, and optical media has a much longer useful life (some purported to be 100 years or more) than magnetic.

phishing   A way of attempting to acquire sensitive information, such as user names, passwords, and credit card details, by masquerading as a trustworthy entity in an electronic communication. Communications purporting to be from popular social Web sites, auction sites, online payment processors, or information technology administrators are commonly used to lure the unsuspecting public. Phishing typically is carried out by e-mail or instant messaging, and it often directs users to enter details at a fake Web site that looks and feels almost identical to the legitimate one. Phishing is an example of social engineering techniques used to fool users, and it exploits the poor usability of current Web security technologies.

PII (personally identifiable information)   Information about individuals that identifies them personally, such as Social Security number, address, credit card information, health information, and the like. PII is subject to privacy laws.

predictive coding   A court-endorsed process utilized to perform document review during the early case assessment phase of e-discovery. It uses human expertise and information technology to facilitate analysis and sorting of documents. Predictive coding software leverages human analysis when experts review a subset of documents to "teach" the software what to look for, so it can apply this logic to the full set of documents, making the sorting and culling process faster and more accurate than solely using human review or automated review.

preservation description information (PDI)   In the long-term digital preservation process adhering to the Open Archival Information System reference model, description information such as provenance, context, and fixity.

process-enabled technologies   Information technologies that automate and streamline business processes. Process-enabled technologies often are divided into two categories that have a great deal in common: work flow automation or business process management. It is fair to say that a good deal of the technology that underpins business process management concepts has its roots in the late 1980s and early 1990s and stems from the early efforts of the work flow community.

project charter   A document that formally authorizes a project to move forward. Having such a document reduces project cancellation risk due to lack of support or perceived value to the company. A charter documents the project's overall objectives and helps manage expectations of those involved.

project management   The process of managing required project activities and tasks in a formal manner to complete a project; performed primarily by the project manager.

project manager   The person primarily responsible for managing a project to its successful completion.

project plan   Includes the project charter and project schedule and a delineation of all project team members and their roles and responsibilities.

project schedule   A listing of project tasks, subtasks, and estimated completion times.

policy   A high-level overall plan, containing a set of principles that embrace the general goals of the organization and are used as a basis for decisions. A policy can include some specifics of processes allowed and not allowed.

preservation   The processes and operations involved in ensuring the technical and intellectual survival of authentic records through time. Preservation involves recording information created, received, and maintained as evidence and information by an organization or person, in pursuit of legal obligations or in the transaction of business.

provenance   In records management, information about who created a record and what it is used for.

records appraisal   The process of assessing the value and risk of records to determine their retention and disposition requirements. Legal research is outlined in appraisal reports. This may be accomplished as a part of the process of developing the records retention schedules as well as conducting a regular review to ensure that citations and requirements are current.

record category   A description of a particular set of records within a file plan. Each category has retention and disposition data associated with it, applied to all record folders and records within the category.

records integrity   Refers to the accuracy and consistency of records, and the assurance that they are genuine and unaltered.

records management (RM) or records and information management (RIM))   The field of management responsible for the efficient and systematic control of the creation, receipt, maintenance, use, and disposition of records, including processes for capturing and maintaining evidence of and information about business activities and transactions in the form of records. It is also the set of instructions allocated to a class or file to determine the length of time for which records should be retained by the organization for business purposes, and the eventual fate of the records on completion of this period of time.

records retention schedule   Spells out how long different types of records are to be held and how they will be archived or disposed of at the end of their life cycle. Such a schedule considers legal, regulatory, operational, and historical requirements.

record series   A group or unit of identical or related records that are normally used and filed as a unit and that can be evaluated as a unit or business function for scheduling purposes.

refreshment   The process of copying stored e-records to new copies of the same media, to extend the storage life of the record by using new media.

return on investment (ROI)   A common investment return measure, where the financial benefit is divided by the cost rendering a percentage or ratio.

risk assessment   An evaluation of the risks and possible bad outcomes an organization faces and the likelihood these may occur.

risk map   A simple identification and ranking of the 10 greatest risks an organization faces in relation to business objectives. The risk map is a visual tool that is easy to grasp, with a grid depicting a likelihood axis and an impact axis, usually rated on a scale of 1 to 5.

risk profile   A listing of risks an organization faces and their relative likelihood; used as a basic building block in enterprise risk management that assists executives in understanding the risks associated with stated business objectives, and allocating resources, within a structured evaluation approach or framework.

secure sockets layer (SSL)/transport layer security (TLS)   Cryptographic protocols that provide communications security over the Internet. SSL and TLS encrypt the segments of network connections above the transport layer, using symmetric cryptography for privacy and a keyed message authentication code for message reliability.

senior records officer (SRO)   The leading records manager in an organization; may also be titled chief records officer or similar.

service-level agreement (SLA)   The service or maintenance contract that states the explicit levels of support, response time windows or ranges, escalation procedures in the event of a persistent problem, and possible penalties for nonconformance in the event the vendor does not meet its contractual obligations.

service-oriented architecture (SOA)   An information technology architecture that separates infrastructure, applications, and data into layers.

Six Sigma   A highly structured approach for eliminating defects in any process, whether from manufacturing or transactional processes. It can be applied to a product or a service-oriented process in any organization. Further, six sigma is a statistical term that measures how far a given process deviates from perfection. The goal of the Six Sigma is to systematically measure and eliminate defects in a process, aiming for a level of fewer than 3.4 defects per million instances, or "opportunities."

social tagging   A method that allows users to manage content with metadata they apply themselves using keywords or metadata tags. Unlike traditional classification, which uses a controlled vocabulary, social tagging keywords are freely chosen by each individual. This can help uncover new categories of documents that are emerging and helps users find information using their terms they believe are relevant.

solid state disk drive   Storage devices that can be built in or external that have no moving parts and are made of semiconductor materials. They are used more often in tablet computers as they are faster and more reliable than magnetic disk drives, although also more expensive. Memory sticks and removable USB thumb or flash drives are also solid state technology.

spoliation   The loss of proven authenticity of a record. Spoliation can occur in the case of e-mail records if they are not captured in real time or if they have been edited in any way.

strategic planning   A systematic process of envisioning a desired future and translating this vision into broadly defined goals or objectives and a sequence of steps to achieve them.

structured data/records   A collection of records or data that is stored in a computer; records maintained in a database or application.

subject matter expert (SME)   A person with deep knowledge of a particular topical area. SMEs can be useful in the consultation phase of the taxonomy design process.

subject records   (Also referred to as topic or function records.) Records containing information relating to specific or general topics. The records are arranged by informational content or by the function, activity, or transaction to which they pertain.

submission information package (SIP)   One of three types of information packages that can be submitted in the Open Archival Information System preservation model.

taxonomy   A hierarchical structure of information components (e.g., a subject, business unit, or functional taxonomy), any part of which can be used to classify a content item in relation to other items in the structure.

technology-assisted review (TAR)   (Also known as computer-assisted review). Includes aspects of the nonlinear review process, such as culling, clustering, and de-duplication, but TAR does not meet the requirements for comprehensive predictive coding. According to Barry Murphy of eDJ Group, here are three main methods for using technology to make legal review faster, less costly, and generally smarter:

1. *Rules driven.* "I know what I am looking for and how to profile it." In this scenario, a case team creates a set of criteria, or rules, for document review and builds what is essentially a coding manual. The rules are fed into the tool for execution on the document set.
2. *Facet driven.* "I let the system show me the profile groups first." In this scenario, a tool analyzes documents for potential items of interest or groups potentially similar items together so that reviewers can begin applying decisions.
3. *Propagation based.* "I start making decisions and the system looks for similar-related items." This type of TAR is about passing along, or propagating, what is known based on a sample set of documents to the rest of the documents in a corpus.

text mining   Performing detailed full-text searches on the content of document.

thesaurus   In taxonomies, a listing that contains all synonyms and definitions and is used to enforce naming conventions in a controlled vocabulary (e.g., *invoice* and *bill* could be terms that are used interchangeably).

time- /date-based disposition   A disposition instruction specifying when a record shall be cut off and when a fixed retention period is applied. The retention period does not begin until after the records have been cut off, for example: *Destroy after two years.*

time, date, and event based   A disposition instruction specifying that a record shall be disposed of after a fixed period of disposition time after a predictable or specified event. Once the specified event has occurred, then the retention period is applied. Example: *Destroy three years after close of case.* In this example, the record does not start its retention period until after the case is closed. At that time, its folder is cut off and the retention period (three years) is applied.

total cost of ownership (TCO)   All costs associated with owning a system over the life of the installation and implementation—usually considered over a range of three to five years. TCO includes implementation price and change orders (and the change order approval process), which occur when changes to the project are made outside of the original proposal. Timing and pricing of the software support fees are also critical TCO components and may include warranty periods, annual fees, planned and maximum increases, trade-in and upgrade costs, hardware maintenance costs, and other charges that may not be immediately apparent to buyers.

transfer Moving records from one location to another, or change of custody, ownership, and/or responsibility for records.

unstructured records Records that are not expressed in numerical rows and columns but rather are objects, such as image files, e-mail files, Microsoft Office files, and so forth. Structured records are maintained in databases.

usage (records) The purpose a record is used for (i.e., its primary use).

ValIT A newer value-oriented information technology governance framework that is compatible with and complementary to CobiT. Its principles and best practices focus is on leveraging IT investments to gain maximum value.

vital records Mission-critical records that are necessary for an organization to continue to operate in the event of disruption or disaster and cannot be re-created from any other source. Typically, they make up about 3 to 5 percent of an organization's total records. They are the most important records to be protected, and a plan for disaster recovery/business continuity must be in place to safeguard these records.

warm site A computer facility location that has all (or almost all) of the hardware and operating systems as a hot site does, and software licenses for the same applications, and needs only to have data loaded to resume normal operations. Internal information technology staff may have to retrieve magnetic tapes, optical disks, or other storage media containing the most recent backup data, and some data may be lost if the backup is not real time and continuous.

work flow, work flow automation, and work flow software Software that can route electronic folders through a series of work steps to speed processing and improve auditability. Not to be confused with business process management systems, which have more robust capabilities.

WORM Write Once Read Many optical disk storage media that is nonerasable and can be written to only one time.

Notes

1. Kathleen Reidy, "The Rise of Information Governance," *Too Much Information: The 451 Take on Information Management* (blog), August 5, 2009, http://blogs.the451group.com/information_management/2009/08/05/the-rise-of-information-governance/

ABOUT THE AUTHOR

Robert F. Smallwood is a founding partner of IMERGE Consulting and heads up its E-Records Institute, a specialty consulting practice, as executive director. Mr. Smallwood has over 25 years of experience in the information technology industry and holds an MBA from Loyola University of New Orleans. He has been recognized as one of the industry's "25 Most Influential People" and "Top 3 Independent Consultants" by *KM World* magazine. He consults with Fortune 500 companies and governments to assist them in making technology decisions and implementations. Some of his past research and consulting clients include the World Bank, Johnson & Johnson, Apple, Miller-Coors, AT&T, the Supreme Court of Canada, Xerox, and IBM. Smallwood was an AIIM International chapter founder and president, and a member of the executive committee of the Board of Direcctors, and is active in ARMA International. He has published more than 100 articles and given more than 50 conference presentations on documents, content, and records management. He is the author of *Managing Electronic Records: Methods, Best Practices, and Technologies* (Wiley, 2013); *Safeguarding Critical E-Documents* (Wiley, 2012); *Managing Social Media Business Records* (CreateSpace, 2011), *Taming the Email Tiger* (Bacchus Business Books, 2008) and several other books, including a novel, a theatrical play, and the first published personal account of Hurricane Katrina.

ABOUT THE MAJOR CONTRIBUTORS

Lori J. Ashley is a Wisconsin-based consultant, writer, and educator dedicated to helping clients improve the performance of their record and information management practices and controls. An experienced business strategist and organizational development specialist, she has codeveloped four continuous improvement methodologies aimed at jump-starting collaboration among stakeholders who share accountability for effective and efficient life cycle management of valued records and information assets.

Barbara Blackburn, CRM, is an electronic records management consultant who assists organizations in defining, researching, selecting, and implementing cost-effective solutions. She assists clients in preparing for technology deployment by providing strategic planning and developing record-keeping programs and taxonomies. Ms. Blackburn has expert taxonomy design skills and has taught AIIM's Electronic Records Management and Electronic Content Management certification classroom courses.

Barclay T. Blair is an advisor to Fortune 500 companies, software and hardware vendors, and government institutions and is an author, speaker, and internationally recognized authority on information governance. He has led several high-profile consulting engagements at the world's leading institutions to help them globally transform the way they manage information. Mr. Blair is the president and founder of ViaLumina.

Charmaine Brooks, CRM, is a principal with IMERGE Consulting, Inc., and has more than 25 years of experience in records and information management and content management. Ms. Brooks is a certified trainer and has taught AIIM classroom courses on ERM and provided many workshops for ARMA. Formerly a records manager for a leading worldwide provider of semiconductor memory solutions and a manager in a records management software development company, today Ms. Brooks provides clients, small and large, public and private, with guidance in developing records management and information governance programs.

Monica Crocker, CRM, PMP, CIP, is the corporate records manager for Land O'Lakes, Inc. Ms. Crocker has also been an information management consultant for 20 years, defining content and records management best practices for organizations across the United States. Her expertise includes SharePoint governance, cloud computing, enterprise strategies for content management, records management, electronic discovery, taxonomy design, project management, and business process redesign. Ms. Crocker is a recipient of AIIM's Distinguished Service Award.

Charles M. Dollar is an internationally recognized archival educator, consultant, and author who draws on more than three decades of knowledge and experience in working with public and private sector organizations to optimize the use of information technologies to satisfy legal, regulatory, business, and cultural memory recordkeeping requirements for digital preservation. He is co-developer of a capability maturity model for long-term digital preservation that incorporates the specifications of ISO 15489, ISO 14721, ISO 18492, and ISO 16363.

Patricia Franks, Ph.D., is a certified records manager and the coordinator for the Master of Archives and Records Administration degree program in the School of Library and Information Science at San José State University. She served as the team lead for both the ANSI/ARMA standard released in January of 2011, *Implications of Web-based Collaborative Technologies in Records Management,* and the 2012 technical report, *Using Social Media in Organizations.* Her latest publication, *Records and Information Management* (ALA Neal-Schuman, 2013), offers insight into a range of topics affecting records and information management professionals.

Randolph Kahn, Esq., is the founder of Kahn Consulting, one the premier information governance advisory firms. The Kahn Consulting team has provided consulting services to major global organizations, including advising U.S. and foreign governments, courts systems, and major multinational corporations on a wide variety of information issues, including e-communications strategies, social media policy, records management programs implementation, and litigation response processes. Mr. Kahn is a highly sought after speaker and a two-time recipient of the Britt Literary Award. He has authored dozens of published works, including *Chucking Daisies,* his new book on defensible disposition; *Email Rules; Information Nation: Seven Keys to Information Management Compliance; Information Nation Warrior;* and *Privacy Nation.* He is a cofounder of the Council for Information Auto-Classification and has been expert witness and an advocate in many industry organizations. Mr. Kahn is an attorney who attained his J.D. degree from Washington University in St. Louis, Missouri, and he has taught at George Washington University.

Barry Murphy is a cofounder of eDJ Group, Inc. and a thought leader in information governance, e-discovery, records management, and content archiving. Previously, he was director of product marketing at Mimosa Systems, a leading content archiving and e-discovery software provider. He joined Mimosa after a highly successful stint as principal analyst for e-discovery, records management, and content archiving at Forrester Research. Mr. Murphy received a B.S. from the State University of New York at Binghamton and an M.B.A. from the University of Notre Dame. He is an active member of both AIIM and ARMA.

INDEX

risk management issues with, 242–243
security issues with, 217–218,
    223–224, 226–227, 233–234,
    241–247
social media distinction from, 257
stream messaging *vs.*, 217–218,
    233–234, 236
technology-agnostic policies on, 243
unstructured information
    management including,
    97–99, 106
Employees/staff:
accountability of, 16, 17, 27,
    28, 30, 35, 36, 53–54, 88,
    133, 192, 267, 309, 311–312,
    349–350
communication with (*see*
    Communication)
corporate culture among, 58, 107,
    124, 199, 304–305
e-mail ownership issues with, 98
executive sponsorship by senior,
    16, 25, 28, 30, 53–55, 63, 65,
    88, 157, 159, 169, 182, 192,
    197, 306, 349–350, 352, 388
IG benefits for, 8
IG continuity plan involving, 350
IG policies for (*see* Information
    governance policies)
IG teams/governance bodies
    including, 11, 35, 38, 55, 56–57,
    62, 88, 124–125, 262–263, 281,
    306–307, 350
information misuse by, 8–10, 26, 208–
    210, 228, 229, 242–243, 258–259,
    291–292, 320–321
inventory team including, 157, 160
risk profile interviews with, 47–48
stakeholder consultation including,
    26–27
training for (*see* Training)
Encryption, 26, 164, 203, 217, 219–220,
    225, 226–227, 228, 276, 277, 281,
    291, 294
Enterprise content management
    (ECM), 149
Environmental Protection Agency, U.S.,
    101, 153

ePolicy Institute, 233, 244
Etsy, Dan, 109
European Union. *See also specific
    countries*
European Broadcasting Union in, 333
mobile devices in, 271
privacy laws in, 398
records and information management
    regulations in, 303
Executive sponsorship:
continuity of, 350
for data governance, 16, 192
for IG maintenance, 349–350, 352
for IG policy development and
    implementation, 88
for inventory of records, 157, 159
for IT governance, 197
key purposes of, 54
as principle of IG, 25, 28, 30
for records and information
    management, 28, 30, 157, 159,
    169, 182, 306, 388
for SharePoint implementation, 306
for strategic planning, 53–55, 63, 65

Facebook, 254, 256, 257, 261, 265
Federal Bureau of Investigation, 9
Federal Deposit Insurance Corporation
    (FDIC), 280
Federal Information Security
    Management Act of 2002, 296
Federal Register, 45, 139, 178
Federal Reserve Bank of New York, 244
Federal Rules of Civil Procedure
    (FRCP):
e-discovery impacts of, 115–116,
    117–118, 119, 150, 265, 303
FRCP 1, 117
FRCP 16, 118
FRCP 26, 118, 119, 265
FRCP 33, 118
FRCP 34, 118
FRCP 37, 118
Federal Wiretap Act, 210
FedEx, 259
FILELAW®, 44, 138, 139, 178–179
Financial Institution Privacy Protection
    Act of 2001/2003, 385